GOODBYE FATHER

GOODBYE FATHER

The Celibate Male Priesthood
and the Future
of the Catholic Church

———

Richard A. Schoenherr

Edited with an Introduction by
David Yamane

OXFORD
UNIVERSITY PRESS

2002

OXFORD

UNIVERSITY PRESS

Oxford   New York

Auckland   Bangkok   Buenos Aires   Cape Town   Chennai
Dar es Salaam   Delhi   Hong Kong   Istanbul   Karachi   Kolkata
Kuala Lumpur   Madrid   Melbourne   Mexico City   Mumbai   Nairobi
São Paulo   Shanghai   Singapore   Taipei   Tokyo   Toronto

and an associated company in
Berlin

Copyright © 2002 by Richard A. Schoenherr

"Editor's Introduction" copyright © 2002 by David Yamane

Published by Oxford University Press, Inc.,
198 Madison Avenue, New York, New York 10016
www.oup.com

Oxford is a registered trademark of Oxford University Press

B+T   29.95   1/03

Library of Congress Cataloging-in-Publication Data

Schoenherr, Richard A.
Goodbye father : the celibate male priesthood and the future of the Catholic Church /
Richard A. Schoenherr.
p.   cm.
Includes bibliographical references and index.
ISBN 0-19-508259-1
1. Catholic Church—Clergy. 2. Catholic Church—Clergy—Supply and demand.
3. Celibacy—Catholic Church. 4. Lay ministry—Catholic Church.
5. Christian leadership—Catholic Church. 6. Power (Christian theology)
7. Catholic Church—Government. 8. Patriarchy—Religious aspects—
Catholic Church. I. Title.
BX1912.S34   1996
262' .142—dc20   95-40074

2 4 6 8 9 7 5 3

Printed in the United States of America
on acid-free paper

To Judy

Dean R. Hoge

T his is a landmark book, and its importance is best appreciated if the reader knows something of its history. Richard Schoenherr and his colleague Lawrence Young worked for years to document carefully the decline in numbers of Catholic priests in the United States. In the 1980s they made some preliminary reports to the Catholic bishops, and in 1993 they published their final analysis in the book *Full Pews and Empty Altars.* Put briefly, they documented a sharp drop-off in numbers of priests from the 1960s to the end of the century, with more decline projected as coming later. For many Catholics, including not a few bishops, this was bad news, and it incited attacks on the authors. Yet the demographic analysis in the book was never challenged.

Meanwhile Schoenherr worked on a companion work, in effect volume 2 of his magnum opus, to be entitled *Goodbye Father.* He finished the manuscript in April 1995 and looked for a publisher. But it was too long to publish, and Schoenherr hated to make the necessary cuts. By this time other sociologists of religion knew about the second manuscript and its weightiness. Some of us urged Schoenherr to cut it down soon before too much time passed. But it was not to be. Schoenherr died suddenly in 1996, and nobody knew if the manuscript would ever be published.

We owe gratitude to David Yamane for taking a big scissors and cutting down the manuscript. He cut it by two-thirds. He tried to make the cuts while minimizing any damage to the force of Schoenherr's argument. It was a success. Now Schoenherr's work is available to all. His first book gave us the numbers, and this one gives us his interpretation. This book answers the big questions: Why is there this shortage of priests? What will it lead to? What else is happening in the Catholic Church, and how is it related to the scarcity of priests? What can be done?

Schoenherr is not afraid of coming to conclusions and making recommendations, and he is not worried about possibly offending somebody. The future of the Church is too important to let such matters get in the way. In this regard, he admires Archbishop Rembert Weakland of Milwaukee for his bold initiatives in opening up discussion in his archdiocese even in the face of Vatican opposition. Schoenherr's conclusions have been attacked by some Catholics in the past, and this opposition may continue. In this book he predicts that we will see a married male priesthood in the next two or three generations, and our grandchildren will see women priests. He thinks both would be good. Statements like these make some Catholic leaders see purple and close their ears to anything Schoenherr has to say. This is a mistake. Schoenherr's work is valuable to study. It is done soberly, carefully, and responsibly. If he criticizes the status quo, it is not out of anger or spite, and he does not hate the Church. On the contrary, he loves the Church and wants to serve it.

It does not help matters that Schoenherr was an ex-priest who resigned to get married. This in itself is enough to make some Catholics dismiss everything he says, arguing that he was an angry man trying to get back at the hierarchy. I urge readers of this book to separate Schoenherr's sociological analysis from his personal life-journey and to focus on the former. I doubt if the analysis in this book was damaged by anger or revenge. It is too deep and deliberate for that. And Schoenherr is not alone in ruminating about these concerns—the priest shortage, the pressures from the feminist movement, the pressures for more lay participation, and so on. Many Catholic intellectuals are doing the same and are making similar recommendations. Schoenherr's views have been echoed repeatedly by other analysts whose love and loyalty to the Church are above dispute. The arguments need to be weighed dispassionately for the good of us all.

I think it is useful to alert readers that Schoenherr's agenda is broad and this book is broad in its scope. I see the book as having two levels, first the analysis of changes in the Catholic Church and second a scientific and philosophical underpinning for understanding religion and religious institutions. The first level reviews trends in church life, movements advocating change, and cultural pressures on the institution. The second level includes expositions of lessons from the works of Mircea Eliade, Sigmund Freud, Max Weber, Erik Erikson, Lawrence Kohlberg, Paul Ricoeur, and others. Both levels are valuable, but some readers may weary of the second level, and if so, they should skim part II and dig into part III.

The question comes to mind as to whether this manuscript, finished in 1995, is still pertinent in the year 2002. Seven years have passed. Has the situation changed enough to make the book's analysis and conclusion out of date? I think not. The situation *has* changed in one respect—the priest shortage has worsened, and the problem of recruiting seminarians has become more difficult. The last few years have seen numerous media reports on priestly pedophilia, a topic that is abhorrent to many and one has certainly not helped recruit new vocations. Otherwise not too much has changed in the Church, and Schoenherr's work is still on target.

My hope is that readers will read Schoenherr's book while keeping in their minds what was foremost in his mind, namely, what would serve his beloved Church in the long run, to keep it authentic and vibrant? This is what's important, and life is too short to tarry over lesser things. Schoenherr says that the Eucharist is the center of Catholic church life, and it must never be denied or deemphasized. For this reason he sorely wants to keep the priesthood as strong as possible. Some steps must be taken. "Goodbye Father" does not mean the end of the priesthood but only an end to the exclusively male celibate priesthood. Keeping the Eucharist and the priesthood strong is Schoenherr's main commitment, and from it flows everything else. The argument is cogent, and I hope it is widely read.

T his book is the product of a truly catholic mind and spirit. Richard Schoen-
herr was a friend and advisor during my graduate studies at the University of
Wisconsin–Madison from 1991 until he unexpectedly passed away in January
1996. At that time, he had spent over half his 61 years studying the Roman
Catholic priesthood, 25 of them as a member of the sociology faculty at UW–
Madison. During his lifetime, Schoenherr was best known, as the *New York
Times* described him in his obituary, as the "sociologist who counted priests."
There is a grain of truth in this description, for it was Schoenherr who was re-
sponsible for the definitive demographic study of the priest shortage in the
United States.[1] That study, published as *Full Pews and Empty Altars,* docu-
mented a 19 percent decline in the priest population between 1966 and 1984
and projected a 40 percent decline by 2005. In recognition of its scholarly rigor
and analytical power, *Full Pews and Empty Altars* garnered accolades among
the Catholic faithful as well as scholars, including the1996 Distinguished Book
Award from the Society for the Scientific Study of Religion.

So Schoenherr was indeed a sociologist who counted priests. At the same
time, those who knew him well always understood his broader theoretical, theological, and pastoral interests. With the publication of this book, others will
have an opportunity to share in his broad vision. *Goodbye Father* is the product
of a lifetime of reflection on the Roman Catholic Church as an organization and
community of faith. Richard Schoenherr's magnum opus sets his demographic
analyses of the priest shortage in its world-historical context. It is a testament
to the power of a mind capable of incorporating the insights of scholars as diverse as the demographers Nathan Keyfitz and Judah Matras, the organizational
theorists Peter Blau and Howard Aldrich, the population ecologists Michael
Hannan and John Freeman, the sociologists of religion Thomas O'Dea and
Robert Bellah, the philosophers Martin Buber and Paul Ricoeur, the historians
Mircea Eliade and Gerda Lerner, the feminist theologians Rosemary Ruether
and Carol Christ, the transpersonal psychologists Abraham Maslow and Ken
Wilber, and others. (Schoenherr's acknowledgments give a full accounting of
his intellectual debts and development.) From his first scholarly publication—
an analysis of power, authority, and celibacy[2]—to this, his last, Schoenherr
proved himself to be single-minded in his devotion to understanding the place
of the priesthood in the church he loved. He was, in Isaiah Berlin's classification
scheme, an intellectual hedgehog. "The fox knows many things, but the hedgehog knows one big thing."[3]

Because of its breadth and depth, this is not an easy book. Profound ideas are rarely simply expressed. It is an important book, though, which will reward the serious and patient reader. Schoenherr argues that the priest shortage, in interaction with other social preconditions for structural transformation, is modifying the internal political economy of the Catholic Church. Therefore, the decline in the U.S. priesthood population is the first in a powerful matrix of forces for change. The second trend at work is a decline in dogmatism and a rise in pluralism of worldviews, bringing with them an array of models of the Church and a variety of plausibility structures. Third, the Catholic Church is witnessing a demise of the cultural hegemony that developed out of its European and Western origins and the birth of a truly worldwide organization that is beginning to be inculturated in a church of six continents. Fourth, doctrinal changes legitimated by the Second Vatican Council represent a major transitional force, particularly those statements that have weakened belief in the absolute superiority of celibacy as a way of holiness and strengthened the importance of the charism of marriage as an equal but different means of grace. Fifth, the feminist movement, especially among nuns and laywomen in church-related careers, is beginning to erode male hegemony over the Church's ministry and to establish a growing sense of female equality. Sixth, the ordained clergy's political monopoly over the technical core of the Church's ministry is being called into question by increased lay participation in ministerial roles. Seventh and last, the sacramental and particularly the eucharistic focus of the Catholic "means of justification" is being dimmed by the growing recognition of the "saving power" of the Scriptures as fewer priests are available for Mass and more laypeople preside at Bible-based Liturgies of the Word. The first three trends are powerful forces whose strength derives from fundamental social processes: (1) change in the *forces of production* inside the Catholic Church, manifested by the priest shortage in recent decades; (2) change in *ideological support* for the ministerial status quo, revealed by a shift from dogmatism to pluralism over several centuries; and (3) change in *population trends* resulting from secularization and the end of colonialism, exhibited by a shift from a predominantly Western to a world church in the latter half of the twentieth century. The rest are current manifestations of the historical conflict surrounding the ideal-typical traits of Catholic ministry.

Many of the individual points Schoenherr makes here have been made recently by others. Eugene Kennedy's book *The Unhealed Wound: The Church and Human Sexuality* (St. Martin's Press, 2001) and Fr. Donald Cozzens's book *The Changing Face of the Priesthood* (Liturgical Press, 2000) both relate to Schoenherr's argument in part III; Gary Wills's *Papal Sins: The Structures of Deceit* (Doubleday, 2000) and John Cornwell's *Breaking Faith: The Pope, the People, and the Fate of Catholicism* (Viking Compass, 2001) bear on the argument in part IV; and so on. One of the great virtues of *Goodbye Father* is that it brings these individual points together with some novel ones into a comprehensive framework and sets it in motion toward a probable end. There is no other book I know of that does all of what *Goodbye Father* does. Of course, making predictions about the future course of history is a risky enterprise, but Schoenherr rushed in, he often admitted, "where angels fear to tread."

The title of this book is perfectly descriptive of its central themes, but in the emotional context of debates about the church and its future, it is easy to misread. Make no mistake: "Goodbye Father" does not mean goodbye to the priesthood. To the contrary, this book is a historical, sociological, and theological defense of the absolute necessity of a professional, hierarchical, ordained priesthood. In this sense, this is a profoundly conservative book. What "Goodbye Father" does mean is goodbye to the *exclusively male, celibate* priesthood. In this sense, this is a profoundly radical book. This seeming contradiction is appropriate since, as the reader will find, paradox plays a central role in Schoenherr's understanding of organized religion (see especially part III).

I often tell my students that before they read any book, they should study its architecture, beginning with the table of contents. Readers of *Goodbye Father* are advised to do this as well, but also to study and make repeated reference to figure 1 (in chapter 1). This figure graphically summarizes the entire causal model presented in *Goodbye Father*. In this figure, we see the pivotal role played by the priest shortage. As the validity of the model of change presented in *Goodbye Father* rests on the accuracy of its constituent parts, I will review some of the recent developments on the key issue of the priesthood since Schoenherr's death. In his argument, it is the priest shortage that is the "linchpin" in the model of change, so if there has been any dramatic change in the state of the priesthood over the past several years, we might begin to question the conclusions Schoenherr draws about the future of the Catholic Church.

The Current State of the Priesthood

In *Full Pews and Empty Altars,* Richard Schoenherr and his student Lawrence Young produced the definitive demographic analysis of the priest shortage in the United States over the past three decades. By creating a registry of 36,300 diocesan priests in 86 dioceses from 1966 to 1984, they were able to document a 19 percent decline in the number of active priests over a 19 year period. To my knowledge, no one has ever challenged this aspect of the study's findings. In a sense, they confirmed what everyone could see happening already. The real power of the study was the ability to use the priest registry data to make "optimistic," "pessimistic," and "moderate" predictions for another 21 years beyond the data—to the year 2005 (see appendix B to *Full Pews and Empty Altars* for a discussion of the assumptions used in making these different projections). Schoenherr and Young projected that by 2005, the number of active diocesan priests would be somewhere between 34 and 68 percent fewer than in 1966—most likely 40 percent (the moderate projection).

In a 1998 article, Lawrence Young assessed these earlier projections using data from the 1996 *Official Catholic Directory*. He found that the Schoenherr-Young predictions for 1995—based on data collected through 1984—were within 1 percent of the actual counts given in the *Directory*.[4] The population projection models in *Full Pews and Empty Altars,* therefore, were quite accurate for the first 10 years of the 20-year period. This accuracy gave Young confidence to extend the projections out an additional 10 years. Young projected that the decline in the size of the U.S. diocesan priest population from 1966 to 2015 would be between 38 and 61 percent, with the most likely estimate being a 46 percent decline over this 50-year period.

Although this work has been generally well received, it has not been without its critics. One line of criticism suggests that when viewed over a longer period of time, the decline in the number of priests is not so great. For example, in 1900, there were 9,000 diocesan priests in the United States; currently there are more than 30,000. However, over the same period, the number of lay Catholics grew even more quickly. In 1900, the number of Catholics per diocesan priest was 1,200. Today it is 1,898. Moreover, this ratio includes retired as well as active priests, and most informed opinions suggest that the percentage of priests who are retired has increased over this period as well (constituting perhaps 25 percent of the priest population).[5] Thus, as Schoenherr argued, the priest *shortage* is relative to the size of the population to be served.

The three main factors affecting the priest population are ordinations, deaths, and resignations. The good news is that resignations have slowed since the "mass exodus" of the early 1970s, and diocesan theologate enrollments seem to have bottomed out in 1997, showing slight growth over the past four years.[6] Still, because of the graying of the priest population, the priest shortage will persist for some time even if ordinations begin to increase. One must also take into consideration that the age of seminarians is increasing, with 57 percent of seminarians over 30 years of age and 17 percent over 40 years of age. These older ordinations will alleviate but not eliminate the graying of the priest population and will give dioceses fewer total years of service per new priest. Thus, as Bryan Froehle and Mary Gautier of the Center for Applied Research in the Apostolate (CARA) at Georgetown University observe, "even if the number of seminarians continues steady or increases gradually, as it has in the past five years, they will not be enough to replace the older priests who are retiring and thus will not substantially affect the total number of active priests."[7] Indeed, the "optimistic" Schoenherr-Young projections of decline are based on higher rates of ordination.

The leading critic of *Full Pews and Empty Altars* among the church hierarchy was Roger Cardinal Mahony, archbishop of Los Angeles. In the Catholic newsweekly *Our Sunday Visitor* (18 November 1990), Cardinal Mahony reacted to a report Schoenherr gave to the U.S. bishops' conference by asserting that "the Catholic Church in our country has been done a great disservice by the Schoenherr report" and that "our future is shaped by God's design for His Church—not by sociologists." This is an unfortunate statement, for Schoenherr never claimed to be able to shape the Church's future. Moreoever, whatever design God has for the Church will be interpreted and implemented by human beings, and sociologists may have something important to say to them.[8] I am reminded of the words of the Second Vatican Council's "Pastoral Constitution on the Church in the Modern World":

> If methodological investigation within every branch of learning is carried out in a genuinely scientific manner and in accord with moral norms, it never truly conflicts with faith, for earthly matters and the concerns of faith derive from the same God. Indeed, whoever labors to penetrate the secrets of reality with a humble and steady mind . . . is being led by the hand of God, who holds all things in existence and gives them their identity. (*Gaudium et Spes,* no. 36)

Indeed, Cardinal Mahony does acknowledge at the end of his essay that "we must utilize sound research techniques in the Church." Unfortunately, in his essay Mahony himself fails to do this. To highlight the "good news" from Los Angeles, he compares Schoenherr's projections for ordinations in Los Angeles from 1990 to 1993 (7.5 priests per year) to the number of seminarians in each of those four ordination classes. He concludes: "Schoenherr Projection: Total—30 priests; Los Angeles Actual Figures—67 priests." Of course, he was writing in 1990, so it would not be for three years that the "actual figures" would be determined. Mahony assumed that all 67 seminarians would be ordained. Furthermore, in understanding the priest shortage, one must consider not just ordinations but resignations and retirements as well. When Young updated Schoenherr's projections in 1995, he found that the actual number of priests listed in the *Official Catholic Directory* for the Archdiocese of Los Angeles was 490, 31 *fewer* than the moderate projection that had been based on the priest registry data; the moderate projections had *underestimated* the decline in the priest population in Los Angeles by about 6 percent.[9] Recently, Cardinal Mahony has come under attack himself as a "liberal" bishop whose diocese is characterized by a decline in vocations. In an essay on the priest shortage in the *New Oxford Review,* high school English teacher Larry Carstens specifically indicts Mahony along with the two heroes of the prophetic coalition (discussed by Schoenherr in chapter 12): Archbishop Rembert Weakland of Milwaukee and Bishop Kenneth Untener of Saginaw.[10]

Debates such as these do not advance our understanding of the serious situation facing the Catholic Church. More helpful is the serious work of social sci-

entists who have offered views of the current situation that differ from Schoenherr's. For example, John F. Quinn, a historian at Salve Regina University, notes
that in 1829 the priest-to-people ratio in the United States was 1:2,150, considerably higher than today's ratio. By the time of the Catholic Church's Third Ple-
nary Council in Baltimore in 1884, the ratio had improved to one priest for every
1,135 Catholics, but only because of a large number of foreign-born priests.
Quinn challenges the "priest shortage panic" by noting that "while in the nineteenth century the Church in America had to rely heavily on French, Irish, and
German priests, in the twenty-first century she may find herself relying on
Nigerian, Filipino, and Indian priests." Indeed, CARA has reported recently
that one in six active diocesan priests in the United States was born abroad, helping to ease the present priest shortage.[11] These empirical facts deserve serious
consideration.

Although it is true that the present priest-to-parishioner ratios are not without precedent historically, just looking at the ratios neglects important changes
in the expectations of both priests and the laity in the recent history of the
Church. For example, the current situation differs from earlier times because of
the Second Vatican Council's stress on the "full, conscious, active participation"
of the laity in liturgical celebrations. Correspondingly, people have higher expectations for the experience of the Mass and sacraments. In addition, Catholics are no longer enmeshed in thick Catholic communities, so the quality of the
parish experience may matter more than it ever has in terms of the transmission
of the faith.[12] For this same reason, an increasing number of foreign-born priests
may not be an adequate, long-term solution. For example, has Quinn fully considered the significance of the change from Latin to the vernacular and the increased importance of the Liturgy of the Word (including preaching) in the celebration of the Mass? It is important to use common measures over time for the
sake of comparison, but we must also keep in mind that the meaning of those
measures may change over time.

Another interesting analysis to consider was published recently by Andrew
Yuengert, an economics professor at Pepperdine University. Yuengert investigates differences in ordination rates between dioceses and finds support for the
idea that the characteristics of the bishops make a difference, even after controlling for demographic characteristics of the dioceses. Analyzing ordination
data from 1986 to 1997, Yuengert finds large and statistically significant differences in the ordination rates between dioceses whose bishops write for *America*
(theologically more progressive) and those who write for *Catholic Answers* (theologically more orthodox). Yuengert summarizes: "Those bishops who wrote
more than once for *America* have much lower ordination rates (31% lower) than
other bishops. . . . Writing once for *The Catholic Answer* is associated with 39%
higher ordination rates; writing more than once is associated with 73% higher

ordination rates." What this translates to in terms of actual numbers is about two fewer new priests every three years for the multiple *America* contributor bishops, one more new priest every year for the one-time *Catholic Answer* contributor bishops, and 1.5 new priests per year for the multiple *Catholic Answer* contributor bishops.[13]

As Young notes in his assessment of the Schoenherr-Young projections, the demographic models they use necessarily sacrifice specificity for generalizability in analysis. And the models succeed quite well in terms of generalizability. Young observes that "the comparative design of employing a single generalizable set of assumptions uniformly in the projection models of every diocese produced results that remain accurate a decade into the projections in over 87 percent of the sample dioceses."[14] Still, Yuengert's analysis of differential ordination rates suggests that there may be some interesting developments taking place that are not fully captured by the generalizable demographic models. An analysis of some "outliers" may be helpful in this regard. A few dioceses in the United States are speaking not of a vocation crisis but of "repriesting" parishes—notably Peoria (Illinois), Lincoln (Nebraska), and Arlington (Virginia). As Quinn argues, what these dioceses "have in common are bishops willing to recruit aggressively for seminarians who are committed to a celibate, male priesthood."[15]

A similar pattern is apparent among religious orders.[16] Consider, for example, a "conservative" religious order like the Legionaries of Christ, which I know somewhat because my brother-in-law is Fr. Daniel Polzer, LC. The Legionaries claim 2,500 seminarians, nearly the same number of seminarians as all of the diocesan seminarians in the United States combined. In 1994, I traveled to Mexico City for Fr. Dan's ordination. After 10 years of formation, he received the sacrament of holy orders along with 56 *other men.* How many dioceses in the United States have even 57 men in seminary in *total?* How many years would it take for the Archdiocese of New York (for example) to ordain 57 priests to serve its two-plus million Catholics?

One consequence of the uneven pattern of selection into seminaries—both within dioceses and between them—is that the orientation of seminarians and newly ordained priests is moving toward greater orthodoxy. This has caused considerable discomfort to some reform-minded Catholics and led to talk of a "generation gap" in the priesthood. The veteran Catholic-watcher and Catholic University sociologist Dean Hoge notes that among priests who were between 37 and 56 years old in 1997 ("Baby Boomers"), 64 percent agreed that "celibacy should be a matter of personal choice for diocesan priests"; among those who were age 36 or less ("Post-Boomers"), only 26 percent agreed that celibacy should be optional. In 1970, by contrast, fully 85 percent of priests under 35 favored optional celibacy. In her analysis of trends and transitions in seminaries and theologates, Sr. Katarina Schuth notes that many seminarians today have only experienced one pontificate: that of John Paul II.[17] Even the *New York Times* has caught onto this emerging pattern, carrying stories about the Catholic priesthood and its turn toward orthodoxy for three consecutive years.[18]

In addition to the generation gap within the priesthood, a gap exists between the emerging priesthood and the existing laity. At the same time that the priesthood is becoming more orthodox, the laity is ever more liberal, at least on certain issues. A series of recent surveys by sociologists Hoge, James Davidson of Purdue, and various colleagues extensively document this. Particularly on the "pelvic" issues—gender, sexuality, and reproductive ethics—lay Catholic beliefs depart significantly from the teachings of the Church. A minority of all Catholics believe with the Magisterium that the following are always wrong: homosexual acts (41 percent agree), abortion (39 percent), premarital sex (33 percent), and artificial birth control (9 percent).[19] In response to the statement "It would be a good thing if women were allowed to be ordained as priests," the percentage of Catholics agreeing increased from about 30 percent in 1974 to over 60 percent in the 1990s. As Schoenherr would expect, the percentage supporting ordaining married men as priests is even higher: 63 percent in 1987, increasing to over 70 percent in 1993. Allowing priests who have married to return to active ministry receives the highest level of support in this survey, with nearly 80 percent of respondents agreeing.[20] Of course, the Holy Father and the Congregation for the Doctrine of the Faith have declared these issues closed for discussion, in *Ordinatio Sacerdotalis* (1994) and *Responsum ad Dubium* (1995), respectively.

Interestingly, this emerging gap between clergy and laity is the inverse of that confronted by mainline Protestant denominations in the 1960s, famously analyzed by the sociologist Jeffrey Hadden in *The Gathering Storm in the Churches*.[21] Although demographic factors like birth rates and the inability to retain children of members seem to be the most important causal factors, the precipitous decline in the mainline Protestant denominations at the end of the twentieth century certainly gives one pause in thinking about this gap.[22] Indeed, if a religious body were to have to choose a gap, it would probably be preferable to have the leadership more orthodox than the membership. Such a situation creates stability through connection to tradition but still allows for gradual change in doctrine and practices in response to developments beyond the hierarchy.[23] In any event, altars full of shepherds more liberal than the dwindling flock is not a model to which most churches would aspire.

It should be noted that the attitude gap between the priesthood and laity in the Catholic Church narrows when one considers only those Catholics who are currently active in the Church.[24] Those who attend Mass or who say that the Church is important to them are more orthodox than those who still identify themselves as Catholics but who are inactive—sometimes called "lapsed" or "cultural" Catholics. (Whether this is a treatment or selection effect, or both, no one yet knows with certainty.) Moreover, many of the core teachings of the Church continue to find strong support among the laity, including young adult Catholics. For example, more than four out of five Catholics agree with the statement "The bread and wine used in Mass are actually transformed into the body and blood of Jesus Christ," including 87 percent of non-Latino young adult Catholics and 95 percent of Latino young adult Catholics.[25] Whether the Eucharist continues to survive as a transgenerational, transideological common ground in Catholic life is precisely one of Richard Schoenherr's driving concerns in *Goodbye Father*.

The Effects of the Priest Shortage

More than a leveling-off of seminary enrollments will be necessary to stem the tide documented in *Full Pews and Empty Altars*. Until a reversal is evident, we do well to consider the manifold effects of the priest shortage—effects that are already here now. In addition to 19,181 parishes, the Catholic Church also sponsors 1,110 hospitals and health care facilities, 1,085 residential care facilities, 1,406 Catholic Charities USA–affiliated social service agencies, 8,170 schools, and 233 colleges and universities.[26] The priest shortage, Schoenherr recognized, "does not only mean no priest in church on Sunday, but also no priest in many of the schools, youth centers, wedding halls, hospitals, funeral parlors, and other locales that host socialization processes, major life transitions, and rites of passage." Indeed, one cannot read the Catholic press without being reminded weekly of the problems created by the shortage of priests, particularly in terms of access to the sacraments.

For Schoenherr the Eucharist was most important, and he notes with dismay the plans in place for the celebration of the Mass in the absence of a priest (chapter 1). Since Schoenherr wrote, Bishop Richard Hanifen—chairman of the U.S. bishops' Committee on Priestly Life and Ministry—wrote a pastoral letter to the faithful of his diocese on "The Service of Priests in the Diocese of Colorado Springs" (27 May 2001). He opened the letter by noting, "it has become commonplace in our nation for bishops to write their people regarding some of the changing expectations required because of the declining number of priestly vocations." A recent example is Bishop James Griffin of Columbus, Ohio, who has issued a document entitled "Guidelines Regarding Expectations of Priests and Sunday Celebrations in the Absence of a Priest." Bishop Griffin writes, "I believe the time has clearly come to prepare the clergy and faithful alike for a new approach, one which acknowledges that there will be times when, due to a lack of an available priest, there may be no Mass on Sunday in a given place." As Schoenherr argues, the "Word and Communion" services that will take place in the absence of a priest are fundamentally different from the sacrifice of the mass celebrated by an ordained priest (chapter 9).

No sacrament is unaffected by the shortage of ordained clergy for adminis-tration. Among other issues addressed in his recent pastoral letter on the con-sequences of the declining number of priestly vocations, Bishop Hanifen urged "reasonable expectations for our priests," including limiting time at liturgical celebrations such as the sacrament of matrimony. The National Association of Catholic Chaplains issued a report recently on the possibility that the sacrament of the anointing of the sick in hospitals and nursing homes is becoming increas-ingly difficult to provide (*National Catholic Reporter*, 7 September 2001). Some have used the shortage of priests as a rationale for the use of general absolution in communal services rather than individual confession to a priest for the sacra-ment of penance (*National Catholic Reporter* article and editorial, 27 July 2001). In my own research on the Rite of Christian Initiation of Adults (RCIA), one of the biggest problems reported by parish RCIA directors and individuals going through the process—a problem directly observed by me and my re-search team this year—is the unavailability of parish priests for sacramental preparation of adults in the process. Of course, these sacraments get adminis-tered one way or another, but the formation of people in the Christian life that should accompany the sacraments of initiation is not what it could be if priests could be more involved. We must keep in mind the quality of the preparation of candidates for reception of the sacraments and not only the quantity of sacra-ments being administered.

Ironically, the priest shortage begets the priest shortage not only in all of the ways that Schoenherr suggests in *Goodbye Father* (chapter 2) but also because priests are too busy administering their parishes and the sacraments to encour-age men to pursue a vocation to the priesthood. Although a 1994 study of priests found that 90 percent would probably or definitely choose to be a priest again and 54 percent find that life as a priest is better than they expected, later work by CARA revealed that less than half of priests actively recruit new vocations. This sits uneasily with Hoge's finding that more than 60 percent of the ordina-tion class of 2001 reported that a priest had initiated a conversation about a vo-cation to the priesthood with them.[27]

According to CARA research for the U.S. bishops' conference, most lay Catholics recognize that there is a shortage of priests, but less than a quarter say that the shortage has directly affected them.[28] This is probably due to a combi-nation of three factors: lowered demand for services, lowered expectations of priests, and the fact that priests are working harder and harder to meet the in-creasing demands made on them. All of these are a cause for concern, but the last factor is most immediately troubling to me; I have read of one parish priest who wearily refers to himself as a "sacramental machine." Or, as Msgr. Thomas Bergin, the vicar for education of the Archdiocese of New York, laments: "The work is lonelier. You have to work harder. It wears you down." Or, as Chester Gillis has written, "in some dioceses and religious orders of nuns and priests, retirement has become a euphemism for death. No matter how old they are, their contribution is needed." These anecdotes lend support to Fr. Francis Dorff's observation that "some of the most dedicated priests I know are killing themselves. They are working themselves to death."[29]

A declining number of priests also creates a situation where more and more Catholic clergy are "home alone." The increasing number of one-priest parishes—and multiple parishes sharing one priest—may foster not only mental and physical problems but problems of discipline as well. For example, drawing on his experience as deputy chaplain of the United States Marine Corps, supervising 250 chaplains from 60 faith traditions, Msgr. Eugene Gomulka observed that "while priests comprised about 20 percent of the chaplains, they accounted for about 50 percent of the serious offenses"—offenses resulting in imprisonment or separation from the military. He attributes this to problems associated with loneliness.[30] Indeed, some have suggested that when priests name "celibacy" as a reason for resignation, what they often mean is loneliness.

Paul Sullins, a sociologist at Catholic University of America, has recently pointed to some areas of growth in the Church that may help to meet the unmet demand created by the priest shortage, in particular the expansion of lay ministry and the permanent diaconate.[31] Certainly the laity has stepped forward to assume many new responsibilities in church life. The National Catholic Parish Survey, released in May 2000, reports that lay ministers outnumber active priests in U.S. parishes by a ratio of 2 to 1.5 (*America*, 13 May 2000). In its *2001 Catholic Ministry Formation Directory*, CARA finds 35,582 students in lay ecclesial ministry programs—up from 20,281 in 1996–97—almost all leading to academic degrees or professional certification. The laity are playing a larger role in every type of Catholic institution, agency, and ministry. A high-profile recent example in Catholic higher education is the appointment by Georgetown University of its first lay president. But as Schoenherr makes clear, there are some things that an ordained priest can and should do that a layperson cannot and should not. Indeed, although it has been spun positively—the appointee is apparently well qualified to lead a university—no one has suggested that a layperson would have been selected over an available and qualified Jesuit to head Georgetown. Unfortunately, among Jesuits—as with other religious orders, male and female—there is a shortage of personnel.[32] That no aspect of the life of the Church is unaffected was brought home to many in September 2001 when New York's cardinal archbishop, Edward Egan, asked Fr. Frank Pavone, the national director of Priests for Life, to resume parish work for the diocese to help alleviate the priest shortage there.

Another area in which there has been tremendous growth recently is in the permanent diaconate, restored in the United States in 1968. Since then, the total number of permanent deacons in the United States has grown from 7 in 1970 to 12,182 in 1998. There is now one permanent deacon for every 1.6 parishes. Still, the permanent diaconate is not a cure-all. Supervising priests are often frustrated because of limitations on hours deacons can work, and lay-people tend to see deacons as "underqualified priests or overqualified laity."[33] More importantly, deacons cannot administer the sacrament of reconciliation, anoint the sick, or consecrate the Eucharist. Their contributions to the Church are a wonderful gift, but, as Schoenherr would say, they are not priests.

In the face of the priest shortage and its various effects on the life of the Church, many favor expanding the priesthood to include married men and women as a pragmatic response to a pressing need. Schoenherr may at first blush seem to say this himself. But the justification for the expansion of the priesthood for Schoenherr is in the first instance theological, not pragmatic. To wit: he began to address these issues in the mid-1960s, when the ordination classes were the biggest in the history of the Church in America. The priest shortage merely draws awareness to the need for doctrinal development on this issue. In other words, it forces the change, but it does not justify the change.

Forces for Stability and Change

Schoenherr's work is indebted to the ideas of German social theorist Karl Marx in ways that go beyond what is reflected in the text and references (due in part to my editing, as I explain later). Marx's work on social change has both deter-ministic and voluntaristic emphases. For example, internally contradictory eco-nomic systems like capitalism inevitably suffer economic crises (deterministic), and those crises create conditions under which the oppressed group will rise up in a revolution against the system (voluntaristic). Revolutionary change results from the combination of material change and social action. As Marx famously wrote in *The Eighteenth Brumaire of Louis Bonaparte* (1852): "[People] make their own history, but they do not make it just as they please; they do not make it under circumstances chosen by themselves, but under circumstances directly encountered, given and transmitted from the past." In assessing the implications of recent developments for Schoenherr's argument, therefore, we must pay at-tention both to the "circumstances" that actors encounter today and to the ac-tors who "make history."

The priest shortage is the engine driving change in the Church, but the di-rection of change is determined by the engineers. For Schoenherr, these engi-neers are the priestly (conservative) and prophetic (progressive) coalitions in the Church (see part IV). The existence of these two coalitional movements in the Church was clearly evidenced in November 1996 in Detroit, where the re-formist Catholic organization "Call to Action" celebrated its twentieth anniver-sary at the same time that a counterreform group calling itself "Call to Holiness" met a few miles away. As journalist John Cornwell summarized the situation,

"The confrontation in Detroit that weekend was symptomatic of the clash among many polarized groups, movements, constituencies, periodicals, and websites which claim that they, and not their opponents, represent authentic Catholicism today."[34] These countervailing movements have also been subject to scholarly elaboration and scrutiny in two volumes edited by Mary Jo Weaver: *Being Right: Conservative Catholics in America* (Indiana University Press, 1995, with R. Scott Appleby) and *What's Left? Liberal American Catholics* (Indiana University Press, 1999).

Since Schoenherr's death, developments have not been kind to the prophetic coalition. Bishop Raymond Lucker of New Ulm, Minnesota, a liberal stalwart among the episcopacy, passed away in 2001. One of the two charismatic leaders that Schoenherr highlights in chapter 12, Archbishop Weakland of Milwaukee, has recently retired. Of course, retirement does not mean disappearance. Weakland himself is not going "gentle into that good night." As the date of his final *ad limina* visit with the pope approached in 1998, Weakland wrote "Reflections for Rome" in *America* (18 April 1998) and was profiled in *Time* magazine under the title "A Firebrand's Valedictory" (25 May 1998). More recently, he was embroiled in a controversy over the renovation of the cathedral in his archdiocese—which he took to be fundamentally about "decisions that were rightfully mine to make as the local bishop of this church."[35] There are unsettling developments outside the hierarchy as well. Although Michele Dillon has documented the remarkable persistence of "institutionally marginalized Catholics"—those "who choose to stay Catholic even though their understanding of Catholicism is denounced in official church teaching"—the recent schism of a Catholic Church in Rochester, New York, over the ordination of women and other issues suggests that the patience of some in the prophetic coalition may be wearing thin.[36]

At the same time, Pope John Paul II has had five additional years since Schoenherr finished *Goodbye Father* to solidify his priestly coalition (chapter 11), furthering his influence on the episcopacy worldwide and on the College of Cardinals that will choose his successor. As of the February 2001 consistory, the total number of cardinal electors (those under 80 years of age) is 135—the highest number in history—of which 125 (93 percent) were appointed by John Paul II (*America,* 12 February 2001). It is certainly possible that John Paul II's successor will be different in orientation, but I don't think most prochange Catholics are counting on that.

Although highly critical of the current state of the Church, this book remains profoundly optimistic. As Schoenherr himself notes: "The book ends with an upbeat scenario." At a time when many Catholics have lost faith in Holy Mother Church, Schoenherr's love for her has triumphed over such pessimism. Some might say this love blinded him to the reality of the ever more deeply entrenched priestly coalition under the pontificate of John Paul II. But one of the virtues of the theory of social change in organized religion elaborated in this book is precisely that if the changes Schoenherr predicts will happen over the course of the twenty-first century do not come to pass, *Goodbye Father* will help us to understand why.

Editorial Strategy

It is the hope of all those involved in this project that this book will draw readers from a variety of audiences: social scientists, theologians, students of religion, church officials, clergy, lay Catholics, and some members of the general public. Creating a text that is challenging yet accessible to these various publics is not easy. The manuscript that Richard Schoenherr completed in 1995 went a long way toward this goal. Its main liability was its length. The last time I saw Richard alive, he was struggling to edit this book down to size. He had produced a manuscript of 1,200 pages—it was his magnum opus, after all—but Oxford University Press thought (quite reasonably) a manuscript of 400 to 600 pages would result in a more readable and affordable final product. A copy-editor had suggested ways of reducing the manuscript by half, but some of the suggestions cut at the heart of the book's argument. The image of Richard sitting at his desk, shaking his head as he thumbed through the pages, scores of which were covered in red, remains vivid to this day. He seemed genuinely perplexed about how to shorten the manuscript while retaining all of its bold theoretical vision and subtle argumentation. Ultimately, he never even had the opportunity to try. Two weeks after I saw him, Richard Schoenherr was born into eternal life.

The task of seeing the completed manuscript through to publication remained and, as he said in his 1998 article (see note 5), Lawrence Young was to take responsibility for this. Ultimately, he was unable to do so. Thus, in January 2000, Judy Schoenherr approached me to ask if I would take over responsibility for editing the manuscript. I immediately agreed. Although I knew Richard for less than five years, my debt to him is profound.[37]

I set about my task with the goal of cutting 800 pages, thinking that I would fall somewhat short but still meet OUP's desire for a 400 to 600 page manuscript. After several months of difficult, even gut-wrenching, work, I succeeded in cutting the manuscript from 1,200 to 400 pages. But it is not possible to reduce a manuscript by two-thirds without some cost. In what follows, I briefly discuss my editorial strategy and highlight some of what was retained and what was lost in the process.

The ideas in this book are uniquely Richard Schoenherr's. I have attempted not to make any substantive alterations in the process of editing. I have added language only where necessary to make the text sensible after deleting material. I have not updated any of the data or references within the body of the text, preferring to bring the text up to date by way of this introduction. What the reader has in this book is what Schoenherr wrote, only much less than in the original.

Wanting to retain the core of the argument, I began by eliminating the 73-page bibliography—a useful resource, but ultimately expendable since full citations are all given in the endnotes. The original manuscript also had seven appendices that contained methodological details and elaborations of arguments that couldn't fit in the body of the text (e.g., "A Note on Theory Construction and Empirical Evidence," "Identifying Conservative and Progressive Coalitions," and "Should Feminists Promote a Married Priesthood?"). All of this was deleted. A dozen tables summarizing the state of the priest shortage—gone. Deletions and other consolidations allowed me to shorten the book from 17 to 14 chapters.

The introductions to each part of the book were deleted, along with much of the introductory and conclusory material in each chapter that summarized the argument. These deletions make the book harder to skim but allowed me to retain more of the original argument and supporting evidence and documentation. Still, much of the evidence and documentation had to go. Within the text, if more than one example was given, I eliminated one or more of them. So too with many of the extended quotations from the work of others. In the notes, if multiple citations were given, some were deleted. Consequently, the book acknowledges less of the secondary material on which Schoenherr drew than it originally did. Almost every parenthetical comment, aside, and elaboration of a nonessential point in the text was eliminated, as were end notes that didn't directly bear on the argument (indeed, the present manuscript has 20 percent fewer notes than the original, in addition to the notes being more succinct).

Although *Goodbye Father* remains meticulously argued and profound, the overall effect of this massive editing of the manuscript is that the argument is less erudite, refined, and subtle than it was originally. I hope readers will not hold this against Richard Schoenherr. I feel I deleted more knowledge and wisdom from the manuscript than I will ever possess myself.

Editor's Acknowledgments

It has been said that economists explain the choices people make, and sociologists explain why people have no choices to make. The expansion of rational choice theory beyond economics into sociology has changed this somewhat. Yet, as a sociologist, my sympathies remain with those who focus on the limitations on our abilities to make "rational" choices. In some instances, we have no choice to make. Editing this book is a case in point: I could not choose *not* to undertake this responsibility. I had a moral obligation to do so.

The responsibility for bringing the publication of this book to completion has been awesome, in the literal sense of the word: it inspired in me a profound and reverent fear. Bearing the burden of this awesome responsibility was made more manageable by a number of individuals. This work would have been more difficult without the encouragement of Maureen Hallinan, a friend and colleague at the University of Notre Dame. Her early and unflagging support of my working on this project prevented any doubt about the wisdom of committing precious time to it from entering my mind. Richard Williams was my department chair when I undertook this work and also supported my efforts, morally and materially. Robert McClory, David McKee, and Robert Mackin read all or part of the edited manuscript and offered their valuable feedback. McClory, Hallinan, Williams, Christopher Shannon, Sharon Schmeling, Paul Perl, Mary Gautier, and Bryan Froehle helped by previewing and commenting on this introductory essay. Finally, I cannot thank Judy Schoenherr enough for entrusting this project to me. I hope the final product begins to repay that trust.

Since confession is good for the soul, according to my friend "Iron" John Bartkowski, I beg the reader's indulgence to conclude on a personal note. Although I am a sociologist by training, I am more fundamentally—in my very personhood—a Catholic Christian. I see the concerns raised by this book as affecting all Catholics. They are global in scope but also touch us on a daily basis in our dioceses, in our parishes, and often in our homes. To wit: the same week Judy Schoenherr asked me to work on *Goodbye Father*, the lead story in the *South Bend Tribune* was on the effect of the priest shortage in the Roman Catholic diocese of Fort Wayne–South Bend, Indiana. The problem is global, but the effects are local. Thus, my prayer for the Church is for a full and vibrant priesthood, a rich sacramental life, and the necessary vision to make these things possible: courage enough to "risk growth" rather than simply "managing decline."[38]

South Bend, Indiana　　　　　　　　　　　　　　　　　　　　　　　　D. Y.
6 January 2002
+ *Solemnity of the Epiphany*

The Roman Catholic Church is facing a crisis of immense proportions. In the United States, the availability of priests to provide essential religious services is being cut in half. By 2005, there will be 40 percent fewer parish priests and 65 percent more church members than there were in 1966. Colleagues and I made these alarming forecasts in *Full Pews and Empty Altars*, the final report of a demographic study sponsored by the U.S. Catholic Conference (USCC) published in 1993.

Besides the magnitude of the priest shortage, there is something else bizarre about the crisis: Most bishops outwardly ignore it and some publicly declare it doesn't exist. Such a dramatic imbalance in supply and demand in other critical occupations would create a public hue and cry. Imagine cutting the supply of doctors, teachers, or garbage collectors in half while the demand for services more than doubled.

Full Pews and Empty Altars was published so that all parties interested in the priest shortage could have access to the same definitive data, which they could use for their own religious, political, or scientific ends. Now that the statistics are available, my aim in *Goodbye Father* is to spell out how interested parties can use the information for their personal and social agendas. The earlier volume combined rigorous empirical research with a strong policy orientation. This companion volume emphasizes theoretical and historical analysis, but still in the service of practical-minded policy.

The demographics of the declining priesthood are startling, but they are only a subplot in a much bigger story. They raise more questions and stir up more conflicts than they resolve. For starters, we're left wondering how the Catholic Church can serve its growing membership. Will nuns, deacons, and laypeople be able to fill the gap left by the vanishing clergy? One spokesman says yes. Bishop Donald W. Wuerl of Pittsburgh, former chairman of the National Conference of Catholic Bishops' Committee on Priestly Life and Ministry, believes that with "the involvement and the appreciation of the gifts and talents of countless laypeople . . . [and] the functioning of the permanent diaconate . . . in parishes where we used to have three priests we find we can provide the same service with two" (Catholic News Service, July 1990). As the shortage gets worse, however, will the two dwindle to one? And will the sole remaining priest become a circuit rider? Or will the eucharistic sacrifice of the Mass become the privilege of the few—perhaps only those in wealthy parishes?

If indeed laypeople are to shoulder more ministerial responsibilities in the Church, other issues follow. To what extent will the locus of Church power shift from clergy to lay ministers? Is a fully empowered laity here to stay, and, if not, how long will the honeymoon of the laity last? These are burning issues for churchgoers struggling to protect and reform the Catholic tradition. So, committed Catholics are the first interested party I hope to reach in this book. They include the laypeople, religious, and priests who together practice Catholicism at the grassroots level; the theologians and Scripture scholars who interpret the ancient tradition in light of contemporary scientific research; and the magisterium or college of bishops who, with the pope as their head, officially teach Catholic doctrine.

The second party I hope to engage is sociologists, psychologists, historians, and philosophers—including feminist scholars—who are interested in theories of social change, the social scientific study of religion, organizational analysis, and, in particular, how organized religion reflects and affects social change. There's also a large third party for whom this story is written: all those interested in the impact of a powerful world religion on their personal, social, and spiritual lives.

My basic premise is that decline in the priesthood population is the engine driving a set of dynamic social forces. Together they form a matrix of pressure for structural change in the Church. Because Catholic Christianity shapes Western culture so profoundly, any radical change in Catholicism is bound to have strong repercussions throughout society. Hence, although I put the Catholic Church in the spotlight, bear in mind that it is playing a role in a universal human drama.

In telling this complex story, the book revolves around several main arguments. First, it predicts that the Catholic Church will lift its ban on ordination of married men in the next few decades. Second, it shows that this radical breakthrough to a married priesthood results from irreversible historical trends. Third, it argues that transformation of the priesthood will strengthen authentic religion within Catholicism. Fourth, it maintains that institutionalization of a married priesthood dismantles one of the strongest supports for patriarchy in human society. And fifth, this book asserts that married priests will pave the way for female priests and, therefore, greater gender equality in the Church and society.

Part I of the book documents the severity and main cause of the priest shortage. The major reason why so few young men are entering the priesthood and why so many are leaving it is compulsory celibacy. The facts are hard to refute or ignore. The Church is simply unable to recruit and retain enough male celibate priests to meet the sacramental needs of faithful Catholics. As their numbers dwindle, the controversy over mandatory celibacy for priests looms ever larger. This age-old dispute, together with the feminist and personalist movements, raises some obvious but threatening questions. Is the male celibate priesthood dying? Will a married priesthood, which eventually includes women, solve the crisis? If so, what are the implications of a married, gender-inclusive priesthood for dismantling other forms of patriarchy in society?

At first glance, the Catholic controversy over celibacy appears to be a parochial issue. This book invites you to take a closer look. What are the deeper structural implications of opening the Catholic priesthood, first to married men and eventually to women? I argue that getting rid of compulsory celibacy undermines the structural foundation of exclusivity as such, paving the way for a more inclusive social structure. Thus, once we look behind the smoke and mirrors used by both sides of the debate, we discover what all the fuss over celibacy is really about: replacing male exclusivity with gender inclusivity in areas of social power and privilege. This book depicts the controversy as an *ultimate* battle because patriarchal religion is the ultimate source of father-rule in society.

The analysis will lay bare the covert connection between compulsory celibacy and patriarchy. It formulates the question about their relationship in a novel way: Can the domination and subjugation of women continue in Western society without the symbolic support provided by an exclusively male celibate priesthood in the Catholic Church? The force of the argument strikes at patriarchy's deepest roots, namely, sacralized father-rule in organized religion. Therefore, what seems to be an internal squabble among Catholics is, in reality, an open battle over the future of patriarchy.

Part II lays out a theoretical framework for explaining the causes and consequences of the conflict and describes historical trends that are driving the Church to the brink of change. My explanation of what ails the Catholic Church stems from a theory of social change based on two major assumptions. First, we live in an organizational society. Thus, society changes only as important large-scale organizations are transformed. Organized religion is chief among them. From this perspective, I see the Catholic Church as one large modern organization among many others that are crucial to human welfare. It is a venerable, transnational, bureaucratic organization that is loved and admired, hated and feared by many. Even in the age of cyberspace technology, the Catholic Church and its leaders are a formidable power the world must reckon with.

The second key assumption is that, despite similarities to other organizations, the Church is unique, sui generis. Why? Because authentic religion deals explicitly with ultimate reality, which transcends ordinary space and time. Hence I also assume that for believers, the Church is the resurrected body of an Incarnate Divinity, the corporate embodiment of the Christ, the People of God on pilgrimage to a transcendent goal. For faithful Catholics, the Church is the sacramental means of human fulfillment, a way to unitive consciousness of Absolute Being. All these poetic images reflect phenomenological facts to be incorporated in the theory.

Regardless of its uniqueness, however, the Church changes in the same way as any other organization: through conflict over its technical core. I will show that, from the viewpoint of organization theory, the priesthood represents the key economic resource and power elite of the Church and therefore forms its technical core. We will discover growing tension in the way religious officials administer the Catholic means of salvation. These tensions well up from deeply embedded social forces that have been gaining momentum over decades, centuries, and millennia. The middle part of the book, therefore, describes the relentless social forces that exacerbate the growing priest shortage: irreversible trends toward greater pluralism in all areas of social life, especially greater autonomy in emerging nation-states; the personalist and feminist movements; and the lay and liturgical movements within the Catholic Church. My point is that the present moment, which future historians will call an axial period, bristles with potential for radical change not only in the Church's ministerial structure but also in all social forms of patriarchal domination.

But in these chapters, I will urge you to see a crisis far deeper than can be resolved by merely adjusting the marital status or gender of the Catholic clergy. Part III calls specific attention to *paradox,* an unfamiliar topic to most of us. The dilemmas facing the Catholic Church and all organized religion are born out of apparent contradictions between unity and diversity, immanence and transcendence, and ultimately, hierarchy and hierophany. I will examine the primal paradoxes of human and divine reality that most of us wrestle with on all sides, but mainly in our religious organizations.

The celibacy debate, therefore, has important repercussions; but settling it does not solve the deeper underlying paradox. Even though Catholics might succeed in achieving marital-status and gender inclusivity in the priesthood, that is not the ultimate goal of authentic ministry. During the struggle we must learn that following the Way—any authentic transcendent way—calls for a personal and communal dying to self. In its deep structure, therefore, authentic religion must be organized around a hierarchical, sacramental, sacrificial ministry. Thus, getting rid of male celibate exclusivity does not—indeed, cannot—mean getting rid of sacerdotal sacramentalism. This is the most important conclusion of the book.

Because paradox is a fact of spiritual life, Catholic piety is grounded in the poetry and ritual of the Mass and sacraments. This book recognizes that authentic sacramental rituals celebrate life *symbolically* and *efficaciously* in its height and depth, at every moment of birth, growth, death, and ultimate fulfillment. Without some form of daily and seasonal sacramental life, the human spirit dies a subtle, slow, but sure death. It is no exaggeration to call the debate over the future of ministry a matter of life and death. For most Catholics, a vanishing priesthood means a dying sacramental life.

No matter how irrational it looks to outsiders, a religious community's sacramental tradition is its most precious possession. The sacred symbols—preserved in some combination of mythic ritual, holy writ, and oral tradition—are protected from corrosion and confusion with utmost care. Proposals to change the tradition are deadly serious. When faced with something new, symbolic clarity and legitimacy emerge slowly and with great effort and pain. Thus, a major goal of this book is to help create new symbols for a new Catholic ministry, ones that sacralize inclusivity rather than male celibate exclusivity.

Part IV explains why the seemingly inevitable change from a celibate to a married clergy is being stymied. Why do bureaucratic guardians of the status quo refuse to say goodbye to celibate fathers? The answer to that question is tangled up in the symbolic nature of religious politics. Resolving tensions that ripple through the Catholic Church, from the pope in Rome to the laypeople in the pews, is no easy task.

Part of the genius of the Catholic Church and organized religion in general is that they provide a battleground for life-and-death struggles in which the major weapons are ideological. Comparative studies of religion and mythology portray a lavish variety of poetry and symbols that religious groups create for their sacramental systems. The Catholic ministerial tradition is one historical solution to the need for external expression of internal spiritual experience. Obviously, it is not the only one, even among Christians. Nor can the social forms of Catholic ministry ever be considered immutable—otherwise they would be dead. As I will show, it is because they live and give life that forms of ministry are the object of intense conflict and debate. Hence this part of the narrative is about coalitional conflict waged on the battleground of legal definition, mystical symbol, and religious paradox in the Church. The moment of crisis is reaching a crescendo as a conservative coalition tries to maintain the status quo defining Catholic ministry and a progressive coalition tries to change it. In the process, coalitional conflict is clarifying the lines of debate.

The last part of the book asks why the conservative coalition—headed by the pope—is so adamantly opposed to a married clergy. My answer is that clerical celibacy provides sacralized support for patriarchy. The papal bloc seems to know intuitively that saying goodbye to celibate exclusivity means eventually saying goodbye to male exclusivity. We will discover that a married clergy is still anathema for most of the Catholic hierarchy because it is the camel's nose under their patriarchal tent. Therefore, the final chapter contends that gender inclusivity must be preceded by the introduction and routinization of marital-status inclusivity in the priesthood.

Many readers will find evidence here showing that married priests are inevitable. It is only a matter of time. In a sense, it brings the Protestant Reformation home to roost. A married clergy in the Roman Catholic Church will reduce the gap between ordained and lay members of the priesthood of all believers, a rallying cry of the reformers, and will be the gateway to further equality for women, who eventually will be admitted to ordination. The transition from ordaining married men to ordaining women in the Catholic priesthood will not take three hundred years as it did in Protestant Christianity, but it may take several generations.

The book ends with an upbeat scenario. If the progressive coalition is successful, the net result will be a new structural form of Catholic ministry that is less Manichaean, less authoritarian, and less patriarchal but still authentically Catholic. In sum, the transformed ministry, marked by vibrant lay participation and a gender-inclusive priesthood, will provide access to authentic means of salvation for mature believers. Ultimately, the renewed Catholic priesthood will provide sacralized support for gender inclusivity throughout human society.

Choices, conflicts, and transformations in my own life have shaped the framework for the story of how the priest shortage produces crisis, conflict, and change in the Church and society. So I offer an autobiographical account that acknowledges the social underpinnings of the analysis in this book. The narrative tells of personal biases, forks in the intellectual road, and milestones in the evolution of my thought. The story begins three decades ago, at the close of the Second Vatican Council.

I had been ordained a priest of the Archdiocese of Detroit only a couple of years when the late John Cardinal Dearden asked me to get a doctorate in sociology at the University of Chicago so I could teach in the seminary. One of my first term paper assignments was to design a research project in a social psychology course with Professor Richard Flacks. The proposal I submitted featured a questionnaire on celibacy in the Catholic priesthood. Flacks liked the paper and urged me to do the survey. I talked it over with Joseph Fichter and Andrew Greeley, both Catholic priests and noted sociologists who were at the University of Chicago. Fichter was there on a sabbatical and Greeley was a program director at the National Opinion Research Center (NORC). It was the mid-1960s. I remember Fichter saying, "You young Turks get right to the heart of the matter, don't you." Greeley said, "To do it right, a study like that will take a lot of money. And it should be done right." Flacks's suggestion soon got lost in the realities of qualifying examinations and a research assistantship with Professor Peter Blau. A couple of years later Fichter published his book *America's Forgotten Priests*. The first American sociologist to pose the burning question, he reported that the majority of U.S. priests were in favor of optional celibacy. Then in 1969, Greeley accepted a contract for another national survey of the priesthood, funded to the tune of $300,000 by the United States Catholic Conference (USCC). "Here's the study you wanted to do on celibacy," he said. "Would you like to be the director?"

I had been reading about theories of social change and complex organizations and working on an exciting research project with Blau. My years in graduate school coincided with the aftermath of the Second Vatican Council, which were electrifying times for Catholics, especially young priests. So much seemed up for grabs in the Church. As a budding sociologist, I began to see the Catholic Church as one of the most powerful complex organizations in the world. I also had a hunch that, somehow, compulsory celibacy was part of its power structure. One of my first published papers dealt with these issues.[1] I was learning a great deal about the structures of modern bureaucracies by studying government employment agencies, which I had chosen for my doctoral dissertation research. I was especially intrigued by how formal structures take on a life of their own and become an "insidious form of power."[2]

While in the final stages of writing my dissertation, I accepted Greeley's offer to be study director for the NORC priest survey. In late 1969 and throughout 1970, we invited some 7,000 U.S. priests to complete a 48-page questionnaire. An amazing 72 percent complied. I had redesigned the project to include an organizational level of analysis. Moreover, I suggested that the sample cover bishops and major superiors, because they represented key power positions in the Church, as well as recently resigned priests, whose views would reveal as much about the state of the priesthood as those of the active clergy. Greeley agreed to the changes in his proposed design after clearing them with Bishop Joseph Bernardin, then general secretary of the USCC. Although he had some misgivings about complicating the research, Greeley was persuaded that the improvements were worth the additional time and effort. Later, however, he complained that the modifications jeopardized our ability to meet the deadline for the final report.[3]

More significantly, in September 1970 I decided—unfortunately and naively as it turned out—to share my intention to marry Judith Woods with my archbishop. I had thought that the chancery would need about six months or so to process my request for a dispensation from the obligations of Holy Orders. The survey report was due in March 1971, so if all went according to schedule, we could be married late that spring or early summer. The plan blew up in my face, however, when Cardinal Dearden commanded me then and there to cease functioning as a priest. Furthermore, he said I would have to be dropped as study director of the priest survey. Greeley and Eugene Kennedy, the director of the companion project at Loyola University of Chicago, came to the rescue. I was grateful to both for their support.[4]

While negotiating with Greeley, Cardinal John Krol, who had responsibility for overseeing relations between the USCC and NORC, also demanded that I be fired from the project. Greeley came to my defense, declaring, "If Schoenherr is dropped, we'll need another year and an additional $70,000 to complete the study." Greeley and Kennedy convinced Cardinal Krol that it was in everybody's best interests for me to continue. Krol backed down but demanded that my name not be publicly linked to the report. Both Krol and Dearden thought that the credibility of the study would be jeopardized if an "ex-priest" was one of the authors. Greeley countered that if my name couldn't be on the byline, neither would his. We would call it a report of the NORC and describe the division of labor in the acknowledgments. Krol agreed, but then—for unknown reasons—the book was published with Greeley listed as its sole author. Nonplussed, he wrote an open letter to Krol published in *America*, a widely read Catholic weekly magazine. He extracted a promise from the USCC that each copy of the book would include an erratum insert—noting a mistake in the authorship. No one noticed it.

With no need to wait until the study was completed, I was married in December 1970. These were emotionally charged months, obviously. I made every effort, however, not to allow anyone to slant or misrepresent the NORC priest data in any way. I claim my share of the credit both for the high quality of the final report and for getting it done on time. No one worked harder or longer hours on that project than I did.

Like Fichter, we found that a majority of clergy favored married priests. We also discovered that the desire to marry was the key reason why respondents were deciding to leave the clerical priesthood. In a comparative analysis, another colleague and I found the celibacy issue was equally powerful in the desire of Spanish priests to leave the clerical ministry. Later, other sociologists would replicate the NORC study. Two decades after the Second Vatican Council had ended, they found that the same conditions, principally mandatory celibacy, still exerted the dominant influence on the decision to leave. The data supported my hunch: the law of celibacy has many structural ramifications.

I finished my Ph.D. in the fall of 1970 and was hired the following year as an assistant professor of sociology at the University of Wisconsin–Madison. A National Science Foundation (NSF) grant awarded in 1974 allowed me to gather additional data on the Catholic Church. Students and I continued analyzing the NORC and NSF data sets throughout the 1970s and 1980s.[5] I also published an article on the bureaucratic and phenomenological aspects of religious power as a sort of prologue to the book about the celibacy conflict that was gestating in my mind since I had entered graduate school.[6] It was a metatheoretical essay dealing with the uniqueness of religious organizations. It also addressed epistemological issues that would help avoid trivializing religion while studying it with quantitative methods.

In the early 1980s, I began a productive relationship with Fred Hofheinz, program director for religion at the Lilly Endowment. He helped heal the wound inflicted during the priest study back in 1970–1971. Late in 1983, Hofheinz persuaded the Lilly Endowment to award me a grant for a study of the priest shortage sponsored by the USCC. It was now 12 years later, and almost no one at the USCC remembered me or my role in the "Greeley Study," as it was known there. Those who did were willing to forgive and forget—and so was I. The following summer we launched the study with a pretest in Milwaukee. Almost a decade later, the archibishop of Milwaukee, Rembert Weakland, would write an endorsement for the cover of *Full Pews and Empty Altars*, the project's final report.

I deliberately kept the theoretical underpinnings of the Lilly-funded USCC project simple. I didn't want to make the mistake of using as elaborate a theo-

retical model as the one I had used for the NSF study. An ambitious comparative structural approach had provided the framework for the NSF project, but
because of its complexity, data collection and processing had consumed so much
time and energy that few resources had been left for analyzing and publishing
the results. I wouldn't let that happen again. I decided to limit the USCC study
to a straightforward application of organizational demography, a new development in the study of organizations. The framework and techniques—stable population theory and life table analysis—were powerful, appropriate, and tried
and true. A decade earlier, the renowned demographer Nathan Keyfitz had
called for applying demographic techniques to the problem of organizational
change but was widely ignored.[7] I became aware of the possibility in an article
published by Judah Matras while he was a visiting professor at the University of
Wisconsin–Madison.[8] Gudmun Hernes had also developed a model for understanding population change as a structural process, and Howard Aldrich applied
his insights to a typology of organizational change.[9] Two of the types of change
were transition and transformation—the former applied to moderate and the
latter to radical change. The type of change taking place in the Roman Catholic
Church was an organization-level demographic transition that could potentially
lead to a full-scale transformation.

Thus, I acquired more of the theoretical vocabulary needed to explain how
the persistent problem of celibacy and the resulting priest shortage might lead
to a radical transformation of the structure of ministry. Integrating the work of
Matras, Hernes, and Aldrich with other literature on organizations provided the
theoretical background for my research on the demographic transition of the
clergy.[10] When the study began, Bill McKelvey and Howard Aldrich were making significant improvements in the population approach to organization analysis. In its original form—labeled the population ecology or natural selection
model and articulated mainly by Michael Hannan, John Freeman, and Glenn
Carroll—the theory was heavily and justifiably criticized.[11] The McKelvey-
Aldrich version, however, answered many of the criticisms and transformed the
approach into a useful sociological model of organizational change.[12]

My earlier work with Blau had alerted me to a profound Weberian insight
about the power of bureaucratic control. But it wasn't until Kenneth McNeil
spelled out the full implications of organizational power that I began to understand the rest of the intellectual legacy of Max Weber.[13] And not until Paul Goldman and Donald Van Houten pointed out that contemporary Marxists could
provide similar insights into organizational forms of domination did I begin to
appreciate the Marxian heritage as well.[14] Charles Perrow's critical essay on organization theory was the final catalyst.[15] The latest results of his sifting and win-
nowing of the organization literature made the theoretical and empirical research that I had been ruminating about for over two decades finally jell. Fully
understood, Weber's theory of the rise of capitalism and rational-legal bureau-

cracy is the story of how modern organizations became the mechanisms of domination and control in the hands of the capitalist class. Organizations as "tools in the hands of their masters" is Perrow's apt phrase. Bureaucratic organization as a mechanism of domination and control is a basic insight that has passed through many minds between Weber and Perrow, who now labels the theory the "qualified power model." It stands at the head of my list of theoretical formulations for understanding modern organizations like the Catholic Church.

Thus, the model I propose in this book combines classic theories of social change with contemporary research on organizations. But because it deals with religious organizations, which are both like and unlike all other types of modern organizations, my model is also heavily influenced by research in the sociology of religion. I was introduced to this exciting literature by Andrew Greeley in one of the first courses he taught just after he finished his Ph.D. at the University of Chicago. I discovered that Weber was also a sociologist of religion par excellence and that Emile Durkheim understood religion as the prototype and paradigm of most modern institutions. Many of their contemporary disciples had delved deeply into the sui generis nature of religion. From Clifford Geertz, I became aware of the importance of symbols and myths; from Thomas O'Dea, of the dilemmas inherent in institutionalizing the sacred; from Peter Berger, of the social construction of reality and especially ultimate reality; from Robert Bellah, of the evolution of authentic religion from archaic to modern forms; and from Rodney Stark, of the importance of rational behavior even among true believers.

I also became amazed by the work of Rudolf Otto, Martin Buber, and Mircea Eliade, all of whom provided sophisticated analyses of the experience of the sacred. Eliade had been a visiting lecturer at Chicago while I was a graduate student, but, regrettably, I was too naive to take any of his classes. Later, his magisterial works became the centerpiece of my own course in sociology of religion and contributed significantly to my understanding of the paradox of hierarchy and hierophany in organized religion. I also stumbled across Paul Ricoeur's hermeneutical analysis of Freud and was intrigued by his developmental model of how individuals and groups relate to religious myths. Believers move from primitive, naive faith through critical distancing to a restorative, critical naivete, which is a rationally integrated faith. From these scholars, it became clear that the positivistic approaches to social science—which I had learned so well at Chicago and practiced so diligently at Madison—had to be integrated with the phenomenology of religion. Otherwise, I would never come up with a comprehensive explanation of social change in the Catholic Church.

Feminist scholars also provided an important missing link. As a graduate student at Loyola, my wife, Judy, avidly read Carol Gilligan, Mary Daly, Rosemary Ruether, Carol Christ, Starhawk, Elaine Pagels, Daphne Hampson, Sandra Schneiders, and Gerda Lerner. Her enthusiasm was contagious, and I read as much as I could. The new data on Christianity, the novel interpretations of history, and the reinterpretations of social science that resulted from incorporating research on the attitudes and behavior of women were stunning. In particular, Gerda Lerner's authoritative analysis of patriarchy clinched my understanding of the historicity of female subjugation, especially in the Catholic Church.[16]

Transpersonal psychologist Ken Wilber, in a series of brilliant works, helped bring it all together. He became the catalytic agent for my thinking in the area of religion, just as Perrow had been in the area of organization studies. Although I had been teaching Abraham Maslow's notions about peak experience for some time, Wilber made me aware that Maslow's research on the farther reaches of human nature was truly pathbreaking. Wilber picked up where Maslow had left off, producing a comprehensive, critical approach for the social scientific study of religion. Wilber's transpersonal paradigm inspired the core chapter and many crucial insights in this book.

The cliché is right: We stand on the shoulders of giants. Whether I see any farther than my mentors have is for readers to decide. In any case, I am delighted to acknowledge their contributions and insights. It is a long list. I personally thank each of you noted here. I am profoundly grateful particularly to my teachers Peter Blau and Andrew Greeley, but also to Robert Bellah, Charles Perrow, Rodney Stark, Gerda Lerner, and Ken Wilber. Your presence was felt while writing every chapter.

I owe a debt of gratitude to many others who steadied me in the last leg of this odyssey. Lawrence Young and I already thanked the sponsors, respondents, and research team in *Full Pews and Empty Altars*. Since this volume completes that analysis, I repeat my thanks to Fred Hofheinz and the Lilly Endowment, the agency that provided generous financial support, and to Father Eugene Hemrick, director of research at the USCC, the organization that sponsored the collection of the demographic data that are the empirical foundation of this work. Only Fred, Gene, and I know how many rough spots were smoothed over by their encouraging personal support. Additional funds were provided by the Graduate School Research Committee of the University of Wisconsin–Madison, which I also gratefully acknowledge.

Lawrence Young began working with me during the data collection campaign for this study and has remained a collaborator, coauthor, and helpful critic ever since. When it comes to work partnerships, few have been as professionally productive and as personally enriching as ours. My hearty thanks to you, Larry. Kathryn Kuhlow and Virginia Rogers helped prepare the bibliography. Anneliese Vandre assisted in typing tables and in collecting data for one of the appendices [deleted from the final manuscript—*Ed.*]. Research assistants Robert Moore and, especially, Lichang Lee took over responsibilities for ongoing projects that allowed me to concentrate on writing. I extend my heartfelt thanks to each of you.

Attentive friends and colleagues read various sections and entire drafts of the manuscript. Fred Hofheinz, Matt Hogan, George Hinger, and Joseph Schillmoeller brought an intimate knowledge of the priesthood to bear with their insightful criticisms. Warren Hagstrom, Lawrence Young, and Tsan-Yuan Cheng applied their different but decisive sociological perspectives, and Leora Weitzman gave her reactions the philosopher's touch. David Roll and Judith Schoenherr wrestled with the jargon and verbiage until it made sense to the general reader. I am deeply indebted to all of you. A singular thanks to David McKee, who read it all—some parts several times. I cherish your untiring enthusiasm, depth of knowledge, and boundless friendship.

My friends and family know best that this book is much more than an objective, scientific explanation of historical events and social change. It is also an expression of who I am and who stands together with me. I wish I could name each of you, but that would be self-indulgence; however, I must thank the St. Paul University Catholic Center, the Community of Benedict, and the Friday Morning Breakfast Group for the joyful moments we share. I am immensely grateful for my children, Andrew, Maria, and Joe. Your presence in my life is a delight. And Judy—to whom this work is dedicated—thank you for reading every word with gentle love, hard-nosed criticism, and close to infallible wisdom. But most of all, for holding onto the basket.

Madison, Wisconsin   R.A.S.
April 26, 1995

CONTENTS

PART V   CONTINUITY AND CHANGE

PART I

CELIBACY, PATRIARCHY,

AND THE PRIEST SHORTAGE

CELIBATE EXCLUSIVITY IS THE ISSUE

M any insist that mandatory celibacy for priests is not the issue behind the malaise plaguing Roman Catholicism. They say that the problem goes far deeper and to suggest that allowing priests to marry will solve the Church's ills smacks of naivete at best.[1] I agree that celibacy is not the issue. I maintain, however, that *celibate exclusivity* is. This distinction is crucial. Understanding the ramifications of compulsory celibacy is the key that unlocks one of the most complex enigmas facing the Catholic Church. Moreover, the law of priestly celibacy has hidden implications for modern society as a whole.

Not everyone recognizes celibate exclusivity of the priesthood as the root problem. For example, the malaise in Catholicism is also blamed on clericalism, especially in the form of limited lay participation in ministry. A recent report on French Canada paints a rosy picture of Catholic congregationalism in Quebec— with decidedly feminine tones. Canadian Catholics report approvingly that "in Montreal, women publicly baptize on Sundays. In St. Jean Longueuil, women preach during Mass regularly. In Valleyfield and Labrador City–Schefferville, women are diocesan chancellors." Montreal Archbishop Jean-Claude Turcotte strongly prefers the new lay-animated church. He affirms, "We have discovered the role of all the baptized people . . . [who] are responsible for the evangelization of the world." The archbishop insists: "To recover a Church of priests could be a facile thing. . . . We would remove celibacy, for example, as a legislation, then we'll find all these wonderful married men, and that would solve our problem, get the Church again in the hands of the clergy. *That* would be a frightening thing to me in the light of Vatican II."[2]

In a similar vein, Monsignor William Shannon, a priest in Rochester, New York, calls for lay participation as the solution to the priest shortage. He writes: "Were this done, it would obviate the necessity of priests becoming 'circuit-riders,' going from one place to another to say words that only they can say." Circuit-rider is "a lonely, depressing position for the priest and a trying situation for the parish communities." The monsignor agrees with one of his friends who said he "would rather pump gas than become a 'circuit-rider priest.'" So Shannon concludes: "How much more sense it would make, in the absence of a resident pastor, to have someone who is known as the leader in that parish community preside at the community's liturgy."[3] Admittedly, congregationalism is one possible solution to the priest shortage. The essential trait of congregationalism is to eradicate the theological distinction between clergy and laity by permitting laypeople to officiate at liturgical services. As a permanent answer, however, it undermines the essential nature of Roman Catholicism.

From another viewpoint, the Catholic emphasis on sacraments may seem to be the issue at stake. For example, in a recent study of reasons why Catholics leave the Church, the sociologist Father Andrew Greeley cites the shoddy celebration of sacraments as the major cause. Greeley writes that "those who were thinking of leaving were troubled not so much by the 'mass media' issues of birth control, abortion, divorce, the ordination of women, and celibacy, but by the absence of spiritual and religious leadership in the Church." His data show that the sacraments "are the strongest predictor of propensity to stay in the Church" and that they "exercise a notable impact in diminishing the effect of those dissatisfactions with the institution (such as lack of respect for women), which incline people to leave the Church."[4]

What, then, *is* the issue? Are the quandaries over mandatory celibacy and the ordination of women only problems trumped up by the media? According to Greeley, "The issue ought to be, rather, how to make the experience of sacrament so appealing, so seductive that those who have drifted to the fringes of the Church will be lured back toward the center."[5] Indisputably, Roman Catholicism is a sacramental church, and as such, Catholic spiritual leadership is inextricably tied to priesthood. The current form of priesthood, however, is locked into male celibate exclusivity. According to extensive research, mandatory celibacy is the most frequently cited cause of poor recruitment and retention of priests. The priest shortage creates understaffed parishes and overworked pastors, a situation that in turn creates the conditions for shoddy sacraments.

If sacraments are what it means to be Catholic—as acknowledged by pope, bishop, theologian, sociologist, and Catholic survey respondent alike—then church leaders face some practical questions. Is the boundary around the pool of talents that are needed to make sacramental encounters appealing, even seductive, drawn too narrowly? How much longer can the ecological niche of Catholic dioceses yield enough celibate men to meet the sacramental demands of a growing and increasingly educated laity? Welcomed advances in education, theology, and liturgy have deepened the appreciation of the Catholic laity for well-celebrated sacraments. With greater demand and deeper appreciation, why should sacraments continue to rely exclusively on the availability of male celibate ministers? If all the traditional elements of Catholic ministry cannot be maintained, which ones are expendable—sacrament and priesthood or celibacy and male exclusivity? And if male celibate exclusivity is abandoned in Roman Catholicism, what effect will that have on patriarchy in the wider society? For committed and aware Catholics, these are no longer rhetorical questions. The current generation of Catholics faces an either-or decision. The Church will *either* have to guarantee this generation its baptismal right of access to the sacraments *or* continue to insist on a male celibate priesthood. The choices are mutually exclusive.

Celibate Exclusivity Is the Issue

Although celibate exclusivity is the issue and decline in the priesthood population is its symptom, the priest shortage is not a story of the faults and failings of latter-day male Catholics too spiritually weak to espouse the celibate state. There is simply no evidence that young priests and candidates for the priesthood are less spiritual nowadays than those of prior generations. Thus, celibacy by itself is not the issue. Furthermore, ascribing the degeneration of an organizational form like the priesthood to the spiritual behavior of individuals is a "grievous misunderstanding" of social reality.[6] The purposive choices of seminarians and priests who decide to enter and remain active in the Catholic priesthood are deeply embedded in social relations that are complex, constantly changing, and riddled with conflict.

The world around the Catholic priesthood has changed dramatically. A matrix of social forces has transformed and continues to alter the core structures of the Catholic Church. The priesthood is at the very center of that structural core. According to my demographic data, the current sociological form of priesthood is in a state of degeneration. Thus, as Catholicism enters its third millennium it faces an imposing dilemma: whether to reinforce male celibate exclusivity in ministry, and thus reproduce the structures of patriarchy, or to reinforce the primordial tradition of eucharistic sacrifice and hierarchy of control that compose the essence of Catholicism.

I contend that the priest shortage brings the issue of celibate exclusivity to center stage. But male exclusivity, which is sorely challenged by feminism, is standing in the wings. Despite the brilliant tactics of the current papacy, Rome cannot withstand the relentless forces of structural conflict generated by demographic and other social changes. Arguably, the right mix of forces precipitating radical change is now reaching a critical threshold. In the near future, a big step toward deconstructing patriarchy in the Roman Catholic Church and, therefore, in the wider society will be taken with the ordination of married men. Optional celibacy for priests will be legitimated amid conflict but will spread and be routinized in the next two or three generations. Once women and children are allowed in the sacred minister's inner chambers, the ordination of women will follow, though with even greater conflict. Nevertheless, gender equality in ministry will spread and also be routinized, but much more slowly than the inclusion of married men in the priesthood. In the end, the world's largest religious organization will allow women to control access to the means of salvation along with men. As the process unfolds, father-rule in Western society will be dealt a severe blow.

Social Change in the Catholic Church

These conclusions follow from a careful consideration of social conditions that are changing the face of Roman Catholicism. I present a sociological argument, based on theories and methods used in classic sociological literature but also drawn from recent developments in organization science, sociology of religion, and social demography. The main thrust of the argument is grounded in empirical evidence. For a full understanding, however, the explanation must go beyond the evidence into theoretical speculation. The speculations are convincing to the extent that the theory and any inferential evidence are compelling.

The diagram in figure 1 provides a map of how the argument unfolds. It incorporates four levels of analysis. The first examines long-term historical, institutional, and ecological trends (segments 1 and 2). The second investigates the sequence of attitudes and behaviors that explain motivation and choice at the social psychological level (segment 3). The third highlights organizational change; this is the major focus of the model (segments 4–6). The last shows the effects of these antecedent changes on structural change in society (segment 7).

Organizational Change

The changing structural form of the priesthood is the starting point of the theoretical argument (segment 6). The defining characteristic of the Catholic priesthood is its fourfold monopoly of ministerial expertise and control. As it is currently structured, the priesthood exercises sacramental, sacerdotal, male, and celibate monopoly over access to the means of salvation for all believers, notions I develop in part II.

I demonstrate that male and celibate exclusivity are the attributes most vulnerable to change. Indeed, during the transformation of the structural form of priesthood that is looming on the horizon, these will be dropped as ideal-typical characteristics. Sacramental and hierarchic hegemony, however, are permanent traits because they compose the deep structure of priesthood. Note, however: The translation of these permanent elements at the level of surface structure is constantly subject to change.

The priest shortage (segment 4) is the driving force that triggers conflict between conservative and progressive coalitions in the Church (segment 5). Sustained loss of critical priestly resources produces an organizational crisis that allows a progressive coalition to succeed in eliminating, first, celibate exclusivity and, eventually, male exclusivity as part of the structural form of priesthood.

Sacramental and hierarchic hegemony constitute the essence of priesthood. So these attributes will not be lost during the organizational transformation of Catholicism, but they will be modified. Social trends have reduced the over-

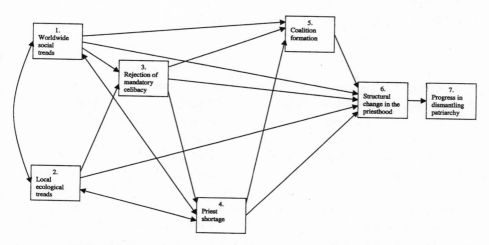

FIGURE 1. Model of social change in the Catholic church and society-at-large

emphasis on sacramentalism in Catholic piety and introduced a new respect for the Bible, thus weakening but not eliminating the sacramental monopoly of control over the means of salvation. With less emphasis on the Sacrament and greater stress on the Word of God, the clerical or hierarchic hegemony of Catholic ministry stemming from priestly ordination is likewise mitigated. As laypeople preside at Bible-based worship services, the priesthood loses part, but by no means all, of its hierarchic monopoly of control.

Social Psychological Change

Widespread rejection of mandatory celibacy has been identified by researchers as the primary cause of poor recruitment and retention in the Catholic priesthood (segment 3). Strong social psychological evidence supporting this statement is presented in chapter 2. This becomes the crux of the analysis: Why are so few young priests and seminary candidates willing to practice lifelong celibacy? Moreover, why has this become a contentious issue at the end of the twentieth century, when mandatory celibacy for priests has been a universal Roman Catholic institution since the twelfth century?

The argument diagrammed in figure 1 stands or falls on whether the disaffection with mandatory celibacy is a temporary or long-range trend. If temporary, adequate recruitment and retention of male celibate priests would be restored once the disaffection passes. The priest shortage would soon subside and along with it the impetus to transform the structural form of the priesthood. If permanent, the shortage will worsen and the pressure for a radical solution to the crisis will mount, as the model predicts.

Historical, Institutional, and Ecological Change

Along with compulsory celibacy, a second major impact on the priest shortage comes from ecological trends in the United States (segment 2). As the priest supply wanes in this country, the lay membership of the Catholic Church continues to grow. Obviously, it takes a dwindling supply and a constant or growing demand to create a shortage. A relatively young age structure along with high fertility and immigration rates are causing steady growth in the U.S. Catholic population. Moreover, moderately high church attendance helps maintain demand for priestly resources. An alternative answer to the priest shortage could come from decline in membership or attendance. This would reduce demand and obviate the need for a large priest supply. But few church leaders would welcome that solution, nor is it likely, given ecological trends.

The impact of ecological change in the United States on the priest shortage is reinforced by a matrix of historical and institutional trends that affect the worldwide Catholic Church (segment 1). These include (1) a shift from dogmatism to pluralism in worldviews, (2) change from a transcendentalist to a personalist construction of human sexuality, (3) decline of a Eurocentric Church and rise in a worldwide inculturation of Catholicism, (4) decline in male superiority and rise in female equality embodied in the feminist movement, (5) decline in clerical control and rise in lay participation embodied in the Roman Catholic lay movement, and (6) decline in sacramentalism and rise in Bible-based worship embodied in the Roman Catholic liturgical movement.

Some of these trends have been gaining momentum for decades, some for centuries, and others for millennia, but they seem to be reaching a critical threshold simultaneously. This confluence of social forces accounts for the change in attitudes and behavior regarding mandatory celibacy. It impacts coalition politics affecting structural change in the priesthood. The decline in the priesthood population is also a direct consequence of these trends. At the same time, the priest shortage acts as a catalyst that exacerbates the strength of the trends and focuses their influence at a common point in history. Thus in figure 1 segments 1 and 4 and 2 and 4 are connected with double-headed arrows.

The first and second trends have their origins in past millennia. The epochal transformations that brought about the shift from dogmatism to pluralism in worldviews laid the foundation for an openness to religious change in modern times. The sweeping changes embodied in the documents of the Second Vatican Council would have been impossible if this shift had not taken place. Similarly, axial transformations occurred in the social construction of human sexuality. Over the past two and a half millennia, our understanding of the place of sexual intercourse in relationships of love and friendship changed from a naturalist to a transcendentalist to a personalist conception. The culmination of these changes was incorporated in the pronouncements of the Second Vatican Council, with volatile consequences for the Catholic theology of marriage and celibacy. These historical data provide evidence that the negative attitude about compulsory celibacy for Roman Catholic priests is not a passing fancy.

The third long-range impetus for change stems from the waning of Western colonialism. Colonial empires appeared in Europe in the fifteenth and sixteenth centuries and established Eurocentrism in the growing Catholic Church. In the twentieth century a groundswell for national autonomy erupted after World War II. During this period, the United States' bid for worldwide hegemony against Great Britain's former hegemony had the latent consequence of fostering national independence in former British and other European colonies.[7] With emerging nationhood came demands from non-European churches for genuine inculturation of Christianity. For Catholics, these demands translated into movements for greater lay participation, Bible-based worship, gender equality, and cultural sensitivity to the married state.

The fourth social trend, embodied in the feminist movement, has been gaining strength in Western society for 150 years. The power of patriarchy has dominated the world since approximately the fourth millennium B.C.E. Father-rule persisted undisputed in all societal institutions, especially organized religion, until the middle of the nineteenth century C.E. The feminist movement has been opposing the subjugation of women with notable and irreversible gains since that time. The latest wave of feminism is creating tension in the Catholic Church that not only raises the possibility of ordaining women but, more immediately, hastens the ordination of married men.

The last two trends, incorporated by the lay movement and the liturgical movement, sprang up in the middle of the twentieth century. Five or six decades in the making, these social forces now span two generations of Catholics. The modifications they have introduced in the hearts and minds of churchgoers are now taken-for-granted elements in the structure of contemporary worship and ministry. That is to say, the almost absolute sacramental and hierarchic monopoly of control that marked the Catholic priesthood half a century ago has undergone an irreversible transition.

Societal Change

The cumulative evidence shows that most, if not all, these trends and changes are irreversible. My argument, therefore, is simple. The priest shortage is the result of irreversible social trends. Riding the crest of the wave of these long-term structural changes is disaffection with mandatory celibacy and demand for gender equality in Catholic ministry. The most obvious solution to the priest shortage, therefore, is the immediate ordination of married men and the eventual ordination of women.

This solution, though simple, is fraught with turbulent consequences for patriarchal domination in the Catholic Church and the wider society (segment 7). I argue that the issue of compulsory celibacy for Catholic priests is but the tip of an iceberg. The iceberg itself or, to switch metaphors again, the smoldering volcano in the background is the feminist antipatriarchy movement. Preserving compulsory celibacy in the Catholic Church is a smokescreen for preserving patriarchy and all that goes with it: fear, hatred, and domination of women. The dispute over mandatory celibacy for Catholic priests is no tempest in a teapot. It represents a titanic struggle between the forces for change in the Catholic Church and the forces that are bent on reproducing the patriarchal structures of human society. The causes and consequences of male celibate exclusivity in the Catholic priesthood deserve serious attention.

Will the Eucharist Survive?

Of all the problems generated by the lack of priests the most distressing for committed believers is the weakening of the eucharistic tradition.[8] The eucharistic sacrifice of the Mass is the heart of Catholic sacramental worship. What is more, worship forms the very basis of all religion. To tamper with the structure of worship, therefore, is to introduce radical change in any religious organization. Change that touches the heart of an ancient sacramental faith is very threatening.

Responding to the growing shortage of priests in many areas, the U.S. National Conference of Catholic Bishops (NCCB) has sanctioned a potentially far-reaching organizational change. This policy has serious implications for altering the structure of worship and ministry that is embodied in the sacramental priesthood. During their fall 1989 meeting, the American bishops authorized a new Sunday liturgy to be celebrated by permanent deacons, nuns, laywomen, or laymen in parishes without priests.[9] This modification, which alters the technical core of the ministry, could signal the most momentous structural change in the Roman Catholic Church since the Protestant Reformation.

Significantly, the new service is not a Mass—although it is easily mistaken for one—because Catholic doctrine holds that only an ordained priest can officiate at the eucharistic sacrifice of the Mass. According to the NCCB guidelines, Sunday service in priestless parishes can now be reduced to a combination of hymns, prayers, Bible readings, a sermon, and Communion using bread consecrated by a priest at an earlier Mass. From the viewpoint of the parishioners, however, the only element that is missing from the new Sunday service is the of-

fering and consecration of the bread and wine. Doctrinally, the offertory and eucharistic prayer that includes the consecration are the sine qua non of the Mass.
Practically, however, they occupy only a few minutes in an hour-long service.

Policy changes, especially those affecting the core technology of large-scale
organizations such as the Catholic Church, have major consequences. Some are
intended, others unintended. The NCCB action legitimating a new order of
Sunday service will create unforeseen and, no doubt, undesirable ripple effects.
An old church proverb, *lex orandi, lex credendi*—paraphrased as "the order of
worship determines the structure of the believing community"—reflects some
hard sociological facts. If there is no priest at a Sunday service, no one in the
congregation is identifying with the role played by the priest. So no one is identifying with the beliefs and values inherent in priesthood and the intimately related ritual of eucharistic sacrifice. Hence, little by little the role of priest falls
out of the social structure of the community as Sunday after Sunday the congregation adapts to an order of worship that does not include a priest. Along
with the disappearing role of priest go the beliefs about the centrality of the eucharistic sacrifice of the Mass, which have been the bedrock of Catholic piety
since the Church's earliest days.

Critical Economic Resources

Shrinking economic resources, whether human or financial, have inevitable political and social ramifications. The more critical the resource, the more far-
reaching the consequences of its decline. As the organization theorists Jeffrey
Pfeffer and Gerald Salancik point out, "criticality" can be measured by the ability of the organization to continue functioning in the absence of the resource.[10]
Until now, there has been no group of members more central to the technical
core of the Roman Catholic Church than its ordained clergy. Therefore, the
priest drain represents the continual loss of its most critical "economic" resource
and, as such, is the most powerful force for structural change within contemporary Catholicism.

Human resources in general and professional employees in particular are the
key element in a service organization's internal economy. For the purposes of
this analysis, a church is a type of human service organization, which, by definition, has a mandate "to maintain and improve the general well-being and functioning of people."[11] The technology of a religious organization centers on the
production and dissemination of a distinctive creed, code, and cult. Traditionally, the priesthood provides the major human resources for the economic production system that makes up the technical core of the Catholic Church.

By no means are religious organizations exempt from the mundane economic
dynamics of social change. German sociologist Max Weber observes that religious "behavior or thinking must not be set apart from the range of everyday

purposive conduct, particularly since even the ends of religious . . . actions are predominantly economic."[12] Despite this important insight, Weber does not reduce religion to economics. On the contrary, he eschews reductionism by insisting that religion is based on a supernatural order. Nevertheless, much if not most of religious activity, though directed at supernatural beings, is focused on "mundane, worldly concerns: health, long life, defeat of enemies, good relations with one's own people, and the like."[13] Even when the "economy of salvation" touches the desired goal of "union with God," believers often rationally calculate the amount of time, energy, and other scarce resources they are willing to dedicate to the pursuit of that goal on a day-to-day basis.[14]

Clergy as Linchpin

The theoretical importance of priesthood is emphasized in Weber's distinction between personal charisma and the charisma of office.[15] The personal charisma of the prophetic role is essential for major "breakthroughs" in religious evolution, and the priestly office is critical for the "routinization" of charisma. Weber's disciple Joachim Wach spells out some of the implications of Weber's basic distinctions in a systematic discussion of the religious roles of founder, reformer, prophet, seer, magician, diviner, saint, priest, and member of a religious order.[16] These role types are fluid, but none is more important for understanding the structures and structuring process of the Catholic Church than that of priest. The priestly role, with its emphasis on sacrifice and ritual in general, most easily appropriates the functions of teacher, lawgiver, magician, diviner, and saint. For centuries, the Catholic priesthood has continued to appropriate all but the most trivial ministerial roles: it is not an exaggeration to note that, at least until the final decades of the second Christian millennium, ministry and priesthood were practically synonymous. This situation is being challenged by the changing beliefs and restructuring instigated by the Second Vatican Council.

In describing the characteristics of the modern rational-legal bureaucracy, of which the Roman Catholic Church is the prototype, Weber links the expertise of the office holder to hierarchy of control.[17] In Catholicism, the fullness of sacramental ministry and decision-making authority is given to the priesthood alone. In John Kenneth Galbraith's terminology, the priesthood constitutes the "technostructure" of the Catholic Church.[18] Subtle changes in the structure of professional ministry produce a gradual evolution in the structures of an entire religious organization like the Catholic Church.

To summarize, clergy decline has become the major driving force for change in the Catholic Church for three key reasons. First, the priesthood is essential to the eucharistic tradition. Second, it is a critical economic resource. And third, it includes the organization's key office holders who have a monopoly on the fullness of religious expertise and hierarchy of control. Decline in the priesthood population spells a loss in the Church's sacramental tradition, economic base, and mechanisms of control. Furthermore, if hierarchical control—firmly grounded in patriarchy that is sacralized by celibacy—is weakened in Catholicism, it is also weakened in other forms of patriarchal domination prevalent in the wider society.

Plan of the Book

Since the priest shortage is the core of the theoretical model, the next chapter summarizes the major findings of my demographic investigations of the U.S. diocesan priesthood population and treats the major cause of the priest shortage: mandatory celibacy. I review the empirical research on the issue and consider whether dissatisfaction with compulsory celibacy stems from short- or long-term attitudinal change.

Part II develops a theoretical model of social change in organized religion. Chapter 3 lays the foundations of the theory, drawing from classic and contemporary analyses of conflict and change in organizations, and applies the general model to the Catholic Church by formulating six propositions based on an ideal-type definition of Catholic ministry. The theory assumes that the most essential element of the Church's ministry is the sacramental, sacerdotal, male, celibate monopoly of control over the Catholic means of salvation. Because religious consciousness transcends prerational and rational consciousness, a new approach is needed to analyze religious organizations. So chapter 4 proposes a new social scientific paradigm, one that can systematically treat unique religious phenomena. In chapter 5 I elaborate on the unique character of organized religion, particularly the transcendent spiritual basis of the faith-events around which the religious group is organized. Chapter 6 advances theory development by analyzing the origin and progress of six interrelated historical trends that form a matrix of forces for change in Roman Catholicism.

Part III examines the convergence of the conflicting forces for change and the resolution of their paradoxical tensions. In chapter 7 I look at the uneasy balance between dogmatism and pluralism and between centrism and localism emerging in the Catholic Church. Chapter 8 assesses the decline of transcendentalism and growth of personalism in the social construction of human sexuality, and the retreat of male dominance and advance of female equality in Catholic ministry. In chapter 9 I examine the conflict between clergy and laity and between sacrament and Bible in the context of the priest shortage. I also describe the convergence of all the other types of conflict and tension in the primal paradox of hierarchy and hierophany.

Part IV is dedicated to understanding the role of coalitions in organizational change. Chapter 10 discusses the peculiar aspects of coalitional behavior in a religious setting and analyzes coalition formation in recent Catholic history. I describe the conservative or priestly coalition in chapter 11 and the progressive or prophetic coalition in chapter 12. The analysis reveals that the conservative coalition is grounded primarily in the papal alliance. The progressive bloc coalesces around charismatic figures like Archbishop Rembert Weakland of Milwaukee, Wisconsin, and Bishop Kenneth Untener of Saginaw, Michigan.

Part V weighs the arguments in favor of continuity or change in the Catholic Church and speculates about the effects of religious change or stagnation on society at large. In chapter 13, I argue that sacerdotal sacramentalism will continue as a defining characteristic of Catholic ministry, but in a modified form. At the same time, however, Catholicism will have to say goodbye to male celibate exclusivity in the priesthood. Chapter 14 reflects on the far-reaching consequences of radical change in the Catholic Church. In particular, I note that the effects of married priests and the ordination of women will reverberate throughout society, making the conflict over patriarchy the main agenda for the new millennium.

COMPULSORY CELIBACY AND THE PRIEST SHORTAGE

Priesthood is the linchpin that links structural elements in the Catholic Church. This link is giving way, however, as the priesthood population steadily declines. In a companion volume, *Full Pews and Empty Altars,* Lawrence Young and I document the extent of the priest shortage in the United States. We report the results of a six-year study in which we collected data from church officials in 86 dioceses and constructed a 19-year census registry of the American clergy covering 1966 through 1984. The registry contains demographic information on 36,300 diocesan priests. It provides original data on the extent and speed of growth and decline in priest populations across the country.[1] These data show that from 1966 to 1984, entrances into the priesthood through ordination and incardination amounted to just over 15,000; exits through leave, resignation, and natural loss totaled just over 22,000; hence the net loss in the number of priests in the United States was a little under 7,000. According to our census counts, in round numbers there were 35,000 active diocesan priests in the United States on January 1, 1966, and 28,000 on January 1, 1985—a 20 percent decline.

We also use these data to describe the demographic transition of the clergy for a period of 40 years, using empirical data for 19 years (1966–84) to make projections to the year 2005. With the presumption that only Catholic males willing to be lifelong celibates will be recruited and retained, we constructed three different projections based on optimistic, pessimistic, and moderate assumptions. The *optimistic projection* assumes that the relatively high ordinations and net migrations and low resignations and retirements experienced during certain specific years between 1966 and 1985 will continue.[2] Furthermore, if any of these events showed consistent trends toward even more optimistic levels in the future than experienced in the past, estimates of their 1990–94 levels are used. The *pessimistic projection* assumes the opposite, namely, the relatively low ordinations and net migrations and relatively high resignations and retirements during certain other past years are likely to continue. Similarly, if any of these events showed consistent movement toward more pessimistic levels, estimates of their 1990–94 levels are used. The *moderate projection* results from assuming that the level of ordinations, net migrations, resignations, and retirements occurring between 1980 and 1984 will remain more or less unchanged from 1985 through the turn of the century. The assumptions about future death rates are based on life tables for U.S. white males produced from national census data. We use the same mortality assumptions for the optimistic, moderate, and pessimistic models. On the basis of our reading of the data and understanding of the American Catholic Church, we make a few other reasonable adjustments to these assumptions.[3]

Even under optimistic assumptions the U.S. diocesan priesthood population would probably show a substantial loss in the four-decade period under study: The number of active priests in 2005 would be over 34 percent fewer than the number recorded for 1966. If the pessimistic assumptions hold true, losses across the country would cut the population by more than half, reaching close to 53 percent fewer between 1966 and 2005. The moderate assumptions, which are calculated to fall approximately midway between the optimistic and pessimistic extremes, forecast a drop of 40 percent in the national population.

Change in Age Composition

Along with the decline in numbers, the average age of priests in the United States is rising rapidly.[4] Between 1966 and 2005, the proportion of active diocesan priests in the 25-to-34 age group will be cut almost in half, from 21 percent to 12 percent. The proportion in the next youngest category, age 35 to 44, will drop from 27 percent to 20 percent. The relative size of the 45-to-54 middle-aged group will remain approximately the same. The oldest age group, which includes all active priests 55 and older, will increase from just under 30 percent in 1966 to almost 47 percent of the entire active priesthood population in 2005. Thus, if the moderate assumptions hold true to 2005, the national distribution will be skewed dramatically toward the oldest age group. Nearly half the active priests in the United States would be 55 or older, while just a little over an eighth would be under 35.

Impact of Change

Because the phenomenon is occurring before our eyes and its full impact will not hit the Church until well after turn of the century, we lack systematic studies of the impact of this decline and graying of the priest population. It is not difficult, however, to speculate on the consequences. A declining and aging priesthood negatively affects the internal economy or resource structure of the Church. Because its human resources have been greatly reduced in absolute size, as well as in quality, which is associated with a young staff, the Church will undoubtedly undergo drastic changes in program priorities. Cutbacks and reallocations mean struggle, conflict, and tension. Fewer and older priests means more stress and burnout in the rectories because of overwork and more frustration and disappointment throughout the parish because of fewer services. These trends also portend greater psychological and cultural distance between Catholic youth—the future of the Church—and a dwindling, aging religious leadership.

The Church interacts with the economic resources in its environment. Reallocations will probably deepen the existing inequalities between rich and poor—when there is a shortage of priestly services in the diocese, who gets them? A plausible hypothesis is that those who can pay for them get them; money interacts with people. The media report inner-city churches being closed and poor rural parishes, especially in areas losing population, also being shut down. Yet suburban parishes in middle-class and upper middle-class neighborhoods thrive. Similarly, first-world countries, where most of the wealth of the industrialized world is concentrated, have the highest ratios of priests to laity. The masses of people in Africa and Latin America, among the poorest populations in the world, have the lowest. Vast priestless areas in these continents are left to lay catechists and superstitious remnants of previous religions. Inequality of access to professional priestly service is cause and consequence of socioeconomic inequality.

The gray-haired priest celebrating Mass as the norm for the community is a strong deterrent to priestly vocations. If a young priest is never present on Sunday, no one in the congregation is identifying with or imagining the attitudes of a young priest. Little by little the young priest role falls out of the social structure. Thus, another critical consequence of a declining and aging priesthood is that it creates a vicious circle: the fewer younger priests, the fewer vocations; the fewer vocations, the fewer younger priests. And so on.

The impending loss of almost half of the U.S. priesthood population and its rapid aging raise serious questions for Roman Catholicism. Will sustained decline and aging of the clergy trigger a major organizational transformation of the Church, that is, a radical change in sacramental technologies, pastoral programs, or operational goals?[5]

Consequences of Decline

The major consequence of sustained loss in the number of priests becomes obvious in view of the growing number of Catholic laypeople. It is the age-old problem of supply and demand. The basic premise of this book is that the decline will result in a pervasive organizational crisis because priests provide valuable services that are in decreasing supply vis-à-vis growing demand. A steady increase in membership has marked the history of the Catholic Church in the United States.[6] According to the *Official Catholic Directory*, between 1925 and 1994 the absolute number of American Catholics has grown from fewer than 20 million to well over 60 million. Catholicism's share of the religious "market" has also increased, from less than 20 percent to about 25 percent during the same period.[7] The number and proportion are still expanding. National polls indicate that high fertility and the influx of Hispanic and Asian immigrants are generating continuous growth in the U.S. Catholic population. By the early years of the twenty-first century, demographic forces will push the number of Americans whose religious preference is Roman Catholicism to over 75 million. The proportion of Catholics among all Americans may come close to 30 percent by the turn of the century.[8] Furthermore, the force of the trends suggests that the Catholic population will continue its historic pattern of growth well into the next century.

A recent study of parish leadership in Catholicism and three comparable Protestant denominations found significant Catholic–Protestant differences in the ratio of clergy to church members.[9] These contrasts epitomize one of the fundamental demographic contradictions within American religion today. Catholicism is experiencing growth in membership but a shrinking priesthood, while major denominations within mainline Protestantism are witnessing declining church membership but a surplus of clergy. Thus, the current priest shortage is a distinctively Catholic crisis. Our data describe the extent of the problem of full pews and empty altars.

Chronic poor recruitment and retention of clergy along with steady growth in lay membership mean that the Catholic priesthood cannot reproduce itself at a rate high enough to meet the increasing demand for priestly services. Moreover, the problem will only get worse before it gets better. The bulk of the active priest population in the 1990s is made up of relatively large cohorts from earlier decades who are reaching retirement age and the limits of life expectancy. Consequently, the parishioner-to-priest ratio—a measure of the priest shortage—gets larger and larger with each passing year. We can only conclude that the priest shortage is severe, chronic, worldwide, and growing. In the balance of this chapter, I continue to focus on the supply side of the shortage, examining the major reason why the priesthood population continues to dwindle in size.

Given Catholicism's long history and complex cultural and political economic structure, unraveling the web of causal forces behind demographic decline in the priesthood is no simple task. If and when the full story emerges, it will be an integration of well-researched *partial* solutions. Poor recruitment and retention as the major demographic components of decline in the Catholic priesthood, providing a segment of the answer. Another step is to eliminate potential explanations by comparing Catholic recruitment and retention with that in other Christian denominations.

Contrasting Trends in Christian Ministry

In their study of patterns of leadership in U.S. parishes, Hoge and his colleagues discovered a stark contrast in the balance of supply and demand between Catholic parishes and Episcopalian, Lutheran, and Methodist congregations.[10] Between 1965 and 1985 the number of ordained clergy for the United Methodists, the Lutheran Church in America, and the Episcopal Church increased, while

church membership for these same denominations declined.[11] Thus, the ordained leadership problems facing Roman Catholics are the mirror image of
those facing mainline Protestants.

These comparative data help solve the puzzle of poor recruitment and retention in the Catholic priesthood by eliminating a wide range of crucial variables
that might otherwise explain the priest shortage. One might hypothesize that
some combination of broad social processes such as secularization, urbanization,
rationalization, industrialization, or a host of other vague forces like materialism,
hedonism, and worldly success are the reasons why young men are not attracted
to professional religious ministry in the late twentieth century. Such an explanation, however, contradicts the facts. Other comparable Christian denominations
are successful in recruiting and retaining an abundant supply, even a surplus, of
ordained ministers. These churches compete for candidates in the same social
environment as the Roman Catholic Church. Therefore, since those environmental conditions are not causing a clergy shortage in other Christian denominations, it is unlikely they are the major cause of the Catholic priest shortage; instead we must look to organizational conditions within Roman Catholicism.

Mandatory Celibacy: The Priesthood's Albatross

The organizational conditions unique to ordained ministry in the Catholic
Church are its eligibility criteria. In Roman Catholicism, priesthood is limited to
celibate men. Many other Christian denominations welcome women to ordination, and none exclude married men. Mandatory celibacy, therefore, is the key
organizational condition distinguishing the Catholic priesthood from all other
Christian ministries. The prohibition of the ordination of women further sepa-
rates Catholicism from a large segment of modern religious organizations. Without exception, recent studies of priestly recruitment and retention document
the persistent and strongly negative impact of mandatory celibacy.

Recruitment

Ordinations are tied to seminary enrollment, which dropped drastically after the
Second Vatican Council. In 1966, according to official figures, 8,325 priest candidates were enrolled in U.S. Catholic theologates (seminaries that include the
last four or five years of training before ordination). By 1994, that number had
plunged to 3,328, a 60 percent drop in less than three decades.[12]

After reviewing other studies of seminary recruitment and his own research
on the issue,[13] Hoge concludes that "the two principal determinants of interest
in vocations remain the 'big two' emphasized by Fee and her associates—the
encouragement factor and the deterrence of celibacy."[14] He continues: "Most
important: The shortage of vocations is not a temporary thing which is self-

correcting or a short-term low point in a cyclical pattern. It is a long-term situation with no end in sight. No large increases in the number of seminarians can
be expected, even if recruitment efforts are expanded and improved."[15] While
these conclusions are not infallible, as Hoge openly admits, they are based on
strong and consistent empirical evidence from one of the largest series of studies on recruitment of professionals in the social sciences.

Findings about the adverse effects of mandatory celibacy on seminary enrollment have been consistent. In one study, a random sample of American youth age
14 to 29 who were not interested in a vocation were asked for their reasons.[16] The
main problem, for both those who had thought about a vocation but not really seriously and those who had never thought about it, was that they were "not allowed
to marry." Of those who had at least considered a vocation, 51 percent said
mandatory celibacy was a "very important" deterrent and of those who had never
thought about it, 55 percent cited the same reason. The second most important
problem cited was "my faith in the Church's teachings is not deep enough" (47
percent and 52 percent) and the third was "lifelong commitment" (33 percent
and 41 percent). Another study surveyed of a random sample of undergraduate
Catholics in both Catholic and non-Catholic colleges and a random sample of undergraduate Catholics active in campus ministry.[17] Of those men not presently
training for the religious life or not seriously considering it, 70 percent of campus
ministry leaders and 61 percent of the general random sample said "not allowed
to marry" was a very important reason. It was, by far, the most prevalent one cited.
When asked "Would you be seriously interested in becoming an ordained priest
if celibacy were not required?" a very large proportion said yes: 35 percent of
male campus ministry leaders and 12 percent of the men in the general random
sample. Most recently, Raymond Potvin, who has been surveying candidates for
Catholic priesthood since the 1960s, conducted a follow-up study of perseverance
rates.[18] In 1985 and again in 1989 he polled U.S. seminarians in their final year of
study before theology or the first two years of theology studies.[19] His findings
show that a desire to marry is a key factor leading seminarians to quit studying for
the priesthood.[20] Another recent survey of 1,300 young men attending Jesuit-run
high-schools and colleges found that "Whites, Hispanics, and Asians overwhelmingly cited mandatory celibacy as a major deterrent to considering a priestly vocation." Furthermore, "the survey showed that if the mandatory celibacy requirement were relaxed, up to half of the respondents would look more favorably
upon becoming a priest."[21] This body of research clearly suggests that recruitment
to the male celibate priesthood will remain a problem for the foreseeable future.

Retention

The Second Vatican Council signaled the reformulation of theology of church
and ministry and at the same time opened what some have called a Pandora's box

of social change within the Catholic Church.[22] One facet of the council's aftermath was the mass exodus of young priests from the clerical ranks during the late
1960s and early 1970s. In response to mounting concerns, the American Catholic bishops commissioned NORC to examine the state of the American priesthood on a wide array of issues, including the relationship between celibacy and
the growing problem of resignations.[23]

Findings from the NORC study showed that resignations were relatively
more frequent among young priests who found loneliness a personal problem,
who would like to marry if celibacy were declared optional, and who endorsed
more modern, nontraditional statements of beliefs and values about the Church
and priesthood.[24] The cost of forgoing marriage was the single most important
explanatory factor. A similar countrywide survey was sponsored by the Spanish
hierarchy that same year. With minor differences, the same set of conditions—
and principally the negative impact of celibacy—explained the propensity to
resign from priestly ministry in Spain.[25] Using many of the same items in the
NORC survey, a follow-up study of the U.S. priesthood in 1985 concluded that
"the dynamics underlying the role commitment process have changed very
little. The cost of celibacy, although weaker than in 1970, is still a priest's principal consideration in the commitment process."[26]

What is remarkable about these studies is not only that they are so consistent
across time and culture but that this consistency was maintained despite the social upheaval affecting Catholicism. During a period in which structural innova-
tion and change in the Catholic Church were the order of the day, the factors
generating the steady exodus of priests from the clerical ranks remained remarkably stable. Given the persistence of this process, in years to come young
priests who endorse modern values, who find loneliness a problem, and who
prefer marriage over celibacy will more likely resign than older clergy who hold
traditional beliefs and values, who are not troubled by loneliness, and who are
content with the celibate lifestyle.[27]

Celibacy and the Social Construction of Sexuality

Why has the prohibition against marriage kept men away from the priesthood
during the last few decades when it has been an eligibility requirement for at
least half a dozen centuries? And why will its negative impact probably persist
in the decades ahead? The celibacy issue emerged in recent decades and will
not go away because of long-term and irreversible changes in perceptions of
human sexuality. The social construction of sexuality in modern society and in
the post–Second Vatican Council Church greatly reduces the positive motivations previously attached to celibacy. In this chapter I begin to explain the increasingly negative impact of celibacy by examining its effects on psychosexual
development during a priest's life cycle.

Life Cycle Development

In sociological studies conducted in 1970 and again in 1985, loneliness was a critical factor in a priest's decision to resign. It can also readily be linked to the set of psychological and psychosexual problems describing most subjects in the Loyola University study of the priesthood. Eugene Kennedy and Victor Heckler discovered that the majority of U.S. Catholic priests were psychologically maldeveloped (9 percent of the sample) or underdeveloped (64 percent), in contrast to the minority, whom they labeled developing (21 percent) and well developed (7 percent).[28] As part of the study, experienced psychotherapists with doctorates in clinical psychology conducted face-to-face interviews with 271 individual priests. They found that maldeveloped clergy often manifest pathological behavior to avoid dealing with their feelings. They have a negative self-image, sexual identity problems, and difficulties with authority. Their psychological problems are severe, stemming from a traumatic past.

Underdeveloped priests show their lack of maturity mainly in relationships with other people, which are distant, stylized, and unrewarding. They have problems with identity formation, principally sexual identity; many are still resolving developmental tasks of adolescence. The maldeveloped or underdeveloped priest, who is likely to be any age, is unlikely to leave the active ministry and marry because priesthood and celibacy provide "a shelter for him against a more fully developed life." Developing priests, most of whom are young or middle-aged, are forming closer personal relationships through more introspection and fewer defense mechanisms than those priests whose growth is arrested. One priest, diagnosed as developing, says he is facing "the developmental challenge of trying to learn, at the beginning of middle age, how to relate to women in a mature manner." Another describes himself as "in a state of flux." A third says he would not have such problems "if he were not growing." A fourth claims he left his overly intellectualized world and has now "begun to grow as a person once more."[29] Developing priests are the ones most likely to leave the active ministry and marry. The researchers found that "the developing person seriously questions celibacy because . . . he has a new appreciation of the values of love and human relationships."[30] The psychologically well-developed priests—who are likely to be any age—affirm their own individuality and enjoy mutually satisfying relationships with others. They are independent, productive men who accept their sexual identity and pursue a strong spiritual practice. They are generally satisfied with the priesthood and do not plan to leave.

Kennedy and Heckler base their analysis on Eriksonian developmental psychology, which calls attention to major crises facing maturing adults.[31] This growing body of theory and research would predict that young priests are facing important adult crises, especially in their early years after ordination but also later at midcareer. For example, underdeveloped priests seem to be arrested in

attempts to face delayed identity crises and so tend not to confront crises of intimacy and mutuality. Developing priests, on the other hand, tend to be han-
dling delayed identity crises in their late twenties and early thirties and then to
be confronting reoccurring crises of intimacy and mutuality through their forties and fifties. Those who resolve these challenges by leaving the active ministry
do so earlier rather than later because alternative job opportunities and the at-
tractiveness of marriage diminish with age.

The resignation statistics for 1966–85 provide support for this view. Resignation rates begin to peak approximately five years after ordination and drop
gradually over the next 10 years but remain moderately high until cohorts reach
age 45. A significant level of resignations continues throughout the late forties,
diminishes during the fifties, and then virtually ceases when priests reach their
sixties.[32] Note, however, that because the age at ordination has been rising steadily since the mid-1980s, priests are now resigning at older ages, though only up
to a point. Social forces, such as fewer job opportunities, marriage becoming
less attractive to someone set in his ways, and other sunk costs of a long priestly
career place limits on the age at resignation.

Obviously, the majority decide to continue in the active ministry, either because the priesthood is a rewarding and fulfilling career, a safe haven in which
to cope with a maldeveloped or underdeveloped personality, or both.

Church Teaching on Human Sexuality

Celibacy and living alone will most probably continue as structural constraints
that have to be met head-on when adult transitional crises manifest themselves
in priests' lives. For young priests—as well as candidates for the priesthood—
the Christian value of marriage versus that of celibacy for meeting the challenge
of intimacy and mutuality must be weighed in a new light. The societywide
trend in cultural values surrounding sexuality is toward integration of person
and sexuality. This involves an easier expression of "equality, warmth, and openness," which Richardson calls the "eroticization" of public behavior.[33]

This more positive view of the relationship between sexuality, love, and friendship is reflected in pronouncements of the council fathers on marriage.[34] The
theological nature of celibacy and marriage as ways of holiness was clarified in
the Second Vatican Council document *Gaudium et Spes*, the pastoral constitution on the "Church in the Modern World." The section on marriage (nos. 48–
52) formulated a new working principle for understanding sex within marriage.[35] The statements stress a more personalist understanding of the marriage
relationship and emphasize love between partners as the context in which children emerge. This principle replaced the older terminology, which identified
the primary and secondary ends of marriage as children and personal fulfillment. This new understanding gave theologians—and priests themselves—the

rationale for replacing the traditional claim that celibacy is the better, if not the only, road to perfection with the understanding that marriage and celibacy are different but equal paths of Christian perfection.[36]

The Future of Mandatory Celibacy

Is this change in social values regarding celibacy and marriage deep and pervasive enough to make a difference in recruiting and retaining priests? Drawing on theological arguments, Edward Schillebeeckx answers affirmatively: "When marriage is given its full value (it is a sacrament), vocations to religious celibate life will decrease."[37] But how strong is the sociological evidence? Over the next few decades, will young Catholic males stay away from the seminary and will young priests continue to resign from the priesthood because of a new appreciation of sacramental marriage and mandatory celibacy? Recent survey data indicate that they will.

What the Polls Show

In a 1966 national sample of Catholic priests, 62 percent of respondents said that priests should be allowed to marry, and 38 percent under 35 answered yes to the question "If a married priesthood were permitted in the Roman rite, do you think that you would marry?"[38] In a 1970 national sample, 56 percent said celibacy should be a matter of personal choice. Of those 35 and under, 84 percent were in favor of such legislation and 33 percent said they would get married if celibacy for priests became optional.[39] In the mid-1980s, the same proportion of seminarians (33 percent) said they would want to be married as priests if celibacy became optional.[40] In a later national poll of diocesan priests, the proportion under 35 who said they would probably or certainly get married if allowed had dropped from 33 percent in 1970 to 25 percent in 1985.[41] In 1993, 58 percent of a national sample of diocesan priests still thought that celibacy should be a matter of personal choice for diocesan priests.[42] Of those under 35, however, only 38 percent were in favor of married priests, in contrast to 65 percent in 1985 and 84 percent in 1970.

Thus, as the 1990s unfolded, younger priests became more conservative on this issue than many of their older confreres and notably more conservative than young priests of the 1970s and 1980s. This growing conservatism deserves a closer look. The 1993 responses from priests under 35 could be evidence that the celibacy problem was, in fact, only temporary. These data show that the majority of young priests no longer want to get rid of mandatory celibacy. Hence we might expect that retention of male celibates will soon be restored to its former level, putting an end to the priest shortage. Counterevidence, however, is more compelling. Note that even in the 1990s almost three out of five priests across the board and two out of five priests in the youngest age category *favor* the ordination of married men. Despite concerted efforts by the papal coalition to reinforce celibate exclusivity, a majority of all priests and a large minority of young ones want new legislation allowing married priests. The younger priests—men ordained during the conservative regime of Pope John Paul II—were recruited by conservative bishops (many selected by the pope because they favored celibate exclusivity) and were socialized and trained in seminaries controlled by the same bishops.

Furthermore, the psychosexual development of priests affects their responses in these polls. In the Loyola study, the depth-interviews showed that the majority favor optional celibacy yet most would not marry if allowed. Kennedy and Heckler's explanations for these findings is worth quoting at length:

> Many of these men seem to realize that marriage is not the automatic answer to their own problems; indeed, it is clear that many of the underdeveloped priests know that they would not be ready for marriage until they were more fully grown as persons. Some feel they are too old or too set in their ways to marry. In any case, they share a conviction that, no matter what they personally do, celibacy should be made optional. This conviction also obtains among the most developed priests who have integrated celibacy in a meaningful and religiously motivated manner in their lives. Although not all of them would marry, they strongly favor making celibacy optional. As a matter of fact, some of those priests most resistant to change in the celibacy law are those who are most threatened by possible contact with women. Their rejection of the possibility of optional celibacy expresses their own desire to preserve it because it is such a functional facet of their own hesitant adjustment to life. It is quite remarkable that most of the priests who do make celibacy a well-rounded value in their own lives are not only unthreatened by a possible modification of the law but are, in fact, strongly in favor of a change to optional celibacy.[43]

The Impact of Homosexuality

Furthermore, it appears that a large proportion of those who do want to keep mandatory celibacy may not be interested in marriage because of their sexual orientation. The sexual orientation pattern among priests has changed over the last three decades from manifestly heterosexual to notably gay or bisexual. Data documenting this change are debatable, but the cumulative evidence from partial studies, anecdotal information, and media reports is convincing.

Richard Sipe's research, based on a long career providing psychotherapy for priests, concludes that 10 percent of priests identify themselves as homosexual, 20 percent express concern regarding their sexual identities, and 40 percent report some homosexual ideation.[44] In a 1989 follow-up study of perseverance rates of 286 seminarians polled in 1985, Raymond Potvin and Felipe Muncada found that a higher proportion of respondents are sometimes attracted to the male body than in the earlier research. They also discovered higher rates of perseverance among those who say they are sometimes attracted to the male body than among those who feel no such attraction.[45] Personal stories of gay priests and a survey of 100 gay priests reveal, minimally, that homosexuality and commitment to the celibate priesthood are not mutually exclusive and that most homosexual priests "have accepted the fact that they are gay and are thankful for it."[46]

The growing prevalence of gays in the priesthood has been the subject of considerable popular attention, in the Catholic media especially. For example, Andrew Greeley worries about it in the *National Catholic Reporter.* In *Commonweal,* the Notre Dame theologian Richard McBrien asks, "Do homosexual bishops give preference, consciously or not, to gay candidates for choice pastorates?" Tim Unsworth reports growing concern over increasing numbers of gay priests, which is openly acknowledged by many and loudly denied by others. He cites an anonymous seminary professor who says, "My hometown seminary is over 50 percent homosexual and it's going higher." Similarly, Katie Leishman claims that at least one-third of priests younger than 45 are homosexuals.[47]

The change toward a more homosexually oriented priesthood is not surprising. Understandably, the all-male environments of seminaries, rectories, and religious communities are congenial for gays.[48] Historian John Boswell argues that throughout history homosexual men have been overrepresented in the clergy.[49] Priestly ministry is an attractive profession for homosexuals, according to Jung and other psychoanalysts, for often a homosexual "may be supremely gifted as a teacher . . . have a feeling for history . . . be conservative in the best sense and cherish the values of the past. Often he is endowed with a wealth of religious feelings which help him to bring the *ecclesia spiritualis* into reality, and a spiritual receptivity which makes him responsive to revelation."[50] Most likely, the percentage of gay men in the priesthood has always been somewhat higher than in the general male population because of the "high correlation between gayness and service professions, especially the celibate ministry."[51] In addition, however, the steady exodus of heterosexuals, who have been resigning to marry, automatically raises the already elevated proportion of homosexual priests. The resulting higher proportion of gays makes the priesthood an even more appealing environment for young men who experience same-sex eroticism.

It is reasonable to conclude that more gays in the priesthood is part of the reason younger priests in the 1990s show less enthusiasm for allowing priests to marry. But this does not mean that rates of resignation will go down. First, heterosexual priests will most likely leave at the same rates in the future as they have in past three decades. Second, the testimony of gay priests shows that they too have left and will continue to leave in a steady stream. Father R. Edwards (a pseudonym) reflects on the experience of fellow gay priests: "Sometimes this [leaving the priesthood] happens as a result of overwhelming feelings of guilt, as the priest realizes he is gay and sees this as absolutely incompatible with his consecrated state of life. . . . Far more often, however, the priest comes out, begins the process of socialization into the gay scene, and realizes that his need for intimacy is much stronger than his desire for priesthood."[52] Accordingly, although the data show that the new generation of priests is less enthusiastic about a married clergy, this is not convincing evidence that the chronic retention problem in the Catholic priesthood is coming to an end.

The decline in percentages of young priests favoring a married clergy makes us expect fewer resignations in the coming decades than during the mass exodus years of the early 1970s. Future resignation rates, however, will continue to be moderately high for several reasons. For 25 years since the Second Vatican Council the majority of priests have consistently called for a change in policy to allow a married clergy. Moreover, large minorities of priests and seminarians persist in stating a personal preference for marriage. The fact that one out of three seminarians would prefer to be married as priests and one out of four young priests actively entertains the idea of marriage demonstrates that mandatory celibacy remains not only an unsettling but also an unsettled issue for the heterosexual American clergy. Hence it will continue to play an important role in their developmental crises of maturity and so have a strong negative impact on priestly recruitment and retention. Moreover, the damaging impact of mandatory celibacy on retention can only be exacerbated by the growing proportion of gays in the priesthood. As I will show in later chapters, the personalist movement is changing the social construction of human sexuality. As a result, both heterosexual and gay priests will continue to be frustrated over the disembodied transcendentalist policy of mandatory celibacy. Significant numbers will abandon the active ministry in favor of personalist lifestyles more in keeping with their views on friendship, love, and intimacy.

Conclusion

Many factors are weakening the institution of mandatory celibacy. The personalist sexual norms in the wider culture exercise a pervasive influence on Catholic priests. Once taken for granted, the spiritual superiority of celibacy over marriage is now viewed with growing skepticism within Catholic theological and priestly circles. When polled, a large minority of priests say they would prefer to be married.

A large proportion of U.S. priests manifest maldeveloped, underdeveloped, or developing psychosexual behavior. A significant number resolve their developmental problems by leaving the active ministry. In the early years after ordination, young heterosexual and homosexual priests face the crisis of intimacy and mutuality. In trying to make that crisis a passage for growth instead of regression, many reevaluate and eventually lose their commitment to celibacy. Given the cumulative evidence, it is reasonable to expect that dissatisfaction with compulsory celibacy will be sustained in the years ahead.

The priest shortage itself is becoming a force for change in the world's largest organized religion. But how do religious organizations change, especially ancient ones like the Catholic Church? Who are the major agents of change? How will the demographic decline of the priesthood transform the structures of Roman Catholicism? I will address these and related questions in the following chapters.

PART II

SOCIAL CHANGE

IN ORGANIZED RELIGION

3

TOWARD A THEORY OF SOCIAL CHANGE

IN ORGANIZED RELIGION

I n many ways religious organizations are just like other organizations. In this chapter, I emphasize their similarities by grounding my analysis of the Catholic Church in classic theoretical models of social change. The writings of Max Weber provide the foundation for the arguments.[1] I add important recent developments, notably from Michael Hannan and John Freeman's population ecology approach to organizational change and from Charles Perrow's qualified power model of organizations.[2]

Weber's Legacy

Much of Max Weber's enormous research efforts were spent analyzing the rise of the capitalist political economy, why it emerged in the West, and why it was destined to dominate worldwide. Weber's explanation stresses the crucial role of tensions and balances between opposing social forces. The main features of Western capitalism did not emerge until certain conflicting historical trends converged in a peculiar balance. For example, a dynamic balance between the democratizing tendencies of self-supplied armies and the centralization of the bureaucratic state was a necessary prerequisite for the capitalist economy, as was an equilibrium between the charisma of priestly office and the participatory communities of monasticism. These and several other seemingly far-fetched political, economic, and cultural relationships are skillfully explained and documented in Weber's analysis. Moreover, not only the emergence but also the dynamism and perseverance of industrial capitalism depends on maintaining a proper balance among competing class, political, and cultural forces. This balance is tenuous but held in place by constant conflict between opposing forces, for conflict enhances their interdependence. Conflict is vital because the victory of any one side of the opposing forces would spell the doom of the capitalist system.

Power and Domination of Rational-Legal Bureaucracy

Weber emphasizes the importance of structurally embedded conflict as the source of both continuity and change. So he extends his theory to explain how a capitalistic society organizes tension and conflict on a daily basis. Critical for the rise of Western capitalism was the emergence and spread of the modern organization, or rational-legal bureaucracy. Modern bureaucracy is the organizational means for controlling the conflict found in a capitalist political economy.[3] The authority wielded by bureaucratic organizations is effective because it is the use of power patterned into everyday behavior and backed by law. Bureaucratic power, therefore, is both extensive and unobtrusive. Usually people submit to it willingly since it is legitimate. But more often they submit unthinkingly because submissive behavior is structured into organizational life.[4]

The modern bureaucracy is organized around two basic principles: division of labor based on expertise and hierarchy of control. Specialized experts—office holders whose expertise is linked to specific tasks defined by the division of labor—are given control over subtasks in their area of expertise. This mechanism of control, in which every office holder is under the supervision of a higher office holder, is reinforced by the other ideal-typical traits of rational legal bureaucracy: written rules, standardization, formalization, and career stability. Together this constellation of structural patterns defines the modern organization in its pure or ideal-type form. Each organizational trait mutually reinforces the other as a mechanism of control, thereby ensuring that the organization will achieve its calculable and predictable goals.[5]

The modern rational-legal bureaucracy is organized around a set of prestated or agreed-on goals. The organization's constitution lists these goals and justifies them by abstract reasoning and law. Reason combined with law yields a peculiar type of rationality, one whose logic leads to the conviction that the more understandable and predictable the goal, the better. Although justified by reason and law, the underlying logic bolsters the relationships of power, for only calculable and predictable behavior is readily subject to domination and control. The modern organization is an efficient bureaucratic tool of control in the hands of its masters. The masters are the key office holders who combine the twin powers of legitimate expertise and hierarchy of control. Therefore, it is the masters of the modern organization who most often establish and achieve *their* goals. Subordinates, who are dominated in organizations controlled by their masters, are often in conflict with these authoritative goals and wish to change the status quo. Thus, conflict, the engine of social change, is endemic because it is structurally embedded in organizational society.

Prophets, Priests, and Social Change

In his sociology of religion, Weber contrasts religious situations in which the priestly role dominates to those that depend on the role of prophet. The prophet is a charismatic figure who proclaims a message calling for a break with the established order, whereas a priest is an office holder who plays a critical role in the routinization and preservation of charisma. These prototypical roles are incorporated in Weber's theory of social change. Office holders are the key actors in structures of domination and control, and their main interests are to support the status quo within which their power and expertise rest secure. A charismatic leader, however, wants to change that status quo and represents a threat to bureaucratic office holders. Hence social change depends on the interaction of the charismatic leader and the office holder. The latter not only tends to resist the impact of the former, but once a charismatic breakthrough occurs, the office holder is the one who must legitimate and routinize the change. The office holder, who embodies the expertise required by an organization and wields the authority and control needed to exercise it, is the most important agent of social change over the long haul. Gradual change, presided over by the office holder, is punctuated now and then by radical change initiated by the charismatic leader. A complete theory of social change must incorporate both phases. Moreover, a major emphasis should be given to understanding how organizations change gradually because radical change is relatively infrequent. Since the characteristics of key office holders before and after a major social change are likely to be very different, the principal empirical question is: How do the characteristics of key office holders change?

An organizational theory of social change, therefore, should focus mainly on that cadre of officials who possess the primary expertise needed by the organization, since those who embody the dominant expertise also tend to dominate the mechanisms of power and control. John Kenneth Galbraith appropriately names this group the technostructure.[6] Not only are capitalist economic organizations controlled by a technostructure, so are all large complex modern organizations—including religious organizations like the Catholic Church.

Paradigm and Prototype

A brief look at these two examples of modern organization—economic and religious—will help illustrate the principal elements in my adaptation of Weberian ideal-type analysis. The capitalist economic organization or business firm is the *paradigmatic type* of rational-legal bureaucracy as it emerged in the West. The Catholic Church, on the other hand, is the *prototype* in that it pioneered all the essential traits characterizing modern bureaucracy.

Weber followed Marx in arguing that the organizational form that dominates the economy has an overpowering influence on other societal institutions. Accordingly, political, military, legal, medical, educational, and even religious organizations in capitalist society take on many traits similar to corporate businesses in order to interact successfully with them. For my theoretical purposes, the major traits I will focus on for understanding the similarities among modern organizations center on (1) the nature of their goals and (2) their key office holders.

The goals of modern organizations are of two types: institutional and organizational. In an analysis of the Tennessee Valley Authority, the only socialist experiment undertaken by the U.S. government, Philip Selznick clarified the important distinction between these two goals.[7] The institutional goals of any corporate group are to provide those goods or services that have meaning and value to society in the context of a substantively rational worldview.[8] Organizational goals, on the other hand, are the actual prestated agreed-on aims achieved by the corporate group through technical rational means—that is, through bureaucratic mechanisms of domination and control.

Paradigm: Economic Organization.   Institutional goals are also of two types: overt and covert. They are distinguished by the ideological intention of the group or class proclaiming the goals. The overt institutional goals of economic organizations, agreed on by all classes in society, are to provide sufficient material products and services to maintain the good life for all. Covert institutional goals, agreed on by those who control the mature oligopolistic firms dominating advanced capitalist societies, are profit and growth. The unstated, mostly unexamined goal of big business—and little ones that aspire to greatness—is to provide goods and services for the private needs of privileged individuals, because this goal best ensures steady profit and growth. Class conflict and other types of power struggles smolder and occasionally erupt because of contradictions between the institutional and organizational goals of modern big business.

Key office holders are those who belong to the technostructure, which is composed of executives, managers, scientists, and technicians who, as a team, control the bureaucratic organizations of big business and other sectors of modern society. These individuals combine the dominant expertise and hierarchy of control needed by the organization. Understanding the changing technostructure is the key to understanding organizational change.

Prototype: Religious Organization.   Most modern churches began as charismatic fellowships and evolved to become either a traditional or rational-legal bureaucracy.[9] The Catholic Church is a prime example of the second type—indeed, its prototype. The overt institutional goals of world religions are variously stated as salvation, enlightenment, nirvana, samadhi, unitive consciousness of Absolute Reality, union with God, and so on. The covert institutional goals of Christianity were unmasked during the early and late Enlightenment periods, mainly through the efforts of modern science, particularly social science. As Marx noted, "Criticism of religion is the premise of all criticism."[10] Chief among these covert goals are the following: to reproduce the stratification and inequality of the existing class structure; to instill attitudes of obedience and discipline needed in modern organizations; and to foster social cohesion, which results in integration for some and alienation for others.

The contemporary organizational goal of corporate religion—exemplified by U.S. Catholic dioceses—is the efficient management of a complex, highly technological system for providing the agreed-on means of salvation to increasingly educated members. A modern religious organization, therefore, needs to employ officials with high levels of expertise who can exercise sufficient hierarchy of control to achieve the "agreed-on" goals. Given their complex goals and the highly technological society in which they function, religious organizations are subject to pressures and tensions that impel them further and further toward technical rational efficiency. These pressures tend to displace overt institutional goals in favor of covert institutional and organizational goals.[11]

Churches are similar to modern business firms not only in their tendency toward goal displacement but also in their reliance on key office holders for expertise and hierarchy of control. Catholic ministry is composed primarily of bishops, priests, deacons, nuns, and brothers and secondarily of volunteer and paid lay ministers. These key office holders represent the technostructure of modern Catholicism. Understanding the changing social structure of the ministry is the key to understanding social change in the Catholic Church.

Weber's Systematized Theory of Social Change

Weber's is a macrosocial theory—it seeks to explain how a whole society changes over time. I adapt it for my purposes in order to theorize about social change at the middle range, that is, in a population of religious organizations. A Weberian middle-range theory of social change follows three injunctions:

1. Identify specific historical trends, chosen on the basis of theoretical interests and drawn from an ideal-type, that are creating background and intervening conditions in a causal chain leading to organizational change.
2. Explain how these trends develop and reach the right threshold simultaneously at some time and place in history.
3. Describe how charismatic leadership and bureaucratic authority interact with the trends to produce, legitimate, and routinize the change.

The historical trends Weber identifies in his theory of capitalism were the material and organizational conditions maturing in the womb of the old social order; these were the ultimate and background causal forces leading to capitalism. His choice of which historical forces to focus on was based on an ideal-type analysis of modern capitalism and its organizational form, the rational-legal bureaucracy. He demonstrates that a unique set of social forces, in critical balance, reached a threshold at a certain time and place—only in Western Europe and only in areas dominated by certain Protestant sects.

Applying other Weberian principles of social change, I further argue that when the critical forces for change reach the correct balance and threshold within a population of organizations, a form of charismatic leadership must seize the historical moment and precipitate a breakthrough. Charismatic or prophetic leadership will be effective, however, depending on its success in interacting with bureaucratic or priestly leadership. The priestly role is responsible not only for preserving the charisma of past organizational breakthroughs but also for routinizing the new charisma introduced by social change. In Charles Perrow's terms, the prophet must not be a stranger in the house of the priestly masters.[12]

The Population Perspective

The matrix of forces generating social change in the Catholic Church is not an ethereal abstraction but a set of concrete historical conditions shaping the environment of actual diocesan organizations. To interpret the dynamism of these social forces, I turn to recent developments in the population ecology approach to organizational analysis.[13] In this approach, one imagines U.S. Catholic dioceses as a population of organizations adapting to their environment and the matrix of social trends as a dynamic ecological niche.

Populations of organizations, like species of biological organisms, emerge, grow, survive, or fail by competing for resources in an ecological niche. Ecological or "environmental *niches* are distinct combinations of resources and other constraints that are sufficient to support an organization form."[14] An organization form, such as that characterizing Catholic dioceses, evolves in cyclical stages involving variation, selection, and retention processes. Sufficient *variation* within and between diocesan organizations and across their environments is the first requirement for organizational change to occur. *Selection* of new or changed forms occurs when diocesan organizations compete amid the variety of resources and constraints of their common environment. *Retention* of certain structures and activities within the diocese, which serves to reproduce or transform its basic structural elements, is a function of external environmental and internal organizational characteristics.

I view the priest shortage as the driving force for structural change in the Church because priests hold key leadership positions in its technical core. Explaining variation in the behavior of individual priests, however, is not my concern as it is in most leadership studies.[15] I am interested instead in the changing *structural form* of Catholic ministry. How does variation in the availability of candidates for the priestly role affect selection and retention of old and new forms of ministerial roles and the relationship between changing ministerial roles and other parts of the organization? The notion of competence elements helps clarify this question. Bill McKelvey and Howard Aldrich define competence elements as the elements of knowledge and skill that, in total, constitute the dominant competence of an organization. Dominant competence is defined as the combined workplace (technological) and organizational knowledge and skills (e.g., differentiation, coordination, control, measurement of effectiveness, and organizing processes) that together are most salient in determining the ability of the organization to survive.[16]

In my view, the priestly role has incorporated the most critical elements of the dominant competence of the Roman Catholic Church—at least until recently.

As part of an ecological niche, the Catholic lay population is the resource pool from which the diocesan organization recruits new members to fill its leadership positions. When the resource pool contains enough individuals with the basic competence needed for the priestly role who are willing and able to acquire other competence elements through education and seminary training, the diocese can continue to select them, fill its key leadership positions, and retain the current form of its technostructure. If, however, the organization cannot recruit and retain sufficient personnel to fill its critical technical positions, it is forced to adapt. One form of adaptation may be organizational decline. Another may be organizational transformation, leading to eventual regeneration with a new organization form in a new ecological niche. When the environment can no longer supply the right cluster of competence elements, the dominant competence of the organizations in that particular niche begins to change. Social change pervades the organization, beginning with its technical core or technostructure and extending to all other parts of the system, including the patterns of beliefs and values motivating its members.

The Qualified Power Model

Seeing organizations as "tools in the hands of their masters" is critical for understanding modern organizations like the Catholic Church. Perrow labels his recent integration of Weber's analysis and contemporary organization research the qualified power model. This synthesis calls explicit attention to bureaucratic organizations as mechanisms of power. His model can be summarized in three principles:

1. Basically, an organization is a tool that masters use to generate valued outputs they can then appropriate. . . . Bureaucratic theory, based on the work of Max Weber . . . is the single most essential element of a theory of organizations.

2. The first and most major *qualification* of the bureaucratic model is . . . bounded rationality: shifting and unclear preferences, limited information, and limited knowledge of cause-and-effect relations. It has consequences for both the master and the employees.

3. Given bureaucracy with bounded rationality, the next most important qualification is group usage, as distinct from individual usage of the organization
by masters and employees. Group usages are internal and external.[17]

The principles of the qualified power model and their corollaries can be readily
applied to the Catholic Church.

The Church is similar to a business firm in many ways, primarily because it
has paid employees. The masters in this case are the employers, usually ordained church officials, whether bishops or priests, although they may delegate
hiring and firing authority to lay officials. From another viewpoint, the Church
is a voluntary association with higher- and lower-level participants. In this case,
too, higher-level clerical participants are the masters, ranging from pope, cardinals, and bishops to rank-and-file pastors and curates. In either case, the laity
are always lower-level participants, and at times the lower clergy are also subordinate to the higher-level episcopal masters and employers.

In an organization governed by qualified power, bounded rationality resides
in lower-level participants; therefore, the masters can use unobtrusive control
over them. Since this rationality affects masters as well, their limited rationality
is a source of power for lower-level participants. Bounded rationality generates
organizational change, but variation in the environment also creates other pressures for change.

Conclusion

The qualified power model provides an integration of classic Marxist and Weberian perspectives with contemporary theories such as the institutional, environmental, and political economic approaches to organizational analysis. Power
theorists like Perrow are also beginning to admit the potential of the population
perspective for understanding certain aspects of organizational change. This approach is strengthened considerably by integrating it with the qualified power
model. In the next chapter I propose a formal theory of social change in the
Catholic Church, one of the world's most powerful religious organizations.

4

THE TRANSPERSONAL PARADIGM

In the previous chapter I discussed the Catholic Church as if it were like any other modern organization. But institutionalized religion is different from all other types of organization in important ways. My aim now is to examine how we can take account of this difference. This chapter begins by observing that most organization theories focus exclusively on mundane rational behavior. Given their philosophical and epistemological assumptions, such theories are inadequate for explaining social change in religious organizations. The second half of the chapter examines the place of religion in social life and describes a newly emerging theoretical paradigm that incorporates the spiritual domain in a model of social change. This new paradigm allows us to examine the stages of social development and the unique character of religious organizations.

Organizational Models of Social Change

My analysis of causes and consequences of the priest shortage in the Catholic Church rests on the premise that ours is an organizational society. The basic functions and institutional forms of modern society, whether economic, political, integrative, or cultural, are all embodied in formally structured organizations.[1] Modern social change at the societal level, therefore, is inextricably linked to social change within organizations and among networks of organizations. Hence the four-level model proposed in figure 1 and formalized in chapter 3 focuses on transformation processes at the organizational level. Because religious organizations are different from any other type, an explanation of social change that involves organized religion must be different from theories that limit their analysis to other types of organizations. Though not often recognized, the main difference between theoretical approaches to the analysis of formal organizations stems from their underlying philosophical assumptions. Thus, I place organization theories in three philosophical categories. The first approach assumes that human behavior is basically prerational, the second that it is predominantly rational, and the third that it is ultimately transrational.

Max Weber's analysis of types of legitimate authority and their organizational forms provides a foundation for distinguishing between prerational, rational, and transrational models of organizations. Different types of beliefs legitimate the authority used in different kinds of organizations. Basically, therefore, organizations take three forms: *traditional,* based on belief in tradition or immemorial custom; *rational-legal* (bureaucracies), based on belief in rational systems of law; and *charismatic,* based on belief in extraordinary or superhuman powers of individuals.

The following sections contain a somewhat formal critique of contemporary organization theories. The point made is that these theories are seriously deficient because they ignore the higher realms of human potential. Readers who prefer to avoid theoretical disputes may wish to skip this review and pick up the thread at the section entitled "Transrational Approach." Those who like theoretical debates are invited to forge ahead.

Prerational Approach

A Weberian analysis of traditional organizations is based on the philosophical assumption that actors, for the most part, behave at a prerational level of human development. For example, in an organization governed by gerontocracy or patriarchy, legitimate domination rests on the belief in immemorial customs, conventions, and norms. The system of rules proposed by the elders or fathers and the manner in which those in command are raised to positions of power are respected and obeyed with minimal objection. Why? Because the corporate group believes in and reveres the way things have always been done. To the extent that justification for these traditional beliefs rests on foundations lost from memory or unexplainable by reason, behavior is based on a prerational magicomythical worldview. In other words, the model assumes that organizational behavior in a traditional organization is basically prerational.

The population ecology approach provides a contemporary example of a theoretical model that assumes human behavior in organizations is prerational.[2] As noted, this theory assumes that social change results from a natural variation-selection-retention process. Natural selection determines the structural form a population of organizations will take, given the resources available in its ecological niche. Social change, therefore, is not a rational process that is planned and coordinated through conscious choices but results from the prerational forces of blind random chance.

Rational Approach

Weber's analysis of rational-legal bureaucracy is the classic model of organizational behavior; it rests philosophically on the primacy of functional rationality. The Weberian principles of modern bureaucracy outlined in the previous chapter lead to predictable, calculable, stable, and, therefore, rationally efficient human behavior. Efficiency in modern organizations is measured against the calculus of time and money, which provides an eminently rational criterion for determining the best or, at least, a better set of means for achieving an agreed-on goal.

Rational behavior can be of at least two sorts, instrumental or substantive.[3] A system of action is instrumentally rational when it is organized to achieve a prestated goal as efficiently as possible. It is substantively rational when the organized behavior is meaningful and valuable in terms of a structured system of ideas and a hierarchy of values—that is, in terms of a worldview or philosophy of life. Theoretical models that assume that social action is limited to enhancing instrumentally rational efficiency cannot raise questions about the meaning or higher purpose of organizational behavior.[4] Most organizational theorists nowadays try to integrate assumptions of both instrumental and substantive rationality in their models. Two well-known examples in the field of organization studies are the institutional school and the qualified power model.[5]

The qualified power model outlined in the previous chapter rests squarely on the philosophical assumptions of bounded rationality and its embodiment in modern bureaucratic organizations. The qualified power model proposes that power relationships are at least partially rational, usually conflictual, and always structurally embedded in modern organizations. Power conflicts are endemic not only because actors disagree on the priorities among conflicting organizational goals and the most efficient means for achieving them but also, more important, because they dispute the substantive meaning and value of the goals themselves. Although members with the most authority have the best chance of realizing their goals, their power is not absolute, for two reasons. First, everyone's power is relative, because all organizational actors have control over some resources, no matter how small. Second, the rational use of power is never optimal, because alternative means and their consequences cannot be fully known (bounded instrumental rationality) and because alternative goals and their interrelationships cannot be fully known or evaluated (bounded substantive rationality). The theory, therefore, assumes that organizational structures emerge, develop, and change in order to enhance the rational use of power. Consequently, power struggles are structurally embedded in organizations. As such, conflict and the mechanisms for managing it are the source of both continuity and change in social organization. Because the rational use of power is both endemic and limited in all organizations, Perrow labels this version of organizational theory the qualified power model.

Generally, therefore, sociological theories assume that organizational behavior is either prerational or rational (even if the rationality is bounded). This brief review also implies that organizations evolve in a hierarchical fashion—over time and in different social settings, organization members seem to increase their ability to create structures that move up a developmental hierarchy. Organizations that enhance prerational behavior are replaced by those fostering substantively rational behavior, and these are supplanted by ones promoting instrumentally rational behavior. A comprehensive evolutionary theory would further posit that organization members develop structures adapted to the spiritual or transrational domains of human behavior. Such a theory, of course, would be based on philosophical assumptions asserting that human development transcends the use of reason and is capable of reaching higher levels of spiritual or transrational consciousness.

Transrational Approach

The vast majority of theorists assume that organizational activity strives to be rational, even though actors' complex behavior is bounded by notable limitations to their rationality. Very few theorists have paid serious attention to human behavior that goes beyond rationality to levels of transrational consciousness. This reluctance may result from philosophical convictions, practical considerations, or both.[6] The implicit philosophy of most social scientists assumes that human beings are rational animals at best. This worldview denies that the human species has the natural capacity to transcend reason, assuming instead that rational awareness is the highest level of consciousness attainable. Another worldview, relatively unexamined by professional social scientists, assumes that a human person is an integrated composite of body, mind, and spirit. The second view assumes a higher level of consciousness beyond reason, a spiritual domain in which human beings achieve awareness of ultimate being by direct perception of nonphysical or spiritual realities.

With his usual breadth of vision, Weber analyzed not only traditional organizations and rational-legal bureaucracy but also charismatic organizations, an organizational form based on belief in supernatural or "superhuman" power. In a charismatic organization, which in reality is a loosely organized fellowship, actors are motivated by a nonrational belief in the exceptional personal sanctity, heroism, or other extraordinary quality of their leader. When faced with "*extra*ordinary needs, i.e., those which *transcend* the sphere of everyday economic routines," we call on leaders with charisma or supernatural gifts.[7] The charismatic hero's extraordinary feats attract dedicated followers willing to obey their master's commands and enact a new vision of the world. Thus a charismatic organization is formed not out of rational economic or other mundane motives but from a suprarational view of the world, a desire to meet needs that transcend those of everyday life. The felt need to realize one's full human potential drives the individual to go beyond the routines of mundane reality, trying to reach a level of consciousness that transcends reason. Most commonly, institutionalized religion is the charismatic organization that attempts to meet such transrational needs.

Founded religions begin as intimate fellowships loosely organized around a charismatic leader. Early in their formation, charismatically organized religions like Christianity undergo a process called routinization of charisma. "The decisive fact is the separation of charisma from the *person* and its linkage with the institution and, particularly, with the office."[8] For example, the marvelous events of Jesus' life and death, his perceived resurrection and ascension, and the Pentecost experience that his followers claimed had opened for them the higher levels of spiritual consciousness—all of this had to be made available to subsequent generations. For Christianity and other religions to survive, somehow the extraordinary has to become ordinary, formalized, and institutionalized. The marvelous happenings that provide access to full human development must be routinized into religious beliefs, values, and rituals that embody these faith-events as a daily routine. So, as we saw in the previous chapter, in a world religion like Catholicism, everyday supernatural events have come to be as highly organized as everyday mundane events in other modern organizations, that is, they are hierarchically administered by trained officials in bureaucratic settings. Most sociological theories, however, focus exclusively on mundane prerational and rational behavior and are inadequate for explaining social change in religious organizations. Some analysts, therefore, are searching for a new paradigm that questions the epistemological limitations and philosophical inadequacies of the orthodox approach, one that provides a basis for reexamining the place of religion in social change.

Bringing Religion Back In

Many, if not most, scholars would agree that religion has been relegated to the periphery of modern society. Ever since the Enlightenment and the emergence of the physical and natural sciences, the majority of intellectuals have been convinced of this fact: Organized religion has become an anachronism, slowly but surely drifting into the backwaters of social life. Religion continues to function to some extent only because it has been "privatized," producing a sense of meaning and belonging in the private lives of individuals. The truth is that the economic, political, and military engines driving modern society are not fueled by religious motivations, nor are they directed toward religiously formulated goals. Modern life is built on reason, science, and technology, and it aspires only to the full actualization of these human potentials.

On the other hand, another view of the place of religion is reappearing, especially among scholars who systematically study it. These analysts do not dispute the evidence that the social impact of traditional religion has notably declined in the last five hundred years. But they interpret the facts differently. Taking a long-range evolutionary view of social change, they see the second half of the current millennium as a two-pronged phase of social development. One side of the phase is a letting-go or distancing; the other is a building-up and intensifying process. Thus, on the one hand, human culture, or the social organization of society at large, is distancing itself from a prerational form of social life grounded in an unexamined magicomythical worldview. At the same time, society is extending and intensifying a fully rational form of social life grounded in an empirical-analytic worldview. The complete rationalization of social life, however, is not the pinnacle of human development. It is an interim launching pad for reaching the highest stage.

The notion that reason governs more and more areas of social life has been endorsed by social scientists from Weber onward. In the last two or three decades, however, some of them have realized the inadequacies of their rational models and begun to direct attention to the surprisingly powerful impact of religion in important psychological and social events. Psychologists and sociologists of religion are exploring new scientific models to explain this unexpected vitality. Taking a comprehensive, historical view, some social scientists propose that the growing rationality of modern society is not the culmination of human potential but instead merely a developmental phase along a distinguishable trajectory. The end points that distinguish the full scale of human potential are assumed from tenets of the "perennial philosophy." This is the name given to the immemorial worldview propounded by the world's wisdom literature and, in modern times, partially expounded by the West's scientific research tradition. When integrated with the findings of Western science, the perennial philosophy provides the foundation for a comprehensive critical social science.

This new transpersonal paradigm views the rational organization of society, which characterizes the modern world, as the middle phase of social evolution, the preparation for entering the transrational stage. To move from the rational to the transrational level of social development, the same two-pronged process is necessary. Human culture would need to distance itself from an exclusively rational social life grounded in a fully elaborated empirical-analytic worldview. At the same time, society must affirm, extend, and intensify a fully transrational form of social life grounded in a psychic-subtle-causal worldview.

A New Paradigm

In a comprehensive paradigm that attempts to explain social change as goal-directed development, the place of authentic religion is critical. Drawing from the perennial philosophy, religion is seen as that institution whereby society structurally adapts to the highest levels of human development, the domain that transcends reason. Furthermore, religion is authentic to the extent that it provides a corporate group with access to the higher, transrational, or spiritual levels of consciousness. Not all religious forms, however, are equally authentic. For example, Freud concluded that historical forms of religion enhance regression to prerational infantile behavior. Marx claimed that organized religion becomes an opiate for subduing the rational autonomy of the masses. In both examples, the new paradigm would agree with the explanations but add that such religious structures and practices would be low on an authenticity scale, a discussion I return to later in the chapter.

The perennial power of authentic religion stems from its role of beckoning a corporate group to the full actualization of human development: the transcendent, transrational domains of consciousness. Drawing from traditional philosophical assumptions and orthodox scientific research, the modern period of rationality is viewed as a transitional stage leading to a higher phase of social evolution.

Transpersonal Theory and Perennial Philosophy

For want of a better name, the comprehensive paradigm is being labeled transpersonal sociology because it derives from humanistic and transpersonal psychology.[9] From one view, the transpersonal paradigm is nothing new. The version known as the perennial philosophy ranks as the oldest and most widespread account of ontological reality available in history.[10] What is new and exciting about the paradigm is its ability to describe an ancient worldview, at least partially, in orthodox scientific language. Moreover, the transpersonal paradigm allows research scholars to deduce and test hypotheses that flow from theory built on age-old metaphysical propositions and accumulated empirical evidence.

The philosophical assumptions of the transpersonal paradigm are not difficult to summarize. Being, in all its forms (i.e., all that we perceive within and around us) is grounded in an ultimate reality. This ultimate is both the ground and goal of all being. Forms of being develop in hierarchical stages, ranging from physical matter to biological, sentient, rational, psychic, subtle, and causal forms, eventually returning to unitive consciousness of the ultimate ground of being. The Great Chain of Being is described with remarkable consistency in the documents of all world religions—Hinduism, Buddhism, Confucianism, Taoism, Judaism, Christianity, and Islam—and in the traditions of local ancestral religions.[11]

Hierarchy and the Pre/Trans Fallacy

According to the perennial philosophy and the emergent transpersonal paradigm, human beings form an intermediate link in the hierarchy of being because they are composed of body, mind, and spirit. The human body exhibits physical matter developed to the level of living sentient being, a developmental stage shared with other animals, and so is said to be *pre*personal. Human mind reflects the level of consciously rational, that is, *personal* being. And human spirit reflects the level of development to transphysical, transrational, and hence *trans*personal being. Thus, human beings develop in three major phases— prepersonal, personal, and transpersonal—with rationality as the criterion dis-

tinguishing them. The fetus, infant, and young child are said to be in the prepersonal stage of development because this is the period in which awareness of the
environment is preconscious and prerational. Under normal conditions, children achieve the full "use of reason" in midadolescence and maintain a personal
or rational level of consciousness throughout adulthood. All individuals have the
capacity to access and develop higher or transpersonal levels of consciousness,
commonly known in Eastern psychology as psychic, subtle, causal, and unitive
stages of human development.

The prefixes "pre" and "trans" convey the notion of hierarchical development. Thus, in the three-stage model summarized earlier, rational consciousness is the middle and not the highest phase of a person's development. It is *pre*-
ceded by a level of consciousness that is dependent on sensorimotor perceptions
and *trans*cended by a level of consciousness that is dependent on spiritual perceptions. Because the prerational and transrational phases are both nonrational,
they are often confused. Once the confusion of "pre" and "trans" occurs, "one of
two things inevitably happens: the transrational realms are *reduced* to the prepersonal status, or the prerational realms are *elevated* to transrational glory."[12]
This confusion, which Wilber calls the pre/trans fallacy, is pervasive in the social
sciences. The transpersonal paradigm helps to avoid the problem.

Epistemology: Finding the Right Scientific Tools

This multistage hierarchical view of ontological reality and the place of full
human development in the Great Chain of Being was lost to many Western
scholars in the excitement of the Enlightenment and the development of the
tools of modern science.[13] Religion, the traditional depository of the perennial
philosophy, became the object of intense scientific scrutiny and criticism and
was found wanting. Science systematically tested the empirically verifiable
truth-claims of religion and rejected those that lacked proof. By association, the
claims about higher domains of nonphysical being were also rejected, even
though they could not be subjected to scientific tests. Among the educated at
least, religion was ignored and the perennial philosophy forgotten. The irony is
that Western science, through its own precise empirical methods, rediscovered
many of the same eternal verities propounded by the perennial philosophy. A
sophisticated understanding of the first two major segments of the chain of
being, which culminate in the prepersonal and personal stages of human development, is provided by modern physics, chemistry, and biology, along with behavioral and developmental psychology and the other human sciences.

But what about the higher domains of being—what Maslow called "the farther reaches of human nature"—the transpersonal stages of social evolution?
This is the edge to which normal science has led Western society. It is also the
fork in the road where Western scientists part company. They divide into three

groups, each espousing a different epistemology. The first group, by far the largest, is often labeled logical positivism. It includes the physical, natural, and biological sciences as well as those approaches in the human sciences that admit only the evidence of sensory data and the linear logic of empirical-analytic thinking. The second group is much smaller; it is limited to social scientists who espouse the methods of phenomenological hermeneutics. This approach to the human sciences often begins with measurable sensory data and linear logic but concentrates more on the further evidence of nonempirical mental data and the logic of empathetic interpretation based on subject-object reciprocity.[14] The third group is the smallest but is gaining momentum. It includes transpersonal psychologists, sociologists, and anthropologists and some mythologists and comparative historians of religion.[15] This approach embodies the comprehensive transpersonal paradigm based on developmental structuralism. It accepts the perennial philosophy as the winnowed wisdom of human experience, a heuristic model of reality or, at the very least, a rich source of working hypotheses for exploring the full range of human potential.

The transpersonal paradigm is both comprehensive and critical. It is comprehensive because it admits not only sensory and mental data but also the further evidence of spiritual phenomena. Likewise, it relies not only on empirical-analytic thinking and phenomenological hermeneutics but also the vision-logic of transrational consciousness and the intuitive knowledge of paradoxical explanations. The paradigm is critical because it allows judgments about higher and lower levels of social and psychological development, along with assessments of more or less authentic and legitimate mechanisms of development.

It is important to underscore that all three analytic approaches are based on the standards of empirical science.[16] The first, however, is limited to only sensory data and empirical-analytic reasoning. The second encompasses both sensory and mental data and combines empirical-analytic with phenomenological-hermeneutic (including narrative) reasoning. The third claims to include all the available evidence and modes of knowing in its explanations: sensory, mental, and spiritual data along with empirical-analytic, phenomenological-hermeneutic, and paradoxical-mandalic reasoning.[17]

Translating the perennial philosophy into scientific language is not too difficult for the first and second major segments of the Great Chain of Being, which correspond to the lower and middle phases of human development: the prepersonal and personal. These ontological segments or developmental phases have been examined by the first two epistemological approaches of Western science. Thus, for example, the physical natural world and its embodiment in the structure and functions of the human body (which includes the brain as a physical organ) have been analyzed with great sophistication and success using the methods of the natural sciences. The experimental empiricism of physics, chemistry, and biology has unlocked the mysteries of physical and sentient matter. Their direct applications to the mechanical functioning of the human body, through the techniques of modern medicine and behavioral psychology, have advanced our scientific knowledge of the lowest stages of human development. Similarly, the hierarchical structure and functions of the human mind have been mapped out in great detail by developmental psychologists, using, for the most part, the same experimental empiricism. For example, Jean Piaget's ingenious experiments with children's modes of perception and cognition led to the "discovery" of the preoperational, concrete-operational, and formal-operational levels of reason.[18]

The human sciences are radically different from the natural sciences because they go beyond sense data to explore the domain of meaning, to think about thinking. The process and content of thinking is not perceptible by any of the senses. The mind, however, can directly perceive thoughts and see relationships among these mental data. Using appropriate scientific techniques, analysts have discovered that the human mind represents an emergent form of consciousness called rational knowing. Formal operational reason is a mode of awareness radically different from the awareness produced by any of the five senses of the human body. Moreover, formal operational reason is not available at levels of evolution lower than human beings. Though linked to the chemical and electrical processes of brain cells, the rational mind is distinct from the physical body and its material brain. Scientists discovered a gap between the material functions of the body and the immaterial functions of the mind. The mind emerges from matter, but rational consciousness is a discontinuous leap from sensorimotor and emotional-sexual levels of consciousness. Thus, the mind has its own proper objects of perception (nonphysical mental data), just as the body has its own proper objects of perception (physical sensory data).

According to the perennial philosophy, however, human development does not stop at the level of reason. Reason is extended and intensified to its limit, and, then, human consciousness yields to the higher mode of knowing, the direct perception of spirit by spirit. So the human spirit, too, has its own proper object of direct perception: spiritual being. According to the wisdom of the perennial philosophy, the evidence provided by Eastern sciences such as yoga and zazen, the testimony of Western contemplative traditions such as Christian mysticism, Jewish kabala, and Islamic Sufism, and the data now being generated by Western sciences following the transpersonal paradigm, conscious reasoning yields to the transpersonal domain of the spirit and, then and only then, to unitive consciousness of Total or Absolute Being.

Organized Religion as Linchpin of Social Change

The province of religion in the scheme of human development is to help the corporate group gain access and adapt structurally to the domain of the spirit. This is the "authentic" function of religion. The structural adaptation of a religious group is *authentic* to the extent that it provides access to the transcendent realm of the spirit. The authentic function of religion is distinct from its legitimating function. Besides providing access and adaptation to the realm of the spirit, a corollary function of religion is to provide a sense of meaning and belonging to the corporate group at whatever level of social and spiritual development it has attained. This function is accomplished with greater or lesser legitimacy at different times by different forms of organized religion.

According to the transpersonal paradigm, a corporate group can be characterized by structural and cultural forms that are based either in archaic, magical, mythical, rational, psychic, subtle, or causal levels of human consciousness. The structural adaptation to each level of human development is *legitimate* to the extent that it provides appropriate exchange relationships, plausible explanations of reality, and genuine feelings of belonging in the corporate group. Thus, religious structures can be legitimate at any level of human development so long as they provide adequate meaning and belonging. Organized religion is *authentic,* however, only to the degree that it offers access and adaptation to the transpersonal levels of human consciousness.

Based on a critical comprehensive paradigm of social change, systematic data could reveal both the authenticity and the legitimacy of the structural forms of organized religion. The notions of authenticity and legitimacy of religion could be used to diagnose critically its level of valid functioning. For example, the religious organization of a corporate group at the magicomythical level of social development may be high in legitimacy but low in authenticity. That is, many members of the society may believe strongly in the explanations of reality provided by the group's myth system and feel strongly attached to the corporate group by participating in the living myth system, but few among them may have achieved the higher levels of transpersonal consciousness. On the other hand, a form of religious organization that is characteristic of a group at the psychic-subtle level of human consciousness may be rated high in authenticity yet low in legitimacy.

Many scholars are making a strong case for the heuristic value of the perennial philosophy and its translation into the transpersonal paradigm. As an evolutionary metatheory of social change, the new paradigm proposes that human development transcends, first, the limitations of the physical body to achieve personal consciousness of the human mind, then, the limitations of rational thinking to achieve transpersonal consciousness of the psychic-subtle-causal spirit, and, ultimately, the limitations of the body-mind-spirit realm to achieve unitive consciousness with Transcendent, Undivided, Eternal, Universal, Ultimate Being. In this analytic scheme, the role of religion in social change is central: Religious organization provides access and adaptation to the higher levels of human development.

Conclusion

Organized religion is both like and unlike other modern organizations. Religious and other types of organizations are similar in their tendency to follow principles of rationality that routinize behavior and allow the pursuit of predictable, mundane needs. Religious organizations are unlike other types, however, in their proclivity to provide access and adaptation to higher spiritual domains of human development. Because the modern organization evolved in the economic sector, it became the model for organizations in all other sectors of society. In many ways, therefore, the Catholic Church is forced to mimic other modern organizations, most of which are rational-legal bureaucracies. Hence, to maintain legitimacy, the Church tends to organize according to rational-legal principles. It also tends to theologize according to empirical-analytic and phenomenological-hermeneutic principles. But in its authentic functions and structures Roman Catholicism attempts to develop organizational forms that provide access to and development of the transrational, spiritual levels of human development. Describing the essential or unique structural elements of transpersonal religious organization is the topic I turn to next.

5

THE SPECIAL CHARACTER OF ORGANIZED RELIGION

The model of social change presented earlier directs our attention to officials who possess the primary expertise needed by the Catholic Church. This group is pivotal because officials with the dominant expertise in modern organizations also dominate the mechanisms of power and control. We identified this group of officials as the clerical ministry, with priesthood at its core, also calling it the Catholic technostructure. So the first premise of my analysis is that to change the form of Catholic ministry is to change the entire organizational structure of Roman Catholicism. The second is that the key traits of Catholic ministry are those structural characteristics of priesthood that are under serious stress and conflict. Pursuing these premises, we found that the priesthood today is characterized by a sacramental, sacerdotal, male, celibate monopoly of control over the Catholic means of salvation.

This chapter begins by trying to show that sacramentalism and sacerdotalism are the primary elements of Catholic ministry. These characteristics are essential because they represent structural forms whereby Roman Catholicism adapts to the transrational, spiritual levels of human development. The explicit recognition of a transcendent domain and development of structures that take it into account is what makes religious organizations different. Authentic religion emphasizes transrational behavior, while other types of organizations center on prerational and rational human behavior.

In discussing these differences, I also demonstrate that religious organizations are unlike others in an additional way: Organized religion relies on two kinds of power. The first is relative because it is based on finite, material resources and human rationality, just like the power structures in any modern organization. In radical contrast, however, the second is absolute. It is based on transrational levels of human consciousness and spiritual resources perceived as infinite. Structural adaptation to an infinite power source establishes the uniqueness of authentic religious organization. The social form characteristic of absolute power is hierophany and that of relative power is hierarchy. In religious organizations, hierophany corresponds to sacramentalism and hierarchy to sacerdotalism. Charismatic persons and other uniquely religious resources embody hierophanic power. Because of their extraordinary spiritual, nonrational source, hierophanic events must be routinized and made accessible to ordinary religious practitioners. In the Roman Catholic tradition, the routinization of hierophany and its integra-

tion with hierarchy result in sacramental sacerdotalism. This chapter concludes
with a descriptive analysis of the routinized hierarchical form of priesthood that
characterizes Catholicism at the turn of the twenty-first century.

Centrality of Sacrament in Organized Religion

Among the four ideal-type elements that characterize Catholic ministry, sacramentalism and sacerdotalism are the most essential.[1] Sacramentalism, which I define as the inevitable need for sacrament, is basic to all religions. Sacrament is the
generic name given to those symbols and rituals that externally express the unobservable spiritual relationship with Ultimate Reality that underlies authentic
religious behavior.[2] Sacerdotalism—the necessity of an ordained priesthood—
stems from the need for sacrament as it is elaborated in liturgical religions.

To understand the need for sacrament, we begin by *assuming* that the core
of authentic religion is an experience of something holy or sacred. Rudolf Otto
provides the unparalleled classic description. It is an encounter with Ultimate
Reality—that is, a numinous presence best described as a *mysterium tremendum et fascinans.* The holy is said to be a *mysterium* because it is perceived as
absolutely and totally "other," like no phenomenon ever encountered or imagi-
nable. The Totally Other is *tremendum* because its presence evokes a trembling
dread, an uncanny awe and fear like nothing known in mundane reality. But it is
fascinans because at the same time the holy numinous presence evokes intense
fascination and attraction, culminating in mystical ecstasy. This strange but ubiquitous harmony of contrasts characterizes an authentic religious experience.

Hierophany and Sacrament

Among comparative historians of religion, an encounter of this type is called a
hierophany, which literally means a manifestation of the sacred. A phenomenon
is sacred if it is deemed the ultimate, that is, the absolutely most perfect and
valuable form of being, or if it provides a link with Ultimate Being. In religious
terminology, *the ultimate* is used interchangeably with *the holy* or *the sacred.*
Therefore, a hierophany is a historical event in which someone experiences a
manifestation of the holy, the sacred, the ultimate.

Documents of world religions and traditions of local ancestral religions are
filled with accounts of hierophanies. They range from an experience of the sacredness of creation to the sacredness of flora, fauna, and human activities of
working, eating, and sexual begetting. Universally, the most stupendous hierophany is described as the creation event, the original manifestation of Ultimate
Being in time and space. All religious systems include a cosmogonic myth—that
is, a highly symbolic story of how the cosmos was generated out of chaos. For instance, a local Australian myth tells of Numbakula, revered ancestor of the

Achilpa tribe. After creating their world and social institutions, he climbed a gum tree back to the spiritual realm, leaving the tree behind as a sacred pole linking the human and divine worlds.[3]

Some important hierophanies focus on transformational events such as the forty-nine days of meditation under the bodhi tree after which Siddhartha Guatama, the historical Buddha, attained complete enlightenment. Others unfold salvational epics such as Moses leading the Hebrews in a Passover from Egyptian slavery to the freedom of a Promised Land. The highly elaborate Christian myth system recounts a new creation and a new Adam, Jesus the Christ, whose life, death, resurrection, ascension, and spiritual outpouring at Pentecost become a new Passover for both Jews and Gentiles.

The need for sacrament derives from the nature of hierophanies, which, by definition, deal with nonobservable supramundane reality in the spiritual domain. Experience of the hierophanic faith-event, whether occurring *in illo tempore* or at the present moment, forms the core of authentic religion. A perceived characteristic of Ultimate Reality is that it is incapable of being limited by or of occupying normal time and space.[4] Sacraments are the physical expressions of an experience of Ultimate Being that happen in a hierophanic event that we cannot perceive by our senses or explain in rational concepts. Sacraments are observable signs, symbols, rituals, and, indeed, the organized community of believers itself, which are the only means of capturing hierophanies and making them accessible now and to future generations.[5] Furthermore, sacraments in this generic sense are the only points of entry into a religious system that are available to normal social science. In their external reality, sacraments are perceived as *sensibilia,* or sensorimotor data. Therefore, the physical aspects of sacraments may become the object of analysis for normal, empirical-analytic science.

Sacrifice and Priesthood

Sacramental symbols take diverse forms, ranging from sacred pole to sand-painted mandala to six-pointed star and jeweled cross, but the paradigmatic sacrament is ritual sacrifice.[6] Religious worship is the human reaction to a hierophany. It reaches its highest form in sacrifice, the ritual surrender of personal and communal being to Ultimate Being. Few have analyzed the significance of sacrifice with more insight and clarity than Henri Hubert and Marcel Mauss.[7] Their analysis draws extensively on anthropological data from Hindu and Hebrew religions and occasionally notes similarities with the Catholic Mass. They argue that sacrifice embodies the essential elements of the relationship with Ultimate Reality more completely and effectively than any other type of religious activity.[8]

The priest is essential for sacrifice, for in this ritual only someone anointed by the community can legitimately act in its behalf. As sacrificer, the priest is chosen from the community and set aside by consecration rites to preside at the awesome communal encounter with Ultimate Reality. Acting in the name of the corporate group, the priest prepares for the sacrifice, touches the very objects that symbolize the deity, performs the ritual death in which divine and human being surrender to each other, and sets out the meal in which their transcendent union is consummated. The priest-sacrificer is distinct from the "sacrifier," the term Hubert and Mauss coin to designate the person or persons who benefit from the ritual. There can be no sacrifice in its complete and full form without the priest-sacrificer and lay-sacrifier.

Sacrament, in its sociological essence, is the outward expression of a nonobservable relation with Ultimate Reality. Sacrament can be simple or complex, as simple as uttering a word, *Alleluia,* or as complex as the eucharistic sacrifice of the Mass. Catholic doctrine, for example, teaches that, ultimately, there is only one Sacrament, the Christ, which is expressed in the living community, the Church. The Sacrament takes personal shape in the individual members of the Body of Christ and communal shape in its seven main liturgical actions. St. Paul formulates the principle of Christic sacrament in the phrase "I live, now not I, but Christ lives in me" (Gal 2:20). The eucharistic sacrifice is considered the culmination of sacramental activity and the very heart of Catholic liturgy. Furthermore, as the fathers of the Second Vatican Council explain, "The liturgy is the summit toward which the activity of the Church is directed; at the same time it is the fountain from which all her power flows."[9] The Church, as the Body of Christ, draws power from its union with Ultimate Being, celebrated and made efficacious in the sacraments.

Thus, through the sacraments of Christian initiation (baptism, confirmation, and Eucharist) the believer ritually dies to self and is reborn into the Body of Christ, a faith-community. This eternal hierophanic moment is celebrated liturgically throughout the believer's lifetime at the eucharistic sacrifice of the Mass. More generally, "According to the sacramental view . . . all human behavior may be regarded as a sign of something else that is approached or appropriated only through this sign."[10] These theological formulations are in accord with anthropological and sociological studies of sacrament.

Priesthood and Power

In Roman Catholicism, priesthood embodies two essential elements of religion. The priest is the sacrificer who provides access to *hierophany,* a source of power embodied in sacrament that culminates in ritual sacrifice. At the same time, the priest embodies *hierarchy,* a type of power conferred by being chosen and set aside to act in the community's name. The hierarchical power of priesthood, as it evolved in the Catholic Church, derives from the need found in all religions to preserve the "definitiveness" of the original hierophanic faith-event. Preserving this faith-event, according to Mircea Eliade, is the function of a living religious myth system.[11] It is not a haphazard process but one that must be handled with extreme care. As I will show, a well-worn path from the definitive hierophanic faith-event through myth to centralized power characterizes all organized religions.

Not One, Not Two Centers of Power

The dual function of priests—as embodiments of both hierophanic/spiritual and hierarchic/temporal power—places them at the locus of tension between two seemingly contradictory forces. Viewed separately, both forces are centralizing tendencies pulling in opposite directions. Viewed together, however, they are inseparable and mutually reinforcing. Two different centralizing tendencies develop in religious organizations because of (1) the historical definitiveness of the hierophanic event on which the religious fellowship is established and (2) the need to preserve this definitive hierophanic event.

Because organized religion wrestles with the paradox of having to adapt here and now to Ultimate Reality, which is universal and timeless, its authority structures derive from not one and not two centers of power. This rational contradiction in describing the power structure of organized religion reflects the Zen formulation of the ageless doctrine of nonduality: Ultimate Reality is "not two, not one." Because the Absolute is "not two, not one," the sacramental community that is in relationship with the Absolute tries to adopt a paradoxical power structure with not one, not two centers of authority. Nonduality is a "concept" totally inaccessible to reason alone. It must be directly experienced, which is possible only in unitive consciousness. Yet nonduality is "the simplest and most fundamental of all mystical doctrines" in the perennial philosophy.[12] It can be described only in poetic or mandalic symbols. Ken Wilber tries to explain the basic paradox: "The absolute—and here we have to speak somewhat poetically—cannot be characterized or qualified because it is not set apart or different from any thing and therefore could not be described as one thing among others."[13] The Benedictine theologian Joan Chittister explains the paradox with a Zen story:

"How does a person seek union with God?" the seeker asked.

"The harder you seek," the teacher said, "the more distance you create between God and you."

"So what does one do about the distance?"

"Understand that it isn't there," the teacher said.

"Does that mean that God and I are one?" the seeker said.

"Not one. Not two."

"How is that possible?" the seeker asked.

"The sun and its light, the ocean and the wave, the singer and the song. Not one. Not two."[14]

Does this paradox reveal some sociological meaning? If so, how are the nondual centers of authority socially established and what kind of social tension do they generate? I begin to explore these questions by examining the more common type of religious power: hierarchically centralized authority.

Hierarchic Power

As we have seen, religious experience tends universally toward expression—first by the individual who encounters the sacred and then by the group who shares the encounter. Group expressions take the form of sacramental symbols, whose primary function is preserving the cosmogonic event manifested in the hierophany. As Eliade has demonstrated, the symbol itself has authoritative respect because it embodies the hierophanic event.[15] Arranged in systems of living myths, symbols are the foundation of hierarchical authority in a religious collectivity. Eliade explains: "Once told, that is, revealed, the myth becomes apodictic truth; it establishes a truth that is absolute."[16] For believers, mythic reality is the only definitive reality. The myth system must be kept alive because the myth system is the sacrament that reveals and generates the link between the human condition and Ultimate Reality.

That which is ultimately definitive is above that which is relative and partially definable. Therefore, all religions are hierarchically authoritative, no matter how informal or relatively decentralized their political structures. The beliefs and rituals that preserve and reactualize what happened *in illo tempore* and those individuals who, because of their personal charisma (prophets) or the charisma of office (priests), are designated guardians of the myth must be given an authority commensurate with their responsibility. For, as Eliade says, the only "true sin is forgetting" the myth.[17] The myth preserves the faith-event that creates the foundation of being, the hierophany that established the center and ground of reality. If the myth is lost, so is the cosmos, that is, the only world that links the believer to Ultimate Being and so gives life meaning and value.[18]

For religious believers, the only alternative to an authoritative myth and hierarchical authority structures for preserving it is the chaos of nonbeing, an existence utterly without meaning and value. As a protection against chaos, hierarchical power and authority are centered in the myth system and those who dominate and control it. Therefore, all religions, no matter how loosely organized, have a central locus of legitimate authority. Entering a living myth system through faith is submitting to the hierarchic power of the authoritative symbol/ sacrament and its designated guardians. Hence religious collectivities engage in the relentless process of developing organizational power and authority sufficient to preserve access to the definitive religious experience that launched and sustains the group. In the history of Christianity, for example, we see that the centralization of power began with the designated 12 apostles, who alone preached the *kerygma* with authority. Centralized authority grew notably with the accumulation of canonical scriptures and the emergence of a powerful sacramental priesthood and episcopate. It expanded as the central cities of Christendom developed, with Rome recognized as the locus of final authority: *Roma locuta est, causa finita est* (Rome has spoken, the case is closed). In recent centuries, the Roman Catholic Church has adapted its organizational form to the principles of rational-legal bureaucracy. In doing so, its organizational form became "the most rational known means of exercising authority over human beings."[19]

Centralized authority in religious systems other than Catholicism has developed differently, but no religion is without the minimal authority of a definitive myth system and rudimentary mechanisms to control it. For example, Protestant free-church congregationalism is no less hierarchic in its submission to the power of canonical scriptures than Roman Catholicism. In fact, in this regard, it is more hierarchic because for many Protestant believers access to the means of salvation depends solely on the authoritative Word of the Bible. Furthermore, social structures for centralizing power are not unique to monotheistic religions, although they tend to elaborate the mechanisms of control and coordination to a greater degree than polytheistic and nontheist religions. Zen Buddhism, for example, exhibits a rudimentary technostructure. The creation, coordination, and control of the means of enlightenment center around the sangha. This is a fellowship of zazen practitioners loosely organized around a specially designated teacher. The teacher guides devotees in the Zen tradition of sitting meditation, speaks with spiritual authority, and elicits genuine obedience. The teacher is also subject to a higher spiritual authority. For no one is designated a teacher or Zen master until the right to this role is authoritatively transmitted by a senior teacher or master.[20]

Beliefs evoke structure in all types of organizations, but in religious organizations the nexus between beliefs and structure is a matter of cosmogonic importance. A full explanation of religious power and authority cannot ignore their cultural basis in the belief system. A major premise following from a comparative examination of definitive religious beliefs is that all religious systems must possess centralized mechanisms of control. Hence they are characterized by a concentration of power in a central locus of legitimate authority. In Catholicism this centralized hierarchic authority resides primarily in the sacramental priesthood.

Hierophanic Power

The strength of the hierarchical centralizing tendency in religious organizations is drawn from the definitiveness and absolute character of the primordial hierophany. Paradoxically, the driving force of hierophany, which is a countervailing second type of centralizing tendency, comes from the same absolute source. The external centralized structures of authority are established for a single purpose:

Hierarchic religion provides a milieu that makes possible a closeness and eventual union between believers and the vital hierophanic force of absolute reality.

The perennial philosophy postulates that ultimate reality is one, providing the unique goal as well as the unique center or ground of all being. In the case of Christianity, the authentic goal of organizational structure is union with God through the Christ-event. Christ in God is "all in all" (1 Cor 15:28) because all become one, in one Absolute Center. This is the primordial and ultimate hierophany: unitive consciousness of Absolute Being. Therefore, ultimate reality is the one source and one goal of two types of religious power. In this paradoxical sense, authentic religious power is not two, not one.

Whatever else it might be, authentic religious experience is profoundly personal. Generally, it is a union gained in solitude and silence. Even when it occurs in social interaction and the actors manifest some type of external transfiguration, the hierophanic event is described as interiorly personal. The experience cannot be empirically observed or verified by the senses. Sacred symbols, persons, and organizational forms are only sacraments pointing believers to or attempting to unite them with something "totally other." For practitioners, however, unitive consciousness of the totally other is infinitely better than the sacred wrappings and trappings of the external religious system. According to most accounts, practitioners progress in the transpersonal domain by approaching the holy in emptiness. Stripped of self and free from attachments, they try to enter or allow themselves to be drawn more personally and deeply into transcendent union.[21] Hence, although religion is inevitably organized around hierarchic centralized power, it nevertheless manifests a radical countervailing force: hierophanic power. Hierophany, the manifestation of Ultimate Reality, draws—indeed, drives—practitioners away from centralized authoritative symbols and structures to the radically personal center or ground of their being.

Religious power, therefore, is intensely personal and inevitably social. To paraphrase Catholic doctrine formulated at the Second Vatican Council: A personal hierophanic or sacramental encounter with Ultimate Being in liturgy is the summit toward which the social, hierarchic activity of the Church is directed; furthermore, sacramental liturgy is the fountain from which all her powers flow, both hierophanic and hierarchic.[22]

Religion and Paradox

Conceptualizing the countervailing forces as two different centralizing tendencies causes confusion. Two centralizing movements drawing in opposite directions within the same bounded system is a logical contradiction. But according to the perennial philosophy, we can view a religious system as the interpenetration of two distinct domains of human behavior, the rational and transrational. Sociologically speaking, organized religion is the structural integration of the rational and transrational levels of human social development. One etymological explanation derives religion from the Latin *religio,* which means to link back. Thus, a religious system links the physical, rational levels of human development back to their foundation in the spiritual, transrational realm; a comprehensive model of social change in organized religion can be satisfied only with a paradoxical explanation that describes not one, not two centers of power.

For the believing community, the unique power that exists in a concrete religious organization is generated from a single source—the foundational cosmogonic faith-event. That event is accessible in two moments. At one moment—the moment of hierarchy—external expressions of this event draw members in the direction of dualistic control centralized in the hands of a visible minority, which in the Catholic case is the sacramental priesthood. At another moment—the moment of hierophany—internal movements draw members away from the center of organizational authority into a living relationship with the invisible reality encountered in the faith-event. This, too, is a centralizing force because all are drawn into a relationship with the same numinous reality, the same unitive consciousness.

Martin Buber's distinction between I–You and I–It relations illuminates the conundrum of two opposite centralizing tendencies stemming from one source of absolute power.[23] His analysis also attempts to formulate tenets of the perennial philosophy in sociological concepts. I–You interactions reflect spiritual, hierophanic moments, each pointing to and including the primordial encounter with an Eternal You. I–It interactions reflect material, hierarchic moments, which coalesce in hierarchic organizational structures. In any social interaction, an I–You relationship exists only in the moment of a mutually personal and dialogical encounter—in a completely holistic relation involving the whole being of both partners. In its pure form, no third party can enter an I–You relation, and certainly not in a manner that would establish hierarchic control, for that would destroy its absolute mutuality and reduce it to an I–It form. I–It interactions are all the one-sided, objective, and abstract relations between self and other beings. In an I–It relation, I "see the other as a means, experience the other as an object, or know the other in an attitude of objective detachment."[24] I–It relationships are not spiritual in the radical sense in which Buber ascribed spirituality to unique I–You relationships. They are the opposite: material, empirical, and interchangeable. All human interactions pulsate dialectically between I–You and I–It, because I–You relationships are necessarily temporary. Buber explained that the I–It relations can either strengthen or weaken the series of I–You relational events. Indeed, strengthening an I–You relation often depends on the activity involved in the I–It relation.

Just so in religious organizations. The purpose of hierarchically controlled sacraments, myths, moral codes, and the organized community itself is to preserve the definitive hierophanic faith-event. These structures make the event

available to potential new members and the faithful who want to strengthen
their relationship with the Eternal You. Thus, for example, baptism plunges the
believer into the death and resurrection of the Christ, and the Mass celebrates
and intensifies this eternal, timeless event from historical moment to historical
moment. Buber observed that the necessity of always returning to physical I–It
relationships is our melancholy fate but the ability of turning again to spiritual
I–You relations our amazing glory. In his view, all I–It relations are only a means
to the same end, namely, strengthened I–You relations, which point to and include the ultimate relation with an Eternal You.

Externalization of the religious experience attempts to link consciousness of
the numinous presence to authoritative symbols, sacraments, persons, and organizational forms. This is an I–It interaction and constitutes the first type of centralizing tendency in religious organizations. Internalization involves a countervailing tendency that we may also view as a centralizing force because it drives
believers toward an absolute center. This process is limited to I–You relations, all
of which have at their center the Eternal You. Hierophanic centralization takes
over when the believer becomes aware of a movement in which the numinous
presence envelops the whole person without intermediary symbols. This is the
transpersonal moment when the radically mutual, holistic, dialogical encounter
of unitive consciousness is centered in the one Ultimate Reality or Eternal You.

The Christ-event is the cosmic center of the Christian belief system. As in all
religions, the I–You relationship must take precedence for the believer over all
external sacraments and symbols, material signs and wonders, and rational philosophical reflection; in a word, over all outward expressions or externalizations of
the encounter with the holy. As Paul tells the fledgling Christians, "Here are the
Jews asking for signs and wonders, here are the Greeks intent on their philosophy; but what we preach is Christ crucified; to the Jews, a discouragement, to
the Gentiles, mere folly; but to us who have been called, Jew and Gentile alike,
Christ the power of God" (1 Cor 1:22–24).

All religious belief systems assume the absolute necessity of a concentration
of visible social power so that the external expressions of the cosmic religious experience will remain authoritatively definitive. In religious power conflicts, many
believers reject centralized organizational power in favor of interior personal
power. After all, hierarchic power is a dualistic, scarce, unequally distributed resource. Hierophanic power, however, is infinitely plentiful and accessible to
everyone through a transpersonal, unitive relationship with Ultimate Reality.

Religious organizations are radically and irreducibly different from nonreligious ones. Religious believers tend to stress a faith orientation in structuring
their formal organizations. When a faith orientation is more salient than cognitive, cathectic, or evaluative orientations, a completely bureaucratic form of organizational control is not possible.[25] In a rational-legal bureaucracy of the pure
type, orientation to everyday actions is predominantly cognitive or rational.

Thus, there is only one centralizing tendency in nonreligious bureaucracies. This single centripetal force leads through the hierarchy to the dominant coalition in the top administrative positions that compose the technostructure.[26] In organizations of living religion, however, two radically countervailing forces prevail. The first, hierarchic centralization, draws its uniquely religious power from the need to externalize the cosmogonic hierophany in a definitive and thus centralizing manner. The second, hierophanic centralization, draws its power from the need to internalize the central faith-event in a movement toward the absolute center of the cosmos. The paradox of all religions and so of all religious organization—emphasized by Buber and paid some attention by Weber—is that one centralizing tendency cannot exist without the other and each pulls in the opposite direction.

Priesthood embodies the paradox of hierophanic power in tension with hierarchic power. These contrasting forces provide the key to understanding why Catholic ministry is dominated by a priesthood that exercises male, celibate, sacerdotal, and sacramental control over the means of salvation. But, although describing priesthood in terms of a transcendent paradox and an ideal type highlights its essential structural traits, it ignores other important characteristics. Therefore we also must examine the priesthood in its most visible form, providing a historical picture of the status quo of Catholic ministry in the late twentieth century.

The Hierarchical Priesthood

For most of its history, Catholic ministry has been equated de facto with the priesthood. Historical reality, however, is enormously more complex; the hierarchical form of Christian ministry unfolded within a history of conflict and change. The story of its evolution begins with the loosely organized, intimate fellowship of apostles and disciples who proclaim baptismal oneness in the risen Christ regardless of ethnicity, class, or gender. It culminates in the male, celibate, sacramental priesthood that is the technostructure of a rational-legal bureaucracy of the late twentieth century. As we know it today, Catholic priesthood manifests a structural form arranged in a hierarchy of pope, bishops, and lower clergy; among the latter, theologians and scripture scholars play a unique role.

A more or less elaborate administrative structure has developed at each level of this hierarchical arrangement of superiors and subordinates. Each member of the priesthood is an official in the ideal-typical sense. Ideally, by church law, at each level of hierarchy the modern priest has a set of subordinate offices at his disposal. Pope, bishop, and parish priest have the right given by canon law to organize and control a bureaucracy, no matter how elaborate or rudimentary, to assist them in carrying out official duties. Change in any part of the complex structure affects the whole priesthood.

Pope and Roman Curia

The papacy represents the pinnacle of monarchical power in the Roman Catholic, multinational, corporate Church. Its primary function is to provide an interface between the Church and its environment. As a component of a specifically religious system, however, the pope is bishop of Rome and, therefore, chief pastor and supreme high priest of Roman Catholicism. Hence, although the papacy evolved into a powerful sociopolitical entity in its own right,[27] its essentially religious legitimation derives from the hierophanic power residing in the priestly pastoral office. This transpersonal view, identifying the pope as priest and minister whose duty is to serve the spiritual needs of the faithful, finds eloquent expression in a lenten sermon of the late Cardinal Joseph Frings of Cologne:

> To have authority in the Church does not mean to rule, but to serve the welfare of the faithful. The Savior said of himself: "The Son of man is not come to be ministered unto, but to minister and to give his life as a redemption for many" (Mt 20:28). In the same way the ministry of priests and bishops does not mean domination, but service, *ministerium,* as the pope makes clear in his traditional reference to himself as the Servant of the Servants of God, *Servus Servorum Dei.*[28]

Although the connection of the papacy to hierophanic priesthood is essential, it is not the most fundamental trait for explaining the pope's role in the social structure of hierarchic priesthood.

The most important characteristic of the modern papacy for understanding social change in the ministry is an ever-expanding centralized control of Catholic dogma, morality, liturgy, and discipline. Creeping hierarchic centralization of the spiritual affairs of the Church in the bishop of Rome began in earnest during the nineteenth century and continued with increased fervor throughout the twentieth century.[29] As the hierarchical importance of the papal office grew, so did its administrative bureaucracy. The top central office of the Church exercises nominal control over a highly differentiated administrative structure known by its Latin name, the curia. Pope Sixtus V was the principal architect of the Roman curia; he restructured it in 1588 as a mechanism to implement the Counter-Reformation. Over its four-hundred-year modern history, the administrative arm of the papacy has continued to evolve into a well-developed modern bureaucracy.[30] Together the papacy and its highly effective curial bureaucracy constitute the most crucial element of the technostructure of modern Roman Catholicism. Despite recent attempts at reform, the curia continues to provide the organizational mechanisms needed to support the longstanding tendencies of the papacy toward hierarchical domination and control of the international Church. Obviously, since the sacramental priesthood is the very foundation of centralized power, the papacy has pervasive interest in and control over the evolution of the structural form of Catholic ministry.

Bishops and Diocesan Curia

According to Catholic doctrine, only the office of bishop enjoys the fullness of priesthood because only he can validly ordain priests and consecrate other bishops. Along with the right to ordain, the bishop has full monarchical authority over the local church.[31] The bishop, therefore, provides the interface between pope and Roman curia above and clergy and laity below him in the hierarchy, as well as between society at large and the local church. At the beginning of 1993 there were 3,275 cardinals, archbishops, and bishops worldwide (more than 900 of them retired); at the beginning of 1994 there were 398 cardinals, archbishops, and bishops in the United States.[32]

The bureaucratic structures commanded by the bishop include the local diocesan curia and recently, as an outgrowth of reforms inaugurated by the Second Vatican Council, international, national, and regional episcopal conferences.[33] In many cases, these are impressive bureaucracies governed by technostructures based on the best available expertise and mechanisms of hierarchical control. Curial responsibilities include overseeing the specifically religious and spiritual affairs of the local churches, social and health care services, education systems, legal and public relations, and even research and planning. In assessing the coalitional power of bishops in any church conflict, one must consider the network of powerful bureaucracies, some with multimillion-dollar budgets. Bishops can and do use these mechanisms of hierarchic power as tools for domination and control of the status quo, as well as for social change in the direction of their values.

Theologians and Academia

The most influential members of the lower clergy are priest-theologians and scripture scholars. Their role in the hierarchical organization of power is best understood as that of "organic intellectuals," a term originating in a Marxist analysis of power and domination. Antonio Gramsci argues that class domination in capitalist societies rests on a balance of two factors: (1) force or coercion and (2) "hegemony," or the consent given "spontaneously" to elite leaders by subordinates.[34] He used the term *organic intellectuals* to refer to those who play an educative or leadership role *within* the ranks of a social stratum or class. Because they are integrated members of the group, these intellectuals can play an organic role in its transformation.

Until recently, the vast majority of influential theologians and scripture scholars in the Catholic Church have been priests. Certainly most intellectuals organically connected to the pope and Roman curia have been priest-theologians, carefully chosen for their conservative views. In the last several decades, however, scholarly ranks within the Catholic Church have become increasingly diverse. They now embrace growing numbers of laymen and laywomen and, most prominently among the latter, feminist theologians and religion scholars. This new breed of theologians can provide intellectual leadership for those struggling against the status quo. Thus members of the modern corps of Catholic intellectuals, now composed of scholars of every ideological stripe, are organically connected to different strata of the Church, not only different levels of the official hierarchy but also various social strata produced by class, race, and gender differences.

Regardless of their ideological leanings, few theologians are without organizational support to protect and further their scholarly interests. Most productive and recognized scholars of religion have ties with colleges, universities, or other formal manifestations of academia such as professional associations. In various ways, academia provides its members extensive bureaucratic support for the production and dissemination of knowledge, oversees their rights and responsibilities, and furnishes them with channels for promotion and other mechanisms for rewarding or sanctioning intellectual accomplishments.

The success of any struggle against the status quo in a powerful organization like the Catholic Church depends on the work of intellectuals and scholars who support the change. Organic intellectuals such as liberation theologians and feminist scholars may create new forms of hegemony in the Church's lower strata. Through personal scholarship supported by a powerful academic bureaucracy, they could help shatter the dogmatic claims of worldviews propounded at the upper echelons by providing challenging alternatives.

Lower Clergy and Grassroots Bureaucracy

Two types of clergy make up the lowest rank in the hierarchical priesthood: secular priests and religious order priests. The organizational function of secular priests is to be the interface between pope and bishops above and laity below. Their institutional function is to act as pastoral and priestly ministers in local parishes. In providing authoritative and legitimate access to creed, code, and cult, the parish priest serves as the hierarchical link necessary for preserving the Church's authentic hierophanic traditions. He is the grassroots mechanism of coordination and control of religious power—both hierophanic and hierarchic.

The parish is also organized as a small bureaucracy with the pastor as its legally appointed head. The technostructure of a large modern parish is composed of ordained priests, professional lay ministers, and volunteer workers. As a grassroots bureaucracy, the parish provides basic religious functions and a wide variety of other social services for the community.[35]

Religious order priests are ordained members of monastic and apostolic communities. Most religious orders in this country have European origins, some many centuries old, while others are indigenous to the United States and only decades old. As these communities usually require vows of chastity (which implies celibacy), poverty, and obedience, members are referred to as religious virtuosi.[36] As ordained ministers, religious priests, like their secular diocesan confreres, also provide access to the authentic creed, code, and cult of the Catholic Church. In fact, many serve as pastors or associate pastors of local parishes and are indistinguishable in this function from secular priests. Historically, religious order priests often fostered reform movements within the Church and even today are considered specialists, while their diocesan-priest counterparts are seen as generalists of Catholic ministry.

Although founded on the transpersonal, hierophanic ideals of Christian charity, most modern religious orders are highly complex rational bureaucracies. Many, such as the Jesuits, Dominicans, and Franciscans, are noted for their professional expertise and intellectual activities. Because of their traditional vows emphasizing communal and personal asceticism, religious order priests are likely resources for charismatic leadership in periods of transition. But their participation in the ordained clergy means that they also lean toward the hierarchic power role of preserving the status quo.

Conclusion

Two types of power characterize organized religion: hierarchy and hierophany. Hierarchy locates the center of religious power at the top of an organizational pyramid. Hierarchic authority is centralized in the technostructure because the technostructure appropriates the primary expertise of the organization and the power that goes with it. Hierarchic centralization of power is inevitable in modern religious organizations because they follow bureaucratic principles. These rules of organization dictate that all officials must possess the expert knowledge appropriate for their job and every lower office must be under the control and supervision of a higher one.

Hierophany places the center of religious power in a spiritual realm, the domain of human development in which religious practitioners establish a conscious link with Ultimate Reality. Hierophanic authority is centralized in a definitive, historical faith-event that makes communication possible with the higher, spiritual, cosmic realm. Hierophanic centralization of power follows from the principle of authentic religion, which says that all believers have an equal potential to achieve consciousness of or union with Ultimate Being.

Conflict and tension is created by the countervailing centers of power in religious organizations. The strain develops because hierophanic power cannot exist without hierarchic power and each pulls in an opposite direction. Hierar-

chic authority draws members toward rational-legal, routinized, predictable behavior. Hierophanic power draws them toward transrational, totally free, unpredictable, unknowable behavior. In the Catholic Church, hierarchic power is
embodied primarily in the ordained priesthood. Hierophanic power, however, is
embodied universally in the priesthood of all believers. According to the perennial philosophy, tension between hierarchy and hierophany and between ordained priesthood and the priesthood of all believers is resolved when, and only
when, all members achieve unitive consciousness of Absolute Reality. In that
timeless moment, hierarchy dissolves in an ultimate cosmic hierophany and,
along with it, all other divisions in the community of believers.

Religious paradox is often the source of bitter conflict. Disputes over changing the historical forms of ministry can take on literally cosmogonic significance
because preservation of foundational faith-events are seen to be at stake. Tension grows because Catholic dioceses and their priestly technostructures are immersed in a matrix of mounting historical forces that are dramatically changing
their ecological niche. At its base, however, the conflict turns on the two types
of centralizing tendencies in organized religion: hierophanic and hierarchic
power. Sacramental priesthood is the linchpin between them. Hence we observe an intense and seemingly contradictory struggle. On the one hand, Catholicism attempts to spiritualize the priesthood by limiting it to men willing to
practice lifelong celibacy, a transrational form of asceticism. On the other hand,
the Church tries to rationalize it by making the priesthood a bureaucratic mechanism of coordination and control. Catholic coalitions are forming, some to protect and preserve the status quo and others to challenge and change it.

The changing structure of Catholic ministry, therefore, is the *explanandum*—
the object to be explained by the theory presented in this and the previous two
chapters. The priest shortage and problems with mandatory celibacy, along with
other social forces for change and the conflict they generate, are the *explanans*—
the explanatory elements of this theoretical framework. In the next chapter I
turn to the explanatory elements of the model, the historical and contemporary
events that are fomenting structural change in Catholic ministry.

6

FORCES FOR CHANGE IN CATHOLIC MINISTRY

In this chapter I examine seven historical trends related to Catholic ministry that have been gaining strength over the latter half of the twentieth century. Each trend comprises two countervailing forces in a dialectical relationship. Together they compose a matrix that is creating tension toward change in the structure of Catholic ministry that will lead first to married priests and then to the ordination of women in the Catholic Church.

Demographic Transition

I list the decline and aging of the priest population first because currently it is the driving force for change in Catholic ministry. As noted in chapter 2, Lawrence Young and I examined the extent, components, and causes of that decline and also discovered that it conflicts with another demographic trend affecting U.S. Catholicism—steady growth in lay membership.[1] This conflict will help bring about a radical change in the structure of Catholic ministry.

The next social trend centers on the ideological apparatus supporting the status quo of the Catholic form of ministry. Have Catholic beliefs and values about priesthood and its relation to ministry changed noticeably in recent decades? If so, how deep are the forces of ideological change and what is the source of their strength?

Shift from Dogmatism to Pluralism

Throughout the institutions of modern society, including religion, blind faith in the received wisdom of the past is being questioned. The Vietnam War shattered the illusion that all Americans uncritically believe in the right to destroy a people to make the "world free for democracy." Watergate ended the belief in the unquestioned right of the president to act outside the law. The inside traders of Wall Street damaged the belief in a free market system. Dogmatism of all kinds is being replaced by pluralism. Dogmatism characterizes an organization's ideology or belief system when a uniform set of truths is taught with absolute authority and accepted with unquestioned obedience. Pluralism characterizes its belief system when a variety of truths are taught with relative authority and those that are convincing are accepted. Both are organizational characteristics. At the

individual level, conformism is the personal response to dogmatism, and voluntarism is the personal response to pluralism.

In the modern era, individuals decide to join a church or continue to participate in organized religion because it provides a favorable environment for their
religious search, not because they want prefabricated answers about Ultimate
Reality. For many, the concern with orthodoxy in faith and morals has been
dropped in favor of being responsible for oneself. Pluralism and voluntarism are
the major characteristics of turn-of-the-century religion.[2]

The primary source of greater flexibility in belief systems is a deep trend that
covers millennia and profoundly shapes the way we construct worldviews in modern society. The freedom for large segments of the same society to hold different
worldviews is only a few centuries old. This newly established flexibility is still opposed by exaggerated notions of dogmatic orthodoxy in some organized religions
and other institutions that take on quasi-religious functions in modern society.

Obviously, however, as Robert Bellah has pointed out, we hold many mort-
gages from prior epochs, and today's freedoms are constrained by holdovers
from previous restrictions.[3] Maintaining outmoded religious formulations has its
roots in the need for dogma in historical religions. In its common meaning,
dogma is a "body of doctrines concerning faith or morals formally stated and authoritatively proclaimed by a church."[4] Religious dogma is necessary because it
preserves the definitiveness of the historical faith-events on which a church is
founded.[5] Religious dogma, therefore, has a paradoxical relationship with reason, because the sociocultural milieu that provides rational symbols for dogmatic statements is constantly changing. A closed society begins to interact with
surrounding cultures once mutually beneficial communication is established.
Open societies must constantly adapt their cherished beliefs and values to the
rational challenges around them. The paradoxical challenge for organized religion is to balance eternal verities with ever-changing symbol systems created to
explain an ever-changing world. I will examine the transition of viewing the
world as a dogmatic "one-possibility thing" to viewing it as a pluralistic "infinite
possibility thing" at three levels: across millennia, centuries, and generations.

Shifts across Millennia

In an effort to understand the modern situation facing organized religion, Bellah
analyzes religious evolution from prehistorical to modern times.[6] He divides the
religions of the world into stages and epochs, marked by their world-rejecting or
world-affirming tendencies. The five stages are labeled primitive, archaic, historic, early modern, and modern religion. The three epochs cover an early period
of world-affirmation embodied in primitive and archaic religions, a middle period of world-rejection that characterized the historic religions, and a later period
of world-affirmation espoused by early modern and modern religions. Protestant

Christianity is the prototypical modern religion, but recently Catholicism and some Asian religions have displayed tendencies similar to Protestantism.

By arranging the massive facts of human history in this fashion, Bellah discovered that prior to approximately the first millennium B.C.E., religion was characterized by a world-affirming symbol system. Primitive and archaic religions during this time were oriented to a single cosmos. Their myth systems did not assume the existence of a wholly different world against which this one is considered worthless. These world-affirming religions were concerned with personal, social, and cosmic harmony—rain, harvest, children, health—not with *salvation.*

Around the first millennium B.C.E., the phenomenon of world-rejection arose all over the Old World. An exalted view of another transcendent realm of reality that alone was true and valuable, coupled with a very negative view of humankind and society, pervaded the religions of India, Israel, and China. The monism of world-affirmation was replaced with the dualism of world-rejection.[7] Then, for a period of two millennia, world-rejection spread over the civilized world and was reflected in the new religions developed in that epoch—Christianity, Islam, and new religious movements in Japan.

Early modern religion, characterized by a new form of world-affirmation, began with the Protestant Reformation. Protestant inner-worldly asceticism did not entirely do away with dualism but made possible a more direct confrontation between the two worlds. Salvation is gained not in withdrawal but in the midst of this world. According to Bellah, modern religions at the turn of the twenty-first century are in a transitional period leading to the total collapse of dualism, which was so central to historic religions. The breakthrough of the modern era involves the very nature of the symbolization process. The worldview prevalent in modern religions has emerged only because of the tremendous intellectual advances of the past two centuries. An infinitely multiplex world has replaced the simple duplex structure of the world-rejecting epoch as well as the nature-bound monistic structure of the earlier world-affirming epoch.

Bellah argues that the world acceptance of the primitive and archaic stages was the only possible response to a reality that invades the self so much that symbolization of self and world are only partially separate. The world-rejecting stance of historic religions made possible the discovery of self. A distinct consciousness of self also marked the beginning of a clear objectification of the social order and thus the ability to criticize sharply the social world. Early modern religion, with its new type of world-affirmation, helped create a self-revising system in the form of a democratic society. This newfound flexibility was balanced by doctrinal orthodoxy and puritanical rigidities. Bellah notes that, ironically, dogmatism and rigidity allowed such flexibility to emerge. In the modern phase, culture and personality are viewed as endlessly revisable. Moreover, since educated individuals in the modern epoch are beginning to understand the physical, biological, psychological, and social structures that underlie the self's own existence, they feel they can and must take responsibility for their own fate.

Bellah makes some bold claims about the symbolization process in today's world. He sees the modern person as "a dynamic multidimensional self capable, within limits, of continual self- transformation and capable, again within limits, of remaking the world, including the very symbolic forms with which he deals with it, even the forms that state the unalterable conditions of his own existence."[8] Thus, the symbolization of humankind's relation to the ultimate conditions of existence are no longer the monopoly of any explicitly religious group, let alone any particular stratum within organized religion.

Christianity played a major role in the creation of the modern situation but no longer controls it. The obligation of orthodoxy is not felt at the leading edge of modern culture where all rigid scientific, political, and religious positions are questioned. This situation, however, generates a more profound commitment to the symbolization process. Now all mature adults share the responsibility of not only constructing social reality but also creating the definitive symbol system that embodies Ultimate Reality.

Change across Recent Centuries

The early Enlightenment period of the seventeenth and eighteenth centuries witnessed the rise of natural science and the decline of myth and tradition as the reigning explanations of reality. Philosophers such as Rousseau and Hume, however, argued strenuously that reason and objective science—that is, a purely rational interpretation—cannot explain all of reality.[9] The late Enlightenment period of the nineteenth and early twentieth centuries was, therefore, dedicated to finding a methodology for the humanities and social sciences, or a modern hermeneutic that would more adequately handle all the data.

In laying out the problems of the traditional metaphysical basis of religion, the Enlightenment philosopher Immanuel Kant argued that reality is not a question of two worlds (a heavenly realm and an earthly realm) but as many worlds as there are modes of apprehending them. Against the exaggerated arguments of objective reason that the newborn natural sciences advanced, Kant demonstrated that explanations based on pure reason do not exhaust the data. Friedrich Schleiermacher corrected the overly narrow rationalism of both Kantian philosophy and the natural sciences and at the same time saw deeper implications of the Kantian breakthrough.[10]

Schleiermacher laid the foundations for the methodology of the humanities and social sciences by emphasizing the importance of the historical approach with its careful accumulation of facts, the personal experiential dimension of religion, and the affinity of the subject with the object of study. The tools of the *Geisteswissenschaften*, or human sciences—first among which was higher biblical criticism—were further refined by Wilhelm Dilthey's hermeneutic approach to interpreting inner experience; Rudolf Otto's classic treatment of the holy and the religious a priori; Edmund Husserl's prescriptions for a phenomenological "bracketing" when judging the factual truth of objects of belief; and finally Mircea Eliade's brilliant melding of the German history of religion (*Religionswissenschaft*) and phenomenology of religion in his monumental studies of primitive and archaic religions.[11]

In the social sciences, Sigmund Freud and Emile Durkheim are generally credited with the discovery of the symbol and its qualities as a unique mode of human understanding and communication. Freud demonstrated that the subconcious and unconscious aspects of the human situation are realities, but realities accessible only through the symbolization process. Durkheim discovered that the realm of the sacred is critical for understanding profane existence. Sacred reality, which is sui generis, can be expressed only in symbols, not in logical concepts of objective reason.

The discovery of the symbol and the true nature of the symbolization process occurred in the West only within the past century. It laid the foundation for further achievements of the historical and social sciences in the twentieth century. The accumulated knowledge of the past dozen decades has revealed the laws of psychological and social development that led to the realization of the modern situation: Human beings are responsible for the social construction of reality, even for creating the symbol systems that provide knowledge of Ultimate Reality and the ground of being. Under these conditions, Peter Berger argues, modern believers not only can but must pick and choose those religious symbols that will legitimate changing the world in the direction of their chosen beliefs and values.[12] Participating in the social construction of reality means knowing more firmly the distinction between unchanging Ultimate Reality and the alterable conditions of one's personal and social worlds. The Marxian proclamation now becomes truer than ever: "Social change no longer occurs behind our backs; we must now make history consciously and collectively."

Change within Generations

The history we make occurs only in our lifetime, though it too has consequences for future generations. The epochal transformations that took place across millennia and the historical changes of past centuries and recent decades all come to bear in developments shaping the current generation. The epic and historic transitions from dogmatism to pluralism allow present-day Catholics, for example, to become responsible consciously and collectively for either reproducing the current form of priesthood or transforming the status quo. An individual's ability to assume that responsibility, however, is also acquired in stages that occur in one's lifetime.

The facility to think rationally, for example, is achieved in roughly four stages, according to Jean Piaget.[13] He describes them as sensorimotor intelligence, preoperational intelligence, concretely operational intelligence, and formally operational intelligence. Only the last stage, which most children in developed societies reach by early adolescence, is considered full human intelligence. It includes the ability to operate with combinations, engage in propositional logic and hypothesis testing, and deal with potentialities or theoretical possibilities. Also among these skills is the ability to participate in creative religious symbolization. Researchers on human development assert that not all adults actually reach full operational intelligence. Although some may have the biological maturation needed, they may lack the necessary social experience, while others, through such deficiencies as malnutrition, may not even develop the biological potency. Roger Brown also notes that not all adults use their full intelligence with the same ease in all areas of life:

> The ability to think scientifically must function as a momentous change in the evolution of culture. It is a prerequisite to the accomplishment of physics, mathematics, biology, and the behavioral and social sciences. The historical order in which these studies have emerged suggests that operational intelligence is not applied to all domains with equal ease; that it is first turned upon realms remote from the self—the non-living world— then upon the living world exclusive of man. Last of all it is turned upon man and his societies. Not everyone in our society who can apply operational intelligence to the stars and to physical mechanics and to white rats can apply it to desegregation and mental health.[14]

And, I would add, to religious reform. The realm most intimate to self is the ground of one's being—the domain of religion.

The magisterial works of Piaget on intelligence and his later studies on the acquisition of morality are matched by Erik Erickson's research on the stages of overall psychosocial development.[15] His well-known model divides the human life cycle into eight stages, from infancy, early childhood, play age, school age, adolescence, young adulthood, and adulthood to old age. Each stage presents a developmental challenge that results in attaining a certain level of positive and negative ego quality. Most are not entirely successful in fully achieving either quality but emerge from each stage with some ratio of the two opposing trends. Corresponding to the eight stages are the following pairs of favorable and unfavorable outcomes: basic trust versus mistrust, autonomy versus shame and doubt, initiative versus guilt, industry versus inferiority, identity versus identity confusion, intimacy versus isolation, generativity versus stagnation, and ego integrity versus despair.

The pioneering work of Piaget and Erickson has been extended by Lawrence Kohlberg to the stages of moral development and by James Fowler to the stages of religious faith.[16] Kohlberg found three stages in his research on moral attitudes: the preconventional, the conventional, and the postconventional. Only in the third stage do children develop the ability to apply universalistic moral principles about justice and similar matters. Once again, further research shows that not all adults reach the level of development where they make moral judgments based on universal principles. Fowler's studies, which build mainly on the work of Piaget, Erickson, and Kohlberg, led to the formulation of six stages of faith. Fowler labels them intuitive-projective, mythic-literal, synthetic-conventional, individuative-reflective, conjunctive, and universalizing. The highest stage, characterized by an emptying of self and a universalizing relation to Ultimate Reality, was achieved only rarely by the people in Fowler's sample and usually only by those over 60. Many adults are permanently arrested in stage 3, which is marked by conformism to the opinions and authority of others.

Fowler found that the majority of adults, however, enter and remain in stage 4, which brings a realization of the relativity of one's inherited worldview along with rejection of the external authority supporting it. Old doctrines and myths are rejected in this stage of faith because they are no longer compelling; in Peter Berger's terminology, they have lost their plausibility structures.[17] Often called a demythologizing faith, this stage allows individuals to reflect critically on their personal identity and construct their own personal but limited worldview. According to Fowler, about one out of 10 adults achieves stage 5, a form of faith that moves away from the rationalistic reductionism of stage 4 to a postcritical attitude. The conjunctive faith of stage 5 allows the believer to reconstruct the traditional belief system about Ultimate Reality, and, in the process, "symbolic power is reunited with conceptual meanings."[18]

Paul Ricoeur's model is useful for integrating research on life-cycle development and its impact on people's ability to reconstruct consciously and collectively their symbolic worlds. In his critique of Freud, Ricoeur describes three relationships believers have with the symbol systems shaping their faith.[19] In the first phase, called primitive naivete, individuals are immersed in their symbols. Believers give literal affirmation to the statements about Ultimate Reality contained in their myth systems. This is well exemplified by the literal interpretation of scriptures demanded by religious fundamentalism. The second phase, labeled critical distancing, is a process in which believers withdraw from the immediacy of the symbols and questioning replaces commitment. Individuals demythologize the "truths" of religion and subject them to the critical scrutiny of scientific reasoning. Only by passing through the stage of critical distancing can individuals enter the final phase of "second naivete." Here believers return to the immediacy of their symbols but without discarding the critical mode. The second naivete restores meaning and therefore renewed commitment to faith and its symbols. Faith is rational because it is critical and interpretive, but it is still faith because "it seeks, through interpretation, a second naivete."[20]

Regarding their beliefs and the ability to restructure organizational forms based on these beliefs, many Catholics may be caught in the phase of primary naivete in which literalism and dogmatism are prevalent. Others may have entered but are not able to transcend the stage of critical distancing; they can only reject the naive understandings of their inherited faith without replacing it with anything more mature. Those who have reached the second naivete, which corresponds to Fowler's last two stages of faith, would be prepared to enter consciously and collectively into the conflict over which symbolic and organizational forms of ministry are most suitable to embody the ultimate realities reflected in Catholic ministry. Ricoeur's insightful analysis was alluded to in a Christmas-season sermon in which the preacher said: "First I believed in Santa Claus, then I didn't believe in Santa Claus, and now I am Santa Claus."[21] It may be that those Catholics who can say, "First I believed in Christ, then I didn't believe in Christ, and now I am Christ" are most ready to transform consciously and collectively the structures of their corporate church.

Some individuals may be trapped in a worldview prevalent in a previous epoch. Their numbers are probably dwindling, however, because the plausibility structures supporting outmoded worldviews are weakening. For example, the unquestioning dogmatism that characterizes religious fundamentalism is weakened by the rationalism of modern society launched during the Enlightenment, particularly the hermeneutics of higher biblical criticism. Others may be caught in arrested stages of intellectual, moral, or faith development. Robert Wuthnow, however, identifies the rising level of education among adherents as the most dynamic and powerful force for social change in modern organized religion.[22] With the help of organic intellectuals, the tools of modern hermeneutics are being learned and applied relentlessly by educated believers to every dogmatic and moral doctrine propounded by the sacred scriptures and endorsed by the techno-structures of corporate religions. Education eventually releases one from the tutelage of educators. John Hannigan explains that the "long-term trend toward increasing individualization . . . means that citizens become more and more emancipated from professional interpreters such as priests, party politicians, and intellectuals whose task it is to define and articulate the interests of other individuals."[23] For example, the moderate and well-respected theologian Avery Dulles has schooled the current generation of Catholics in a variety of sociological models of the Church.[24] The believing community need not be patterned after the triumphalist, monarchical view of the institutional model but can reflect the servant model or the community model of the People of God on pilgrimage.

Catholics are also becoming aware of diverse theological perspectives such as redemptionist, creationist, and liberation theologies, each eliciting a different set of ecclesiological forms. Their vistas are widened even further by visions of Christian ecumenism and even "deep" ecumenism across major world religions.[25] The pluralism and voluntarism of modern religion and the individualization in the wider society are not abstractions. Mature, educated believers make individual choices among diverse religious ideologies—they are not restricted to a "one-possibility thing" imposed by a dominant coalition. More and more believers may be not only entering the phase of critical distancing but also continuing on into a stage of second naivete. Increased numbers of Catholics interested in ministry may be discovering a level of faith in which they proclaim "I live, now not I, but Christ lives in me" (Gal 2:20).

Shift from Western to World Church

The third set of causal forces for change has taken shape in recent decades as a decline in the political, economic, and cultural dominance of Western Christianity has confronted a rise in membership, autonomy, and creativity of Christian churches in the Southern Hemisphere. For Roman Catholicism, this dialectical shift creates pressure for a basically European Church to relinquish its privileged status and become part of a truly multicultural Church.[26]

Western Church

As a new religious movement, early Christianity made a significant step toward catholicity when, in principle, it rejected the tribal constraints of Judaism and became the church of both Jews and Gentiles. Nevertheless, the fledgling community turned its back on Asia (see Acts 16:6–7) and became in fact a Greco-Roman, Mediterranean, European, and thoroughly Western Church. Beginning in the fifteenth century, Christian European nations systematically colonized Asia, Africa, South and North America, and finally Australia. Throughout a four-hundred-year colonial period, Christian theology, liturgy, and church discipline that developed out of indigenous Western cultures were exported from Europe by missionaries and imposed on "barbaric pagans" with almost no adaptation. A few early experiments to adapt Christianity to indigenous cultures in Asia were thwarted by Rome. Mateo Ricci (1552–1610) in China and Roberto de Nobili (1577–1656) in India made successful attempts at genuine inculturation of the Christian religion. But their efforts were eventually condemned by the papacy and systematically rooted out by subsequent missionaries, who had to take oaths against such ventures.[27]

World Church

European hegemony in a transnational political economy had peaked by World War II and then began to disintegrate. During the 1950s colonial imperialism collapsed, from Jamaica to the Cape of Good Hope to Singapore. When the United Nations was established at the end of World War II, it comprised 51 nation-states. By the turn of the twenty-first century, there were 189 UN member states. In their efforts to reclaim ancient precolonial cultures, many new nation-states asked foreign missionaries to leave and denied them visas if they tried to return.

After the beginning of the twentieth century and especially after World War II, the center of gravity for Roman Catholicism moved from a predominantly Western Church located in the First World to a predominantly Southern Church situated in the Third World. At the start of the twentieth century, 85 percent of all Christians lived in the West. By 1970, 51 percent of all Catholics were in southern continents: Latin America, Africa, and Asia-Oceania. According to estimates, at the turn of the twenty-first century Catholics living in the Southern Hemisphere may account for 70 percent of church membership.[28]

Inculturation

Recent decades have witnessed not only a shift in Catholicism's demographic center of gravity but also a cultural transformation of its clergy. In a remarkably short time, the colonial Church with its predominantly foreign clergy has been replaced by a native hierarchy. In Asia, 95 percent of Catholic bishops are now indigenous, and in Africa native bishops constitute 75 percent of the episcopacy.[29] In symbolic recognition of the world Church, Popes Paul VI and John Paul II visited all six continents. No previous pope ever left Europe.

Decrees of the Second Vatican Council and their implementation in the decade immediately following it acknowledged the emergence of a radically new form of worldwide catholicity, the Church in six continents. Walbert Bühlmann sees evidence that the Third World Church has potential for creative leadership in the world Church.[30] He notes that bishops and theologians from the Third World dominated the 1974 Synod of Bishops, which dealt with evangelization in the modern world. In contrast, during the Second Vatican Council and the three synods between it and the 1974 synod, leadership was definitely under control of the First World churches. Pronouncements of the Second Vatican Council spoke cautiously of cultural accommodation in the Church. But *Evangelii Nuntiandi,* the document issued after the 1974 Synod of Bishops, proclaimed boldly that legitimate pluralism is essential in a Church of many cultures. The issues clarified in *Evangelii Nuntiandi* were raised and eloquently defended by African, Asian, and Latin American delegates, all from the new Church of the Southern Hemisphere.

Centrifugal Forces

A major responsibility of Church leadership, increasingly embodied in the papacy, has been to safeguard Church unity. This task proved difficult enough when Rome had to control only the diversity inherent in Western Christendom. The emergence of a Church on six continents, however, brings with it a profoundly deepened and radically new responsibility. Now church leadership must also safeguard pluralism, which traditionally has been the responsibility of local bishops. Given the 2,000-year history of European cultural uniformity and papal monarchical control centered in Rome, safeguarding unity continues to have the upper hand.

In view of the historic shift to a world Church, imbalance in church leadership—strong papal primacy versus weak episcopal collegiality—looms as a critical issue for Catholicism in the new millennium. Bühlmann describes the problem as follows:

> As soon as a local church wants to take concrete steps to become really a local church, not merely a carbon copy of the Roman church, it is told by authority: in the name and in the interests of unity, that will not do. This tension between documents and deeds constitutes the testing and trial for the Church in the present time. . . . One pole of the Church, central power, concentrates on unity. This is its right and duty. All the more, however, must the other pole, the bishops and episcopal conferences, enter into dialogue defending their interests and their complementary viewpoints so that genuine parity and balance can come between the two poles. Unity certainly, but within pluriformity.[31]

The pleading tone of Bühlmann's description (he begs the pope for recognition of diversity and the bishops for courage to champion it) bespeaks his many years as missionary priest, professor of missiology in Freiburg and Rome, editor of missionary journals, and secretary general for the Capuchin missions.

Bühlmann's analysis also reflects the tension inherent in the dual forces of hierarchic and hierophanic religious power described in chapter 5. If faith-events that form the basis of Christian religion are to be accessible so as to infuse believers with hierophanic power, then the symbol system in which these events are embodied must be truly inculturated for all indigenous groups. But if these cosmogonic events are to remain definitive and to be proclaimed authentically, they must also be safeguarded by hierarchic power. Hierarchic control is needed so that the authenticity of the myth is not lost in the inculturation process. Yet the hierophanic power of the myth stands the risk of being lost in the centralized control process. To paraphrase Eliade, the true sin is killing the myth either by too much uniformity or too much pluriformity. Is the sacramental, clerical, male, celibate priesthood—the sociological form of ministry that emerged in and served the Western Church moderately well for almost two millennia— adequate for the multicultural world Church of six continents?

Celibacy and the Growing Personalism of Human Sexuality

The priest shortage, the trend from dogmatism to pluralism, and the shift from a Western to a world Church are not operating in a vacuum. They are part of a larger mass of storm clouds gathering over the Catholic world. Arguably, celibate hegemony is the eye of the hurricane brewing over the structure of Catholic ministry. It is the focus of the fourth set of trends creating a dialectical force for change. The turn of the twenty-first century is marked by growing tension in the Catholic Church between the institutions of compulsory celibacy and marriage—a tension created by the decrease in the credibility of celibacy as a necessarily superior lifestyle for ordained ministry and the growth in credibility of the holiness of marriage.

Change inside the Church

Priests, seminarians, and those who should be encouraging vocations have become increasingly aware that the institution of compulsory celibacy is theologically nonessential, uniformly repudiated by all other Christian churches, and widely resented by secular priests.[32] Moreover, it has recently become the most cited and documented cause of poor recruitment and retention of diocesan priests in the United States. At the same time, Christian marriage is newly extolled as a sacramental means of fostering love and friendship within a sexual relation, which deepens the believer's relationship with God.

The historical reasons for imposing celibacy on the priesthood have their roots in Manichaeism, a third-century heresy emphasizing the soul as good and the body as evil. Simply declaring Manichaeism a heresy, however, did not eradicate from Christianity the negative attitudes toward human sexuality and their effects on the institution of celibacy. Puritanism in the Anglo-Saxon churches and Jansenism in the French, Irish, and North American churches were a variation on the same theme, with strong holdovers in modern U.S. Catholicism.

In his convincing defense of the *ideal* of celibacy, however, Richard Sipe argues: "The history of Western civilization, peopled with intellectual giants and bold liberators, thoughtful curators, and institutions of beauty and value, is partially dependent on and indebted to celibate practice and organization."[33] Nevertheless, he also demonstrates with equal vigor that the present teaching of the Church on sex—in which much of the motivation for celibacy is still embedded—is not credible:

> Pronouncements do not conform to the sexual nature of man [*sic*] for several reasons. (1) The teaching is based on an archaic anthropology. (2) There is no realistic moral framework in which the developing and even mature single person can work out his or her sexual potential. (3) Informed experience (validated by pastoral practice) shows that there can be

sexual acts that are free of sin even outside the marital state. (4) Scripture scholarship has neglected the exploration of the sexuality of Christ and the apostles. (5) The Church has chosen to speak essentially in the prophetic voice (thou shalt/shalt not) in isolation from the objective voice and the lyrical voice.[34]

Sipe and many others consider reform of Catholic doctrine on human sexuality one of the most pressing problems facing the modern Church. I see the institution of compulsory celibacy—not the ideal of celibacy itself—standing at the center of that debate.

Some contradictions in Catholic doctrine on human sexuality were addressed by the fathers of the Second Vatican Council. Doctrinal changes promulgated in the "Pastoral Constitution on the Church in the Modern World" significantly redefined the goals of marriage.[35] These teachings weakened belief in the superiority of celibacy as a way of holiness and strengthened the importance of the charism of marriage as an equal but different path of perfection. The new understanding of marriage—a sacrament wherein the union of husband and wife symbolizes union with God in Christ—emphasizes the Christian relationship between love, friendship, and sexuality.

Change in the Wider Society

The tensions that exist between human love, friendship, and sexual activity, according to Herbert Richardson, have been resolved in a strikingly new way in the modern era.[36] Richardson argues that during the first preaxial epoch of the human community, which lasted until approximately the seventh century B.C.E., human sexuality was tied to the cycle of nature. The social structure of human sexuality flowed from biological urgency and the consciousness that human destiny depended on sexual begettings. Sex was a necessity of nature, not a component of love or friendship. Human sexual behavior was instinctual and aggressive, and hence true love or friendship between men and women was extremely difficult if not impossible.

The second epoch followed the axial shift from a matrilineal to a patriarchal culture and corresponded roughly to the Hellenistic, early Christian, and medieval eras. In this postaxial epoch, human sexuality was structured on the basis of a new level of consciousness that recognized human destiny as part of a transcendent, transtemporal order. The new worldview held that all humans are equal in their personhood because all possess spiritual transcendent souls. Engaging in genital sex could be considered accidental, not essential for fulfilling human destiny. Hence renunciation of coitus was highly valued during this epoch since sexual activity was still seen as based on instinctual aggressive behavior. The relationship between sexual intercourse, love, and friendship that

characterizes this epoch reached its epitome in the love trysts of the trouba-
dours, in which modified forms of sexual gratification were honored but coitus
between lover and beloved had no place.[37] Another and undoubtedly more
widespread manifestation of this form of human sexuality was celibacy practiced
by monks, nuns, and priests, whereby union with God—the ultimate human
destiny—was deepened through permanent renunciation of sexual intercourse.

The third epoch affecting the structure of human sexuality began with a second axial shift, which ushered in our modern technological era. Rational technology allows unprecedented freedom for humans to refashion the world of nature to accord with human vision. Technology creates material and symbolic
products that affect how humans socially construct their reality. We now can rationalize and moralize our own sexual behavior, breaking it down into parts,
studying and rearranging it so that sexual behavior is capable of integration with
the personal and voluntary values of life. The chief novelty of modern human
sexuality is the growing consciousness of the integration of sexual intercourse
with love and friendship. Instinctual aggressive behavior can now be controlled
through personal romantic love. Coitus is transformed, becoming part of a complex relationship based on equality, so that it is understood that sexual intercourse fully satisfies its potential only when integrated with personal love.

In analyzing change in the normative structure of organizations like the Catholic Church—organizations that record their age in centuries and millennia—it
is important to see the big picture. To the extent that Richardson is correct in
mapping axial shifts and epochal changes in the social structure of human sexuality, the declarations of the Second Vatican Council are beginning to bring
Catholic doctrine on marriage and celibacy into the modern epoch. This is no
small feat.[38]

Personalism and Celibacy

This step forward, though, needs reinforcement from a complete overhaul of
Catholic teaching on sexuality, according to Sipe and many like-minded Catholic
scholars.[39] Bishops too are beginning to realize that the Church's teachings on
human sexuality are woefully outmoded.[40] Richardson's analysis also implies that,
in comparison to past centuries, relatively fewer heterosexual Catholic males who
might aspire to the priesthood will highly value renunciation of coitus, perhaps
not even enough to staff a burgeoning and highly diverse world Church.

Recent spurts in the trend toward greater personalism in human sexuality
have gained the attention of social scientists.[41] Research on the youth culture of
the 1960s lends support for Richardson's broad overview. It may be argued that
the sexual revolution of that decade, epitomized by the slogan "Make love not
war," has its roots in epochal shifts in the social construction of sexuality. Posi-

tive attitudes toward sexuality in general, tolerance of extramarital sex, awareness of natural sexual preferences that encouraged the liberation movement
among gays and lesbians, the ideal that sexual expression may be combined with
love and friendship in marriage are all expressions of greater personalism.

In keeping with the modern era's social construction of sexuality, all Christian churches except Roman Catholicism have abandoned compulsory celibacy
as a requirement for ordination. My data on the demographic transition of the
clergy prove conclusively that poor recruitment and retention of priests became
endemic in the U.S. Catholic Church during the waning decades of the twentieth century. Official Vatican statistics show that this is a worldwide problem and
one getting steadily worse. Studies consistently document mandatory celibacy as
one of the major causes of the growing shortage.

Further evidence of conflict over the relative merits of celibacy and marriage
for priests emerged in the first congress of the European Society for Catholic
Theology, which met in Stuttgart, Germany, in 1992.[42] Affirming the charismatic
nature of marriage, the Tübingen moralist Dietmar Mieth noted: "Despite buf-
fetings from divorce, never has the unitive meaning of marriage been so clear,
since never before have people lived so long after their procreative period was
over."[43] Defending the superiority of celibacy, Jósef Tischner, the Polish theologian and supposed protégé of Pope John Paul II, said the issue of a celibate or
married clergy is a question imposed on the east European Church and does not
arise out of their situation.

Obviously, the ecological niche of most Catholic dioceses has changed with
the times, and their ability to produce sufficient Catholic males motivated to become and remain celibate priests is being called into question. The social construction of human sexuality in modern times raises serious doubts not only
about the superiority of celibacy over marriage but also involving patriarchy and
gender inequality in all its forms.

Feminist Movement

If compulsory celibacy is the eye of the storm, the feminist movement in the
Church threatens to become the hurricane itself. Gender oppression in all societal institutions, not just within love and marriage, has receded considerably
by the turn of the twenty-first century. Female equality, at least in principle, is
guaranteed through legislation in growing numbers of institutions and countries,
though de facto gender discrimination is still widespread.[44] The feminist movement is a primary manifestation of the changing structure of human sexuality.
As reflected in the Catholic Church, it embodies both the decline in emphasis
on male supremacy in ministry and the growth in consciousness about female
equality.

Equality in Theory, Misogyny in Fact

Gender equality is most patently opposed in Catholic Christianity through its pro-hibition of female ordinations. But by no means has equal privilege for women been fully achieved in Protestant denominations either. Edward Lehman's re-search, for example, shows that female pastors and ministers are decidedly sec-ond-class citizens in Protestant technostructures, achieving lower-status jobs, pay, and benefits than their male counterparts.[45] The monopoly of ministry by men runs deep—the chasm reaches down at least six millennia.

Some effort to begin to fill the awesome gap between the Christian principle of gender equality and the social reality of male domination began within Roman Catholicism in the 1950s with the Sister Formation Movement.[46] At that time, Catholic nuns in the United States began a professionalization campaign with a vengeance. They expanded their efforts after receiving a mandate from the Second Vatican Council in its "Decree on the Appropriate Renewal of Reli-gious Life." The movement focused primarily on earning academic degrees commensurate with their teaching positions. In the process, however, religious women moved out of their convents into secular universities and thereby opened career opportunities and vistas of modern society previously closed.[47] American sisters gradually became a highly educated and politically socialized cadre of professionals in the Church; simultaneously, however, their numbers dramatically declined.[48]

Indeed, during the 1970s and 1980s their professional and organizational skills were sometimes resented by secular feminists because religious women were found at the forefront of the feminist movement in the Catholic Church. Somehow this seemed to be a contradiction since history and experience judged religion and feminism to be very odd bedfellows, especially Catholic religion and feminist nuns.

A decade after the Second Vatican Council, the papacy issued its declaration "On the Question of the Admission of Women to the Ministerial Priesthood," which had a catalytic effect on the feminist movement in the Catholic Church. Rome pronounced that the Church "does not consider herself authorized to admit women to priestly ordination."[49] The official prohibition greatly heightened the controversy over male domination, especially among feminist theologians.[50]

Launched among Catholic women by the Sister Formation Movement and galvanized by papal opposition to women's ordination, the feminist movement continues to erode male monopoly of power over the Church's ministry in two major areas. First, the role of "organic intellectuals" played by theologians and scripture scholars has been, until recently, an almost exclusively male (and priestly) preserve. Second, a growing number of tasks within the ministerial technostructure that were handled exclusively by priests are now the domain of lay ministers, the vast majority of them nuns and laywomen.

Feminist Organic Intellectuals

The feminist movement in the Church is spearheaded by women theologians and scripture scholars whose works cover a wide range of views. They vary from radical condemnations of Christianity because it is intrinsically flawed in its basic teachings about a male God to conservative pleas for tolerance and patience with the glacial rate of change in male domination, with every shade of moderation in between. A visit to any feminist bookstore finds shelves of critical scholarly works on religion, mainly Christianity; the pathbreaking publications of scholars such as Mary Daly and Rosemary Ruether in the 1960s and 1970s are joined by hundreds of similar books from a wide variety of leading feminist scholars of the 1980s and 1990s.[51]

Syllabi for women's studies courses in secular universities often contain the work of feminist theologians and scripture scholars, and Catholic women's colleges, particularly, emphasize feminist authors in their religious studies programs and social science curricula. The structures of male domination in the Church and wider society are topics of conversation for growing numbers of college-educated Catholics. More and more of the intellectuals organic to this stratum of the Church are female scholars who are either dedicated or sympathetic to the feminist movement.

The Lay Movement

The dialectic inherent in the lay movement reflects the pressure created by the erosion of clerical monopoly of power (based on ordination) coupled with the growing empowerment of lay people in ministry (stemming from baptismal rights and responsibilities). The driving force behind the lay movement is threefold: the priest shortage, the feminist movement, and the doctrinal statements of the Second Vatican Council. Obviously, as fewer and fewer ordained ministers are available, the Church makes more concerted efforts to recruit lay ministers.

For the most part, the lay movement is a women's issue in the Catholic Church. The fullness of ministry is open to males, which goes a long way to dull the edge of the controversy over clerical hegemony for men, although some married men undoubtedly feel the strain of the lay–ordained split. These forces, though powerful, are up against the most theologically essential elements defining Catholic ministry—sacramentalism and ordained priesthood.

Narrowing the Clerical–Lay Gap

The Catholic Church endured a long history of conflict over clerical and lay control in temporal and even certain doctrinal matters. After the second century, however, little if any dispute remained regarding monopoly of the clergy over the Church's sacramental life.[52] Not until the Second Vatican Council was the doctrine of "no salvation outside the Church" publicly repudiated by Roman Catholicism, thus weakening somewhat the exaggerated importance of ordained priesthood.[53] Likewise, lay participation in all aspects of church life, with the careful exception of the sacraments or any official priestly ministry, was also given strong emphasis.[54]

The hegemony of the ordained clergy reigned supreme in Christianity for 14 centuries (from about the third to the sixteenth century) and was attenuated considerably by the Protestant Reformation but then continued virtually unchallenged for four more centuries in Roman Catholicism. The lay participation movement fostered by the Second Vatican Council further weakened clerical hegemony over Catholic ministry in general but left intact monopoly of power over the central elements of the technical core of the Catholic Church—providing, coordinating, and controlling access to the sacramental means of salvation.

The irrepressible paradox of the Christ and the sacramental minister or *alter Christus* is that the *other Christ* is the source of both hierophanic and hierarchical power and yet he and all those he ministers to are equal in God. Only the priest brings the consecrating power of the foundational sacraments—baptism, confirmation, and Eucharist—to the believing community.[55] Yet Catholic doctrine asserts that those who are consecrated through the baptism-confirmation-Eucharist initiation rites and those with authority to perform the rites have the same Parental source. All Christians are absolutely and indisputably equal in their kinship with God. This religious paradox is profound, and the sociological dilemma it creates is painful. The question raised by the lay movement in the contemporary Catholic Church is: Has the lay ox been gored too often and too long?

Given the past record, pronouncements of the Second Vatican Council calling for lay participation would probably have remained idealistic rhetoric in many parishes if sufficient priests had been available to handle ministerial and pastoral tasks. Growing numbers of congregations are now served by pastoral teams with more lay than clerical members, while some are facing the prospects of either an all-lay staff or no parish at all.[56] A few studies describe these lay ministers, their attitudes, and the job characteristics.

Zeni Fox surveyed lay ministers in nine dioceses and discovered that 57 percent were directors of religious education (DREs) and 24 percent coordinators of youth ministry.[57] The remaining were pastoral ministers (4 percent); directors of music (3 percent), liturgy (2 percent), and social ministry (1 percent); and combinations or others (9 percent). Thomas Walters found that DREs are the fastest growing segment of lay ministry; he estimated 4,685 in U.S. Catholic dioceses in 1981.[58] He learned that they were mostly women, mostly nuns, and mostly poorly paid, but the vast majority had moderate to high morale. In 1992, Philip Murnion and his colleagues completed an extensive study of lay ministry in the United States.[59] These researchers found that, apart from personnel in

Catholic schools, about 20,000 laypeople and religious work at least 20 hours per week as parish ministers in half the country's parishes. Of that number, 85 percent are women, and almost 50 percent belong to religious orders. About 40 percent of the religious but only 8 percent of the laypeople are over 60. Hence fewer religious and more laypeople are expected among future ministers.

The growth and complexity of the lay ministry population provide part of the foundation for a new form of Catholic ministry. Furthermore, the restructuring process, involving mainly women, is taking place in a previously monosexual setting reserved only to males. These innovations are calling into question the ordained male's monopoly of control over the means of salvation.

The Liturgical Movement

The dialectical tension in the final set of trends lies at the crux of the matter: How can the Church achieve a proper balance between the power of the Sacrament and the power of the Word? An ironic development of the modern liturgical movement is that the ancient Catholic emphasis on the eucharistic sacrifice of the Mass is being notably dimmed by the growing recognition of the saving power of the Word. The interaction effect of the liturgical movement and the priest shortage, however, is producing the irony. As fewer clergy are available for Mass, more laypeople—mainly women—preside at liturgies of the Word and communion.

Generally, these liturgies are worship services composed of just the first and last ritual phases of the Mass, using bread consecrated at an earlier Mass. In a regular Mass the first phase of the ritual is devoted to hymns, prayers, readings from the Bible, and a sermon; the last involves consuming the sacrificial elements at Holy Communion. In a worship service without a priest, the intervening sacrificial phases of the ritual—the offertory and consecration of the bread and wine—are omitted.

Although worship services presided over by a layperson are nonsacrificial rites, they nevertheless benefit greatly from the rich, creative resources of the liturgical movement. The renewal of Catholic liturgy reached fruition shortly after its flowering at midcentury, but by century's end the movement had all but dissipated. In addition, priests are now overextended because of growing demands and so have less time and energy to devote to vibrant liturgies. In contrast, Ruth Wallace reports that many parishioners appreciate the communion services presided over in priestless parishes by female pastoral administrators. One female parishioner declares, "The sisters have done such a good job with the eucharistic service, I am not missing the consecration part of the Mass, and we have everything else. So it really hasn't bothered me.[60] Although liking sister's "eucharistic service" demonstrates a preference for better liturgy, it also reveals some confusion about the difference between a communion service and a eucharistic sacrifice. The liturgical movement may have come to fruition, but with troubling implications for upholding and appreciating the traditional Catholic means of salvation. Reforming the liturgy opens old wounds inflicted during the centuries-old debate over clerical and lay access to the means of salvation.

Historical Developments

Sacrament and Word have always been honored as Christian means of salvation. But Catholicism is noted for overemphasizing the former and Protestantism for overchampioning the latter. With its focus on preaching, Protestantism fostered the development of modern hermeneutics and other methodological tools of the social sciences in a systematic and scientific approach to biblical studies. These efforts were strenuously resisted by Rome from the early Enlightenment up until the groundbreaking publication of *Divino Afflante Spiritu* in 1943. This *motu proprio* of Pius XII fully legitimated modern hermeneutics for Catholic scholars.[61] It also finally sounded the death knell to the antimodernist movement and opened the floodgates of higher biblical criticism in the Catholic Church. The flurry of research and publications that ensued became the intellectual foundation for the Second Vatican Council two decades later. At the same time, Bible-centered study groups and worship services flourished. Thus the liturgical reform movement itself was a related development coinciding with the official lifting of restrictions on modern scholarship.

During the 1950s and 1960s, the names of renowned liturgy scholars such as Romano Guardini, Godfrey Dieckmann, and Pius Parsch became familiar not only in seminaries, rectories, and convents but also in the homes of educated laypeople. Priests, seminarians, and nuns as well as notable numbers of laypeople flocked to national liturgical conventions and returned to experiment with new forms of liturgies in churches and homes. For example, the NORC survey of priests and bishops included items on liturgical innovations. The results showed that almost half the priests had "notably modified the rubrics [of the Mass] to fit the occasion" and well over a third had "said Mass without the proper vestments."[62] These were proscribed activities that few priests and fewer laypeople would have tolerated before the liturgical movement but were commonplace because of it. Creating animated liturgies became an important priority in parish life. Much of the creativity centered on the Liturgy of the Word, however, if only because it allowed greater lay participation and has fewer legalistic restrictions.

The liturgical movement was strongly reinforced by the Second Vatican Council, particularly by replacing Latin with the vernacular at Mass. In the aftermath of the council, church architecture was altered dramatically in almost every Catholic parish in the United States. The altar was moved from the far wall to the center of the sanctuary so that the priest could face the people, since he now was speaking their language. The lectern and pulpit were resituated, making the locus for the Liturgy of the Word both prominent and distinguishable from that of the Liturgy of the Eucharist.

As the movement progressed, scriptural research and Bible study groups reached a zenith, with positive effects on the Liturgy of the Word and especially its central activity, preaching. By the 1980s, in many parishes it was a rare event when weekday Mass was celebrated without having a priest give a homily, whereas in the 1950s parishioners would have been shocked and annoyed at such an occurrence. In some parishes today, nuns, laymen, and laywomen regularly take turns offering a "scriptural reflection" during Mass. This advanced form of lay participation is officially discouraged in many dioceses, however, where only the priest is allowed to preach.

A Demographic Boost

The attempts within Catholicism to narrow the gap between Sacrament and Word progressed steadily throughout the latter half of the twentieth century, spearheaded mainly by the liturgical movement. Some progress, however, resulted from the demographics of underdeveloped countries and the withdrawal of foreign missionaries in favor of native clergy.[63] In Africa and South America, for example, the Catholic Church became notoriously understaffed by ordained clergy. As table 1 documents, the availability of priestly services in Africa was cut in half between 1965 and 1990, when the clergy-to-laity ratio dropped from 5.4 to 2.3 priests per 10,000 Catholics. In response, local parishes developed a thriving lay-catechist movement, which incorporated a Liturgy of the Word or Bible-centered worship service in place of the Mass. Similarly, in South America the Catholic Church witnessed a 41 percent decline in the clergy-to-laity ratio (from 2.3 to 1.4 priests per 10,000 Catholics) during the same two-decade period. Mass is a rare event for most Catholics in Latin America. But the amazing spread of ecclesial base (grassroots) communities, especially among the poor, has been accompanied by lay pastoral agents regularly presiding over enthusiastic Bible-centered Liturgies of the Word.[64] The demographic boost to liturgical change in Africa and Latin America was unintended and for the most part viewed as theologically unfortunate. Furthermore, it was not limited to the Third World.

Emphasis on preaching and Bible-based liturgies took another great leap forward during the 1970s and 1980s, when Catholics in Europe and North America began to feel the pinch of the priest shortage. This time the impetus was provided not only by demographics but by the Catholic bishops themselves and, once again, with unintended consequences. National hierarchies, particularly in France, Canada, and the United States, and even the Vatican began to issue official guidelines for Bible-centered Sunday services in priestless parishes.[65]

TABLE 1. Number of diocesan and religious priests per 10,000 Catholics and percentage of change, 1965–91, by year, nation, and continent

	Year							% change
	1965	1970	1975	1980	1985	1990	1991	1965–91
Western nations								
Austria	11.1	9.3	9.0	9.3	8.8	8.3	8.0	−28.2
Belgium	17.2	15.0	15.4	14.3	12.8	12.2	11.8	−31.3
Canada	16.9	15.1	13.1	12.2	10.7	9.9	9.7	−42.5
France	12.3	9.9	9.3	8.5	7.7	6.8	6.6	−46.1
Great Britain	20.4	16.4	15.9	15.3	15.0	13.9	13.8	−32.3
Ireland	19.6	17.6	17.4	16.4	14.8	14.4	14.6	−25.7
Italy	12.3	12.4	11.5	11.5	10.9	10.3	10.3	−16.4
Netherlands	17.5	14.2	11.8	12.3	10.8	9.5	9.2	−47.7
Poland	5.6	5.8	5.8	5.9	5.9	6.4	6.6	17.7
Spain	11.0	10.7	9.6	8.9	8.4	8.3	8.3	−24.7
United States	12.9	12.1	11.7	11.6	10.7	9.8	9.7	−25.0
West Germany	—[a]	8.2	8.2	8.2	7.8	7.6[b]	—[a]	−7.0[c]
Southern continents								
Africa	5.4	4.3	3.3	3.0	2.5	2.3	2.3	−58.1
India	11.6	11.2	11.0	10.4	10.0	10.5	10.4	−10.1
South America	2.3	1.9	1.7	1.5	1.4	1.4	1.4	−40.9

[a]Separate data for West Germany are not available for 1965, 1990, and 1991.
[b]Data for 1989.
[c]For 1970–89.

Balancing Sacrament and Word

The Catholic Church has preserved a strong sacramental tradition for 18 centuries. That emphasis was undermined during the last four centuries by the spread of Protestantism. And, in the last five decades, a closer balance between Sacrament and Word has been struck throughout Roman Catholicism. The increased consciousness of the saving power of the Word, fostered by the liturgical movement and further heightened by the priest shortage, reminds Catholics of their full Christian heritage. Paul told the first Christians, "Receive this message not as the words of man but as truly the Word of God. For God is at work in you who believe" (1 Thes 2:13). Even Catholics are discovering that preaching the Word allows God to be at work in believers directly, without intermediaries of priest and sacrament. A reform movement in Christianity was organized around this doctrine in the sixteenth century and has flourished in Protestant churches ever since. The Catholic liturgical movement has succeeded in bringing the reform back home.

The power of the Word is penetrating the Catholic Church today as never before. At the same time, the priesthood population is shrinking while the lay population expands. After an analysis of the seriousness of these trends, a stinging question was posed at the "Future of the American Church Conference" held in 1990. A dynamic young priest in tie and sport coat asked over 1,000 attendees, mostly nuns and laywomen: "Can the Eucharist survive?"[66]

Conclusion

The survival of the Eucharist, the very capstone of Catholic piety, is a rhetorical question that dramatizes the startling implications of the social forces affecting modern Catholic ministry. Undoubtedly, what has already survived two millennia can hardly be on the brink of extinction. But in view of the seven dynamic trends I have just delineated, the eucharistic priesthood has embarked on a period of severe conflict and notable change. Resolution of this conflict must take into consideration deeper religious paradoxes underlying the dialectical trends, the topic I now address.

PART III

CONFLICT AND PARADOX

7

UNITY AND DIVERSITY

Kindness and truth shall meet;
justice and peace shall kiss.
Truth shall spring out of the earth,
and justice shall look down from heaven
                              Psalms 85: 11–12

The issue of structural strain in organized religion is a prism refracting the psalmist's vision of truth and justice. It creates a rainbow of conflict and paradox. How does the truth of reality spring from the earthly community and interact with salvific justice looking down from heaven? The kindly truth of earth is a diverse, immanent, hierarchic force, and the peaceful justice of heaven a unitive, transcendent, hierophanic force. How do the material forces of earth and the spiritual forces of heaven meet? How do they sacralize their conflicting elements with a holy kiss? For religious organizations as well as individual persons, conflicts within and between material and mental forces are confronted and transcended only by paradoxes within spiritual forces.

The first trend in the matrix of social forces affecting Catholic ministry is decline in the priesthood population combined with growth in church membership. This dual force bears a catalytic relationship to the others, so must be treated separately. In effect, the priest shortage is the key to understanding why other social forces are reaching a critical threshold simultaneously. Thus, I will first show that each of the other trends is reaching a state of balanced tension and then, at the end of chapter 9, that the priest shortage is a catalyst creating convergence among them.

In this chapter I treat the second and third trends in the selected matrix: (2) the decline of dogmatism coupled with the rise of pluralism and (3) the decline of Eurocentrism coupled with the emergence of the Church inculturated in six continents. They have a direct bearing on the tension between unity and diversity in the Catholic Church. First I show that the increasing tensions between dogmatism and pluralism help account for changes in expressive social forces, that is, the cultural and motivational transformations occurring in Ca-

tholicism. Then I describe how conflict between organizational centrism and localism helps account for changes in utilitarian social forces, that is, the internal
political-economic transformations facing the Church.

Dogmatism and Pluralism

Recall that, according to Bellah, modern religions are characterized by a new
kind of world-affirmation, which replaces the dualistic world-rejection of historical religions and the pristine world-affirmation of the prehistorical epoch.
When the historic religions emerged between the second and first millennium
B.C.E., they replaced the monistic world-affirmation of primitive and archaic religions. Liberal Protestantism, post–Second Vatican Council Catholicism, and
some Eastern religions are numbered among the modern religions at the turn
of the twenty-first century. These religions are in a transition leading to the
total collapse of dualism, the world-rejecting view central to historic religions of
the past four millennia.[1]

When modern religions overemphasize dogmatic uniformity they are taking
a step backward in the evolution of religious symbol systems. To counterbalance
a strong tendency toward dogmatism, creedal religions must allow for pluralism
in symbolizing the faith-events of their living myth. Tolerance of religious pluralism developed gradually in the Judeo-Christian tradition. Its foundation was
laid with the development of ethical prophecy among the Hebrews, which
began the transformation of tribal religions. Then, through its emphasis on
Pentecostal proselytization, Christianity, a Jewish sect, broke down the ritual
barriers between Jews and Gentiles and further opened the tribalism of Hebrew
religions to universalism.[2] Ushered in by the Protestant Reformation, the Enlightenment, and the Industrial Revolution, the modern era destroys the absolute nature of historically and socially determined symbol systems. These developments set the stage for greater diversity in formulating religious beliefs.

At the turn of the twenty-first century, despite the rearguard action of the
papacy of John Paul II, Roman Catholic Christianity is judiciously embracing
these trends. Catholicism has loosened its rigid dogmatism by allowing a cautious pluralism of views to develop among scripture scholars, theologians, clergy,
religious, and educated laypersons. Legitimation for pluralism was introduced
a half century ago in a critical papal document, *Divino Afflante Spiritu.* With this
famous *motu proprio,* Pius XII opened the floodgates of Catholic scholarship
to higher biblical criticism and the natural and social sciences. Pluralism was
notably advanced by the Second Vatican Council's pronouncements rescinding
the doctrine of *extra ecclesiam nulla salus* (outside the Church there is no salvation), especially the document proclaiming freedom of religion.[3]

Given the long-range sociocultural developments culminating in the modern
era, the symbolization of faith-events has become more complex and sophisti-

cated. Religious myth systems can now handle their primary symbols—for example, sacred time and space—with more subtlety and insight. Greater complexity in symbolizing primary concepts like time and space accelerates the disappearance of dogmatic dualism. For example, official formulations of unique historical happenings, such as "the incarnation of God in Jesus Christ," can be held in tension with interpretations stemming from a second naivete that sees them as timeless, transpersonal, transcultural faith-events.[4]

In his essay on human discoveries, Daniel Boorstin demonstrates that time and space are primordial dimensions expressing one and the same reality, both in the religious and the scientific imagination. What we as Westerners take for granted about the difference and sameness of time and space was discovered and institutionalized slowly over millennia and crystalized only in the sixteenth century C.E.[5] The measurement of time and space by means of clocks, maps, and precision instruments spawned the age of geographic discovery and indeed the modern notions of historicity and the scientific revolution. Religious notions of time and space took a back seat. Unfortunately for organized religion, so did consciousness of Eternal and Universal Being, which transcends the time-space grid of historicity and modern science.

Long before Galileo conceptualized time and space as dimensions of reality that could be subjected to precise measurement, "here and now" represented interchangeable moments of universality and eternity. At the burning bush, "Moses said to God: If they should say to me: What is his name? What shall I say to them? God said to Moses: I am who am (Yahweh)" (Ex 3:13–14). For Jewish believers, God is given a name that connotes an Eternal Living Presence, Absolute Being here and now. With this ineffable name in mind, Jesus said to the pharisees, "Before Abraham came to be, I am" (Jn 8:58). He was accused of blasphemy for claiming to transcend time and space and exist in oneness with Absolute Being. Similarly, Lao Tsu said, "Since before time and space were, the Tao is. It is beyond *is* and *is not*."[6] Philo expounds the same paradox: "Today means boundless and inexhaustible eternity. Months and years and all periods of time are concepts of men, who gauge everything by number; but the true name of eternity is Today."[7]

Maturity through Naivete

Recall that Ricoeur introduced the notion of second naivete to describe religious maturity (chapter 6). Wilber calls religious maturity the stage of transrational or transpersonal consciousness. Mature believers achieve a second naivete or transrational consciousness only after transcending two earlier stages in their conscious relationship to the faith-events and symbol system informing their faith. Ricoeur calls the first stage primary naivete and Wilber labels it prerational consciousness.

In the first phase of development, a believer is immersed in his or her faith-events, mythic symbols, and sacred rituals, affirming their magical truth content without hesitation, in a childlike fashion. Divine or demonic beings live and intervene in the natural world as if they shared the same time and space as human beings. In the Santa Claus myth, a child truly believes that a jolly old elf delivers toys through the chimney on Christmas eve. That is, Santa Claus shares the same time-space dimensions as the child. During the second stage of development, called critical distancing or rational consciousness, the believer replaces childlike religious faith with rational questioning. Mythic faith-events are subjected to scientific analysis and generally found wanting. Obviously, Santa Claus does not exist in time and space like other phenomena. As an intermediate level of development, both Ricoeur and Wilber recognize the rational distancing stage as necessary for clearing away the cultural distortions that become mixed with mythic events during symbolization, a process fraught with sociopolitical conflict. Individuals must pass through a stage of rational criticism before they can enter the final phase of second naivete or transrational consciousness. Combining Ricoeur's and Wilber's models, I call the third phase the stage of transpersonal naivete.

In mature faith, the believer reaffirms the immediacy of the mythic events and symbols with a deeper commitment, forged in the critical rational mode. Thus, transpersonal naivete includes rational thinking but transcends the limitations of reason. In the stage of transpersonal naivete, the hermeneutics for interpreting the myth are neither infantile nor reductionist but restorative. A transpersonal naivete restores transcendent meaning to the symbols and so renews commitment to the mythic events they signify. Transcendent symbols make efficaciously present and operative the events they signify and so constitute a living myth system. Reflecting all three phases of development, the parent says, "First I believed in Santa Claus, then I didn't believe in Santa Claus, and now I am Santa Claus." Echoing Saint Paul, the mature Christian in a state of transpersonal naivete says: "First I believed in Christ, then I didn't believe in Christ, and now I am the Christ."[8]

Transcending the ordinary dimensions of time and space by experiencing Absolute Reality is a prerequisite for transcending dualism. The ability to be consciously aware of transpersonal reality and to symbolize it is not achieved through the primary naivete of primitive monistic religion or the reductionistic rational criticism of the Enlightenment. Instead, transcending the dualism of prerational and rational consciousness is achieved through the transpersonal naivete of modern pluralistic religion.

Because of long- and short-range sociopolitical and cultural developments, pluralism in symbolizing faith-events is possible. It can emerge when the believing community is able to share a common relationship to definitive faith-events, regardless of sociopolitical and cultural heterogeneity. The doorway to modern religious pluralism is a transpersonal naivete, in which believers balance a rational interpretation of religious beliefs and a transcendent religious experience of definitive faith-events. Such a precarious balance is hard won and its price is constant tension. The tension arising from the pluralism of worldviews in modern religion is transcended by the transpersonal naivete of united believers. The juxtaposition of pluralism and transpersonal naivete allows subgroups in a unified universal Church to experience historical yet timeless and spaceless faith-events in diverse but complementary ways. This diversity, if it is genuine, reflects the historical, cultural, and sociopolitical contingencies affecting each subgroup. The unity, if it is authentic, is experienced in the state of transpersonal naivete, in which believers recognize that no single cultural and social explanation can exhaust the reality of the *mysterium tremendum.*

Indeed, neither one nor a thousand symbolic interpretations can describe the Ineffable Absolute.[9] According to Lao Tsu, "The tao that can be told is not the eternal Tao. The name that can be named is not the eternal Name."[10] Ultimately, symbolization and interpretation become dispensable, for "after those days, says the Lord: I will place my laws in their minds and I will write them upon their hearts" (Heb 8:10). The state of transpersonal naivete is a mode of consciousness in which Ultimate Reality is indelibly written in the believer's body, mind, and spirit. There is no longer need for clocks, maps, precision instruments, or religious symbols to point to the Here and Now.

Balancing Tensions

The shift from dogmatism to pluralism within a historical world religion like Christianity had to await the discovery of the tools of rational science, modern hermeneutics, and the widespread awareness of the social construction of reality. Change from a dogmatic worldview to pluralistic worldviews in religion is part of the paradigm shift from Cartesian to Kantian philosophy that occurred during the Enlightenment.[11] It is similar to the shift from Newtonian physics to quantum mechanics that took place during the twentieth century. Both shifts have had literally earth-shattering consequences. They represent a move from a time-and-space framework that is absolute to one that is relative, while the framework simultaneously continues to be based on concrete historical or physical events.

The Kantian revolution in philosophy introduced the notion that the mind contributes to the construction of reality. The space/time grid in which we perceive reality is never absolute because our beliefs about space and time are true *relative* to our own forms of perception. Social scientists extended these notions on the premise that whatever the mind does is socially conditioned. As a social construction, therefore, human reality is viewed *relative* to a group's sociocultural conditions. The quantum mechanics revolution in physics introduced a different kind of relativity. In the new physics, material reality is viewed as the relationship between matter and energy in a time-space grid but *relative* to the speed of light. Both revolutions make the same point: What is relative is no longer absolute. Thus, there were three important shifts from the absolute to the relative. The first was in philosophy, the second was in physics, and the third is happening in religion. In modern society, neither philosopher nor physicist nor religious practitioner can claim an absolute view of the world. Herein lies the problem for modern religion: relativism.[12]

Not only dogmatism but also pluralism has its strengths as well as its limitations. The trap of pluralism is relativism. Falling into the trap of religious relativism is dangerous because it sounds the death knell for definitive faith-events. The historical manifestation of the sacred, the hierophanic event on which the religious group was founded, is called into question. The trap of dogmatism, on the other hand, is narcissism in its personal consequences or totalitarianism in its social consequences. In this snare the world is closed to all views but one's own, that is, the one gained in a historically and culturally determined socialization.

In modern religions that are authentically transpersonal, both relativism and totalitarianism are overcome by a balanced tension between dogmatism and pluralism. For Ultimate Reality transcends both dogmatism and pluralism, just as It transcends time and space. Modern religious practitioners can achieve consciousness of Ultimate Reality when, and only when, they are permitted to view definitive faith-events from every possible angle. In modern creedal religions, pluralistic interpretations of eternal/universal Reality can and must be held in tension with dogmatic formulations of the same divine verities. The mechanism for achieving the balance is transpersonal naivete, an increasingly widespread phenomenon in modern religion. Transpersonal naivete brings awareness of the unity of opposites, dissolves dualism, and rests in unitive consciousness of Universal Being.

Paradoxically, therefore, genuine pluralism is possible only if it is balanced by a sufficiently strong dogmatism.[13] The power of dogma offsets the tendency of pluralism to deny the definitiveness of the faith-events, that is, dogma allays the fear of forgetting the myth (chapter 5).[14] As the second millennium of Christianity wanes, dogmatism has developed to a sufficient level in the Catholic Church. It can serve as a mechanism to protect the uniqueness of historical faith-events on which Christianity's entire symbol system is based. Eliade, following Schleiermacher, Dilthey, Husserl, and others, points out that the crucial elements of living myth systems have their foundation in some type of historical reality. Historicity grounds reality in unique time and space coordinates. At the same time, however, historical uniqueness is transcended by religious reality, which is eternal and universal, that is, beyond ordinary space and time.

The historical uniqueness of a faith-event, after it has served its purpose, gives way to religious universalism. As we have seen, a religious group becomes aware of this paradox by maintaining a peculiar balance between dogmatism and pluralism in symbolizing its living myth system. Individuals internalize the balance by achieving the stage of transpersonal naivete. Though it is a state of religious maturity, relating to definitive faith-events with naive immediacy informed by reason is not the final goal of the religious quest. Behavior stemming from the state of transpersonal naivete is an intimation of the end state of human development: unitive consciousness of Absolute Being.

Widespread personal ability to achieve, recognize, and analyze transpersonal consciousness and the social ability of organized religion to adapt its structures to the transpersonal stage of human development call for another paradigm shift in the human sciences (chapter 4). The new transpersonal paradigm must take account not only of the higher levels of self-consciousness that transcend reason but also the ultimate level of unitive consciousness that transcends the self.

Self and No-Self

The event in which human awareness of Absolute Being is achieved is called the experience of the Holy in traditional religious terminology and the experience of no-self in both esoteric religious and transpersonal psychological terminology.[15] This experience is the ultimate solution to the paradox of unity and diversity and goes beyond the psychic, subtle, and causal levels of transpersonal human consciousness, described in Eastern psychologies. The passage to this ultimate experience is generally said to unfold only after achieving transpersonal consciousness, which accompanies awareness of the true self. The ability of Western creedal religion to provide a social context in which individuals might transcend the paradox of unity and diversity has come to depend on a twofold collective consciousness: communal awareness of (1) the psychosocial developmental process of achieving selfhood and (2) the spiritual path providing passage to no-self.

According to the perennial philosophy underlying most religious symbol systems, the ego and self give way to no-self in the moment they bring a person to consciousness of Ultimate Reality.[16] The passage to no-self, therefore, is the process of gaining consciousness of the Universal Self. Without a strong ego and self, however, transcendence to universalism or no-self is blocked. One cannot lose the self one does not possess. The paradox of gaining and losing the self is evident in the writings of Hindu, Buddhist, Taoist, Zen, Kabala, Christian, and Sufi contemplatives, in the research literature of humanist and transpersonal psychologists, and in social scientific studies of the stages of faith.[17] The process is also viewed as a paradox because those experiencing it report that it takes place both in time and eternity, in physical and universal space.

Achieving and transcending selfhood is a human process and so unfolds in a social context at historical moments during the life cycle. Each moment is identifiable in its chronological-physical time and space coordinates. Yet, because it is also a religious event, each moment transcends ordinary time and space and reflects an eternal now and a universal here. As a religious event, the series of moments whereby one gains and loses one's self is eventually experienced as one Eternal Universal Moment. Gaining and losing the self are usually identified by scholars as a social psychological or a religious process; they are rarely described in a conceptual framework combining both approaches. The aim of social science, however, is to explain human behavior in all its dimensions. Consequently, social scientists studying religion attempt to gather and interpret valid data about religious activity no matter what their source.

Integrating the Human and Spiritual Sciences

Because of their different philosophical worldviews and analytic frameworks, social science (*Geisteswissenschaft*) and religious knowledge have traditionally been indifferent if not antagonistic to one another.[18] Our systematic knowledge of the stages that lead to psychosocial maturity, therefore, is primarily the result of Western social science, particularly developmental psychology. Systematic knowledge of the stages leading to spiritual maturity, on the other hand, proceeds from the contemplative tradition of world religions, particularly Eastern mysticism. Western social scientists interested in religious phenomena are beginning to develop an integrated approach, tentatively labeled the transpersonal paradigm. It combines both conceptual frameworks—scientific and religious— that deal with the mature self and no-self.

Obviously, the religious conceptual framework explaining human maturity is much older than the social scientific framework. In modern society, however, the scientific approach is more accessible to the majority of intellectuals and other power elites, including religious leaders. Hence most scholarly integrations of knowledge about the mature self move from familiar studies of Western social science to unfamiliar analyses of Eastern contemplative traditions.

Sigmund Freud and Carl Jung were the first to unlock the mysteries of the inner life with the keys of Western science. Freud discovered the unconscious through his systematic research on dreams. His theory of the ego and superego launched depth psychology and laid the foundation for modern developmental psychology. Jung's research focused more explicitly on the concept of self, a pivotal element in the psychosocial developmental paradigm. In an insightful analysis of Jung and Teresa of Avila, John Welch summarizes the Jungian theory of self:

> The self is the center of the personality and the circumference. It expresses the unity of the personality as a whole. The conscious and unconscious, together, form the self. It is the central archetype in the collective unconscious calling the personality to order and unity. As an objective of the psyche, the self is the goal never reached. The goal of the individ-

ual is to achieve selfhood, self-realization, or, in Jung's term, individuation. This achievement necessitates a shift from ego to self as the center of the psyche.[19]

The center of the psyche shifts from ego to self through individuation, a two-phase process in Jung's theory. The initial phase corresponds to the first half of life; it is an expansion of the personality and an initiation into outer reality. The other phase coincides with the second half of life; it is a restriction of the personality and an adaptation to the inner life.[20] In Jung's view, as one's personality is "restricted," one transcends ego, achieves selfhood, and becomes aware of inner reality.

Developmental psychologists draw from Freud's and Jung's pioneering discoveries and from the work of Wilhelm Wundt and William James. These early investigations have been extended and systematized by Erikson, Piaget, Kohlberg, and Fowler. According to contemporary developmental psychology, gaining selfhood during the life cycle is achieved not in two but as many as eight critical stages. Maslow significantly narrowed the gap between the findings of developmental psychology and competing claims that religion provides another path to human maturity. Maslowian transpersonal psychology corrects orthodox developmental psychology by claiming that full maturity is achieved only when selfhood is transcended by the experience of no-self.

In his research on peak experiences, Maslow demonstrated the difference between what he called D-cognition and D-love and B-cognition and B-love.[21] Knowledge and love in everyday human interaction are motivated by the desire to overcome deficits in oneself (D-cognition and D-love). Maslow found that these ordinary modes of perception and affection are intrinsically different from the knowledge and love achieved in peak experiences. Maslow's respondents consistently described their peak experiences in terms of knowing and loving Being in Itself and for Itself. Hence he called these levels of consciousness B-cognition and B-love. A peak experience, therefore, is a developmental moment in which selfhood is transcended by conscious transpersonal participation in Absolute Being—Being that is known and loved in and for Itself. Maslow further notes that a plateau experience is a prolonged moment in which B-cognition and B-love become the ordinary modes of consciousness.[22]

Most recently, Wilber and others are proposing an integration of Jungian depth psychology, Eriksonian developmental psychology, and Maslowian transpersonal psychology, along with the systematic studies of ancient contemplative traditions. This synthesis is labeled the transpersonal paradigm. Wilber is recognized as its foremost spokesperson. What is distinctive about the transpersonal paradigm is its positive use of spiritual knowledge and data. Spiritual evidence is incorporated in the framework as long it meets the standards of science—but science in an expanded definition. Hence, if we assume that the human person is compounded of body, mind, and spirit, then human beings have direct experience not only of sensory data (sensibilia) and mental data (intelligibilia) but also of spiritual data (transcendelia). Furthermore, the validity of all three types of experiential evidence can be confirmed through communal consensus achieved by following methodological standards of science that apply to each realm of data. Thus, because of the spiritual component in the human person, spiritual data (direct experiences of transcendent reality) are permissible evidence in a scientific paradigm. Wilber turns to Eastern rather than Western religion in search of such systematic knowledge and data because of the East's contemplative tradition.

Becoming aware of no-self is fostered by all world religions; however, continuity of the contemplative mode of religiosity is stronger in Eastern religions (Hinduism, Buddhism, Taoism-Confucianism) than in Western ones (Judaism, Christianity, Islam). Hence, the phrase "awareness of no-self" is more familiar to Eastern than Western religious scholars and practitioners. Nevertheless, Christian contemplatives easily recognize the same reality, though they express it in different terms: dying to self, being born again, "I live, now not I, but Christ lives in me," and so on.[23]

Why has the contemplative tradition been disrupted in Western but not Eastern religions? The answer lies in their contrasting sociopolitical and cultural developments, evident in the history of Christianity. The Christian contemplative tradition emerged in apostolic times, exhibited by the mystical tone of John's Gospel. Contemplation was lauded in the patristic era and recognized as an important element of the Gnostic movement. At the same time, the Desert Fathers and Mothers institutionalized mystical contemplation as the central feature of the cenobitic life.[24] By the fifth century, monasticism was established in the Western Church through the pioneering efforts of Saint Benedict of Nursia (480–547) and his sister, Saint Scholastica. In the following centuries, monasticism made contemplation an institutionalized way of life for large self-sustaining communities throughout Christendom.[25] The Benedictine motto is *"Ora et labora,"* that is, prayer and work are one and the same. Western monasticism reached its zenith in the Middle Ages, when monks became cardinals and popes and the mystical writings of male and female contemplatives were considered the Church's crowning glory.

The brilliance of the Christian contemplative tradition in the West was overshadowed by the corruption of the medieval papacy, the overwhelming accomplishments of the Enlightenment and modern science, the polemics of the Protestant Reformation and Catholic Counter-Reformation, and the rational technology of the Industrial Revolution. As Weber noted, the other-worldly asceticism and mysticism of monastic life were replaced by the inner-worldly asceticism of the Protestant ethic and the spirit of capitalism. Though minimally preserved in small cloistered religious orders and rare orders of hermits in Western Catholicism, and by monasticism among Eastern Catholics, the contemplative tradition has had little impact on the Catholic Church for at least the last four centuries. Contemplation was reemphasized in the mid–twentieth century by the liturgical movement and monastic renewal in Western Catholicism. I already discussed the impact of the liturgical movement on Catholic ministry (chapter 6). Monastic renewal advanced in the United States, notably through the efforts of thoroughly modern monks like Thomas Merton, David Steindl-Rast, and Thomas Keating. At the turn of the twenty-first century, the ideal form of Catholic piety reflects these trends, balancing prayer and contemplation, liturgy, and charity, or agape.[26]

As a result of progress in modern psychology and religious reforms, Catholic piety has come to be defined as a spiritual practice through which one gains an autonomous mature self and progresses to the awareness of no-self or Universal Self. Prayer and contemplation, along with participation in the annual liturgical cycle (primarily through the Mass but secondarily through the Prayer of the Hours and *lectio divina*), are the first two mutually reinforcing pillars of Catholic piety. Because modern religion balances the tension between inner-worldly and other-worldly asceticism and mysticism in a new way, these forms of spiritual practice are equally important for all believers, whether clergy or lay, living inside or outside the monastery. The third pillar of Catholic piety is agape—charity or sisterly/brotherly love. The spiritual power of prayer and contemplation and liturgy flows from and back into love of neighbor, especially as it is manifested in concern for peace and social justice.

With the Christian contemplative tradition largely forgotten by Western intellectuals and only recently reemerging among practicing Catholics, Wilber and other transpersonal social scientists have turned to the Far East, where the conceptual apparatus, store of knowledge, and systematic gathering of spiritual data are more highly developed. Readers who are tone-deaf to Far Eastern mysticism need to adapt to a distinctive harmonic blend to appreciate the new paradigm of transpersonal and transcultural social science. The key concepts, however, are easily recognizable. Jung, for example, who viewed psychological maturity in terms of self-awareness, defined religion as "obedience to awareness." Teresa of Avila imagined Christian maturity as arrival at the center of the self's interior castle where the human and divine embrace in perfect union. She wrote: "The gate of entry to this castle is prayer and reflection."[27]

Centrism and Localism

The third trend creating tension for change in Catholic ministry is another combination of declining and growing social forces: decline in the political, economic, and cultural dominance of Western Christianity and increase in the membership, autonomy, and creativity of Christian churches in the Southern

Hemisphere. This trend also affects the problem of unity and diversity in universal religions. Just as modern universal religions need to maintain a peculiar balance between dogmatism and pluralism in belief and ritual, they also must resolve the tension between centrism and localism in social organization.

Like dogmatism and pluralism, centrism and localism have their strengths as well as limitations. In the context of religious organizations, the trap of organizational centrism is homogenism or sameness, the very antithesis of universalism and unity. There is no need to unite things that are all the same. In Catholicism, for example, Rome's insistence on centralized theological, liturgical, and organizational control results in homogenizing the myriad possibilities for religious expression generated at the local level. Rome's vision becomes a homogenized view of multiplex reality, changing the world back into a "one-possibility thing." The trap of localism, on the other hand, is isolationism, the antithesis of diversity. The local church's insistence on its own unique style means cutting itself off from the world Church, the communal reality that is an "infinite-possibility thing." But at the right threshold and in balanced tension with each other, centrism and localism manifest sound organizational reality as well as religious reality.

Balancing Tensions

To transcend the contradictions of unity and diversity, the organizational centrism of the Roman Catholic Church had to reach a certain level of strength before it could incorporate the further diversity of a Church inculturated in six continents. Historically, the Church's highly centralized structure has balanced the heterogeneity of Western cultures in a relatively successful manner. But now the Eurocentric Church has to struggle to free itself from the cage of isolationism, and Roman Catholicism faces the same challenge confronting the world's most powerful nations. Since the fifteenth century, several European nations have attempted to administer far-flung empires with varying degrees of success.[28] After World War II, a shift from imperial colonialism to national independence began to occur all over the modern world. The collapse of the Berlin Wall, the exposure of the shamble of Russian communism, and the fall of state communism throughout Eastern Europe are but the death rattle of national colonialism in the Western world.

These world-shaking events give added weight to trends toward pluralism in other world-influencing institutions like Roman Catholicism. Inspired by the *Zeitgeist* of decentralization, the Catholic Church is beginning to balance its exaggerated forms of organizational unity with greater diversity. Breaking the cultural, geographic, and demographic hold of its Western origins, the Church is slowly becoming inculturated across the world. In the process, its center of gravity is shifting to the Southern Hemisphere. The end of Eurocentrism spells the beginning of pluralism in the organizational structures of Catholicism.

I will argue that Church leadership, perhaps too exclusively identified with the papacy, has been mesmerized by its responsibility to safeguard Church unity. The existence of a world Church, however, radically alters the overall responsibility of its leadership. As the new millennium unfolds, Church leadership is also looking to safeguard pluralism, a job too exclusively identified with the episcopacy. The Catholic Church has entered an era when the forces of unity embodied in a strong papacy and the opposing forces of diversity inherent in a strong local episcopacy have reached a threshold of power at which one can balance the other. This balance would transcend the limitations of centrism and localism in a synthesis of unity and diversity. Bühlmann's summary of the situation is worth repeating: "One pole of the Church, central power, concentrates on unity. This is its right and duty. All the more, however, must the other pole, the bishops and episcopal conferences, enter into dialogue defending their interests and their complementary viewpoints so that genuine parity and balance can come between the two poles. Unity, certainly, but with pluriformity."[29]

Conclusion

Balancing the tensions between dogmatism and pluralism, centrism and localism in Catholic ministry is a structural solution to a religious paradox: the strain between the particular and the universal in psychosocial development. The paradox is superseded as the ego yields to the self and the self to no-self. As increasing numbers of religious practitioners achieve unitive consciousness of the one and the many through transpersonal naivete, this stage of human development calls for a structural adaptation in organized religion. Thus, a balanced coincidence of dogmatic faith-events and pluralistic understandings of them along with a balanced coincidence of the unifying papacy and diversifying episcopacy have been slowly emerging in Roman Catholicism.

As the Catholic Church adapts its organizational structures to its members' transpersonal development, we see the material, rational, diverse forces of historical reality combine in a holy kiss with the spiritual, transrational, unitive forces of absolute reality. I turn, now, to assessing the threshold of change in the next two trends of the matrix.

8

IMMANENCE AND TRANSCENDENCE

This chapter continues the discussion begun in the last, explaining why each trend gaining strength in the Catholic Church consists of a pair of social forces in dialectical conflict and how balancing the tension between them can resolve the conflict. The fourth and fifth trends in the matrix affect the tension between immanence and transcendence: (4) declining transcendentalism and growing personalism in the social construction of human sexuality, reflected in the conflict over celibacy and marriage in the priesthood, and (5) declining male dominance and growing female independence in relations between the sexes, reflected in the conflict over male hegemony and gender equality in Catholic ministry.

The Personalist Movement and Celibate Hegemony

Resolving the apparent contradictions between immanence and transcendence is not an offhand theme in religion or in my analysis of the social forces for change in the Catholic Church. The polar opposition of immanent and transcendent divine forces permeates all religious systems. It is nowhere more apparent than in the social construction of human sexuality, a process that is closely connected with religious evolution. So we need to review the development from primitive to modern religion, this time probing for the paradoxical tension between immanence and transcendence as it affects the social construction of sexuality.

Some religious systems emphasize one side of the paradox over the other. Primitive and archaic religions stress immanence by espousing a world-affirming symbol system. They tend to emphasize the pervasive immanent presence of mana, nature spirits, and other animistic powers. Anthropologists and historians of religion insist, however, that even though primitive myth systems may accentuate divine immanence, imaged as a nearby, nurturing Mother Goddess or Mother Earth, they are not blind to overpowering, distant, transcendent forces, imaged as Sky God, Sun God, or Moon God.[1]

The world-rejecting view of historical religions emphasizes the absolute otherness of a transcendent being or universe, imaged as an all-powerful father god or Absolute Being. But this view does not totally deny the immanent presence of divine power, imaged as Incarnate Compassion or Love and ritualized in sacraments. The worldview of modern religions attempts a new blend of immanence and transcendence, a balanced tension that avoids primitive monism and historical dualism. The modern worldview is often labeled humanism or personalism in the West and awareness of the true self or absolute mind in the East. In this view, the tension between the natural immanence of body and mind and the supernatural transcendence of spirit is overcome in the self-actualized or self-transcended human person. The paradox of blending divine immanence and transcendence is imaged by the Christian symbol of the Incarnate God.

Immanentist, Transcendentalist, and Personalist Sexuality

How do the relationships between immanence and transcendence affect the social construction of sexuality? For religion in general, the nub of the issue is a spiritual yet physical relationship with transcendent yet immanent Being. For present-day Roman Catholicism, the problem gets translated primarily into conflict over celibacy and marriage in the priesthood and, in a closely related way, into conflict over male hegemony and female equality in ministry.

I have tried to capture the sociological problem that underlies these religious conflicts by understanding them in terms of long-range transformative trends of decline and growth and by noting that they are reaching a critical threshold of strength. The pattern of relationships among the trends is creating a balanced synthesis of forces that will radically transform the structure of Catholic ministry. The change will include, first, married priests and later the ordination of women. This organizational transformation will have pervasive consequences for altering the patriarchal structures of the Church and wider society. The transformation and its consequences stem from and cause further change in the social construction of human sexuality.

In chapter 6 I examined the production, reproduction, and transformation of beliefs and behaviors regarding not only expressions of intimacy, erotic desires, and genital activities but also the whole gamut of social action appropriate to males and females across different time periods and social settings. I focused on two dimensions of sexuality. In treating the personalist movement, I examined the beliefs and behaviors appropriate for abstaining from or engaging in coitus, as spelled out in the conflict over celibacy and marriage in the priesthood. In dealing with the feminist movement, I focused on the beliefs and behaviors appropriate for defining the division of labor between the sexes, as applied to Catholic ministry.

According to the evidence, personalism is a growing social force in modern society. It developed as a result of epochal changes in the social construction of human sexuality. For Catholics, personalism enhances the balance between celibacy and marriage as paths to Christian holiness. The personalist movement allowed the sacramental charism of marriage to unfold in the Catholic Church, notably through pronouncements of the Second Vatican Council. Likewise, the feminist movement made significant inroads by advancing gender equality in the Church's ministerial division of labor, especially in the areas of sister formation and parish ministry.

As personalism and gender equality pervaded more and more aspects of Church life, mechanisms opposed to them, like the male celibate exclusivity of priestly ministry, gradually weakened, and so did the stark opposition between immanence and transcendence in the Catholic symbol system. To examine the relationship between these trends and the forces of divine immanence and transcendence I investigate here the impact of personalism on celibate exclusivity first and then turn to the issue of gender equality and male exclusivity.

The Power of Personalism

Modern religions, characterized by a new kind of world affirmation, make possible a personalist conception of human sexuality. In a personalist construction of sexuality, males and females are equal as full human persons. This equality extends to both the immanent realm of nature (body and mind) as well as the transcendent realm of the supramundane (spirit). As a religious conception, personalism balances the immanence and transcendence of Absolute Being in the one human person.

Personalism recognizes that each human being is a unique composite of spiritual and physical parts in tension, as polar opposites. In genuine personalism, propounded by the *philosophia perennis,* the spiritual pole has a paradoxical priority—one that is effective only when negated by its opposite. Buber elaborated the philosophical foundations of personalism for social science in his treatise on I–You and I–It modes of being. The human person is a composite of spiritual I–You and material I–It relationships, in which the spiritual relationships have priority. The material relationships are absolutely necessary but find their fulfillment in spiritual I–You encounters with nonsentient, sentient, human, suprahuman, and divine beings.[2]

Wilber describes spiritual priority in terms of involution and evolution.[3] The process of involution is described in most religious worldviews: In the beginning, according to the perennial philosophy, Absolute Reality manifested Itself in spiritual reality, then causal, then subtle reality, and next in mind, body, and, finally, material reality. That is, the spiritual has precedence over the material as reality unfolds through involution, because the process is a movement down the scale from spirit to matter. Evolution is the inverse process because through evolution reality evolves up the scale from matter to spirit. Evolutionary development is explained by natural science, transpersonal psychology, and transpersonal sociology in four basic stages: Material reality evolves (1) physically and biologically from inert matter to living and sentient body; (2) psychosocially from prerational to rational mind; (3) religiously from rational to transrational spirit; and (4) ultimately from dualistic to nondualistic Absolute Reality. Thus, material has precedence over spiritual as reality unfolds in the process of evolution. In the end, however, temporal, logical, and causal priority are meaningless because Absolute Reality is without time, logic, or cause. But in the meantime, when human beings live in the context of ordinary space and time, priority is crucial.

Regarding priority, note the similarity and difference in the use of the terms *prepersonal, personal,* and *transpersonal.* These terms emphasize the priority of the physical in the hierarchy of human development. From the viewpoint of evolution, "prepersonal" designates the launching stage of the developmental hierarchy and, from the viewpoint of involution, the stage of consciousness farthest away from awareness of Absolute Reality. From either the evolutionary or involutionary perspective, "personal" designates the central stage of a three-stage hierarchy: prepersonal, personal, and transpersonal. The terms *transpersonal, transpersonalism,* and *transpersonalist* are used to emphasize the priority of the spiritual in the hierarchy of human development. From the viewpoint of involution, "transpersonal" designates the launching stage of the developmental hierarchy and from the viewpoint of evolution, the goal of human development, namely, unitive consciousness of Absolute Reality. Thus "prepersonal" highlights the sensorimotor dominance of the body over the spirit in human beings. "Personalism" stresses the wholeness of the human being who is body, mind, and spirit. And "transpersonal" indicates the precedence of the spirit over the mind and body.

In the personalist and transpersonalist worldview embraced by a modern Christian, the spiritual element of personhood has priority, because Spirit empowers the resurrected Christic person. Paradoxically, however, the human person is integrally body, mind, and spirit in the original creation, as well as in the rebirth to a new resurrected person. So priority doesn't matter in the end-time, ushered in by the New Creation and the New Adam. But in historical time, the spiritual element is the foundation of the integral human person, regardless of the person's sex, gender, or any other physical, psychological, or sociocultural trait.

Balancing Tensions

The personalist construction of sexuality in the modern era radically alters the relationship between marriage and celibacy in the Catholic Church. At the same time it changes the balance of tension in symbolizing the immanence and transcendence of God. The modern understanding of person contrasts with the view held in early Christianity. Peter Brown documents conclusively that, in their worldview of the new person reborn in Christ, the early Christians considered celibacy superior to marriage; they esteemed continence and perpetual virginity as preeminent signs of holiness.[4]

The historical record of early Christianity reveals a truncated transcendentalist view of personhood. The new converts to Christianity had been recently reborn by baptism and the Spirit. They were incorporated into the Resurrected Christ, who was to return at any moment to take them into his kingdom. While waiting for the *parousia* (the end-time when the Glorified Christ would return to earth), giving and taking in marriage became unimportant. Moreover, keeping one's body pure was a sign of willpower befitting a person who is longing for Christ's Second Coming. Sex was carnal and pertained to the old person bound to the material body. Abstinence from sex was spiritual and characterized the new person reborn in the Christ and freed from material constraints. In this worldview, the immanent power of a Creator God who made human persons "to his own image . . . male and female" (Gn 1:27) and saw "that they were very good" (Gn 1:31) is overshadowed by a transcendent glorious resurrected God who ascended into Heaven "to prepare a place" for them (Jn 14:2).

The symbolic meaning of sexuality is critical for defining the human person. In the early epistles of Paul, the married person was considered a "half-Christian."[5] The early Christian worldview altered the Jewish construction of sexuality and human personhood but remained tied to Jewish dualism. This dualism, however, was turned on its head. Jewish dualism overemphasized the immanence of the body as opposed to the transcendence of the spirit, creating a dualistic material inferiority. The Christian construction of sexuality overemphasized the transcendent spirit to the neglect of the immanent body, creating a dualistic spiritual superiority.[6]

The Christian transcendentalist view of sexuality was soon institutionalized by consecrated virginity and monastic celibacy and later by mandatory priestly celibacy. Obviously, and by necessity, marriage had to become the norm, for Christianity survived and prospered. But even though it was sacramentalized, for almost two millennia marriage was not considered as spiritual or charismatic a symbol of the Christian person's relationship with the Incarnate God as celibacy was. Transcendentalism went unchallenged by most Roman Catholics until the Second Vatican Council. Since the council, the new theology of marriage, reinforced by a personalist view of sexuality, has contested the privileged position of celibacy in Catholic spirituality.

The religious power of personalism and transpersonalism emerged as a synthesis of earlier views of human sexuality. Primitive and archaic world-affirming religions emphasized the indwelling and immanent force of nature. So human sexuality and especially marriage were conceptualized in terms of natural and necessary begettings, nothing more and nothing less (see chapter 6). Historic world-rejecting religions introduced an emphasis on the transcendent realm and, within Christianity, abstention from coitus became its preeminent charismatic symbol.

The personalist conception of sexuality that developed in the modern era supersedes the more restricted naturalist and transcendentalist notions prevalent in prior epochs. To supersede, as Hegel reminds us, is to both negate and preserve.

The personalist/transpersonalist worldview negates the contrasting limitations of naturalism and transcendentalism but preserves the natural and transcendent capacities of the human person. Most important for this analysis, the personalist construction of sexuality denies that celibacy is superior to marriage as a way of Christian perfection. For personalist Catholics, personalism annuls the exclusive bond between the charism of celibacy and the charism of priesthood.

Symbol and Paradox

In a personalist conception of sexuality, the charisma of celibacy and that of marriage are equally potent religious symbols. Together they signify the synthesis of immanence and transcendence of Divine Being. Thus, in the new Catholic theology of sexuality and sacrament, the full erotic genital expression of sexuality in sacramental marriage is just as spiritual as abstaining from it in consecrated celibacy. This is true because the human persons joined in a marital union are each unique integrated composites of the physical and spiritual, the immanent and transcendent aspects of Reality. At the transpersonal level of consciousness, the physical does not preclude the spiritual; on the contrary, they compose an inviolable unity.

As a Catholic sacrament, the marital union connotes this physical-spiritual and immanent-transcendent integration significantly and efficaciously. At another level of symbolization, marriage and celibacy complement each other. Marriage efficaciously signifies the immanent fullness of union with Absolute Being. Consecrated celibacy symbolizes the polar opposite: the transcendent emptiness of Infinitely Possible Being. The theology emanating from the Second Vatican Council reaffirms the sacramental nature of marriage, recognizing that the erotic union of married lovers not only signifies but encourages union with God. Thus, the charisma equality of celibacy and marriage was acknowledged by the council fathers, at least in theory.

The charismatic power of marriage and celibacy achieve equality in the paradox of the immanent and transcendent God of Christianity: a Person in human and divine nature, a Being in potency and act, a Reality in emptiness and fullness. Charisma equality, like gender equality, attempts to express the multiple paradox of Absolute Being. The *Tao Te Ching* uses similar language to describe the relationship between immanence and transcendence, emptiness and fullness, potency and act, nonbeing and being:

We join spokes together in a wheel,
but it is the center hole
that makes the wagon move.
We shape clay into a pot,
but it is the emptiness inside

> that holds whatever we want.
> We hammer wood for a house,
> but it is the inner space
> that makes it livable.
> We work with being,
> but non-being is what we use.[7]

Reality is both transcendent and immanent: center and movement, emptiness and holding, space and living, nonbeing and being. One is not better than the other, for they can be reality only together. Likewise, celibacy is not better than marriage, neither in reality nor in symbol. For celibacy and marriage can express immanent-transcendent reality only together as balanced charismatic equals.

Nowadays, restricting the highest sacramental functions to celibates continues to signify that celibacy is better than marriage in the Catholic symbol system. Few informed Catholics, however, continue to believe in that outmoded view of sexuality. A personalist sexuality, embracing the sacramental immanence of marriage, can challenge the exclusivity of celibacy as the highest form of holiness. The Catholic Church maintained consecrated virginity and monastic chastity for almost two millennia, and the institution of compulsory priestly celibacy for eight centuries. As the third millennium of Christianity dawns, social trends signal that the strength necessary to maintain the symbolic power of celibacy has reached a threshold high enough to counterbalance the charismatic power of marriage. Accordingly, growing minorities of bishops and the majority of theologians, priests, and laypersons agree that both celibacy and marriage should be permitted in the priesthood.

I hasten to add that opening the priesthood to married men does not signal the end or even the weakening of the charismatic power of Christian celibacy. On the contrary, the transcendent power of celibacy as charismatic symbol is increased when counterbalanced by the immanent power of marriage as charismatic symbol. The increased power of both stems from a personalist conception of sexuality that assumes that women and men differ in sex and gender but are equal as persons. In their biologically determined sexes and socially constructed genders they reflect opposite poles of the dialectic: males archetypally signify transcendence and females immanence. In their compound persons they equally unite the opposites: immanent physicality and transcendent spirituality.

From a personalist viewpoint, celibacy as a way of holiness represents one side of the dialectic and marriage the other. The synthesis, which I call charisma-equality, balances the transcendent way to holiness signified by celibacy and the immanent way signified by marriage. In reality, however, there is no exclusively transcendent or exclusively immanent way to the Holy. For Christians, there is only one immanent-transcendent way, whether followed by the celibate or married path: Jesus Christ, the Human God, who says, "I am the Way" (Jn 14:6).

Both celibacy and marriage become stronger symbols when they enter a relationship of charisma-equality. Celibacy is enhanced because it is freed from the cloud of legal compulsion and the false claim of spiritual superiority. Marriage is enhanced because it is freed from the suspicion of base instinct and the false accusation of spiritual inferiority. Only the charisma-equality of celibacy and marriage can symbolically express the immanent-transcendent Way of an Incarnate God.

The Feminist Movement and Male Hegemony

When it comes to the issue of immanence and transcendence in Catholic ministry, the personalist movement and feminist movement are so closely related that it's hard to treat them separately. Nevertheless, I make a distinction between their effects on male celibate hegemony. Personalism has its greatest impact on celibate exclusivity and feminism on male exclusivity. In turning to the issue of male exclusivity, therefore, I examine not only feminism's primary effects but also those combined with the impact of personalism.

In the powerful intuitive logic of Christian symbols and archetypes, female goes with marriage and male goes with celibacy. The symbols turned out this way not by necessity but through sociohistorical processes. The Christian view of sexuality was deeply influenced by Augustine's Manichaean negativism. Manichaeans held that the soul and all goodness come from God and that matter, the source of all evil, comes from the Devil. Furthermore, "matter was concupiscence, a 'disorderly motion in everything that exists.' Matter or concupiscence was female, the 'mother of all the demons,' and the soul was imprisoned in it."[8]

If matter was female in mythic symbolization, the soul was male. Augustine taught that before the creation of Eve the male archetype, Adam, originally ruled his body, "the inferior part," with the rational soul, "the better part of a human being."[9] For Augustine, celibacy was a way to reject the material world and gain control of the rational soul. Marriage meant contact with and contamination by the material and thus female world. Thus, keeping marriage out of the priesthood helps keep females out as well. The distinction between the effects of personalism and those of feminism is analytically useful, but it dissolves when examining the practical problem of division of labor in Catholic ministry.

Immanentist, Transcendentalist, and Personalist Division of Labor

Until recently, the division of labor in Catholic ministry was characterized by male celibate exclusivity stemming from a transcendentalist worldview. Pressures for changing this pattern are reaching a critical threshold in the modern era. As I've just shown, personalism, reinforced by the feminist movement, brings Catholic ministry to a point at which it can balance the charismas of marriage and celibacy. In a similar way, feminism, backed up by personalism, is forging a division of labor that integrates the religious talents of male and female ministers.

In many Protestant denominations and sects, women already participate in the full gamut of ministerial jobs available, including those reserved to the ordained.[10] Since the Second Vatican Council, many Catholic ministerial activities that were once exclusively male are now open to women. These jobs range from top appointments as chancellors of dioceses and pastors of priestless parishes to such simple privileges as reading the Bible at Mass.[11] In 1994, John Paul II expanded the list to include altar servers; formerly the job had been limited to males.[12] An extensive lay ministry is the proud boast of the post-conciliar Catholic Church—and it is predominantly a female phenomenon.[13]

The feminist and personalist movements laid the foundation for gender equality in the Christian churches. A specific goal of the feminist movement is gender equality in the workplace. In the Catholic context, therefore, the movement strives to increase female participation and power in Catholic ministry. Gender equality in any social situation results from a balanced interdependence of males and females stemming from equal independence as mature human persons. A prerequisite of gender equality is the taken-for-grantedness of both male and female independence.

Balancing Tensions: Personalist Gender Equality

At the turn of the twenty-first century, the personalist and feminist movements are developing a new type of independence for males and females. The new independence leads to genuine interdependence based on gender equality. At this stage of the modern patriarchal era, male independence, in terms of psychological confidence vis-à-vis the female, is strong enough to accommodate a strong female independence. At the same time, because of the personalist and feminist movements, exaggerated male dominance is waning in other areas of social life.

Likewise, female independence is increasing as a result of the transformations affecting the male. First, as an accompaniment of patriarchy, male psychological confidence is sufficiently strong to handle the anxiety before the sexual mana of the female. So male dominance, maintained on an exaggerated scale under patriarchy by institutionalized forms of avoidance of and hostility toward females, is no longer generally needed. Second, the personalist movement has established the ethic of human equality of male and female. This equality extends to physical, mental, and spiritual abilities and is not negated by biological and sociocultural differences. Third, the feminist movement has raised consciousness, exerted political pressure, and found ways to transform the structures of male dominance into structures of male/female interdependence based on gender equality. Obviously, as emerging social constructions of reality, these transformations are not completely institutionalized. So patterns of attitudes and behaviors reflect a mixture of the modern construction of female independence and holdovers from the past. This new construction of sexuality and gender, emphasizing interdependence based on equality, is spreading gradually in the wider society. Gender equality is slowly beginning to make inroads even in religion, historically one of the strongest institutional supports of patriarchal dominance.

Roadblocks in Religion

In comparison to other social institutions—business, politics, the military, education, medicine—the transformation to gender equality lags behind in religion. Modern religious organizations maintain two impressive roadblocks to female equality: first, a gender-based division of labor deriving from deep-seated cultural and theological beliefs; second, a unique resistance to social change stemming from the legal separation of church and state.

Men and women work at being religious in different ways, and, generally, women work harder at it than men. In patriarchal cultures, males tend to appropriate the cognitive, evaluative, and control aspects of religion, females the affective, cathectic, and more subtly spiritual aspects. Weber noted this widespread tendency, particularly in historical, world-rejecting religions and among the privileged classes in all religions.[14] Empirical studies consistently show that women engage in common religious activities (public worship, financial support, volunteer labor, spiritual reading, ascetic practices, almsgiving, etc.) in notably higher proportions than men. That is not to say, however, that men are not prominent in religious organizations. On the contrary, men occupy the positions of prominence and power, exercising control in governance, official teaching, and public ritual.

Traditional gender barriers affecting the division of labor in religious groups are reinforced in the United States by law and politics stemming from the separation of church and state. In nonreligious settings, many aspects of gender discrimination are illegal and others are subject to democratic politics. But no such mechanisms operate in the Catholic Church. The ascriptive barriers governing the division of labor in ministry are determined by theology and canon law, both dominated by a male celibate papacy and episcopacy. To cite civil rights in demanding the ordination of women and married men in the Catholic Church is unthinkable in the United States. That would violate the Constitution. Nor can Catholics elect bishops who endorse gender and status equality in the priesthood. That would violate canon law.

Though insulated in ways that dampen the forces of change, religious groups nevertheless gradually transform their social structures. As noted, major internal mechanisms of social change for organized religion are developments in symbolization, ideological persuasion, and charismatic coalition formation. Moreover, religious organizations exist in an ecological niche, which is constantly in flux. The organization's environment, therefore, is the external and perhaps most important source of social change. Catholic dioceses are transforming their ministerial structures because the personalist and feminist movements are radically transforming their ecological niche. As population ecology theory predicts, in most cases the structural transformations result from blind chance and so occur regardless of the knowledge or affirmation of church leaders.

Conclusion

The transformation from gender dependence to independence to interdependence hangs on the resolution of seeming contradictions between divine immanence and transcendence. Advances in both religious and social scientific symbol systems help resolve the religious paradox affecting human sexuality and provide an escape from exaggerated egoism and altruism. According to traditional theories of human development and the recently emerging transpersonal paradigm, human beings acquire full maturity through a series of "small" and "great" transcendences.[15] In the small transcendences, the ego emerges out of a primordial immanence or fusion with matter, passing from matter to ego-body to ego-mind. In the great transcendences, the self surmounts the gross consciousness of ego-mind and passes to subtle to causal to ultimate consciousness of reality. In the Ultimate Transcendence, the self experiences no-self and becomes one with Ultimate Immanence, or Absolute Reality.

For males and females alike, the path to full maturity and Absolute Reality is a social psychological and religious process that unfolds in a societal context. To pass from male or female dominance to gender independence and then to gender interdependence is to become conscious of human reality. To transcend all forms of immanence and transcendence is to become part of Immanently Transcendent or Absolute Reality. Only under the conditions of gender interdependence are human reality and Absolute Reality one and the same.

Because celibate exclusivity in the priesthood is a structural and symbolic mechanism of support for patriarchal dominance and gender inequality in the Catholic Church, its days are numbered. For Catholics, the sacralization of the charisma of marriage in balance with a completely free commitment to voluntary celibacy is becoming the structural and symbolic mechanism of support for male and female interdependence based on gender equality.

Balance between both the tensions of personalist sexuality and celibate monopoly and the tensions of gender equality and male monopoly in the Catholic Church are manifestations of structural solutions to the paradoxical strain between immanence and transcendence in organized religion. In Catholicism, the structures affected most are those that compose the monopolistic priesthood. Next, I assess the threshold of change in the last two trends and analyze the full matrix of historical forces for its impact on the primal paradox of hierarchy and hierophany in Roman Catholicism.

9

HIERARCHY AND HIEROPHANY

Take this, all of you, and eat it: This is my body.
Take this, all of you, and drink from it: This is the cup of my blood.
Do this in memory of me.

Roman Catholic Mass

The Catholic lay movement and Catholic liturgical movement, the sixth and seventh trends in the matrix, draw their dynamism from the conflict between hierarchic and hierophanic power in religious groups. Introduced in chapter 5, this is the culminating paradox that recapitulates all the tensions impinging on Catholic ministry. Thus, the countervailing powers of hierarchy and hierophany are bound up with the tension between the forces of unity and diversity and the tension between the forces of immanence and transcendence. The decline in the priesthood population brings these tensions to a head. As this decline continues, it acts as an catalyst provoking a series of far-reaching changes, most notably the loss of the sacrificial focus of the Mass.

The Lay Movement and the Liturgical Movement

The lay movement reflects the dynamic tension between clergy and laity produced by the Catholic Church's division of labor. One pole of the dialectic is charged with clerical power arising from the sacrament of Holy Orders; the other involves lay empowerment stemming from the sacrament of baptism. Decline in the priestly monopoly over ministry and growth in the ministerial prerogatives of the layperson are the opposing forces affected by the lay movement. The dialectic in the liturgical movement reflects the tension between sacrament and scripture in Catholic worship. The sacramental side of the dialectic gains its dynamism from the power of ritual and the scriptural side from the power of the written word. Decline in the Catholic Counter-Reformation emphasis on sacrament, especially the eucharistic sacrifice of the Mass, and growth in the Protestant emphasis on the biblical Word are the opposing forces affected by the liturgical movement. Both sets of dialectical forces lie at the very core of our sociological problem: the primal tension between hierarchy and hierophany in organized religion. The conflict between clericalism and laicism flows primarily from the problem of hierarchy, and the conflict between ritualism and biblicism stems from the problem of hierophany.

Sacerdotalism and sacramentalism are the most deeply embedded elements defining Catholic ministry because ordained priesthood embodies hierarchy and sacrament embodies hierophany. Moreover, given the awesome nature of sacramental sacrifice in the Catholic tradition, sacrament is socially impossible without an ordained priesthood. Sacrament is as inextricably linked to ordained priesthood in Catholicism as hierophany is to hierarchy in all organized religions.

Clericalism and Laicism

In Catholicism, the dichotomy between clergy and laity is created by the contrasting and complementary powers of ordination and baptism. But lay ministerial power has been strengthened vis-à-vis clerical power by long-range and recent trends in Western society and the Catholic Church. Beginning in the mid-twentieth century and spurred on by pronouncements of the Second Vatican Council, the lay movement transformed the ministerial division of labor in the Church. Religious ministry in which the ordained priest has a monopoly of control over most, if not all, of the ordinary means of salvation has become a thing of the past. A division of labor in which both priest and layperson participate in a wide variety of ministerial tasks according to their expertise and availability was delayed until the level of education and theological formation of the laity had progressed far enough to support it.

Although advances in the rational division of labor along with a successful Catholic lay movement have narrowed the lay-ordained split in ministry, it nevertheless remains an unbridgeable chasm. A genuine dilemma is maintained because both conflicting forces have theological foundations and sociological functions. As we have seen, organized religion is universally characterized by some form of hierarchy because only by safeguarding the definitiveness of its foundational myth can a believing community provide access to hierophanic faith-events from one generation to the next. Safeguarding the living myth is the function of hierarchy. Minimally, the absolute paradigmatic truth of cosmogonic events is preserved by a central symbol system of word and ritual in the care of elders or other elites like shamans, sages, and gurus. Centralizing mythic beliefs and values in a symbol system and designating elites by age or charisma to be responsible for preserving it constitute the rudiments of hierarchy. Thus, myth is an authoritative religious symbol system preserved by hierarchy. In Catholicism, the paradigmatic reality of the Christian myth is authentically preserved by the hierarchic priesthood.

The religious need for hierarchy is reinforced by sociocultural imperatives. In industrialized societies, even religion tends to be organized according to rational bureaucratic principles. Hence, although the explicit goal of organized re-

ligion is transpersonal holiness and not rational technical efficiency in ministering the means of salvation, corporate religion is nevertheless organized on bureaucratic principles of control and expertise.

Although spawned by religious necessity and supported by many bureaucratic advantages, hierarchy has its limitations. These are evident in the distinction between clergy and laity that is generated by hierarchy of control in a religious group. An overemphasis on clergy can spring the multiple trap of elitism,
rationalism, and esotericism. Under *clericalism* the religious group can fall into
a pattern of attitudes and behaviors in which only the clergy are capable of leadership (elitism), the transcendent elements of the symbol system are reasoned
away (rationalism), and the beliefs and rituals become arcane and inaccessible
to the faithful (esotericism). On the other hand, an emphasis on laypersons in
ministry can lead to dilettantism, emotionalism, and magic. Thus, under *laicism*
leadership passes from experts to amateurs (dilettantism), historical definitiveness of faith-events is sacrificed to here-and-now feelings (emotionalism), and
the purpose of doctrinal formulas and rituals changes from worshiping to ma-
nipulating Divine Being (magic).

The tendency toward either clericalism or laicism is an inescapable dilemma
as religious groups try to optimize the strengths and minimize the weaknesses
of hierarchy in their social organization. Catholicism has tended to err on the
side of clericalism, but a new balance is being struck by internal and external social forces affecting the structure of ministry. Since the Second Vatican Council,
for example, priests see themselves as belonging to, not set apart from, the
People of God. In Latin American churches, witness the frequent mention of
the "preferential option for the poor" and liberation theology in episcopal documents as well as the widespread development of "base communities" in pastoral ministry.[1] In developed countries, these attitudes are apparent in less distinctive clerical dress, reduced isolation in seminary training, decreased reliance
by priests on laypersons in menial roles such as housekeeper and cook, and more
reliance, generally, on laypersons in positions of power and prestige.

For their part, Catholic laypersons are gaining greater expertise in religious
knowledge, pastoral care, and liturgical skills. In the contemporary U.S. Church,
the priest is no longer the only educated person in the parish.[2] Growing numbers of lay Catholics are earning degrees not only in secular disciplines but also
in sacred scripture, theology, pastoral ministry, and liturgy. These newly acquired credentials are providing entry to a wide variety of ecclesiastical jobs
once reserved for priests.[3]

Biblicism and Ritualism

Because the aims of the lay movement and liturgical movement reinforce each
other, laity are prepared not only to participate in but also to preside over litur-

gical functions. Having laypersons take leadership roles in the sanctuary and pulpit inevitably narrows the gap between clergy and laity, thus balancing the tension between clericalism and laicism. Ironically, however, because these developments also interact with the priest shortage, they intensify the tension between Word and sacrament. Hence, in many parishes today, priest and laypersons continue to share liturgical tasks at Sunday Mass, with the priest presiding over major activities and laypersons taking responsibility for minor parts of the ceremony. This is the norm and ideal—indeed, the fruition of the liturgical movement.

The term *sacrament* can be used generically to denote any external physical expression of an interior spiritual encounter with the Holy. Words, music, bodily movements, and material objects are all sacramental elements when used to express a hierophanic faith-event. As we also have seen, a living myth system preserves the foundational hierophany of a religious group. Myths are kept alive by means of communal sacramental celebrations that combine word, song, ritual movement, and material objects, all symbolizing religious faith-events. In its fullness, therefore, a sacramental event is a holistic expression of body, mind, and spirit—that is, an activity involving the whole human person.

Theological conflicts of the sixteenth century introduced analytic distinctions between different elements in Christian sacramental worship and different degrees of importance across sacraments. The sacramental tradition divided into two camps, one grounded in the power of the sacramental priesthood and the other in the power of the biblical Word available to all baptized believers. As a result of Reformation and Counter-Reformation polemics, Catholics stressed ritual movement, sacred matter, and ordained liturgists as the most essential elements of sacramental worship. Protestants, in contrast, championed the power of Word and song and the priesthood of all believers. Furthermore, Catholics insisted on the priority of Eucharist and defined it as sacrificial worship presided over by an ordained priest. Protestants, for their part, either limited the frequency of eucharistic celebrations, eliminated the eating of bread and wine altogether, or emphasized it as a memorial supper. These developments widened the gap between Word and sacrament and fortified the traps of biblicism and ritualism within Christianity.

An exaggerated emphasis on the written word describing a mythic event is *biblicism.* An exaggerated emphasis on ceremonial gestures and material objects used to reenact the mythic event is *ritualism.* To the extent it existed in prior ages, the delicate balance of body, mind, and spirit in sacramental worship was seriously weakened by the Protestant Reformation and Catholic Counter-Reformation.

Biblicism, defined as an overemphasis on the book, attempts to capture the spiritual element of the Christian faith-event mainly by reading, preaching, and singing the Word of God. In the context of Western culture, biblicism tends to overemphasize the mind, reason, logic, and mental vision. Since the Enlightenment, its major traps are historicism, scientism, and privatism. If the religious group tries to encapsulate its foundational hierophany solely in the written word, to the practical exclusion of oral and ritual tradition, it runs the risk of choking the life out of it. The mythic event is reduced to merely a historical or scientific account, available to any private individual who can read. Left standing on its own merits, the written document can be subjected to the canons of historicity, scientific proof, or private interpretation; often it is criticized according to any one of these standards and is found wanting.

Ritualism is defined as an overemphasis on the correctly designated celebrant, formula, gesture, and physical matter. It is an attempt to capture the spiritual element of a faith-event through officially prescribed ceremonies. Thus, a dominant teaching among Catholic theologians—challenged by the liturgical movement—was that sacraments worked *ex opere operato*.[4] That is, if the designated celebrant and recipients have the correct intentions and the prescribed ritual is performed with the correct words, gestures, and physical matter, the sacrament unfailingly has its spiritual effect. Ritualism, carried to its logical conclusion, overemphasizes the body, emotion, imagination, and sensory vision. Its principal traps are irrationalism, emotionalism, and magic. Irrationalism in religious worship emphasizes blind mental submission to the exclusion of reason. Emotionalism gives unbridled reign to the sensory and affective aspects of religious consciousness. And magic reduces religious ritual to manipulation of supernatural forces.

When writing entered civilization those religions that survived prehistory and those that emerged during the historical period adapted their ritual celebrations, drawing from oral tradition, written documents, and other human artifacts. Therefore, a vibrant living myth system is one that transcends the tendency of biblicism to overemphasize the mind, reason, logic, and mental vision and the tendency of ritualism to overemphasize the body, emotion, imagination, and sensory vision. The worship of a faith-community structurally adapted to a transpersonal myth system maintains an adequate balance between Word and sacrament. Recently, the liturgical movement has attempted to free Catholics from the traps of biblicism and ritualism and to restore the balance between Word and sacrament in Christian worship.

Balancing Tensions

How does a faith-community adapt its organizational structures to maintain a transpersonal myth system? For Christianity, part of the answer lies in its periodic reform movements. The Protestant Reformation and Catholic Counter-Reformation, along with the modern Catholic liturgical movement, altered the tension between hierarchy and hierophany as it is played out in the distinction between sacrament and Word. Reformation politics drove a sharp wedge into the Church's sacramental tradition. Recently, however, Catholic biblical scholarship and the liturgical movement have created new appreciation for the Word of God among churchgoers, correcting the overemphasis on priestly sacramentalism.

As noted, the exaggerated accent on sacraments in the Roman Catholic tradition has a long history. The Reformation generated a free-church tradition that championed the priesthood of all believers. To emphasize this basic Christian doctrine, new sects abolished the ordained priesthood and along with it all the sacraments except baptism. The Bible and preaching the Word of God were substituted as the exclusive means of salvation. The Roman Catholic Church countered these reforms at the Council of Trent, pronouncing the importance of the seven sacraments controlled exclusively by the ordained priesthood. Thus, since the sixteenth century, Catholicism has been rigidly sacramental to the practical exclusion of Bible-based piety.

The restoration of a dynamic balance between the power of the sacrament and the power of the Word in the Catholic Church had to await the flowering of the liturgical movement. The modernist heresy had blocked Catholic biblical scholarship until the 1940s, when Pius XII promulgated *Divino Afflante Spiritu*, which effectively lifted the ban on modern hermeneutics and the social sciences, allowing the use of these tools in the Catholic study of sacred scripture. Serious biblical research soon had a strong impact on the liturgical movement and revitalized the first part of the Mass called the Liturgy of the Word. Now, after half a century of biblically based liturgical reform, sacrament and Word can stand side by side in Catholic piety without one overshadowing the other. Bible-based worship services, homilies at daily Mass, and Bible study groups were novelties in the 1950s and 1960s but became commonplace during the 1970s and 1980s. As the liturgical movement gained momentum, many Catholics were introduced to the Bible in its entirety for the first time. Seminarians took catch-up courses in higher biblical criticism, hermeneutics, and biblical archeology.[5] Young priests experimented with new forms of liturgy at Mass and paraliturgical services at other times, with the Bible taking center stage. Nowadays, the book of Bible readings is enshrined in the sanctuary of parish churches and held high in processions at Mass, while paperback Bibles are sold in grocery stores to eager Latin American Catholics learning about liberation from oppression.

Thus, the liturgical movement itself achieved a new balance between scientific scholarship and rational respect for the written word and the revitalization of ritual, preaching, and embodied spirituality in Catholic worship. The Mass and sacraments are not to be watched by passive observers or received by uneducated clients who do not understand their underlying mysteries. They are to be celebrated by persons who fully integrate body, mind, and spirit in the sacramental action. Moreover, they are to be celebrations of fully responsible Christians engaged in ministries they are called to by virtue of their baptism.

Participation in the Mass and sacraments became the watchword of the liturgical movement, just as participation in other aspects of ministry was the rallying cry of the lay movement. Both movements soon reached their zenith and were fully legitimated in the documents of the Second Vatican Council. Of all the new developments in Roman Catholicism during the last half century, lay participation in the Church is the most welcome and least controversial. In the vast majority of Catholic dioceses, lay leadership and responsibility are growing trends, championed by bishops, priests, and laypersons alike.

Sacrificing Sacrifice

Among the many consequences of increased lay participation, one stands out as most critical for changing the core structure of ministry: Significant numbers of laypersons are leading parish worship groups, even on Sunday. Lay leadership at principal religious functions like Sunday service, however, is an aberration in liturgical religions like Catholicism. Lay participation was a legitimate goal of both the Catholic lay movement and the liturgical movement, and lay leadership in certain "nonpriestly" areas of ministry, too, was a desirable aim of the lay movement. But full lay leadership at Sunday service was never a conscious aim of the liturgical movement, precisely because of the tension between sacrament and Word in the Catholic tradition.

The lay and liturgical movements within the Church, in combination with the priest shortage, have had the unintended consequence of increasing the prominence of the Liturgy of the Word at Mass and decreasing the centrality of the eucharistic sacrifice. The Catholic Church faces a historical situation in which a serious shortfall of ordained priests is occurring while church membership is growing. At the same time, the supply of motivated laypersons skilled in liturgy and other ministerial tasks is on the upswing. A reasonable response is to create a new form of Sunday worship, one in which the role of lay leaders can be emphasized and that of priest sacrificer can be diminished.[6]

When the pendulum of tension between clergy and laity and Word and Sacrament swings to laicism and biblicism, the essential function of the priest falls out of the picture. Hubert and Mauss demonstrated that in sacrificial worship the priest, as sacrificer, plays the sine qua non role.[7] Although Holy Communion is usually included in a lay-led Sunday service, the eucharistic meal is taken out of context. It is no longer the culminating phase of mystical sacrifice in the Catholic tradition. It cannot be sacrifice because the priest is not present.

When Communion is served outside of Mass, the natural sequence of the ritual is violated. The bread has been consecrated as sacrificial victim at an earlier Mass in which the offering is accepted and reciprocated by God when the participants consume the bread and become the Body of Christ. So eating the sacrificed elements outside of that context is not interpretable as mystical sacrifice—that is, surrendering one's self to God and consummating one's union with the Divine Center and through this union deepening one's membership in the religious community. It is not a sacramental participation in the sacrificial Passover from life to death to resurrected life in the Body of Christ. Instead, Communion is seen as participating in a memorial supper, as in the free-church Protestant tradition.[8]

In his famous studies of Ndembu religion, Victor Turner spelled out the inviolable processual nature of sacred rites.[9] All religious rituals are passages from one mode of being to another, with each phase having its critical importance. Interrupting those phases destroys the passage and vitiates the purpose of the ritual.[10] The Eucharist as memorial supper is also a time-honored Christian ritual, but it is not sacrificial worship. Catholic bishops, theologians, and liturgists may or may not be aware that Sunday service without a priest sacrifices the Catholic sacrificial tradition. Simply put, nonordained liturgists protestantize Catholicism. Lay celebrants presiding at a parish's principal worship service completes the Protestant Reformation, whether Catholics realize it or not.

Turner further emphasizes the importance of proper phasing when a story is told and cherished by a community. In contrast to chronicle, which is a historical account claiming facticity, story is an "arrangement of events into the components of a 'spectacle' or process of happening, which is thought to possess a discernible beginning, middle, and end."[11] Parts of chronicles may be transformed into stories "according to their nodal location in the life process of the group or community that recounts them. It all depends where and when and by whom they are told."[12]

To be an authentic Catholic story, the eucharistic sacrificial event must be told only in the proper setting, at the proper time, and by the proper people. All this is decided by the community; only they know what is proper and what is not. The story relates a spectacle, a life process; it has a beginning, middle, and end. No one part of the story relates this particular life process; wrenched out of context it becomes something else, part of another story. A Communion service following a Liturgy of the Word is another story altogether; it is not the sacrificial Eucharist in the Catholic community. It may be something important and beautiful for the group, a memorial supper, a celestial banquet, but it is not the sacrificial Eucharist. How can it be? For it is not told in the proper setting, in the proper order, by the proper people. The service necessarily excludes the symbolic gestures and physical objects of sacrifice reserved to the priest, and thus the full ritual process of mystical sacrifice is lost. The Catholic community can no longer tell its story.

The Primal Paradox

The entire analysis in this book is based on the postulate that priesthood is the linchpin that holds together the structures and animates the structuration of the Roman Catholic Church. Furthermore, the incorporation of a sacramental priesthood is the mechanism the Church developed to transcend the paradox of hierarchy and hierophany inherent in all religions. We have seen that the opposition between hierarchic and hierophanic power is the primal paradox in organized religion. Thus, the conflicting pressures intrinsic to all the dialectical trends I have been analyzing have their source in the tension between hierophany and hierarchy as it is played out in the Catholic Church.

The priest shortage draws attention to the various pressures represented in the matrix, releases them from dormancy, exacerbates them, and demands a new synthesis among them. For the Catholic Church, priesthood is the structural mechanism by which the believing community normally gains access to its foundational hierophanic faith-events. By means of the socially constructed hierarchic power invested in it, priesthood accesses, coordinates, and controls hierophanic power. The only authentically religious use of priestly hierarchic power, however, is to produce, disseminate, and maintain the ascetical and mystical means of fostering awareness and submission to the Ultimate Source of hierophanic power: Divine Being.

Unity and Diversity

In chapter 7 I discussed the tension between unity and diversity in terms of centrism and localism. How do the countervailing forces of hierarchy and hierophany manifest themselves in the tension between centripetal and centrifugal structures in the Catholic Church? The Christian faith-events that infuse believers with hierophanic power cannot be universally accessible unless the symbol system recounting the events is skillfully transposed into different cultural contexts. Inculturation, by definition, takes into account the needs of individuals in all their sociocultural diversity. Thus, hierophanic power is tied to localism precisely because hierophany is operative only when it infuses believers here and now.

In addition, for cosmogonic events to be operative they must be proclaimed authentically and accepted as definitive. Therefore, the function of hierarchy in religion is to safeguard the authentic expression of definitive faith-events. Hierarchy takes many forms, some with stronger tendencies to centrism than others. Hierarchy, in this sense, is evident even in primitive religion. Members of tribal societies develop their beliefs and normative behaviors from a commonly held myth system that is preserved through stories and rituals controlled by elders and shamans. Hierarchy is even more obvious in the elaborate form it takes in corporate religion. The modern religious organization is a rationalized bureaucracy in which a hierarchy of expert office holders legitimately produces and administers a complex creed, code, and cult for educated, rationally motivated members of a believing community. Thus, whether religion has a simple or complex structure, the principle of hierarchy is manifest in a central myth safeguarded by legitimately designated elites.

Hierarchic power tends to generate centrism because legitimately desig-nated leaders must be chosen to safeguard the authenticity of the myth system. In contrast, hierophanic power tends to generate localism because the myth must be kept personally alive in the hearts and minds of individual believers. Thus the dilemma: Hierarchic control is needed so the authenticity of the common myth is not lost in the pluralistic inculturation process; at the same time, the intimately personal hierophanic power of the myth must not be lost in the centralized control process.

Immanence and Transcendence

Likewise, the ethereal notions of immanence and transcendence can be cap-tured in the more concrete relationship between hierophany and hierarchy in organized religion. In religious imagery, hierophany signifies the vertical or spir-itual dimension of a religious group and hierarchy its horizontal or material di-mension.[13] A hierophany makes possible an encounter with an absolutely tran-scendent Being or Universe. Otto describes the encounter with the Holy as an experience of the *totaliter aliter,* Totally Other. It culminates in unitive con-sciousness, dissolving the distinction between self and other. The hierophanic encounter with Absolute Transcendence is expressed as a faith-event by the be-lieving community. It is a vertical event because a hierophany allows passage to and from the higher and lower divine/demonic realms of reality.

Sociologically speaking, the faith-event is preserved, safeguarded, and made accessible for future generations through a hierarchically organized group. Re-ligiously speaking, however, these social activities are horizontal events because they all occur at the same level of reality, the realm of the human and mundane. Thus, hierarchy makes encounter with Immanence possible, while hierophany—and sacrament—make encounter with Transcendence possible.

Priesthood as Linchpin

In Roman Catholicism, the hierarchic, sacramental priesthood is given power and responsibility to mediate conflict between the demands of unity and tran-scendence on the one hand and diversity and immanence on the other. In the eyes of the Catholic faithful, priests legitimately exercise hierarchical control because of their expert training and their consecration in the sacrament of Holy Orders.

Practicing Catholics concede, at times grudgingly, that the hierarchic priest-hood has the primary authority to interpret the central dogmas and rituals to the local community. Furthermore, the community expects the hierarchic priest not only to proclaim the dogmas and celebrate the rituals authentically but also to make the Christian myth come alive. In a complex multicultural society, the priest has to make the Living Myth of transcendent reality accessible to a variety of worldviews so believers can personally partake of its immanent hierophanic power. Moreover, the Catholic priest must also interpret the local community's diverse needs to the central powers for the balance between unity and diversity and transcendence and immanence to be maintained. As pastors, preachers, and sacramental presiders, priests serve as intermediaries between the "deposit of faith," safeguarded primarily by the official magisterium, and the living tradition preserved primarily in the believing community.[14]

The many translations and inculturations of its central faith-events throughout a group's history compose its living tradition, or living myth. In a highly organized church like Roman Catholicism the myth stays alive to the extent that its symbolic expressions are based on a respectful, mature I–You dialogue between the teaching magisterium, pastoral priesthood, and committed laity (chapter 5). Viewed from the angle of hierarchy, priesthood is pivotal in Roman Catholicism. Catholic priesthood is not only hierarchic, however. It is also sacramental and therefore hierophanic. Religion is a social institution that attempts to span the realms of the holy and the human, the transcendent and the immanent; hence hierophany is inextricably linked to hierarchy. The indivisible bond between them is symbolized—becomes significant and efficacious—in the priest. A hierarchic sacramental priesthood, therefore, is imperative for liturgical sacramental religions and absolutely essential for those who emphasize mystical sacrifice as the highest form of worship. Hence, for Roman Catholics, there can be no hierophany nor sacrament without consecrated priesthood. And the opposite is also true: There can be no priesthood that is not hierarchic and sacramental.

A Catholic Tragedy

A tragedy, in the classic sense, is being played out on the Roman Catholic stage. The plot revolves around a religious community that clings desperately and vociferously to celibate hegemony and male exclusivity while calmly and quietly rejecting priesthood and sacrament. In a classic drama, the tragic hero is unaware of impending disaster. There are at least four classes of unsuspecting heroes in the Catholic tragedy: the alert laity and clergy, feminist leaders, conservative bishops and clergy, and the contented laity and clergy.

Many educated laypersons and even some priests see the priesthood as an anachronism, a privileged role that can be filled by equally well-trained and committed lay ministers. They are puzzled by the argument that a consecrated priesthood is essential to modern Catholicism. Feminists are disturbed by an argument that sacrificial surrender to God (especially a male-imaged deity) constitutes the height and depth of worship and, moreover, that hierarchy is essential to organized religion. Incredulous popes, bishops, and priests are threatened by the need to let go of celibate hegemony and male exclusivity. The idle laity and clergy are uncritical of the status quo and content to be loyal to the official magisterium, especially to papal preferences. So the alert laity and clergy in general and feminists in particular may rejoice over the trends generating decline in the priesthood population. Conservative bishops and priests, for their part, may simply deny the trends described in *Full Pews and Empty Altars* and this book, confident that male celibate hegemony cannot be in jeopardy because it is the will of God. Lay and clerical loyalists, by definition, take their cue from the dominant papal coalition and, therefore, also support male celibate exclusivity.

The tragic irony is this: Each polar camp risks throwing out the sacred baby with the profaned bathwater. Alert Catholics are willing to let go of a clericalized priesthood in favor of lay ministry and the priesthood of all believers. Feminists are willing to abandon sacrifice and hierarchy to gain gender equality. Conservative bishops and priests, along with Catholic loyalists, are willing to forgo the hierophanic vitality of the priesthood itself to hold onto male celibate exclusivity. Seemingly oblivious to the ironic consequences of their actions, each of the tragic heroes is throwing out the same precious baby: the Eucharist—the sacrificial tradition—the foundation of Catholic piety. The villain in this tragedy, a veritable wolf in sheep's clothing, is male celibate exclusivity: limiting the priesthood to unmarried men. The next section deals with this villainy by examining the interaction between the sacred symbols and hierarchic and hierophanic powers attached to the Catholic priesthood.

Balancing the Symbolic Structure of Priesthood

Because the priestly role is structured to absorb the tensions between unity and diversity, immanence and transcendence, hierophany and hierarchy, the religious symbols adopted to signify this complex reality must be carefully chosen. The tension between hierarchic and hierophanic power is more clearly evident in the manner in which Catholic priesthood symbolizes the paradox of unity and diversity than in how it symbolizes the paradox of immanence and transcendence. Ideally, the priest is chosen from the people, reflecting the Church's diversity, and ordained into the hierarchy, reflecting its unity. As symbolic forces, unity and diversity are thus balanced in one and the same person, the priest.

The same symbolic balance between immanence and transcendence, however, is not achieved in today's priesthood. Symbolically, the celibate priesthood signifies the transcendent emptiness of infinite possibility and overlooks the immanent fullness of union in God, signified by marriage. The male priesthood symbolizes transcendent power, imaged as Father Creator, and rational power, imaged as Incarnate Logos. But it overlooks immanent nurture, imaged as Mother Goddess, and the intuitional transrational power of Spirit/Wisdom, symbolized by femaleness.[15]

Male celibate exclusivity rules out a balance between the symbolic expression of immanence and transcendence in the priesthood. Otto explains that ascribing both immanence and transcendence to the Holy seems contradictory at first. He concludes, however, that only in a religious encounter, in which the overpowering majesty of the *mysterium tremendum* is transcended by union with the numinous presence, can both immanence and transcendence be known *experientally* as two essential aspects of the same Divine Reality. What is true at the individual level is also true at the social level. To be complete, the symbolic structure of the priesthood must include and span both the transcendence and immanence of Divine Reality. As we have seen, in the patriarchal worldview of Catholic Christianity, transcendence is symbolized by maleness and celibacy, while immanence is signified by femaleness and marriage. Only a priesthood open to males, females, celibates, and married persons can symbolically contain and express the full paradoxical reality of Transcendent and Immanent Being. To balance its symbolic structure, therefore, the exclusively male celibate priesthood must be replaced by one that incorporates four types of ordained persons: male and female, celibate and married.

Conclusion: Catalyst for Change

The great fear for Roman Catholics is that losses in the priesthood spell the loss of the Mass because they are inextricably linked. As the priest shortage progresses, the distressing question raised in the first chapter and elaborated here becomes inescapable: Will the Eucharist survive? The priest shortage, lay movement, and liturgical movement interact to create a new and much deeper trap for Catholicism than either clericalism, laicism, biblicism, or ritualism could on their own. Ironically, maintaining the status quo of a male celibate hegemonic priesthood is likely to result in sacrificing the sacrificial tradition, the raison d'être of priesthood itself. The continued loss of the Church's most critical resource, the sacramental priesthood, has become a powerful locomotive for pervasive social change. Will it continue, or can it be turned around? Are the demographic trends powerful enough to produce the catalytic reaction needed to bring the matrix of forces to a threshold of radical change? Or can the conservative forces hold the line? The direction the transformation will take depends on the outcome of coalitional politics, the subject of part IV.

COALITIONS IN THE CATHOLIC CHURCH

10

BUREAUCRATIC COUNTERINSURGENCY

IN CATHOLIC HISTORY

R eligious conflict is highly charged because it deals with ultimate reality. In his study of the politics of heresy, Lester Kurtz captures some of the intensity by labeling behavior that promotes doctrinal change *insurgency* and behavior that defends the status quo as *bureaucratic counterinsurgency*.[1] I use the term "progressive coalition" for insurgency and "conservative coalition" for counterinsurgency. As used here, *conservative* and *progressive* are sociological concepts and should be understood in their restrictive meanings. A progressive coalition moves the social order in the direction of new productive forces and away from those that are old and spent. A conservative coalition, in contrast, tries to keep the social order centered in the productive forces that constitute the status quo.

Catholic Coalitions

Contrasting values distinguish conservative from progressive behavior, but a basic agreement lies beneath them. Most of us value productive forces that foster life and support human well-being, at least once we put aside our class, ethnic, gender, or other self-interests. We are motivated by "good" conservative values when we believe that productive forces in the current structures are still vibrant and so we strive to conserve the status quo. With the same "good" intentions, we act out of progressive motives when we see new forces and relations of production generating in the womb of the old social order and we strive to give them birth by opposing the status quo.

In organizational terms, conservatives call for a bureaucratic reproduction of Catholic ministry; progressives seek a charismatic breakthrough. Simply by carrying out their religious commitments, practitioners engage in political behavior. Sometimes they actively support either continuity or change, but most often they only passively support one option. Thus, whether consciously or unwittingly, Catholic leaders and their followers create the two kinds of coalitions common in organizational politics.[2] In the ideal-typical sense, active and passive conflict over the status quo tends to group actors in either conservative or progressive alliances. I thus assume that a conservative coalition exists in the Catholic Church that wants to reproduce the current sacramental, hierarchic, male, celibate priesthood. At the same time, a progressive coalition is striving to muster sufficient charismatic resources to transform the ministerial status quo.

Disagreement over productive forces in an organization like the Catholic Church is resolved by conflict between coalitions. Catholic coalitions are similar to those that operate in other organizational settings but at the same time are unique to organized religion. In religious organizations, progressive coalitions are formed by charismatic leaders who draw mainly on hierophanic power. As defined earlier, the source of hierophanic power is a relationship with ultimate reality or a numinous presence that is unobservable and unverifiable in normal categories of space and time (see chapter 5). Conservative religious coalitions are composed of bureaucratic leaders who rely on hierarchic power—that is, rational-legal bureaucratic authority as defined by Weber (see chapter 3). Neither type, however, exists in its pure form. In every concrete historical situation, religious coalitions exercise domination by drawing on both of these countervailing sources of power. But progressive religious coalitions tend to rely more heavily on charismatic and hierophanic than bureaucratic and hierarchic power. Conservative religious coalitions, on the other hand, build their strength primarily on bureaucracy and hierarchy and only secondarily on charisma and hierophany.

How can we distinguish between conservative, bureaucratic, and priestly behavior on the one hand and progressive, charismatic, and prophetic behavior, on the other? The primary actors in most debates over the status quo of Catholic ministry are pope, curia, bishops, and theologians. The outcome of their debates has ramifications throughout the international Church. Most conflicts at this level are couched in terms of papal primacy versus episcopal collegiality—or uniformity versus pluralism in its various forms. Given the history of centralized power in the Church, behavior that preserves uniformity is a logical way to maintain the status quo; it identifies the conservative, bureaucratic coalition. Behavior that champions pluralism is a logical expression of the desire for progressive change; it typifies the charismatic, prophetic coalition.

For example, the popes in office since the mid–twentieth century have espoused contrasting values about preserving or transforming the status quo. Regarding papal primacy and Romano-European uniformity, John XXIII and Paul VI were mainly progressive or prophetic, while John Paul II is mainly conservative or priestly. In most cases, the Roman curia has been on the side of papal primacy and Roman uniformity, thus forming the backbone of the conservative coalition. The international episcopacy has been split. Some bishops consistently side with the conservative coalition and strongly insist on papal sovereignty because they see it as the guarantee of Romano-European uniformity and male celibate hegemony. Others argue prophetically for episcopal collegiality because they regard it as the mechanism that safeguards pluralism and recognizes the world Church. Theologians tend to support either coalition depending on their ideological leanings. For the most part, local and national conflicts reflect the international debates over papal sovereignty versus episcopal collegiality, or Roman uniformity versus pluralism.

Coalitions in Catholic History

Three recent studies analyze the role of the conservative coalition in shaping and controlling change in the modern Catholic Church. Gene Burns's investigation recounts how loss of the papacy's temporal power, particularly that of the Papal States, led to an unprecedented coalescence of papal control over the Church's spiritual affairs. In the study that inspired the title of this chapter, Kurtz describes the mobilization of the papacy and international episcopacy in an attempt to stamp out modernism in the Church. John Stephens analyzes the impact of conservative Catholic forces on the transition to and breakdown of democracy in Western Europe.

Papal Battle against Liberalism

Burns provides extensive evidence describing papal opposition to liberalism and how such developments furthered the centralizing tendencies of the Vatican.[3] He describes the pronounced but futile attempts of the papacy during the nineteenth and early twentieth centuries to safeguard its longstanding temporal power in the European sociopolitical order. The Catholic Church, mainly through the efforts of the popes, fought a bitter rearguard battle against the modernist impulse toward republicanism, rationalism, freedom of thought, and freedom of religion.[4]

Separation of church and state, nevertheless, proceeded relentlessly and culminated in a series of events between 1864 and 1870. During this period Pius IX issued the infamous *Syllabus of Errors* roundly condemning modern liberalism in all its forms, lost all the Papal States, including Rome, and declared himself a prisoner of the Vatican, where he remained until he died in 1878. The separation of church and state became a *fait accompli*. With no temporal domains to distract them, the popes turned to internal church affairs—especially consolidating internal organizational control of spiritual powers—with renewed zeal. In the process, according to Burns, the popes not only "subordinated sociopolitical issues to more purely religious and moral issues" but also constructed "a new ideological opposition to liberalism."[5] The enormously popular Pius IX had launched the offensive with the declaration of papal infallibility at the First Vatican Council (1869–1870).[6] Each of his successors gradually extended Vatican control to as many aspects of Catholic spiritual life as possible.

Although Burns focuses primarily on the activities of the popes, in some cases he also describes or implies the coalitional support of a wide range of powerful

actors. Cardinals, high-ranking members of the curia, papal nuncios, key members of national episcopacies and politicians, especially in Italy and other predominantly Catholic countries, were all heavily involved in the papacy's efforts
to slow down the spread of liberalism.[7] Furthermore, countervailing forces
within the Church—in favor of the modernizing trends of republicanism, capitalism, and rationalism—existed but were not powerful enough to organize and
prevail against Rome. This was true particularly in the area of rationalism and
modern scholarship.

Bureaucratic Counterinsurgency

Kurtz zeroes in on one aspect of the Church's opposition to liberalism in his
study of the heresy of "modernism."[8] He describes the coalitional forces of ecclesiastical elites who opposed the modernist movement and those of scholarly
elites who propelled it forward. He provides a balanced view of the fierce power
struggle that began in the nineteenth century, climaxed in 1907 when Pius X
condemned modernism as the "synthesis of all heresies," and finally began to
subside only in 1943 when Pius XII issued a personal pronouncement, *Divino
Afflante Spiritu,* lifting the ban on modern scholarship for Catholic theologians
and scripture scholars.

   The conservative Catholic coalition was able to halt the spread of modernism
for over a century by mounting a massive mobilization of its defenses. In this
case the alliance was remarkably monolithic. It was composed of the papacy, the
Roman curia, and practically the entire international episcopacy, all backed by
the full force of their bureaucratic technostructures. Kurtz describes the major
activities of the coalition of bureaucratic counterinsurgents as follows:

> The Holy Office, successor to the Inquisition, placed numerous modernist
> books on the *Index of Prohibited Books.* Rome ruined the careers of Cath-
> olic clergy in order to punish and deter those labeled as modernist
> heretics. An antimodernist oath was administered to all clergy. A secret in-
> ternational organization (the Sapiniere) and diocesan "vigilance commit-
> tees" were instituted to detect and report heresy throughout the Church.
> Countless individuals were harassed and censured, relieved of their posts,
> and stripped of their credentials.[9]

The targets of this impressive campaign were all loyal Catholics who supposedly
had formed an international conspiracy against orthodoxy. Yet, as Kurtz argues
and most scholars agree, the alleged conspiracy "was actually a caricature of the
modernist movement."[10]

   The liberal Catholic modernists were never able to organize a coalitional
force to help forward their views. At most, toward the end of the nineteenth
century, "a loose-knit network of relationships did begin to form . . . among

Catholic intellectuals who were concerned with reconciling the Church and modern culture."[11] The papal reaction labeling the movement a heresy, however, meant that no bishop or any other powerful Catholic, even if sympathetic to democracy, scientific methods, and modern hermeneutics, could openly support the modernist movement and remain in the Church. The politics of heresy had intervened to prevent a liberal coalition from forming.

Insulation against Democracy

The Catholic Church can be passively subject to change simply by ignoring transformations taking place in its ecological niche. Because members and clients live in a changing environment and because organizational boundaries are permeable, in many ways the Church changes gradually and unconsciously. The permeability of the Church, however, does not negate its power to insulate itself and its members from the full force of social conditions in the environment. The ability of actors consciously to adapt their organization to the environment or, conversely, to insulate it from the environment is an assertion of the qualified power model (introduced earlier). Both Burns and Kurtz provide ample evidence that coalitional action within the Church can slow down the impact of powerful environmental forces even for several generations.

In his study of the transition to democracy and its breakdown in some but not other Western European countries, Stephens makes a similar argument about the Catholic Church.[12] In this situation, however, an international papal and episcopal alliance did not act in unison. Instead, local episcopacies and other Catholic groups formed coalitions based on different alliances and ecological circumstances unique to their countries. During the European transition to democracy, the Church hierarchy occasionally opposed civil authoritarianism and advanced the establishment of democratic rule (e.g., in Belgium). For the most part, however, liberal alliances were forged with socialist Catholic political parties and based in working-class Catholic groups, not in the papacy or episcopacy. At the higher echelons, however, the Church maintained a firm stance against most forms of liberalism. For example, during the transition period (before World War I), the papacy opposed Catholic working-class support of democratic reforms. Burns comments on the antiliberal actions of Pius X (1903–1915):

> Pius X wanted hierarchical control over any political group that claimed Catholic inspiration, especially liberal groups; he was more lenient with the semifascistic *Action francaise,* in that its royalism was compatible with his idealization of the ancien regime. . . . Pius X prohibited the reformist *Sillon* in France and the Christian Democrats in Italy, and he prohibited Christian democratic priests from serving on legislatures . . . or, in general, from being active politically.[13]

Stephens cites the Italian Marxist Antonio Gramsci's argument that the capitalist class rules in part because of its reliance on hegemony or ideological domination. In the transition to and breakdown of democracy in western Europe, Catholic coalitions helped produce and maintain ruling-class hegemony in some ways while opposing it in others. Stephens contrasts the role of the Church during the breakdown of democracy in Germany and Austria-Hungary:

> The Catholic Church . . . organized an institutional culture for its believers. Clearly, the class content of this culture was quite different from that of the working-class institutional culture. At one extreme, when the Church was a minority and under attack by the state-building elites, it did insulate its believers from ruling-class hegemony. At the other extreme, where the Church itself allied with the state and the large landed class, the Catholic institutional culture became a conduit for ruling-class ideology.[14]

Stephens shows that the Catholic regions of southern and western Germany were insulated against the ruling-class ideology forged by the pro-Nazi state/Junkers/bourgeoisie bloc. In Austria, however, the Church formed an alliance with the Hapsburg state and the landed oligarchs and became the conduit for ruling-class ideology. Generally speaking, the Catholic Church opposed authoritarian Nazism in Germany and Austria-Hungary, but for different class-based and ideological reasons.

Thus, when the Church tries to influence trends in macropolitics, Catholic coalitions can be selective, choosing partners in local power conflicts depending on ideological and class-based affinities. Ecological conditions affecting organizations, such as minority and majority status of church membership, also play their part in shaping outcomes—no doubt unconsciously and unintentionally. Furthermore, in those countries where democracy broke down, the papacy and episcopacy generally supported either reestablishing authoritarian rule or preserving its own authoritarian privileges. For example, Burns writes: "Pius XI clearly admired Mussolini from early on not only as a man who could guarantee the Church's independence, so Pius XI thought, while unpredictable democratic governments could not, but also as 'a man who lacked the prejudices of the liberal school,' that is, hostility toward the Church."[15] The conservative Catholic coalition in Spain provided similar support for the return to authoritarian rule under Franco.[16]

A consistent pattern emerges from all three studies. Powerful coalitions in the Catholic Church draw their strength mainly from the hierarchical power of papacy and episcopacy. Tightly centralized, they have an impressive array of bureaucratic counterinsurgency resources at their disposal, which they use skillfully. With considerable success, conservative coalitional forces in Catholicism in the twentieth century upheld or reestablished authoritarianism.

Religious Coalitional Power in Action

The ability to form powerful coalitions and shape the course of social change both inside and outside the Church is deeply embedded in the history of Roman Catholicism. Secularization has greatly weakened the possibility of outright church–state alliances that were the focus of most coalitional activity before the twentieth century. Ironically, however, secularization—principally the separation of church and state—has released new energies for tightening centralized control of the Church's internal affairs.

Mechanisms of Coalitional Power

How do coalitions translate their potential power into influence on events creating social change? Stephens identifies three mechanisms: structural determination, conscious instrumentation, and ideological hegemony. Structural determination involves constraints embedded in social networks and organizational patterns of behavior. Conscious instrumentation is direct intervention through funding, legislation, political pressure, and the like. Ideological hegemony is domination by shaping the beliefs and values of political actors.

The influence of the conservative papal coalition is structurally determined: it takes the form of centralization of power in Rome. The modern form of papal centralization was fashioned with the disputed doctrine of infallibility as its cornerstone.[17] Its progress was fostered by the loss of the papacy's temporal powers and fomented by an unprecedented personality cult of the pope made possible by advances in transportation and media technology.[18] Similarly, given the relentless development of papal centralization over the last century, progressive coalition formation in Catholicism faces severe structural constraints. Between the mid–nineteenth and mid–twentieth centuries, the balance of power in the Church changed radically. It became extremely difficult, if not impossible, for any coalition to exercise power in opposition to the personal wishes of the pope. Personal loyalty to the pope became a twentieth-century Catholic fetish.[19] Thus, the power of a conservative Catholic coalition is exercised through centralization of power in the papacy, a mechanism that not only has its roots in the nineteenth century but is also deeply embedded in the structure of ministry. The more closely tied to the papacy, the more powerful the coalition.

Along with structural determination, coalitions employ direct intervention and ideological hegemony to translate potential power into real influence. Thus to be effective, Catholic coalitions not only can utilize the centralized structure of the papacy but also can use the politics of heresy, bureaucratic counterinsurgency, and other tactics involving social isolation. The complex relationship between these tactics and coalition formation in organized religion bears closer examination. Religious corporate groups use the strategy of insulation and the politics of heresy to protect not only their structural but also their phenomenological or hierophanic core (chapter 5). Ostensibly they are used to safeguard the foundational faith-events, but covertly insulation and heresy are mechanisms for the centralization of power.

Coalition, Hierarchy, and Hierophany

Dual centralizing tendencies—hierophanic and hierarchic—are fundamental to organized religion. A believing community is formed to preserve the definitiveness of cosmogonic faith-events, that is, hierophanic events that provide the ground of personal and social being and the source of meaning and value in life. Destroying the cosmogonic myth constructed by the community is destroying the sacred cosmos, the foundation of reality. Maintaining the myth, however, is accomplished at the cost of routinization of charisma and institutionalization of hierophany. As the external expressions of faith-events are routinized by the believing community, its institutional structures become more differentiated. Orthodox teachings, canonical scriptures, and ordained officials emerge as embodiments or guardians of the definitive faith-events, and so, paradoxically, all these forms serve as both hierophanic and hierarchic centralizing mechanisms.

To survive in its sociocultural environment, a religious movement must find a supportive niche—it must adapt to its environment. Routinization of charisma involves adjusting the external expressions of the cosmogonic faith-events to the resources available in the environment. Unless the religious group accommodates well enough to recruit new members and select and retain other organizational resources, it cannot survive. In the course of institutionalization, the original faith-events and their message of ultimate meaning and value are not only routinized and formalized but also often diluted, desiccated, and compromised. Under certain conditions, therefore, reform movements develop to protest the overaccommodations. Reformers claim they are trying to keep the corporate group faithful to the original message. Elite defenders of the status quo insist on their version of orthodoxy and often use social insulation and accusation of heresy as mechanisms of control against the insurgents. The higher strata, whose responsibility is to guard the definitive myth system, try to insulate from error not only themselves but also those lower-level participants whom they can influence or dominate. Branding the reformers heretics is an extreme insulating measure whose origins and consequences are rooted in social conflict, as Kurtz demonstrates in his anatomy of the modernist heresy. Heretics are expelled from the community, thus insulating the remaining members from the deleterious effects of the attempted heretical reforms.

Social insulation and heresy are, therefore, primarily mechanisms that conservative coalitions use for protecting the status quo, which they believe is a faithful expression of definitive faith-events. As Kurtz points out, social conflict surrounding a heresy usually has the positive effect of redefining orthodoxy in more intelligible and, for many, more acceptable language. In countering the insulation strategies of institutional elites, charismatic coalitions can open the believing community to the wider society through the incorporation of new modes of expressing the definitive faith-events.

Conclusion

The twentieth century began in bitter conflict between the champions of authoritarianism and liberalism. With the Church's temporal power gone, one of the bitterest struggles was between science and religion, which the conservative Catholic coalition resolved by extreme measures. Insurgents were labeled heretics, scholarly careers destroyed, and key actors excommunicated. The papacy and episcopacy successfully insulated themselves and many of the faithful from the progress of modern science through forms of bureaucratic counterinsurgency: book censorship, loyalty oaths, antimodernist seminary curricula, and international and local vigilance committees. At the dawn of a new century, the modernist heresy is an embarrassment to most Catholics, both high- and low-level participants.[20] Kurtz is correct in his observation that "one generation's heresy is the next generation's orthodoxy."

On the face of it, the major crisis facing Roman Catholicism in the current generation appears to be a strictly internal issue. A closer examination, however, reveals that it touches the very core of the Church, with ramifications for society in general. Since Christianity is the world's largest organized religion and Catholicism the largest body in Christianity, a crisis affecting the core structures of Catholicism cannot help but spill over into the wider society. The controversy centers on the structure of ministry and the ideological apparatus maintaining it. The centrality of ministry in the organizational structure of the Catholic Church is strongly underscored by theologians. In his magisterial work *Ministry to Word and Sacrament,* Bernard Cooke insists: "Acquiring more accurate understanding of Christian ministry is not an incidental item on the agenda of the Church today; it is basic to everything Christianity claims to be and attempts to do. In a world of staggering problems and 'mind-blowing' potential, it would be foolish to waste time and energy on what is not the genuine ministerial role of the Church."[21] The real bone of contention for Catholic coalitions today is the form of ministry in the Church.

I assert that the priest shortage and six other transformational forces have increased in strength since the Second Vatican Council, making it impossible for the Church's environmental niche to support much longer the status quo of Catholic ministry. As more and more Catholic leaders become aware of the forces for change and their consequences, particularly the mounting conflict that surrounds them and its link to antipatriarchy, the probability that a coalition for change will form increases. "Become aware" means not only consciousness-raising—though that is the first step—but also learning the skills of how to use ambivalent cultural symbols to move behavior and structure in the direction of one's values. The direction of the change, therefore, depends on the religious values and the personal, gender, and class interests of leaders who seize the historical moment.

If the values and interests of the dominant coalition continue to support status quo, it will continue to be reproduced. If the challenging group successfully becomes the new dominant coalition, an organizational breakthrough will ensue. In the next chapter, I describe how the conservative coalition is currently engaging in bureaucratic counterinsurgency to preserve the status quo of Catholic ministry.

11

PRIESTLY COALITION

The decisive aspect here . . . is the *leveling of the governed* in face of the governing and bureaucratically articulated group. . . . In the Catholic Church . . . all independent local intermediary powers were eliminated. . . . The transformation of these local powers into pure functionaries of the central authority . . . was based on the political party organization of Catholicism.

Max Weber, *Economy and Society*

Authoritarian leaders are . . . comfortable with unambiguous concrete faith, and ill at ease with mystery, the central identifying component of all true religion. . . . That is why such leaders possess so little spiritual authority.

Eugene C. Kennedy, *Tomorrow's Catholics, Yesterday's Church*

Leadership in religious coalitions is either priestly or prophetic. Historically, the main function of a priest is to solemnize an established social order. The role of the prophet, in contrast, is to urge believers to change their attitudes and behavior. A priestly coalition relies primarily on hierarchic and bureaucratic forms of power. It is dedicated to leveling opposition and conserving the status quo.[1] A prophetic coalition draws mainly from hierophanic and charismatic forms of power. It is bent on breaking through old organizational structures to establish something new. Hierarchic power leads to authoritarian leadership characterized by permanence and taken-for-granted legitimacy. Hierophanic power generates spiritual authority, characterized by instability and ambiguity.

Although priests try to preserve and prophets try to change the status quo, both believe they are acting in the name of God. Symbolically, both priest and prophet are the human embodiment of divine action. The prophet literally speaks for God, particularly in uttering the word that creates something new. The priest is the divine caretaker, preserving and celebrating what God has wrought. Thus, by labeling one type of coalition priestly and the other prophetic, I call attention to their religious functions. Though always in tension, both coalitions are essential for the well-being of religious organizations.

For the most part, the priestly coalition dominates organized religion. As we have seen, the papacy lies at the center of the dominant priestly coalition within

Roman Catholicism. Indeed, one of the major documents of the Second Vatican Council reiterates what has been unquestioned for many centuries: The major aim of the priestly coalition is to ensure that the pope "is the subject of supreme and full power over the universal Church" (*Lumen Gentium,* no. 22).[2] Historically, however, local bishops exercised extensive power and were by no means "pure functionaries of the central authority."[3] The same Council document asserts that the college of bishops participates in the exercise of "supreme and full power," thus grounding the structures of unity in the pluralism of local churches (*Lumen Gentium,* nos. 22–23). Nevertheless, the tension in local–universal church relations has been resolved in favor of papal concentration of power ever since the early Middle Ages.

Eliminating the intermediary power of bishops and their local churches "was begun by Gregory VII and continued through the Council of Trent, the [First] Vatican Council, and it was completed by the edicts of Pius X."[4] The nature of papal power changed dramatically during the millennium begun by Gregory and ended by Pius X. The efforts of Gregory VII (d. 1085) and the Council of Trent (1545–1563) were directed more toward the external political economic affairs of society than to the internal spiritual concerns of the Church. But, as I showed in the previous chapter, after the de facto separation of church and state in the late nineteenth century, Rome launched pronounced and unprecedented efforts to concentrate not temporal but spiritual power in the papacy.

The strength of the conservative coalition is structurally determined by the centralized papacy. To bolster its own structurally based power, the current papacy is closely allied with the Roman curia, certain conservative segments of national hierarchies, and key theologians. In addition, such organized lay groups as *Opus Dei, Comunione e Liberazione,* and the Knights of Malta play an important role in the papal coalition.[5] Thus, as the new millennium dawns, the papal coalition is dominant, priestly, conservative—and formidable. This is exemplified in the aborted reforms of the Roman curia, growing pains of the newly established Synod of Bishops, retrenchment in the appointment and promotion of bishops, and constraints on the autonomy of bishops, scholars, lower clergy, and nuns.

Reforming the Curia

Although awesome personal power resides in the papacy, the pope—even when he wants to—never stands alone. The Roman curia is the organizational extension of the papal office. It reinforces the papacy as a structural mechanism constraining the outcome of coalitional power. Since its establishment in the sixteenth century, the curia has gradually acquired a life of its own. Recently, popes began to see that the tail was wagging the dog. Pius X tinkered with some minor restructuring in 1908, but it was not until the Second Vatican Council (*Christus*

Dominus, nos. 9, 11) and the apostolic constitution *Regimini Ecclesiae* in 1967 that the curia was subjected to serious and far-reaching reform.[6]

Paul VI presided over the early attempts to carry out the decrees of the Second Vatican Council. He had the advantage of being former Vatican secretary of state and so knew the Roman curia's intricate workings from the inside. Responding to the cries of many bishops at the Second Vatican Council, the reforms called for by Paul VI in *Regimini Ecclesiae* touched the heavy-handed centralization, overelaborated specialization, careerism, parochialism, and other severe problems plaguing the curia. According to Peter Hebblethwaite, through his bold reforms "Paul VI 'liberated the papacy' from the heavy downdrag of the curia," earned himself "the title of 'second founder of the curia' and forged an instrument to realize the implications of Vatican II."[7]

This restructuring of the curia was hailed as an auspicious beginning. Dismantling the rigid centralized structures that had developed over the centuries, however, was easier said than done. The sweeping reforms were resisted by career bureaucrats and then effectively thwarted by John Paul II, who succeeded Paul VI in 1978 (discounting the month-long interim reign of John Paul I). Hebblethwaite describes how the current pope, in his 1988 Apostolic Constitution *Pastor Bonus,* restored key curial procedures to their pre–Second Vatican Council conditions. This document became a major part of the pope's so-called Restoration Program.[8] A major "restoration" of *Pastor Bonus* was to reinstate centralized control by making all other offices in the curia subject to the Congregation for the Doctrine of the Faith (CDF), whose head is Cardinal Josef Ratzinger.[9] Another reform called for bishops to submit themselves to extensive curial inspection during their required quinquennial *ad limina* visits to Rome, inspections that could now be controlled by Cardinal Ratzinger and the CDF.

Thus, John XXIII tried to get around the curia by calling a council, Paul VI to reform it by decree, and John Paul II to restore it as a mechanism of centralized papal control. Enfolding the curia in the tight control of the papacy and its chief agent, Cardinal Ratzinger, appears to have been a key part of Pope John Paul's strategy to insulate the episcopal elite from suspicious and harmful changes in the environment.

Social Insulation and the Synod of Bishops

According to Stephens, one of the strategies in coalitional politics is to insulate organizational members against reform by means of ideological domination.[10] Insulation against a changing environment is thickest at the top of an organization, for two reasons. First, the ability to insulate is directly related to the size and diversity of the group to be protected. Second, scarce insulating resources will be used to safeguard the organization's most important and powerful elements. Given the diffusion of modern technology and education, it is increasingly difficult to insulate a billion lay members of the Catholic Church scattered across continents, cultures, and communication networks. It may be feasible, however, to shield the relatively small and homogeneous episcopal elite from undesirable encroachments of a perceived hostile environment. Moreover, since bishops enjoy the fullness of priestly power along with extensive bureaucratic means of domination and control, insulating them can have trickle-down effects on the lower clergy and laity. Thus, examining efforts of the papal alliance to maintain ideological domination over Catholic ministry, particularly those aimed at bishops, provides a way of assessing the strength and scope of the conservative coalition.

One of the few structural innovations stemming from the Second Vatican Council was the permanent establishment of the Synod of Bishops. It was to meet every three years as a forum for elected bishop-delegates to "inform and give advice" to the pope (see *Apostolica Sollicitudo*).[11] Since the Second Vatican Council, nine ordinary and three extraordinary synods have been called, the first in 1967 and the last in 1994. All dealt with issues germane to the gathering crisis in Catholic ministry. Given the charged nature of the times, the new Synod of Bishops bristled with potential and ambiguity. Depending on who gained control, it could strengthen either the entrenched conservative coalition or the newly emerging and fragile progressive coalition. The main contenders for dominating the synod were the pope, the Roman curia, conservative or progressive bishops, liberal theologians, or some combination of these groups. During and after the Second Vatican Council, conservative bishops enjoyed the strong assistance of the Roman curia. Progressive bishops had come away from the Council allied with liberal theologians who significantly shaped most council pronouncements. The role of the papacy, however, had become ambiguous.

Throughout the twentieth century the papacy consistently created a conservative coalition, allying itself with the curia, large segments of the episcopacy, and the majority of theologians. But John XXIII (1958–1963), by calling for *aggiornamento* (an updating of the Church) through an ecumenical council, had transformed the papacy into a wild card. Formerly part of the conservative coalition, papal power could now be played either way. Paul VI (1963–1978) embodied this ambivalence. He accepted the Johannine mantle of *aggiornamento* with considerable reluctance and not a little courage.

For the most part, Catholics are not surprised when papal pronouncements are used as mechanisms of social insulation. So progressive bishops suggested that the Synod of Bishops might serve as an opening in the thick walls protecting the papacy from the changing environment; it might help the pope carry out the council's mandates. Ideally, the synod would put the pope in contact with the unique problems facing local churches. Conservative bishops, particularly cardinals and bishops who were members of the curia, saw it in a different light: The synod could become an even more effective mechanism of social insulation.

Not surprisingly, the outcomes have been mixed. According to Hebblethwaite, the four synods celebrated under the auspices of Paul VI were genuine though ambivalent attempts at collegiality.[12] Those held under John Paul II were thinly veiled attempts to reinforce papal supremacy.

Synods under Paul VI

Barely off the drawing board, the synod became the object of intense debate. To outsiders it may seem an arcane struggle, but according to ecclesiologists, "it concerns the very nature of the post-conciliar Church. Is it to be a monarchical Church in continuity with Vatican I or a collegial Church in continuity with Vatican II?"[13] Created by Paul VI as a compromise to appease the world's progressive bishops yet not offend the Roman curia, the synod came to embody the ambivalence of the times. While he would only allow it to be an advisory body "immediately subject to the Roman pontiff" (*Apostolica Sollicitudo,* no. 3), the pope acknowledged it could be granted increased powers later since "like all institutions, [it] can be still more perfected with the passage of time."[14]

In the spirit of John XXIII, Paul VI cautiously tried to move the Synod of Bishops toward updating the Church. His waffling, however, brought hope and despair to liberals and conservatives alike. For those who favored greater collegiality, hope marked the first synod convened in 1967. The delegates flexed their muscles by rejecting an offensive document "On Dangerous Modern Opinions" prepared by the curialist Cardinal Ottaviani and by electing their own leaders to draft a new one. Further, the pope welcomed the synod's help in getting the extensive liturgical reforms mandated by the council off the ground. But the tide quickly turned. Liberals swapped their short-lived hope for the conservatives' earlier despair. The first meeting was followed by three extremely controversial encyclicals, all issued by Paul VI *without* collegial input from the new Synod of Bishops: a letter on celibacy in 1967, one on birth control in 1968, and another on the papal diplomatic service in 1969. Conservatives were vindicated.

Humanae Vitae, the 1968 encyclical reasserting the absolute prohibition of "artificial" birth control, drew such an intense reaction that Paul VI convoked the Extraordinary Synod of 1969 to deal with the conflict.[15] The outcome this time was the establishment of a permanent synod council to set agendas for future synods, which took this key responsibility away from the conservative Roman curia. It also put some collegial teeth in the synodal proceedings. Even though the encyclical had reinforced the conservative teaching on birth control, the structural reform pendulum was swinging back to the progressive side.

Ambivalence, ambiguity, and outright contradiction marked the 1971 synod. It was convoked to deal with the growing problems of the priesthood, which had received minimal attention at the Second Vatican Council. In the council's aftermath, many countries were witnessing massive resignations of young priests along with dwindling ordinations. In other ways, however, the Church was still riding the crest of a wave of enthusiasm created by the Second Vatican Council, so the 1971 synod was being watched with great interest. It was even preceded by some grassroots consultation; several national hierarchies commissioned comprehensive studies and convened conferences on the state of the priesthood.[16]

Although the topic was not officially scheduled for discussion, an impassioned debate over compulsory celibacy ensued and practically dominated the synod. Edward Schillebeeckx, one of the *periti* (experts) in attendance, describes the bishops' behavior in terms of ambivalence over their loyalty to the celibacy tradition and their pastoral sensitivities about the priest shortage.[17] Loyalty to tradition won out. As a result, the statement favoring the ordination of married men—if the needs of the faithful warranted it and the pope approved–failed by a vote of 87 for and 107 against. A majority of the *elected* delegates, however, were in favor of the ordination of married men. Opposition came more from the delegates who were members of the curia and appointed by the pope.[18] The results were ambiguous at best.

Ambivalence and ambiguity were followed by contradiction. The pope chose to ignore and even contradict the tenor of advice contained in the voting. At the synod's closing, Paul VI said, "From your discussions it emerges that the bishops of the entire Catholic world want to keep integrally this absolute gift by which the priest consecrates himself to God; a not negligible part of this gift—in the Latin Church—is consecrated celibacy."[19] Reflecting the dismay of the elected majority who had pleaded for allowing priests to marry, Hebblethwaite comments on the speech: "There was not a word about the ordination of married men. This raised the question: if the Synod of Bishops cannot put a question on the Church's agenda, who can?"[20]

It is also clear from Schillebeeckx's extensive analysis of synod speeches that all the bishops definitely did *not* agree on an absolute prohibition of married priests. He reports that a veritable *cri de coeur* arose from pastorally minded bishops who made "passionate pleas" for the ordination of married men. Although officially the synod's agenda was much broader, "in fact, tacitly this was the issue for the whole of the synod—whether the law of celibacy should be reaffirmed or 'opened up.'"[21]

Failure to address honestly the celibacy issue was symptomatic of a greater failure. The synod was incapable of affirming the possibility of pluralistic solutions to the complex problems facing a worldwide Church. If some bishops' conferences felt the desperate need for ordaining married men and others did not, why not allow different solutions depending on local needs? Schillebeeckx notes: "The fact that the Synod was not brave enough to take account of this possibility may perhaps be described in subsequent history as the 'great refusal' which explains its failure."[22]

In effect, the next synod, held in 1974, was Paul's last. (He convened the 1977

Synod on Catechesis but it was brought to conclusion after his death.) The pronouncement coming from the 1974 Synod, *Evangelii Nuntiandi,* is considered by some the best synodal document produced so far. Its topic is evangelization in the modern world and its tone creative and tolerant of local developments, particularly liberation theology. Bühlmann notes that procedures at this synod reflected genuine collegiality at work: "Bishops and theologians of the Third World took over the leadership in the 1974 Synod. It was they who raised the burning issues that finally went into *Evangelii Nuntiandi.*"[23] Hebblethwaite agrees with Bühlmann:

> For here was a text that was at once synodal and papal, and therefore deeply collegial. The Synod provided the raw experience and many of the insights, while Paul VI articulated them using his 'charism of discernment'. . . . [*Evangelii Nuntiandi*] is very different in tone and content from *Ecclesiam Suam,* Paul's first encyclical. If he went on learning throughout his pontificate, this was largely because of the Synod.[24]

Paul VI at least managed to keep the progressive agenda alive. His successor, in contrast, attempted to turn back the tide permanently. For John Paul II, the synod was to be a mechanism of ideological hegemony at the service of papal centralization.

Synods under John Paul II

John Paul's pattern for the Synod of Bishops was to use it as a forum for airing his personal worries and reinforcing traditional conservative doctrine. The 1980 synod addressed Christian marriage and restated the prohibition against birth control from *Humanae Vitae.* In 1983, the topic was the Sacrament of Reconciliation; the resulting pronouncements insisted on individual confession and downplayed "general absolution." The Extraordinary Synod of 1985 was convoked to review programs launched by the Second Vatican Council. Many observers, however, saw it as an attempt by the Vatican to correct "excesses" in the interpretations of the council teachings such as lay preaching, clergy in politics, and discussions of women's ordination.[25] Preparation for the synod was perfunctory, the agenda was preset by Rome, and little of substantive value emerged other than cautionary pronouncements. The topic of the 1987 synod was the role of the laity, a potentially progressive issue. It dealt mainly, however, with suspicious lay ministries, the need to maintain a clear-cut distinction between ordained and lay ministries, and the need to encourage conservative lay groups such as *Comunione e Liberazione* and *Opus Dei.* A further irony of the 1987 synod was that, despite the extensive prior "consultation" of laypeople, the views of the faithful were introduced at the synod and then totally ignored.

The 1990 synod was hurriedly called to deal with priest formation programs, another potentially critical topic. Once again the curia preset the agenda. It was decidedly lackluster and allowed for no serious preparation by bishop-delegates. The sessions were also dominated by curialists, particularly Cardinal Ratzinger. It was declared a "waste of time" by many bishop-delegates. Discussion of celibacy, for example, was expressly and strictly proscribed. Nevertheless, during the sessions the Brazilian bishop Valfredo Tepe did manage to plead for permission to ordain married men. A small number of other bishops supported his efforts, but the majority acquiesced to Vatican pressure, and the issue was tabled. Pronouncements of the synod called for more traditional forms of seminary training that emphasized the unique necessity of ordained priesthood and the need for separation between priests and the nonordained.

The 1994 Synod on Religious Life was more of the same. Officially entitled "The Consecrated Life and Its Role in the Church and in the World," the ninth Synod of Bishops was attended by 244 bishops (i.e., voting members), a group of listeners (*auditores,* 51 of whom were women), and a group of helpers (*adjutores,* 20 of whom were women).[26] Sister Doris Gottemoeller, president of the U.S. Leadership Conference of Women Religious, who was allowed to speak but not vote, summed up the reaction of many women who lead the "consecrated life." Critical of the "message" from the synod, she wrote that the rhetoric about women's value in the Church "is meaningless unless they put some more teeth into it." She continued: "You would never know from reading this [message] that there was any struggle over an issue, that there was any new insight, that there was any complexity over anything, that there were any unresolved questions."[27] Once again, the document issued after the synod represented a consensus agreeable to the pope: no struggle, no new insight, no complexity, no more questions.

The fourth Extraordinary Synod met in 1994 to handle the problems of Africa's 95 million Catholics. Significantly, it was held in Rome, to which some three hundred African bishops dutifully traveled. The problems they brought for discussion were monumental: dire poverty, bloody wars, rapid growth in church membership, and cultural contradictions over African marriage traditions, priestly celibacy, and irrelevant sacramental rituals.[28] The solutions, however, were mundane and predictable. The Church must "take deeper root in the African culture," but there is to be no change in any essentials: African marriage traditions must yield to European norms, priests must be celibate, and the matter and form of the sacraments must be recognizable to Europeans.[29] The hopes of a Namibian bishop, Bonifatius Haushiku, and many like-minded colleagues were gently set aside. Bishop Haushiku said: "Yes, our Namibian African people have accepted Christ. But this Christ walks too much among them in a European garment. People have made some progress in Africanizing the liturgy. . . . But this kind of inculturation must be carried deeper than just music, drums, and clapping of hands."[30] Not much hand-clapping celebrated the accomplishments of the African synod.

Hebblethwaite's overall evaluation of the short history of the Synod of Bishops rings true:

> Thanks to Paul VI's compromises, the Synod had always been somewhat ambivalent: was it the organ of the bishops or the Pope? Of course, a dialectic was involved which we have seen at work in the Synods of Paul VI, and the institution could be said to have grown towards maturity in his pontificate. But in the pontificate of John Paul II, one-half of the dialectic seems to be suppressed, and the Synod became simply the organ of the Pope.[31]

Conceived in compromise and born in ambivalence, the Synod of Bishops may be maturing into another mechanism of social insulation protecting clerical elites from the modern world.

Appointment and Promotion of Bishops

Another primary insulating mechanism available to the papal coalition is the selection and promotion of bishops, a prerogative that modern popes try to control as completely as possible. Indisputably, at least since the early Middle Ages, the pope has the sole right to appoint bishops (canon 377, 1).[32] A wide range of participation in the selection process, however, has been the rule, even after the papacy appropriated exclusive appointment powers.[33] Until recently, the local church has played a major consultative role, with Rome choosing one of three candidates submitted by a diocese. John Paul II, however, has made concerted efforts to dismantle even this participatory tradition.[34]

In the first 15 years of his pontificate (1978–1994), John Paul appointed more than 1,600 bishops, almost three-fourths of the world's active bishops. Appointing new bishops from among those priests who conform closely to his model of the Church allows the pope to insulate himself and the existing episcopacy from the changing environment and the immediate impact of potential conflict. According to Vatican officials in charge of screening candidates for the episcopacy, the most important general criterion applied is orthodoxy.[35] Orthodoxy, of course, is determined by the degree of loyalty to the Holy See and the pope's personal version of Catholic doctrine. Thus, along with ensuring adherence to the teaching of *Humanae Vitae* against birth control, bishop-candidates are routinely probed for their firm opposition to the ordination of women and married men. Maintaining the status quo on sexual morality and Catholic ministry is uppermost among the criteria of orthodoxy. The pope also reminds bishops regularly of these priorities, earning the reputation among bishops of being, in Archbishop John Roach's words, "a stern pontiff bent on taking us to task."[36] For example, in 1983 during their *ad limina* visit to Rome required of bishops every five years, John Paul II told the U.S. bishops: "A bishop must give proof of his pastoral ability and leadership by withdrawing all support from individuals or groups who in the name of progress, justice or compassion, or for any other alleged reason, promote the ordination of women to the priesthood."[37]

Carefully selecting and promoting those men who support male celibate hegemony in the ministry is one part of the insulatory strategy of the current papacy. Other selection and promotion criteria are geared to maintaining a conservative authoritarian hierarchy: ties with *Opus Dei,* elite landowners, and nobility and the upper class in general. A pattern of ideological hegemony and authoritarian control emerges from recent examples of episcopal appointments.

In his analysis of the conservative reaction to the Second Vatican Council, Michael Walsh provides a résumé of events surrounding the appointment of bishops in Latin America:

> From as early as 1971 Roman appointment to bishoprics in Latin America, as they become vacant, have reflected a choice of clergy who can be identified as being in the conservative tradition. The complexion of Bishops Conferences is changing across the continent—quite swiftly in Peru, for example, with a relatively small number of bishops; more slowly, but inexorably, in the much more radical Brazil, which has the world's largest conference of bishops. . . . An increasing number of bishops have been chosen from among Opus clergy, and of clergy sympathetic to Opus, for sees in Latin America and elsewhere.[38]

Although most of the sources documenting the papal strategy of shaping a conservative episcopacy are journalistic, they paint a story consistent with Walsh's evaluation. For example, while he served as papal nuncio to Chile, Bishop Angelo Sodano (now Vatican secretary of state) was recognized as an authoritarian servant of the pope's wishes in appointing bishops. "He was particularly effective in shifting the balance inside the bishops' conference with a series of conservative nominations."[39] Sodano's choices were generally better-educated, upperclass nominees with traditional theological leanings.

Media reports indicate that only a few bishops sympathetic to the "Church of the poor" are left in Mexico. A priest-informant told a journalist: "Since the arrival of the apostolic delegate 12 years ago, 35 new bishops have been named. Most of them have two things in common: They are enemies of liberation theology and have strong relationships with the rich and the government." During the pope's 1990 visit to Mexico, Bishop Samuel Ruiz of San Cristóbal de las Casas, Chiapas, one of the few remaining advocates of the "preferential option for the poor," was attacked in the national press by ranchers. They claimed his "diocese was full of 'political clergy' who supported land reforms that violated landowners' inherent rights."[40]

One of the most lamented examples of trying to turn back the liberal tide involved the world-renowned and revered champion of equality and social justice

Archbishop Dom Helder Camara, the so-called Red Bishop of Recife, Brazil. On his retirement he was replaced by an equally well-credentialed archconservative, Archbishop Jose Cardoso Sobrinho. The appointment was followed by shock and dismay as Dom Helder's progressive reforms were quickly dismantled.[41]

The current pope is now revoking historical agreements that formally granted local churches the privilege to participate in the selection of candidates for episcopal appointment. For example, the ancient rights to participation were rescinded for the Archdiocese of Salzburg, eliciting a loud cry of protest. John Paul appointed a new archbishop there "who prefers to say Mass with his back to the people," a custom rendered obsolete by liturgical reforms of the Second Vatican Council.[42] In a similar vein, the Diocese of Coire, Switzerland, continues to be in "open rebellion against Wolfgang Haas, imposed as bishop in 1980. But the Pope refuses to reconsider this extremely unpopular appointment, even after a personal appeal by the president of the Swiss bishops' conference."[43] In a comparable situation, the priests of Bacolod in the Philippines have appealed the naming of a bishop "linked to members of the upper bourgeoisie known for their continual undermining of our pastoral efforts."[44] That appeal, too, goes unheeded in Rome. The once progressive Dutch hierarchy has been systematically transformed into one of the most conservative bodies in Europe through the appointments and promotions of John Paul II. Likewise, the conservative nature of the Spanish hierarchy was greatly reinforced by elevating the notoriously right-wing *Opus Dei* movement to the status of a personal prelature of the pope, a move without precedent. Similar examples of insulation through selection and promotion of bishops abound.

Autonomy of Bishops

Another mechanism of power and influence available to the papal coalition is harassment of boat-rockers in the episcopacy. Three celebrated cases of this form of direct intervention involve two U.S. prelates, the archbishops Hunthausen and Weakland, and a French bishop, Jacques Gaillot.[45]

The retired archbishop Raymond Hunthausen of Seattle had a reputation for espousing a life of simplicity and poverty while promoting the pastoral care of the disenfranchised in the Church, among them women, resigned priests, and homosexuals. He was a much-admired leader in the American hierarchy who seemed to ignore Roman rigidities when they conflicted with his notions of sound pastoral care. In a tradition-shattering reaction, the papacy stripped Hunthausen of key decision-making powers by appointing Bishop Donald Wuerl, a carefully chosen conservative, as auxiliary bishop.[46] The new auxiliary bishop was given responsibility for decision-making in sensitive areas, which had the effect of declaring Hunthausen incompetent. Rome communicated that Hunthausen was to delegate to Wuerl power over the marriage tribunal, liturgy,

priestly formation, former priests, medical ethics, and ministry to homosexuals—
all areas that have direct or indirect bearing on the male, celibate, sacramental,
and hierarchical power of the priesthood.

Reaction was strongly negative and volatile. Initially, U.S. bishops did not act
decisively as a body, although their own prerogatives were threatened by the
papal attack on one of their number. A compromise solution was reached after
a commission composed of Cardinals Bernardin of Chicago and O'Connor of
New York and Archbishop Quinn of San Francisco investigated the situation.
Bishop Wuerl's appointment was rescinded, and Bishop Thomas Murphy, who
shared many of Hunthausen's beliefs and values, was named as coadjutor.
Hunthausen's full authority was restored, and the new appointee took on responsibilities traditionally granted a coadjutor archbishop.

Nine years later, the Vatican tried this extreme measure again: firing a bishop
who challenges its views. After repeated warnings that his attitudes on homosexuality, abortion, the use of condoms, and a married clergy were not in keeping
with Rome's position, Bishop Jacques Gaillot of Evreux, Normandy, was relieved
of his duties by the Vatican. He "retains his title but no longer has any churches
or parishioners under his jurisdiction."[47] The French bishops' conference has
taken no official action, but several French bishops, Catholic lay groups, and the
media have protested loudly.[48] Once again, the incident threatens the canonical
prerogatives of bishops and shatters tradition. If Bishop Gaillot lacks the support
that Archbishop Hunthausen received from his episcopal colleagues, Rome's
show of power might work this time.

Another incident involves the harassment of Archbishop Rembert Weakland
of Milwaukee, who had gained the Vatican's attention by participating in "listening sessions" on the abortion issue.[49] Prior to writing a pastoral letter on the
topic, he and his staff listened to Catholic women relate their views on birthing
and rearing children. Weakland announced that he had gained important insights and recommended more listening on the part of the magisterium. In
Rome, Weakland's recommendation to listen to women's views was considered
superfluous, if not threatening to the official teaching on abortion. The listening
sessions were also part of a consistent policy Weakland follows in actively supporting the feminist movement.

One of Rome's reactions to Weakland's controversial activities was refusal to
allow the University of Fribourg in Switzerland to grant him an honorary degree. The Vatican declared the archbishop an unacceptable recipient of honors
from a Catholic university because his statements about abortion had caused
"a great deal of confusion among the faithful."[50] The Vatican snub, as it was
called, was not only humiliating but appeared to be part of a systematic harassment effort. Denying Milwaukee's archbishop the honorary degree was followed by the appointment of a "watchdog" to the vacant see of a neighboring
Wisconsin diocese. According to observers, Robert Banks, the new bishop of

Green Bay, "worked closely with Boston's Cardinal Bernard Law, who is widely viewed as the American bishop with the closest ties to Rome. 'Now whenever the bishops of Wisconsin get together, they won't be talking as freely,' one source said, referring to Bank's presence at conferences. 'The feeling will be there that whatever they say will be reported back'"[51]

A particularly thorny intervention in the autonomous jurisdiction of local bishops involves the seminary formation of priest candidates. It is difficult for the Vatican to interfere directly in the day-to-day operations of local seminaries, if only because of their sheer number. But controlling priest formation programs in particularly threatening situations can be handled through episcopal appointments. Hence, the appointment of Dom Helder Camara's successor in Recife, Brazil, was immediately followed by a seminary closing. The seminary in Recife and those in many other Brazilian dioceses have been noted for their open informal structures, emphasis on liberation theology, and attempts to reduce the gap between seminarians and laity. The new bishop closed the "open seminary," dismissed the faculty, and began to structure a new program following strict Vatican guidelines.[52]

Correcting local "excesses" in seminary training through episcopal appointments is a slow process, but other methods may be used. The Vatican recently devised an evaluation program in which a committee visits each seminary, reviews its curriculum and programs, and makes recommendations for improvement.[53] Although Rome provides guidelines for the evaluation, the national hierarchies appoint the review committees. Thus, all the elements of social conflict are present. Little is known about the success or failure of the evaluation program. It warrants careful research, however, since it has the potential for becoming a bureaucratic mechanism of insulation and control. Furthermore, coalition activity would be involved in the appointment of the committees, the reaction of seminary officials, and the use of information and recommendations.

Autonomy of Scholars

Persecution of those who veer from official Vatican policy is used not only to insulate the episcopacy from the changing world but also to safeguard orthodoxy against the dissent of Catholic theologians. Among the most celebrated cases of scholar harassment was the Vatican censure of the internationally renowned theologian Father Hans Küng.[54] In 1979, Küng was barred from his chair of dogma and ecumenical theology at the State University in Tübingen for his criticism of ecclesiastical authority, especially regarding the dogma of infallibility. Within days after the Sacred Congregation for the Doctrine of the Faith pronounced against him, theologians from the United States and Spain, as well as Küng's own bishop, came to his defense. The Vatican censure stood, nonetheless.

More recently and closer to home, in 1990 the moral theologian Father

Charles Curran was ousted from his tenured position at the Catholic University of America.[55] Considered a moderate theologian by most colleagues, Curran was nevertheless expelled from the university because his teachings on birth control, premarital sex, and masturbation depart from strict Vatican doctrine. Once again, fellow Catholic theologians as well as secular academicians—since the action violated rules of the American Association of University Professors— raised a public outcry, but to no avail. Curran had great difficulty finding another academic position. He was refused tenure after winning an appointment at Auburn University and finally secured a permanent position at Southern Methodist University, a chaired professorship in Christian ethics.[56]

Several other influential scholars who strayed from the neoscholastic formulations of Vatican theologians have been attacked by Ratzinger's Congregation for the Doctrine of the Faith.[57] For example, the Brazilian liberation theologian Father Leonardo Boff has been subjected to severe scrutiny several times; he has since resigned from the active ministry.[58] The Dutch theologian Father Edward Schillebeeckx was similarly harassed.[59] Both Boff and Schillebeeckx are internationally renowned. They are respected and revered not only for their prodigious and impeccable scholarship but also for their undying loyalty and compassionate service to the Church. The treatment they received from Rome has prompted dismay and heartache along with vociferous protest in the Catholic intellectual community. Fathers Küng, Curran, Boff, and Schillebeeckx are only some of the most celebrated cases of the Vatican's curtailment of academic freedom among Catholic theologians. Patrick Granfield describes similar kinds of harassment of other lesser-known but highly respected scholars: Anthony Kosnik and colleagues, John J. McNeill, Jacques Pohier, Anthony Wilhelm, Phillip S. Keane, and Matthew Fox.[60] As the list of interventions grows, the power of the conservative papal coalition expands accordingly. So does the wall of insulation around the male, celibate, sacramental, and hierarchic hegemony that marks the Catholic priesthood.

Other bureaucratic control-nets have been cast to catch not only the big but also the little scholarly fish tempted to swim beyond the official ideological stream. In 1989, the Vatican instituted a loyalty oath for theologians and a year later issued a restrictive "Instruction on the Ecclesial Vocation of the Theologian." The instruction raised alarm from Hans Küng, Charles Curran, Elizabeth Schüssler-Fiorenza, Richard McBrien, and a host of other liberal and moderate theologians around the world.[61] In fact, Catholic scholars found it hard to take the instruction seriously in these days of widespread academic freedom. Embarrassment and frustration were more frequent reactions than anger and fear over the threat of a loyalty oath. Some said that so preposterous an attempt to curtail scholarly autonomy may be the last futile efforts of a dying cause. Others called this wishful thinking and saw the Vatican vise getting tighter as it squeezes out opposition to its views.

Autonomy of Lower-Level Participants

The multitudes of lower clergy and religious sisters and brothers in the Catholic Church rarely attract Rome's negative attention—except when their questionable activities are reported heavily in the media and the local bishop cannot or does not want to handle the controversy. In his forthright and balanced analysis of the "possible limits to papal primacy," Granfield documents Roman interventions in the lives of lesser-known priests and nuns who became targets of ideological control. One focus of concern was political activity, which John Paul II had clearly and often proscribed for priests and religious. The new Code of Canon Law issued in 1983 reinforced the pope's predilections. Four cases stand out as examples of how the Vatican enforces these laws.[62]

Father Robert Drinan, a Jesuit priest and Democrat from Massachusetts who served five terms in the U.S. House of Representatives, was directed by the Vatican in 1980 not to run for reelection. He complied without a fuss. In 1982, Agnes Mary Mansour, a Sister of Mercy for 30 years, was appointed director of the Department of Social Services for the State of Michigan, an agency with a large abortion program. In a complicated case involving the local archbishop, the Sisters of Mercy administration, and another bishop appointed by a Vatican congregation at the direction of the pope, Sister Mary Agnes was forced to resign from the directorship or face canonical trial and dismissal from her congregation. She left her religious congregation and three years later resigned her state government post to work for the Mercy Sisters in their Health Services in Detroit.

Sister Arlene Violet, a Sister of Mercy for 23 years, resigned from her congregation in 1984 to run for the office of attorney general in Rhode Island. The local bishop refused to grant her an exemption from canons 285 and 672, which would have allowed her to run and remain in religious life. She won the election as a Republican candidate in 1984 but was not reelected in 1986. In another instance, four priests who held high office in the Sandinista government in Nicaragua were issued an ultimatum by the Vatican in 1984 to resign their government posts in accordance with canon 285 or be disciplined. They refused, and Rome suspended them (i.e., they could not celebrate Mass and the sacraments).

Another well-documented case of strong negative sanctions against the lower clergy and religious involves 24 nuns and three male religious whose names accompanied a statement about the abortion debate that appeared in the *New York Times* on October 7, 1984. The Vatican reacted to this "flagrant scandal" by directing the religious superiors of the signers to obtain statements from them declaring their loyalty to the Church's teaching on abortion. The men immediately retracted, but despite the efforts of a Roman congregation, a cardinal, and their local superiors, the sisters delayed and waffled. Two sisters of Notre Dame de Namur publicly refused to comply. Humiliated and saddened by the events, they eventually left the order.[63]

Centralization is most effective, however, when the conservative coalition based in Rome can exercise bureaucratic control not over a few notorious dissenters but over them all. The most pervasive example of bureaucratic counter-insurgency against reform-minded nuns is reflected in recent dealings between the Congregation of Institutes of Consecrated Life (CICL) and all the religious institutes of women in the Catholic Church. The CICL is the curial office overseeing papal approval of revised constitutions being written by religious institutes. Communities of religious women have changed considerably after decades of reform following the Sister Formation Movement of the 1950s and the mandates of the Second Vatican Council. Meanwhile, the revised *Code of Canon Law* (1983) has intervened. The code sets a distinctly retrogressive tone and severely restricts governance options available to religious communities.[64] Many communities of Catholic nuns feel caught in the middle, first being told to reform their outmoded constitutions and now being told to go back to the status quo ante.

To ensure compliance with the new code, all religious institutes have been instructed to submit their constitutions to the CICL for approval. The ensuing conflicts have been severe and prolonged. Marie Augusta Neal, a sister of Notre Dame de Namur and noted sociologist of religion, has been studying the changing social structures of religious institutes of women in the U.S. and elsewhere for over 25 years. In her analysis of the situation, she concludes that the main issues at stake in this controversy are centralized control by the Vatican and male hegemony.[65]

In the last few decades, sisters throughout the country have completed a long and painful process to restructure decision-making within their institutes. Neal documents that, as a result of reforms began at midcentury, the majority of U.S. sisters prefer participatory, decentralized, collegial forms of decision-making to the traditional monarchical structures they were subjected to in the past. These preferences have been translated into new constitutions that are approved by legally constituted governance bodies of the institutes but that Rome is now rejecting because they stray from the new code.

Canon 601, for example, calls for "submission of the will to legitimate Superiors, vice regents of God, who rule according to the particular constitutions." Another canon refers to the "supreme moderator," which describes the role of superiors who "should rule over their subjects as children of God and, promoting voluntary obedience of their subjects with reverence for the human person, they should listen to them willingly and foster their harmony for the good of the Institute and the Church but always with their authority for deciding and planning for what must be done remaining intact" (canon 618). Women religious perceive these injunctions as a twofold attack on their maturity and dignity as educated professionals dedicated to serving the Church. They see the canons as perpetuating an outmoded model of monarchical domination and gender inequality.

Neal reports the bitter frustration of Catholic sisters who are being commanded to submit to a type of language that is so foreign to their new understanding of ministry and the Church:

> Women have experienced a sexist authority wielded over them and their institutes during the long history of the Church. For this reason, they are more seriously affected by the use of this language of sovereignty. More specifically, organizations with real power have been consistently controlled by men. In the Church, this remains so today. When such archaic language is used now, it inspires, confirms and encourages the old relationships of dependency and unquestioning submission of women to men.[66]

Along with continued decline in membership of their institutes, analysts foresee growing disenchantment and alienation among vowed religious women, some of the Church's most able and committed ministers.

On the other hand, Neal sees the possibility that the looming crisis could lead to coalition formation and creative forms of loyal dissent. In her opinion, "many Catholic sisters face a serious dilemma of obedience in the 1980s and will continue to do so in the 1990s." They will have to decide whether to honor Second Vatican Council mandates to prophetic ministry that are now built into their collegial structures or "archaic" laws imposed by men that idealize superiors with monarchical ultimate authority, "expressing what is presumed to be God's will for the governed."[67] The lines of conflict have been drawn by hierarchical, male, celibate hegemony on the one hand and the lay movement and feminist movement on the other. The possibility of effective coalition formation grows as these tensions mount.

Conclusion

Through social insulation and forms of direct intervention the conservative priestly coalition attempts to maintain the status quo of Catholic ministry. But it is impossible to insulate the entire clergy and laity from the impact of changes in the environment. An organization is always dependent for survival on resources in its ecological niche. When those resources are changing, the organization is changing too, either through decline and death or by transformation and growth. As the priest shortage worsens, and our projections indicate it will, these coalitional forces will gain greater momentum and move toward their critical threshold precipitating change.

Can conservative coalitions successfully dampen the forces for change? Can the resources of bureaucratic counterinsurgency tone down what conservatives see as overly enthusiastic interpretations of policies and programs stemming from the Second Vatican Council? The energy and scope of the efforts at "restoration" and the conflict they generate bear witness to the contrasting alliances in the Church. Even if it were true in earlier historical periods, the coalitional structure of present-day Catholicism is not at all monolithic. The dominant papal alliance is frequently opposed by challenging groups. These charismatic reformers may be creating a powerful prophetic coalition to foment change within the Catholic Church, the topic of the next chapter.

12

PROPHETIC COALITION

Samuel grew up, and the Lord was with him, not permitting any word of his to be without effect. Thus all Israel from Dan to Beersheba came to know that Samuel was an accredited prophet of the Lord.

I Sm 3:19–20

The "natural" leaders in moments of distress were . . . the bearers of specific gifts of the body and mind that were considered "supernatural."

Max Weber, *Economy and Society*

Deciding whether charismatic leaders are prophets or heretics is a perennial problem for organized religion. For believers, the criterion of legitimacy is whether the leader is "accredited" by the Lord or, more generally, by the supernatural source or ground of the religion's myth system. The charismatic leader who is called to be a prophet in a religious organization must manifest hierophanic power at its highest and purest (see chapter 5). The litmus test of accreditation is the effectiveness of the prophet's utterances; for the Divine Being does not permit "any word of his to be without effect" (1 Sm 3:19). In times of religious distress, like the crisis generated by the priest shortage in the Catholic Church, how do charismatic leaders gain acceptance? How do their teachings, policies, and programs become effective? This chapter presents vignettes of charismatic church leaders and their attempts to establish effectiveness for reforming Catholic ministry.

Prophetic Coalitions in the Catholic Church

Because of enormous pressures of loyalty to the pope, groups that challenge the Church to go beyond its bureaucratic routines must be discreet. They tend to keep a low profile. Nevertheless, large components of the international episcopacy, Catholic scholars, clergy, religious sisters and brothers, and well-informed and vocal laity often make concerted efforts to oppose strongly—if respectfully—many policies propounded by the papal alliance.

Conflict and tension are endemic in religious organizations, and these disputes are necessarily conflicts over sacred texts and symbols—by nature ambivalent and subject to diverse meanings and feelings. Coalitions form to capture the hearts and minds of believers, to convince them that a particular view of faith-events is best for them and the whole community. Frequently challenge groups carefully word their public pronouncements to evoke contrary meanings and feelings. And so do the defenders of the status quo. Just as Pope John Paul uses "restoration" to denote retrenchment to pre–Second Vatican Council patterns of centralized control and "freedom" to mean adherence to papal teachings, those seeking change rely on phrases like "listening sessions" to allow Catholics to reexamine the forbidden topics of abortion or same-sex erotic behavior.[1]

Because of the need for a low-profile, informal structure and heavily nuanced ideological exchanges, the coalitional structure of progressive Catholic elites has attracted little attention. Much of the work on how prophetic coalitions relate to the U.S. priest shortage remains anecdotal and journalistic. A deeper knowledge of what constitutes charismatic leadership is essential if we are to understand and recognize prophetic coalitions.

The Nature of Charismatic Leadership

In Weber's view of social change, a charismatic coalition has seven qualities. First, charismatic coalitions can develop only in times of distress stemming from extraordinary needs. Weber argues that when faced with *"extra*ordinary needs, i.e., those which *transcend* the sphere of everyday economic routines," we call on leaders with charisma or supernatural gifts.[2] Priestly or bureaucratic coalitions, on the other hand, gain their legitimacy in the administration of routine affairs, which rests on rational legal authority.

Second, the leader's source of legitimation is a specific set of gifts of body and spirit—that is, a personal charisma. These are extraordinary gifts, whose ultimate source is believed to be supernatural. Legitimating charismatic leaders in an association like the Catholic Church involves an extra challenge because all leaders, by their very office, are supposed to have supernatural powers, or at least be able to provide access to supernatural powers. The charismatic leader must seek legitimation based not on the power of *office* but on superextraordinary *personal* powers.

The third attribute of a charismatic leader is that he or she gains recognition only by virtue of a specific mission and success in achieving that mission. A prophet's success in providing some needed service determines whether he or she gains followers. A reciprocal reinforcement occurs. The power to lead comes from being recognized, yet the prophet gains and maintains recognition only by proving his or her strength.

The fourth property is that those to whom the prophet proposes a new vision have the *duty* to recognize and follow her or him as their charismatic leader. The hierophanic power that resides in all believers—from pope to peasant—recognizes the hierophanic power in the potential charismatic leader. As "deep calls unto deep," this recognition generates the obligation to take heed. In the Hebrew scriptures, the prophet is literally a mouthpiece for Yahweh. Charismatic leaders in the Judaeo-Christian tradition bear the burden of claiming to speak for God, whose word cannot be ineffective (1 Sm 3:19). Those who hear the prophet's message as the word of God have the *duty* to obey. In contrast, Weber points out that rational-legal authority prevalent in modern bureaucracy comes from the *will* to be governed. Though a powerful motivational constraint, the will to be governed is a weaker force than a divinely inspired duty to obey.

Fifth, a genuine charismatic leader is *responsible* to those whom he or she influences—"responsible, that is, to prove that he himself [sic] is the master willed by God." Meng-tsu (Mencius) refers to this trait when he says: "The people's voice is God's voice." According to Meng-tsu, the people's voice is "the only way in which God speaks." In contrast, a bureaucratic or priestly coalition draws from monocratic rational legal authority in which every lower office is subject to the authority of a higher one. Thus, in a priestly coalition the superior's voice, not the people's, is God's voice.[3]

Sixth, prophetic or charismatic leadership is not supported by formal organization. Rather it emerges as a loose set of relationships among devoted followers. The power of a charismatic coalition does not draw on expert training, hierarchy of control, division of labor, rules and regulations, and career advancement. It has no permanent structure, and its leaders seek no approval from those who govern permanent structures.

Last and most important, a charismatic coalition is revolutionary. The leader rejects all ties to an external order in favor of the exclusive promotion of the mission. The prophet claims that the new vision is a break with the old traditions and rational norms: "It was said of old, but I say unto you." Because charismatic authority is limited to fulfilling a specific need, the revolutionary force of a charismatic coalition is transitory.

Coalitional Activities of Bishops

From the U.S. episcopacy I highlight two examples of potential charismatic leadership in the Catholic Church: Archbishop Rembert Weakland of Milwaukee, Wisconsin, and Bishop Kenneth Untener of Saginaw, Michigan. Of the two, Weakland presents the more towering figure, perhaps because of the maturity that comes with age and the stature gained by his experience as abbot primate of the 1,500-year-old Benedictine Order. The mission that has brought these men national recognition focuses mainly on solutions to the priest shortage. Their vision for leading the Church out of this stressful situation makes them prime candidates for leadership in a charismatic coalition.

Weakland's leadership, in particular, appears to be broad-based, whereas other nationally known liberal bishops have demonstrated a more limited potential for prophetic leadership, at least among the grassroots. In a two-part series in the *New Yorker,* Paul Wilkes observes that Weakland "has avoided being typecast . . . as a categorical liberal, like Thomas Gumbleton, of Detroit, and Francis Murphy, of Baltimore."[4] Although both Bishop Gumbleton and Bishop Murphy are recognized as progressive leaders in the U.S. Catholic Church, they are sometimes dismissed as too radical. Since they are expected to take an extreme stance on controversial issues, any solution to the priest shortage they offer is likely to be met with suspicion by moderate and conservative members of the Church. When leaders ask too much too often, they lose their followers. Archbishop Raymond Hunthausen of Seattle might have been another possible charismatic leader, but counterinsurgency attacks by the Vatican, described in the previous chapter, forced him into early retirement.[5] Weakland expressed the feelings of fellow bishops about these events: "Take Hunthausen—Dutch, we call him. Rome broke him, and the point was made that anyone who follows in his footsteps will be similarly broken."[6]

If they are as outspoken as Hunthausen and other progressive bishops, why have Archbishop Weakland and Bishop Untener been able to avoid being broken by Rome? Will they, or others with similar traits, emerge as significant charismatic leaders needed to help lead the Catholic Church out of its current distress? To what extent do Weakland, Untener, or unidentified others like them embody the Weberian characteristics of charismatic leadership?

Archbishop Rembert Weakland of Milwaukee

Archbishop Weakland first entered the limelight in the mid-1980s when he wrote the U.S. bishops' pastoral letter entitled "Economic Justice for All." After the vote in which the final draft was overwhelmingly approved, his colleagues at the NCCB demonstrated their appreciation for his work with a standing ovation. The widely acclaimed document gave Weakland national media exposure. He was immediately invited to address an assembly of Wall Street financiers and the Joint Economic Committee of Congress. Some thought the pastoral letter he drafted was "not only more complete in its analysis of thorny economic issues but also more Scriptural and pastoral in spirit" than Pope John Paul's encyclical *Centesimus Annus* on the same topic.[7]

In 1987, Weakland was elected by his episcopal confreres to attend the Synod of Bishops in Rome. He raised the issue of male exclusivity in ministry. He told the synodal fathers, "Women who are loyal to and love the Church express dis-

may and discouragement if their talents and contributions to church life are sti-
fled or rejected. They want church leaders to treat them as Jesus treated
women. . . . Women in the Gospels ministered to, with, and for Jesus."[8] He
called for women to assume all liturgical roles not requiring ordination and to
be appointed to the Roman curia and the Vatican diplomatic corps. He did not,
however, directly call for the ordination of women.

The Synod had been preceded by grassroots consultations involving hundreds of thousands of laypeople, but all this was ignored in the pope's final statement summarizing the synodal proceedings. Weakland commented that the
document could have been written without any input from the synod delegates
and promised he "would never go through such a charade again."[9] The same
year he was one of four archbishops who addressed John Paul II during the
papal visit to Los Angeles. Weakland used this opportunity to repeat the conviction he had voiced in Rome: Women should be treated as equal partners in
the Church's ministry. He also bluntly told John Paul: "An authoritative style
is counterproductive, and such authority for the most part then becomes ignored."[10]

He put his criticism of autocratic leadership into practice by launching an extensive dialogue on abortion in his archdiocese. His listening sessions and a subsequent statement about women's views on abortion gained Weakland further
national attention in 1990 when Roman officials forbade the Swiss University of
Fribourg to grant him an honorary degree (see chapter 11). Thousands of letters
arrived, some supported his statement on abortion and others were hate mail
from strident prolife advocates. The story about the Vatican snub broke while
the U.S. bishops were attending an annual meeting in Washington. Reporters
cornered Weakland between sessions for comments on the Fribourg affair, and
many fellow bishops made efforts to show their empathy and support. He was
again the center of positive attention. Weakland quipped that he made the *New
York Times* twice in one year for doing nothing: first for listening to women on
abortion and then for not receiving an honorary degree.[11]

In early 1991, Weakland released the first draft of a pastoral letter addressed
to his local archdiocesan church. In it he called for priestly ordination of married men, causing another national media event. The letter is a 25-page tightly
reasoned theological and scriptural analysis of the priest shortage. Weakland
writes that he would be willing to ordain suitably qualified married men under
certain conditions if no celibate priest were available. He said he would "present such a candidate to the pastor of the universal Church [the Pope] for light
and guidance." He knows John Paul is adamantly opposed to a married priesthood but, nonetheless, with this letter Weakland becomes the first American
bishop to call publicly for the removal of compulsory celibacy from the structural form of priesthood.[12] He joins his request to the desperate pleas from bishops in Africa, Brazil, Indonesia, and Canada to open the priesthood to married

men.[13] Weakland undoubtedly also knows how many of his American confreres have written privately to the pope with similar requests. The revolutionary aspects of his actions are recognizable: He publicly mentions the unmentionable, regardless of consequences.

Extraordinary Personal Gifts

Weakland is bright, articulate, and savvy in church politics and in the use of the media. Many say he possesses these qualities to an extraordinary degree. But, in Weber's understanding of charisma, are these "gifts of body and mind" to be "considered 'supernatural' (in the sense that not everybody could have access to them)?"[14] Wilkes, who spent several months in close contact with Weakland, makes a number of insightful observations about the archbishop's personal qualities. He draws a picture of Weakland as one who is indeed the bearer of extraordinary gifts.

After an impromptu lecture to Wilkes in which the archbishop analyzes ecclesiastical, philosophical, and scientific history, Weakland concludes by saying that he rejects the principle of preserving the status quo for its own sake. Referring to the counterinsurgency activities of the Church's present bureaucratic coalition, Weakland argues: "If there is truth it will win out. . . . If an idea is false, it will fall away. It makes no sense to do battle with new ideas just because they don't fit neat little categories codified by some council hundreds of years ago."[15] Instead, Weakland adheres to a radically different principle and formulates what might be labeled the Charismatic Manifesto: "But if . . . a situation presents itself that is not right, you have to do your best to say or do something about it. Regardless of whom it pleases or displeases."[16] This is a deceptively simple and profound statement that, when viewed in its historical context, bespeaks extraordinary inner strength. To do or say something about what is not right takes unusual courage when the opposition is as formidable as the papal coalition. Like Archbishop Hunthausen and Bishop Gaillot, you could be fired. If Wilkes's evidence is reliable, Weakland may be the bearer of personal gifts that for many believers would be "considered supernatural, in the sense that not everybody could have access to them."[17]

After the Vatican's slap on the wrist for his listening sessions and statement on abortion, Weakland said "That's the role of a bishop—to say it as you see it."[18] Another time, however, he confesses that he's no hero. The heroic Christians today, in Weakland's opinion, are those who are dying for their faith. After his pastoral trip to El Salvador he reflected on the courageous people he had met in villages under constant siege in the government's efforts to eliminate the opposition guerrillas. Not only had Archbishop Oscar Romero, six Jesuit priests, their housekeeper, her daughter, and other priests, nuns, and lay ministers been assassinated in El Salvador but hardly a single family in a village he visited had not had a husband, son, brother, or some other relative killed in the resistance. Weakland's musings on El Salvador reflect important aspects of his own approach to a situation that is not right: "A martyr, to me, is someone who just did his best and, because of circumstances, was killed. The Salvadoran martyrs . . . were working in the ordinariness of each day, looking at the events around them, reacting, trying to do—in some small, usually unnoticeable way—something they thought was right."[19]

After the denial of the Fribourg degree, he said that "if he were a Catholic college president he would be a bit leery about speaking out" against the Vatican. But after returning from El Salvador his tone had changed; he said he could not imagine keeping silent "unless you take out my tongue."[20] This statement takes the basic manifesto a significant step further. Here Weakland displays an extraordinary inner determination that may fall short of his definition of heroism but nevertheless shows a level of courage accessible to only a gifted few. He once made a simple assessment of himself: "I have a certain sense of my own personal integrity and that means a lot to me."[21]

Recognition, Duty, and Responsibility

Has Archbishop Weakland been recognized for successfully implementing his visions for the Church? Weakland has performed several demanding and courageous missions for which he received extensive active recognition. Authoring "Economic Justice for All" gained him international renown for his pastoral daring and scholarly erudition along with a warm standing ovation from his peers. His public stature was quickly reinforced by being one of four U.S. bishops elected to attend the 1987 Synod of Bishops in Rome and again by being selected as one of four archbishops to address the pope in Los Angeles the same year. A couple of years later, reports of his listening sessions and his compassionate statement on abortion were also carried by the national media. The resulting sanction by Rome turned the entire series of events into another occasion for demonstrating recognition for his outstanding services. Most recently, Weakland's bold assessment of the priest shortage, in which he publicly suggests ordaining married men as the reasonable solution, received instant national media attention.

But can we detect a sense of duty on the part of supporters? Most church watchers know that John Paul II has commanded Catholic bishops to avoid open discussion of the problems of compulsory celibacy and the ordination of married men. So when Weakland issued the first draft of his pastoral on the priest shortage, journalists undoubtedly had a hard time finding bishops willing to comment. Despite the risk, Bishop Francis Quinn of Sacramento showed courage by his enthusiastic endorsement, saying: "Archbishop Weakland has always been a man who speaks his mind openly, so it's quite in keeping with his approach to crucial matters in the Church. Weakland will find supporters among the American Catholic hierarchy."[22] Two months later, the Saginaw presbyteral council, endorsed by Bishop Kenneth Untener, encouraged Catholics to study and discuss Archbishop Weakland's "bold prophetic" letter examining the possibility of ordaining married men.[23]

A particularly poignant and telling display of support for Weakland came from the American hierarchy at the close of the fall 1991 NCCB meeting. The story about the Fribourg degree was in the news, reporters wanted comments from the bishops attending the Washington meeting, and colleagues were going out of their way to assure Weakland of their backing. The tension seemed to demand a demonstration of solidarity if it really existed. Bishop James Malone of Youngstown, Ohio, took the floor and invited his fellow bishops to register "moral support for Rembert at this moment." They gave him "a sustained standing ovation."[24]

Weakland's openness to discussing abortion with Catholic women could have easily generated rejection by his colleagues instead of support, for Rome is adamant that this topic does not deserve further discussion. Yet even the "conservative Catholic columnist James Hitchcock bitterly concluded that there are signs that the 'moderate middle' of the American episcopacy welcomes Archbishop Weakland's 'breakthrough' and will attempt to give it respectability."[25] Hitchcock's statement calls attention to a form of passive recognition that fellow bishops provide simply by not publicly rejecting Weakland's actions. Overall, Weakland's followers display an unusual level of devotion. Support under intense pressure comes from conviction akin to religious duty rather than more superficial motives.

Weakland also feels more responsibility to his supporters than his superiors. A friend and admirer of Weakland, Bishop Raymond Lucker of New Ulm, Minnesota, expresses the dilemma all bishops face.[26] Asked to comment on why more bishops don't stand up to Rome, Lucker responded: "This is our home—we can't burn it down. This is our mother—we can't defy her. We were trained to be loyal." The other side of the dilemma is equally piercing. According to Bishop Lucker, "for those in power in Rome, the Church is not 'the People of God' that Vatican II talked about. It is an imperial monarchy that must maintain absolute control." So how should a bishop handle this dilemma? Lucker responds with another question: "How long can I be concerned only about this Church as my home, and not about the people who are being hurt by it and leaving? I ask myself that almost every day."

Archbishop Weakland has asked himself the same question and on several critical occasions has shown that his primary responsibility is for the people being hurt by Rome. One such incident involved the extremely popular appointment of Father Richard Sklba as auxiliary bishop of Milwaukee. Between the time Sklba's appointment was announced and the day of his consecration, Rome communicated that the appointment was to be canceled. Sklba had chaired a committee of U.S. scholars commissioned to study the prohibition against ordaining women. The commission concluded that there was no scriptural basis for the ban. Rome discovered this "indiscretion" at the last minute and concluded that Sklba was unfit for episcopal consecration. Weakland was outraged and declared, "I couldn't let this happen. Should a line or two in a document . . . be allowed to ruin a man's life?"[27] Weakland and Sklba flew to Rome immediately. After an acrimonious exchange between Weakland and Pope John Paul—carried on by messengers and written statements, since Weakland and Sklba were refused an audience—the pope acquiesced, and Sklba's appointment went through.

Weakland knew the consequences of being responsible to the people. Referring to Sklba's appointment, he says, in an understatement: "That incident, obviously, made Rome distrustful of me. And I imagine that other stands I have taken—from advocating a fuller role for women in the Church to what I have said about abortion—do not correspond with what the Vatican wants put forward."[28] Since the time of Auxiliary Bishop Sklba's appointment, Rome has ignored all of Weakland's suggestions about who should be made a bishop. Nevertheless, he continues to press the issue. Weakland confronted the U.S. pronuncio, Archbishop Agostino Cacciavillan, reminding him that the appointment of Robert Banks to Green Bay had gone against the grain, and complained about the pronuncio's pattern of ignoring local input in the appointment of new bishops. Weakland conveyed that he and other American bishops felt "that it is totally useless to present names, and I find it offensive that one is expected to go through a procedure that is a charade."[29] He noted further that many of his U.S. colleagues "had hoped that the appointments of bishops would not continue to be controlled by Cardinal Law, Cardinal O'Connor, and Cardinal Krol."[30] No priest from Milwaukee has been elevated to the episcopacy in over a decade.

With the Roman curia in mind, Weakland reflected on the consequences of his actions: "Yes, I'm sure they are thinking up ways to keep me in line, to criticize me, to isolate me. Nobody likes someone standing up to him and challenging what he says. So my career is over. I will die the Archbishop of Milwaukee."[31] Weakland's decision to follow Meng-tsu's dictum, "The voice of the people is God's voice," was not made in the dark. Reflecting on why bishops tend to look over their shoulders at Rome rather than at their people, Weakland said, "I spent thirteen years in Rome; the Vatican is demythologized for me. It is not the repository of truth and right thinking that some make it out to be—not at all. I know what happens in the back rooms there, so, frankly, I spend little time forecasting what Rome may think."[32]

Being responsible to Rome would probably have won Weakland the red hat of a cardinal, since appointment as archbishop of Milwaukee has traditionally been a stepping stone to the cardinalate. Being responsible to the people, however, has won him the potential for charismatic leadership in the Church's moment of distress.

Loose Organization

Weakland does not rely openly on the powerful organizational strength of the official Church but instead assists in developing a behind-the-scenes loose association of devoted supporters. He knows the difference between a bureaucratic strategy devised by the Vatican and the informal charismatic approach. Recalling the early years of John Paul's pontificate, when the pope was making known his agenda to restore centralized control, Weakland remarked:

> When it became apparent to me what the years under John Paul II would be like, I didn't sit down and line up a master plan of confrontation for the next few decades. That was Rome; I was Milwaukee. I had my own work to do, and, just as I had done as abbot and then as primate, I simply went about my business, listening to what people were saying, watching the tide of human events.[33]

Many bishops consider much of the agenda at their annual meetings trivial and many of the debates, in which they try to achieve consensus as the authentic teaching voice of the Church, nothing more than a charade. Although he respects the role of prime teacher played by the college of bishops, Weakland seems to take a negative view of the formal structures used in exercising that role and outlines his strategy for developing the loose structures of a charismatic coalition. Referring to the fall 1990 meeting of the NCCB, he says: "You quickly learn that these public meetings are not the place to make policy. You make policy at home, quietly. You try to move things there, not in Washington. If I can ever get the third section of my pastoral letter on the priesthood together, I think that it might serve as a good example."[34]

A few months later Weakland did publish his pastoral letter, with its daring policy statement on the need to ordain married men to the priesthood. He thus set the example of how prophetic coalitions get things moving outside of formal bureaucratic structures. Actually, in promulgating this letter he followed the same strategy he used earlier when he initiated listening sessions and wrote the statement on abortion. This calm approach to reform helps produce the pattern of attitudes and behaviors that constitute the loose informal structure of charismatic coalitions. Other bishops and church leaders learn from these examples and, by following them locally, reproduce the same patterns in their own dioceses. So the potential coalition gains momentum.

I personally observed another mechanism that could contribute to the production of the loose association that characterizes the structure of charismatic coalitions. During a meeting I had with Archbishop Weakland in December 1990, the phone rang in his inner office. He excused himself to answer it, even though several staff members were available. When he returned, he explained that he gives that number to only close friends and colleagues. This was a call from a bishop friend who wanted Weakland to speak to a group in the friend's diocese. Weakland remarked that he likes to keep speaking engagements to a reasonable number but tries to accept requests from fellow bishops because they offer an opportunity for mutual encouragement and support. If this was not an infrequent incident, it points to the existence of a support network of like-minded bishops and other influential individuals. Members of the loose association make unobtrusive contacts among themselves, especially with leaders like Weakland, to encourage and help one another carry out the work of policy formation and structural change "at home, quietly."

Revolutionary Action

I have already described the radical character of Archbishop Weakland's attempts to say or do something he thinks is right when the occasion demands. But do his visionary activities provide evidence of the revolutionary quality associated with charismatic leadership? Revolutionary action in a tightly controlled ideological organization like the Catholic Church is relative. Of course, Weakland could be more revolutionary by more openly defying the pope on these key issues. But the challenge is to balance loyalty with truth, to act according to one's convictions no matter what the sanctions.

A progressive Catholic bishop living the truth of his pastoral convictions would produce a string of quiet revolts not much different from those ascribed to Archbishop Weakland. Even quiet protests, however, can be very forceful in the long run. For example, opposing the authoritarianism promoted by the papal coalition in the Catholic Church can be compared to opposing the ideological repression of the communist regime in the former Czechoslovakia. In his analysis of the Czech human rights movement, Václav Havel describes the exceptional courage needed for seemingly small gestures of protest. Havel imagines the actions of a greengrocer who posts communist slogans in his window because he fears losing his job:

> Let us imagine that one day something in our greengrocer snaps and he stops putting up the slogans merely to ingratiate himself. He stops voting in elections he knows are a farce. He begins to say what he really thinks at political meetings. And he even finds the strength in himself to express solidarity with those whom his conscience commands him to support. In this revolt the greengrocer steps out of living within the lie. He rejects the ritual and breaks the rules of the game. He discovers once more his suppressed identity and dignity. He gives his freedom a concrete significance. His revolt is an attempt to *live within the truth*.[35]

Havel reminds us that the costs for these actions would be great: job demotion, lower pay, loss of vacation time, no higher education for one's children, harassment by superiors, and wonderment from fellow workers. The rewards, however, would be the dignity of living in the truth and eventually, perhaps, the chance to participate in a peaceful revolution and the election of the first non-communist president of Czechoslovakia in 40 years.

Charismatic activity is a series of ordinarily nonrevolutionary events that add up to a revolution. As a whole, Weakland's protestations of truth take on the revolutionary nature of a charismatic mission. Further, we saw that he possesses prophetic leadership qualities, demonstrates loyalty to his supporters who are religiously devoted to him and his causes, and plays a dominant role in an informally structured association of church leaders. The evidence indicates that resources for a charismatic coalition are forming in the U.S. Catholic Church. To be effective, however, this coalition would need a broader base of both leadership and followership than that provided by Weakland and his supporters. So I examine the extent to which another U.S. bishop might extend the charismatic coalition to another locale, mission, and set of actors.

Bishop Kenneth Untener of Saginaw

Bishop Untener shows many of the same qualities as Weakland. The area of stress and tension that seems to be shaping Untener's mission of reform for Catholicism is male hegemony in ministry and, more generally, male domination in a patriarchal society. His most prophetic activities center on various facets of these problems.[36]

Human Sexuality

At the November 1990 meeting of the NCCB, the U.S. bishops debated the final draft of "Human Sexuality: A Catholic Perspective for Education and Lifelong Learning." The document reasserted the Church's firm stand against artificial birth control, which upset Bishop Untener. In an uncharacteristically passionate interchange, Untener "seemed on the verge of tears as he proclaimed that the issue had cast the Church as 'a dysfunctional family that is unable to talk openly about a problem that everybody knows is there.'"[37] The problem known to all, but mentioned by only a few bishops like Untener, is that most Catholic couples continue to ignore the Church's teaching on birth control and many if not most theologians support their right to do so. In issuing the encyclical *Humanae Vitae* that contains the doctrine, the pope went against the advice of a commission he had established to study the birth control question, and bishops around the world "mitigated" the encyclical's teaching.[38]

Untener manifests his revulsion for continuing the farce that a consensus exists on so controversial an issue. He realizes that the U.S. bishops are supposed to speak as the Church's authentic teaching voice, yet few seem disturbed that their voices are used to distort the real problem and, moreover, to generate indifference if not scorn among many of the faithful. No doubt many bishops were agitated about this pretense, but only a handful expressed their feelings and fewer still with the depth of emotion that marked Bishop Untener's comments. This incident reveals a level of courage and conviction in the face of opposition that exemplifies Untener's personal charisma.

Theology and Gender Equality

Untener also uses his skills as a writer and theologian to help advance the mission of creating structures of equality for women in the Catholic Church. In *Worship* magazine he presents a carefully reasoned argument, concluding that the Catholic Church's rationale for banning the ordination of women lacks a scriptural basis.[39] He claims that the official interpretation—that a priest must be male because he acts "in the person of Christ"—is based on faulty exegesis of the Pauline text in which the phrase occurs and on limited theology of the last half century. Untener's argument implies that the writings of recent popes and the documents of Roman congregations began emphasizing the maleness of Jesus as a prerequisite for Christian priesthood precisely at the time when social practice and feminist scholars began to question male exclusivity in all important occupations and professions. He concludes that the meaning of "acting in the person of Christ" as applied to priesthood is far from clear: "Thus a phrase used very infrequently for 19 centuries has become standard terminology for our times. This raises a theological question that deserves careful examination. Theologically speaking, the usage of this phrase is relatively recent and relatively unexamined. A great deal of work is needed on this crucial point."[40]

The next few issues of *Worship* carried responses to Untener's article by the theology professor Father Charles Meyer, Bishop John Sheets, and the noted French theologian Father Hervé Legrand. Although Legrand agreed with Untener's analysis, Meyer and Sheets challenged it, deducing the official prohibition of women in the priesthood from the New Testament.[41] That Bishop Untener's call for an examination of male exclusivity in the Catholic priesthood got a speedy answer from the theologians Meyer, Sheets, and Legrand demonstrates that he was successful in drawing attention to the nonordination of women as a problem in need of research. He was also mindful that Pope John Paul has commanded bishops to avoid any public discussion whatsoever of this burning issue. It must be noted that examination of theological issues in scholarly journals like *Worship* is not considered public discussion. Nevertheless, when a bishop takes a theological stance that is contrary to that of the pope and his advisors, especially on such a vehemently proscribed topic, he is taking a notable risk. Given the acrimony of the conflict over androcentrism in the Church and society, this is another incident exhibiting the familiar traits of charismatic behavior.

Ordination of Women

Untener's plea for open theological discussion of gender inequality preceded an even more clarion statement that something beyond theologizing was required. Later that fall, at the 1991 NCCB meeting in Washington, Bishop Untener made an impromptu reply to a reporter's question about women's ordination, saying: "I won't waffle on this. . . . I can't see any reason why women should not be ordained. And as far as I'm concerned, I think women ought to be ordained."[42] The next day, however, he clarified his position with a formal statement for the press. Yes, he endorses the ordination of women, but as his personal opinion, not as a demand for action.

A formal statement to the press is definitely part of a public discussion. This time, it seemed that Untener had stepped over the line. The front-page story in the *Detroit Free Press* defines the situation as it appeared to the general public: "Saginaw Bishop Kenneth Untener . . . became the first U.S. Roman Catholic bishop to publicly call for the ordination of women, thus risking censure from Pope John Paul II." The archbishop of Detroit, Adam Maida, seized the occasion to side with the pope, saying: "I totally agree with our Holy Father. There is no question about it: Theologically it is not possible [to ordain women]. And there is just no reasonable hope for any change in our discipline or our teaching on this." Untener explained that the catalyst precipitating his endorsement of women's ordination is the priest shortage. Maida again disagreed. "'This problem can be licked,' Maida said. Talking too much about the shortage is 'negative thinking that just invites a disaster to happen.'" The disaster, of course, would be the continued decline in numbers of male celibate clergy and the pressure it causes to open ordination to women. Maida clearly wanted to place himself in the papal alliance and separate himself from his neighboring bishop and the progressive coalition.

A few colleagues, however, were willing to be identified as supporting Untener's position. Bishop Lucker of New Ulm, Minnesota, said he too has been urging the bishops to study women's ordination. Bishops Thomas Gumbleton and Francis Murphy likewise favor a frank discussion and, implicitly, opening the priesthood to women. Yet all three "have been careful to stop short of urging women's ordination." Bishop Murphy explained why: "The present official teaching on the exclusion of women is that this is of divine origin—that God, through Christ, has bound the Church to the practice of ordaining only men." Bishop Lucker wistfully agreed: "Unless a major change is made at the Vatican . . . the clear and official position of the Church now is that we should not ordain women, and as a bishop, I must follow the official teachings of the Church."

By saying that he will not waffle on the issue, Bishop Untener would seem to be at the forefront of those supporting women's ordination. His resolute stand may be braced by his feelings of responsibility to women he knows personally who want to be ordained. The week after Untener's endorsement of women's ordination in Washington, the *Detroit Free Press* ran a feature story on Sister Jane Eschweiler, pastoral associate at St. Andrew's parish in Saginaw. A member of the Sisters of the Divine Savior for 30 years and niece of three aunts who were nuns and three uncles who were priests, Eschweiler has longed to be a priest since "all the way back. All the way. Since childhood."[43] Although immersed in pastoral ministry, she feels a painful sense of incompleteness. She says, "I can be with people when they're dying, but I can't anoint them. I can listen to their sins, and frequently do, but I can't officially forgive them. I can counsel engaged couples, but I can't marry them. I can advise the parents of newborns but not baptize the babies. And, of course, I can't celebrate the Eucharist, the core of the community. I pray not to be resentful."

A similar story involves the forced resignation of Sister Teresita Weind as pastoral minister at the St. Catherine–St. Lucy Catholic church in Oak Park, Illinois.[44] The plot in this drama includes the repressive and restrictive interpretation of liturgical rules by Cardinal Joseph Bernardin of Chicago and the obvious efforts of Father Edward K. Braxton to become a bishop through his rigid loyalty to Rome. Sister Weind is a gifted liturgist, preacher, and counselor with 13 years experience in parish ministry. She felt pressured to resign by Bernardin and Braxton, who wanted her to stop deviating from Roman guidelines about women's leadership roles. After her resignation, Bishop Untener immediately appointed her as pastoral administrator in a five-parish cluster in Saginaw's predominantly poor and black inner city. She too would like to be ordained a priest "if the circumstances were appropriate."

To the extent that he is a charismatic leader, Bishop Untener feels more responsibility to women like Sisters Eschweiler and Weind than to the unexamined theology of his superiors, which claims that because they are women they are not worthy of priesthood. It takes uncommon courage for a bishop to face head-on the inequalities of androcentrism, which not only are rampant throughout Roman Catholicism but also are theologically justified and structurally reinforced by higher echelons in the Church bureaucracy. Untener's prophetic actions manifest responsibility to his people rather than his superiors. He is endorsed enthusiastically by his priests and people and cautiously by a few bishops. He and his loose association of followers work quietly at home, not only without the support but usually against the opposition of the national and international church bureaucracy.

Bishops like Weakland and Untener are charismatic leaders who address the priest shortage as a serious crisis in the Catholic Church. But are their activities isolated examples of episcopal efforts to reform the structures of Catholic ministry? On the contrary. An examination of media accounts reveals that a limited but noticeable number of other bishops in the United States and around the world may be forming a progressive coalition.

Other Bishops Join Rank

The most obvious and frequently proposed progressive remedy for the priest shortage is the ordination of married men. In the U.S. episcopacy, immediate public endorsement of Weakland's suggestion to relax the rule on compulsory celibacy came from Untener, Francis Quinn of Sacramento, California, Raymond Hunthausen of Seattle, and Matthew Clark of Rochester, New York.[45] Scores of others in the U.S. hierarchy, like the bishops Raymond Lucker of New Ulm, Thomas Gumbleton of Detroit, Francis Murphy of Baltimore, James Malone of Youngstown, Ohio, and Richard Sklba of Milwaukee support the ordination of married men. An examination of Catholic publications for 1989 through 1992 uncovered the names of 30 U.S. bishops who had publicly declared or acted in favor of the ordination of married men; a few also announced that they approve women's ordination to the priesthood.

The U.S. publications I consulted reported similar events in which bishops in other countries endorsed relaxing male celibate exclusivity in the Catholic priesthood. For example, in Germany even the conservative Cardinal Georg Sterzinsky of Berlin and Bishop Walter Kaspar of Rottenburg-Stuttgart were quoted as questioning the necessity of celibacy for priests. In Brazil, much to their dismay, Cardinal Aloisio Lorscheider of Fortaleza and Bishop Adriano Hippolito of Nova Iguacu were ordered to dismiss married priests from their seminary faculties.[46] Allowing married priests to teach in the seminary may be interpreted as an implicit rejection of mandatory celibacy. In a manner similar to the Vatican's intervention in the case of Archbishop Hunthausen, Rome divested Archbishop Bartolomé Carrasco Briseño of Oaxaca, Mexico, of his authority in key areas because of concerns over "Oaxacan's priests violations of celibacy."[47] It seems the bishop of Oaxaca had reported the violations to Rome in a manner that did not manifest sufficient disapproval of the situation; hence he was severely sanctioned. In all, I was able to identify 21 bishops in 10 foreign countries whose actions reveal that they support the ordination of married men; some would also favor ordaining women.

Not only are individual bishops concerned about the detrimental effects of compulsory celibacy but national bishops' conferences have also been begging for change in the ruling. Bishop Valfredo Tepe, representing the Brazilian hierarchy at the 1990 Roman Synod of Bishops, pleaded for permission to ordain married men. In 1967, 1970, and again in 1988 the Indonesian bishops asked Rome's permission to ordain married tribesmen, for whom celibacy is unthinkable if their society is to survive.[48] The Canadian bishops' conference is also frequently recognized for asking the pope to consider married priests.[49] Since the end of the nineteenth century, African bishops have petitioned Rome for a married clergy, a request that was repeated in the late 1960s and early 1970s by the bishops of Zambia, Tanzania, Gabon, Chad, the Central African Republic, Congo-Brassaville, and the Cameroons.[50] The problem was mentioned again at the 1994 Extraordinary Synod on Africa but, of course, not resolved.

Based on frequency of mention in media reports, it seems that the number of bishops publicly concerned about women's ordination is much smaller than the number who endorse and even emotionally beg for optional celibacy. But even here there are some notable exceptions. In 1992, Bishop Murphy published an article in *Commonweal* in which he condemns patriarchy and sexism as destructive. He says that he is "personally in favor of the ordination of women into a renewed priestly ministry."[51] Bishop Michael Kenny of Juneau, Alaska, makes a similar argument in *America,* declaring that the prohibition of women's ordination "is an expression of a patriarchal era that tended to view females as inferior to males."[52] In an address on feminism to the Catholic Press Association, Archbishop Weakland said: "The ordination of women to the priesthood is the key issue . . . not to face it and all the issues surrounding feminism could lead to the loss of so many wonderful women who have contributed so much to the life of the Church."[53] *Churchwatch,* a quarterly report of the Call to Action Catholic reform movement, claims that Bishop Raphael Fliss of Superior, Wisconsin, supports ordaining women to the priesthood along with optional celibacy for priests.[54]

Beyond the United States, Bishop Norbert Werbs of Schwerin recently urged his fellow German bishops to question the exclusion of women from positions of authority in the Church.[55] I know of no national bishops' conference, however, that has requested an open discussion of the scriptural and theological foundations for banning women's ordination, let alone one that has endorsed female priests. As Bishop Kenny notes, given the adamant opposition of the vast majority in the hierarchy, when an individual bishop declares his approval of women's ordination, he realizes that he is "one small voice in one small part of the world."[56]

Theologians Speak Out

Within the past several years, theologians in western Europe and North and South America have begun to challenge the overly conservative teaching and highly centralized leadership style of the current papacy and the hierarchy that supports the Vatican's approach. Among the complaints was the much publicized 1989 Cologne Declaration, signed by 485 theologians, including such prominent scholars as Hans Küng, Bernard Häring, and Edward Schillebeeckx. According to their statement, the growing concerns of theologians include: "The overruling of local opinion in the naming of bishops, moves to silence independent and left-leaning theologians, the systematic weakening of national bishops' conferences, a narrow interpretation of sexual morality and the Pope's authoritarian style of rule."[57] Two years after the Cologne statement appeared, the

Catholic Theological Society of America issued the eighth and final draft of a similar document, "Do Not Extinguish the Spirit."[58] In it, U.S. theologians criticize Rome for departing from mandates of the Second Vatican Council, especially its disregard for collegiality of bishops, harassment of theologians, antifeminism, and hostility toward ecumenism.

Each of these general categories of criticism can be linked to problems stemming from the structural form of the priesthood. For example, local opinion is ignored in naming bishops so that Rome can be free to appoint only those priests who agree with the pope's position on male celibate exclusivity in the priesthood and birth control in marriage. Narrow interpretation of sexual morality and deep suspicion of feminism are mandated by Rome because they support celibacy and gender exclusivity. Bishops conferences and theologians are emasculated because they challenge the pope's authoritarian style of rule, which is used, above all, to maintain the ban on ordination of women and married men. In stating their opposition to these restrictions, theologians join forces with like-minded members of the hierarchy. Together they may be forming a coalition of charismatic resistance in the Church.

Lower Clergy, Religious, and Laity Unite

The lower clergy are also beginning to be more open in taking positions that run counter to Rome's wishes. They express their concerns collectively through professional associations that are either exclusively or predominantly clerical in membership. In 1991, the U.S. National Federation of Priests Councils adopted a report on priestless parishes that advocates the ordination of women and married men.[59] The statement received strong support among the 265 priest delegates attending the annual meeting. The federation is composed of presbyteral councils and priests associations that represent 26,000 priests in over half the dioceses of the United States. The highly respected Canon Law Society of America created a task force to study issues related to the ordination of married men.[60] The Federation of Diocesan Liturgical Commissions recently petitioned U.S. bishops to broaden access to sacramental leadership.[61] This request, though couched in highly nuanced language, calls for an end to male celibate monopoly over presiding at the Eucharist.

Perhaps the most outspoken U.S. group demanding optional celibacy is an association of ordained Roman Catholic priests who have resigned from the canonical ministry, most of them to marry. They call themselves the Corps of Reserved Priests United for Service (CORPUS): National Association for a Married Priesthood. Founded in 1974, CORPUS now claims 11,000 members, issues a quarterly newsletter edited by a full-time national coordinator, and held its seventh annual national conference in 1995. This organization is one of several associations of married priests that banded together in 1986 to form the International Federation of Married Catholic Priests. The federation held its sixth international conference in 1995 and now claims a membership of 30 groups in 25 countries. The Latin American Congress of Married Priests is another international association with affiliated organizations in Brazil, Paraguay, Argentina, and Mexico. The Latin American organization celebrated its second international convention in 1992.

The progressive activities of religious sisters focus mainly on advancing gender equality in the Church, notably by trying to eliminate patriarchal control in the governance of their congregations and opening the priesthood to women. The most conspicuous and effective group is the Leadership Conference of Women Religious (LCWR), composed of the heads of the vast majority of religious congregations of women in the United States.[62] In the previous chapter I recounted the battle LCWR is waging against Rome's interference in their internal affairs. Spurred on by mandates from the Second Vatican Council, most U.S. congregations of religious sisters have rewritten their constitutions along less monarchical and more collegial lines. The Vatican is now pressuring them to restore clearer lines of monarchical authority.

Religious sisters and brothers, along with committed laypeople, are important to the new progressive coalition in at least two ways. First, they give support to the more visible and powerful episcopal leaders. Second, they provide leadership at a different but equally important level of the hierarchical Church. Laypeople have a grassroots effect on one another that no pope, bishop, or priest can match. The Second Vatican Council provided a rallying cry for the laity: The Church is the People of God. Grassroots organizations, spearheaded mainly by lay leaders but also composed of clergy and religious members, are trying to transform the hierophanic power received at baptism into the people power restored to them by decrees of the council.

In the United States, Call to Action (CTA), Women's Ordination Conference (WOC), Catholics Speak Out (CSO), and the Association for the Rights of Catholics in the Church (ARCC) are among the most active progressive lay-dominated organizations. A Chicago-based group that grew out of the Call to Action meetings held in Detroit in 1976, CTA in 1994 claimed a membership of 10,000, distributed three quarterly newsletters, employed a full-time national coordinator, and held its fourth annual national convention that drew over 3,000 attendants.[63] Segments of the 1994 gathering were recorded by Mike Wallace and the CBS staff and aired on *60 Minutes* in January 1995.

Founded in 1975, WOC's membership stands at about 3,600. It regularly distributes a newsletter, *New Women, New Church,* and sponsors advertisements like the ones appearing in the *New York Times* in 1989 and 1990 that called for the ordination of women and married men. In 1992, WOC sent a delegation of its members to Czechoslovakia to interview women priests secretly ordained by bishops in good standing; they served the underground Church during the com-

munist regime. The Vatican has tried to cover up the significance of these ambiguous events, declaring their orders invalid, so WOC felt the need to document the facts from the ordained women themselves.[64] In 1995 WOC celebrated its twentieth anniversary with its third national conference.

The CSO group is a project of the Quixote Center in Hyattsville, Maryland.
In 1991, they completed a study of the "priestless parish" problem, called a press
conference to present the results to the media and the U.S. hierarchy at their
fall meeting, and sent a copy of their research report to all the bishops in the
country.[65] The following spring they and a group of cosponsors commissioned a
Gallup poll on controversial aspects of church reform, particularly the ordination of women and married men. The results, showing that 67 percent of adult
Catholics favor women's ordination and 70 percent support a married priesthood, were released at a press conference during the U.S. bishops' 1992 spring
meeting. Both events received wide media coverage.[66]

Since its establishment in 1979 the ARCC, spearheaded by the feminist theologian Rosemary Ruether, has promulgated and sought signatures for a charter
of human rights for church members on various occasions. Rights nos. 26 and 27
call for the ordination of women and married men. In all, my scrutiny of Catholic publications yielded the names of 26 grassroots Catholic reform organizations in North America. The national groups range from ARCC to VOCAL (Vic-
tims of Clergy Abuse Linkup), and the regional groups from CCW (Chicago
Catholic Women) to NYRCC (New York Renewal Coordinating Committee).
The North American groups are matched by like-minded organizations in several European countries. According to U.S. media accounts, there are at least 19
grassroots associations for Catholic reform in nine different countries. The most
dynamic appears to be the Eighth of May Movement in the Netherlands.

The North American groups have formed two international roof organizations: Catholic Organizations for Renewal, with 30 reform groups in the United
States and Canada, and Women Church Convergence, an alliance of 35 organizations in several countries. Women Church Convergence held its third international conference in 1993, preceded by extensive local dialogue. Abroad, the
European Conference on Human Rights in the Church has distributed its
"Lucerne Statement" in eight languages. Among other reforms, the document
demands an end to sexism and all discrimination excluding women from offices
in the Church.[67]

Conclusion

The examples of progressive activities and lists of charismatic leaders and followers presented here are not exhaustive but are intended simply to show that
the emergence of a charismatic coalition is a distinct possibility. A critical mass
of Catholic charismatic resources is developing in many countries around the

world. An informal alliance seems to be forming not only at the level of the episcopacy (where I assume the resources are strongest) but also among theologians, lower clergy (both celibate and married), religious sisters and brothers,
and at the grassroots lay level of the ecclesial community. As the isolated parts
of this charismatic coalition become aware of their mutual interests and their
varied strengths, it is likely that large numbers of responsible and committed
Catholics, clerical and lay, will not shrink from a program of Church reform.
They may soon become the quiet revolutionary force needed to confront the
dominant papal coalition and enact radical change in the structural form of
priesthood.

PART V

CONTINUITY AND CHANGE

13

THE COLLAPSE OF CELIBATE EXCLUSIVITY

Show your favor graciously to Zion,
rebuild the walls of Jerusalem.
Then there will be proper sacrifice
to please you.

> Ps 51:18–19

I contend that we are witnessing the collapse of celibate exclusivity in the Roman Catholic priesthood. Mandatory celibacy has been identified as the major cause of decline in the priesthood population. The falling numbers represent the collapsing walls of the Church's technical core, the Church that biblical poetry calls Zion and the New Jerusalem. Catholic tradition is bound more deeply to sacerdotal sacramentalism than to male celibate exclusivity, and the majority of Catholics would welcome a married (and gender-inclusive) priesthood that would restore their rightful access to the sacraments, especially the eucharistic sacrifice of the Mass. In this chapter I address a central research question guiding this work: Will the Catholic Church bid farewell to celibate exclusivity in the priesthood, and if so, how soon? I argue that married men will be admitted to the priesthood during the lifetime of this generation of churchgoers. In the concluding chapter I explore the implications of this change in the structure of Catholic ministry for the dismantling of patriarchy in the Church leading to the ordination of women.

Celibacy in the Spotlight

The demographic imbalance between the supply of priests and the demand for priestly services—enumerated in *Full Pews and Empty Altars* and summarized in chapter 2—is like a loaded tanker in the open sea. Once momentum is gained, it takes a long time to slow down and turn around. Even if the conservative coalition finds a successful program for improving recruitment and retention of priests, it would take several decades to decelerate and reverse the downward trend. Several decades, however, is a relatively short time for an organization like the Catholic Church, which measures its age in centuries. Many church leaders, especially those composing the conservative coalition, are content to take a wait-and-see approach. Others mix the wait-and-see attitude with tried-and-true solutions for the business-as-usual approach. Thus, while waiting to see what happens, some dioceses are improving their recruitment techniques and launching prayer campaigns to increase vocations to the male celibate priesthood. Others are urging deeper spiritual programs for priests and seminarians and calling for renewed lay support, hoping such efforts will foster the retention of young men who are at risk of leaving the active ministry. Still others are hoping that large numbers of older men will choose priesthood as a second career and older priests will postpone retirement.

At their proactive best, these approaches assume that the challenge facing the Catholic Church is to change the environment, not adapt to it. If the environment no longer yields enough committed male celibates to staff its growing parishes, then the Church must mount an effort to transform its ecological niche, making it more supportive of male celibate exclusivity. Unfortunately for these strategists, the Church and society have been spending their best efforts in exactly the opposite direction. In chapter 2, I explain that the declining demographic trends in the priesthood are propelled by a deep-seated dissatisfaction with mandatory celibacy. The next step in the analysis, therefore, is to prove that the tide has turned against celibate exclusivity in the priesthood.

Here, too, we encounter a mountain of supportive facts. Study after study executed over the last three decades concludes that poor recruitment and retention of priests is caused, in great measure, by problems with mandatory celibacy. The review of the empirical evidence in chapter 2 provided overwhelming proof that celibate exclusivity is a major intermediate cause of demographic decline in the Catholic priesthood.

The Axial Drama Unfolds

Other links in the argument reach further back in the causal chain. The rejection of male celibate exclusivity gains strength from antecedent religious, social, and environmental trends. From the theoretical view proposed in chapter 3, the priest shortage and the problem with celibacy are riding the waves of irreversible social trends. Shifting numbers in the demographic picture and changing attitudes toward celibacy must be examined against the constant flux of social change affecting both organized religion and society in general. Not just the mandatory celibacy issue but a powerful matrix of inexorable social forces is propelling the priesthood population in its downward trajectory. The full weight of history and social change is turning against male celibate exclusivity in the Catholic priesthood.

Society as a whole, and the Catholic Church along with it, is experiencing an axial epoch. As these historical trends come to bear on the Church, they are producing a unique balance of countervailing pressures for change. In this momentous era of societal transformation, the Catholic Church is trying to adapt its structures to incorporate a better balance between dogmatism and pluralism and between centrism and localism (chapter 7); between male and female equality and between personalism and transpersonalism (chapter 8); and, finally, between clericism and laicism and between sacramental and biblical means of salvation (chapter 9). While adapting to the new era, the Church tries to forge new social mechanisms for transcending the paradoxes of unity and diversity, immanence and transcendence, and hierarchy and hierophany. The priest shortage acts as a catalyst, forcing the trends and paradoxes to reach a threshold of change and inciting Church leaders to conflict and action. A successful solution to the conflict would restore balance in the supply and demand for priestly services in the Catholic Church.

Celibate exclusivity has taken the lead role in the drama currently playing in the Catholic Church. Three main threads of argument explain why mandatory celibacy attracts so much attention. The first holds that material support for mandatory celibacy is waning in the ecological niche of most Catholic dioceses. The second thread combines insights from Marxist and Weberian principles of social change and Perrow's qualified power model: Ideological support for mandatory celibacy grows more critical as material support for it wanes; hence the theology of celibacy and marriage has become a contested ideological terrain where conservative and progressive coalitions fight over the status quo. The third thread suggests that organizational change results when a charismatic coalition successfully resolves conflict over the status quo.

Material Support Wanes

The first thread of the argument reveals that the time for celibate exclusivity in the priesthood has run out. Many of the economic and political conditions supporting mandatory celibacy are less salient nowadays than in the past. In prior centuries, for example, inheritance and landholding traditions in Catholic countries used to provide structural support for priestly celibacy. These customs directed that the first son inherit the family property, encouraging the second or third to enter the priesthood. Under feudalism, large family size was dictated by economic and technological constraints. A traditional agrarian economy is based on a system of farms that requires a relatively large but cheap stationary workforce. Big families supplied the necessary labor for the farm and an abundance of sons for the Church. Although mandatory celibacy was the price to pay, priesthood was nevertheless an attractive avenue of upward mobility in the rigidly controlled feudal system. (Note, too, that a priestly career serves the same latent function in underdeveloped regions of industrializing countries.)

Denied family property that went to the eldest son, ambitious younger sons could satisfy their desire for power and wealth by acquiring a church benefice. Talented younger sons could obtain a higher education in the priesthood. Even homosexual sons could satisfy their need for dignity and respect in the same way.

With the change from an agricultural to an industrial economy, most of the structural supports for mandatory celibacy crumbled. Generally, the *need* for large families is gone, and the widespread availability of effective birth control techniques makes the *choice* of small families possible. In addition, the avenues of upward mobility for men are wider and the chances for power and wealth are greater.

The separation of church and state is another structural support for mandatory celibacy that is weakened by the spread of rational-legal behavior. The Constitution of the United States, for example, protects the Catholic Church's right to maintain celibate exclusivity in the priesthood, although marital-status exclusivity is illegal in all other occupations. If the Church wants to maintain celibacy as a job requirement, the state has historically not interfered; however, over the past half century more and more people have come to question taken-for-granted norms that deprive citizens of their civil rights. As a sign of the times, even church privileges have come under close scrutiny. Witness, for example, the pressure to remove tax exemption from business operations conducted by religious orders and other church-affiliated groups.[1] Thus, although the separation of church and state and religious freedom are still honored in this country, churches have been put on notice not to abuse their privileges.

Stories abound in the liberal Catholic press about Church officials allegedly violating the civil rights of Catholics who take the celibate exclusivity of the priesthood too lightly. A Catholic school teacher who marries a resigned priest loses her job, and other Church employees who attend the wedding are threatened.[2] Married resigned priests cannot be hired for jobs in the Church. As these cases are taken to court, the structural supports for celibate exclusivity in the priesthood are weakened. The taken-for-granted privilege was once so strong that it used to be honored even in its abuses. Not any more. Catholics are wondering about the conflict between their civil rights and churchmen's strong-arm attempts to maintain celibate exclusivity in the priesthood.

While structural supports in favor of mandatory celibacy are waning, structural pressures against it are growing. Obviously, marriage is the norm in contemporary society, and this norm is enforced by widespread suspicion of those who choose not to enter wedlock. This general suspicion has recently increased because of the fear of pedophilia among priests. Whether the celibate priesthood has a higher incidence of pedophilia than similar helping professions that provide access to young children is questionable. In fact, there is some evidence that married men are more prone to pedophilia than single men.[3] Whatever the data show, however, the celibacy of priests is under suspicion. Whether empirically grounded or not, the fear is real. Suspicions about unmarried priests are heightened because of homophobic interpretations of the growing proportion of homosexuals in the Catholic priesthood (chapter 2).

In the final analysis, the most telling structural pressure against celibate exclusivity are losses in the Church's critical economic resource, the priestly workforce. Like any other modern bureaucracy, the Church is organized around its technical core and cannot continue her far-flung operations without an ample supply of priests. The Church must decide, therefore, whether the Catholic tradition of eucharistic worship should be sacrificed on the altar of mandatory celibacy. The conflict over which is the better strategy—keeping mandatory celibacy or retaining the eucharistic sacrifice of the Mass—results in intense ideological struggle.

Ideological Debate Waxes

As the material basis for mandatory celibacy declines, celibate exclusivity becomes an open debate in the Church. Ideological arguments are taking over as the major weapons in the battle, and whose ideology wins is the outcome of a sophisticated political contest. The classic arguments about the political power of ideology are nicely summarized and applied by Rhys Williams and Jay Demerath.[4] They studied a battle over the status quo waged by city politicians in Springfield, Massachusetts, against a religious challenge group. Their findings have direct application to the conflict over mandatory celibacy.

Williams and Demerath note that all political issues go through a life cycle. First, the issue area must be named and defined. How an issue is categorized is a political process. For example, the pope tells bishops to avoid public discussion of mandatory celibacy. This keeps the issue area from evolving because bishops cannot name and define celibate exclusivity as a problem worthy of attention. The debate over a married priesthood may be defined as either a bureaucratic or pastoral issue. Whenever open discussion is permitted, the pope and his agents define the problem as a bureaucratic issue. They couch it in arcane theological language, calling celibacy a "most precious jewel." They announce authoritatively that the theological issues are closed, not in need of further study. They argue that the priest shortage is temporary. Better recruitment techniques, better support groups, better in-service training, better discipline and asceticism, and so on will solve the crisis. This approach is distinctively bureaucratic, not pastoral in tone.

Many bishops, however, define mandatory celibacy as a pastoral problem involving access to the sacraments, especially the Eucharist. They give priority to immediate pastoral solutions. For example, Archbishop Weakland, Bishop Untener, and others in the progressive coalition take a public stand against bureaucratic solutions supporting the status quo. They go on record in favor of the people in the pews, not officials in Rome. They argue that the wait-and-see strategy is wrong. The present generation of practicing Catholics should not be deprived of the Mass because of the scarcity of celibate priests. They propose the immediate and simple pastoral solution of ordaining qualified married men when a celibate priest is unavailable to celebrate Mass (see chapter 12).

In such an ideological battle, Williams and Demerath point out, definitions imply solutions. That is, defining a problem determines who has the authority or responsibility for addressing, deciding, and acting on the issue. Thus, to be granted the right to reduce the complexity of an issue to its essence is a hotly debated political process. If compulsory celibacy is really a pastoral issue, then it must be addressed immediately in those terms. If conservatives can keep attention off the pastoral implications by defining the issue in other terms, then the status quo remains intact.

Describing the battle over celibacy as a political struggle brings up the issue of pressure politics. Should charismatic coalitions use pressure politics to move their agendas forward? No, a much more delicate process is needed, according to Williams and Demerath. Even in city politics, moving away from moral authority toward pressure politics usually backfires for groups that challenge the status quo. Note, however, that the papal coalition is allowed to engage in pressure politics. According to Williams and Demerath, pressure politics exercised by the dominant bureaucratic coalition have an aura of legitimacy precisely because they are orchestrated by those with legitimate authority. "But challenge groups cannot take the solid low ground of pressure politics because that is seen as a reprehensible affront to legitimate authority."[5] Thus challenge groups have to stay close to the moral high ground. The choice of weapons for the progressive coalition favoring a married priesthood must be cultural resources based in pastorally grounded theology and morality.

Thus, progressives argue that the conservatives' insistence on celibacy over marriage creates an artificial, useless barrier between priest and people. Both the call to abstain from sexual intercourse within institutionalized celibacy and the call to engage in it within sacramental marriage have the same spiritual goal—Union with God. The progressive position asserts that the celibate ascetic and the married lover "have" the Divine Lover in different but complementary ways. As Meister Eckhart explained, the mature Christian is both virgin and wife, embracing God not only in divine emptiness but also in divine fullness of Being. Likewise, members of the ordained priesthood can be called to "have" God in celibacy or marriage (chapter 8).

Progressives advocating a married priesthood note that all Christians are pilgrims on the same journey to transpersonal holiness. In this regard, the ordained priesthood is no different from the priesthood of all believers—throughout history, all Christians have been called to "have" God, whether in celibacy or in marriage. Generous response to God's love, no matter what the call or where it leads, is the only test of Christian love. Above all, the test cannot be limited to invidious comparisons between the ascetic difficulties of celibate or married life. Celibacy as such has been and will continue to be a viable, respected path to transpersonal holiness *for those who are called.* A call to priesthood, however, can no longer be equated with a call to celibacy.

Most of all, therefore, allowing priests to marry puts them on the same spiritual plane as the laity. In reality, this means bringing priests down from an unwarranted pedestal and lifting laypeople up from an undeserved inferiority. The conservative transcendentalist view of human sexuality—dominant in Catholicism until recently—casts a shadow over the sanctity of marriage. Allowing married ministers to enter the "holy of holies" lifts the shadow, so all can see marriage as an authentic call to holiness. Marital-status equality of clergy and laity means admitting that all Christians are called equally to the highest levels of spiritual development. Some are called by the path of celibacy, others by marriage. One is different from but not better than the other.

Sorting out higher and lower states of being, whether levels of hierarchy or stages of hierophany, is serious business. Hierarchy implies relative power, dominance, and submission. Hierophany implies higher and lower levels of awareness of Absolute Being and Absolute Power. Mature adults struggle to be free of dominance, submission, and lack of awareness of their full human potential. Paradoxically, mature freedom comes only through stages in which one willingly submits to physical, intellectual, and spiritual leaders who have more strength, more knowledge, and more awareness than oneself. No one ever has enough strength, knowledge, or spiritual awareness to be self-sufficient; even mature adults willingly submit to others who have more of what they need and want. Accordingly, Catholics are willing to submit to authentic hierarchic and hierophanic power embodied in the ordained priesthood.

Catholic priests of the future will continue to exercise sacerdotal and sacramental power because mature laypeople need and want them to. But many mature Catholics no longer need or want to submit to celibate exclusivity in the priesthood. To be authentically religious, Catholic ministry must open itself to the charismatic transformative power of marriage as well as celibacy. Because marital status has nothing to do with access to the highest levels of transrational hierophanic power, it should have nothing to do with access to the highest levels of rational hierarchic power. The radical equality of hierophanic power demands marital-status equality in ministering the means of salvation.

Continuity and Change

The last thread, explaining why the celibacy issue torments the Catholic Church, is spun from the theoretical model's fifth proposition: Social progress results when structural tension creates conflict over the status quo, a charismatic coalition resolves the conflict, and the organization moves in the direction of the charismatic coalition's progressive values. So, we ask, if the progressive coalition is victorious in the coalition conflict buffeting the Church, which aspects of the status quo will change?

Of the interrelated traits constituting the current form of Catholic ministry, two flow from the essence, or deep structure, of religion: sacerdotalism and sacramentalism. The other two stem from historical and cultural circumstances, or the surface structures, of religion: celibate and male exclusivity. Because celibacy has become the most vulnerable trait defining the priesthood, it takes on an exaggerated importance. Just as a chain is only as strong as its weakest link, the weak commitment to mandatory celibacy makes this aspect of the status quo likely to be broken first, after which the structure of ministry will change dramatically as married men are ordained to the Catholic priesthood.

Although highly probable, the ordination of married men in the immediate future is not inevitable. Conflict over the structural form of Catholic ministry is far from being resolved. The conservative coalition vigorously dedicates itself to preserving the status quo, while the progressive coalition cautiously tries to change it. The very intensity of this conflict indicates that transformation is already underway. Social transformations are marked by change as well as continuity.

Because they are part of the deep structure of religion, hierarchy and sacrament will always be part of the definition of Catholic ministry. Thus, the sacramental priesthood will remain intact. And, despite greater participation of the laity in Catholic liturgy, approaching the *mysterium tremendum* in the eucharistic sacrifice remains an awesome hierophanic event. Because it must be celebrated communally, sacrificial worship requires a properly designated sacrificer. Thus, in keeping with the unique rights and responsibilities flowing from ordination, priests will still be called to preside over sacramental celebrations, principally the eucharistic sacrifice of the Mass. Even the rites that require a priest, however, are no longer rigidly controlled by them.

Laypeople now help plan the liturgy, which is not only celebrated in the vernacular but also in other ways adjusted to local culture and custom. Catholic laypeople actively participate by reciting prayers, singing hymns, reading the Scripture passages, serving at the altar, even preaching homilies and distributing the bread and wine at Communion. Furthermore, such activities are open to both men and women. These modifications, unheard-of a few decades ago, have become routine in Catholic parishes. Moreover, they will endure because they fit the needs of an educated, pluralistic community moving away from its Eurocentric origins.

Once in place, modifications in the order of worship have far-reaching structural consequences. Following the iron law of *lex orandi, lex credendi* (the order of worship determines the order of the believing community), if the ordained priesthood shares hierarchic control of worship with the priesthood of all believers, other transformations follow. Genuine participation in creating and controlling the order of worship demands greater participation in hierarchic co-ordination and control of the structure of the believing community. Decision-making power over the hierophanic actions of worship necessarily spills over into decision-making power governing other hierarchical activities. Note, how-ever, that hierarchic power continues, even though it has been adjusted to in-clude participation of the laity. Hierophanic power continues, too, even though it has been modified to balance the power of sacrament and word.

The continuity of hierarchy and hierophany is guaranteed as long as practi-tioners recognize that these traits are part of the deep structure of authentic re-ligion. They can be adjusted and modified but not eliminated without destroy-ing the essence of religious organization. Though inextricably tied together, hierophanic power has priority over hierarchic power. Thus the wisdom in the law of *lex orandi, lex credendi:* The hierophanic structure of worship determines the hierarchic structure of the believing community, not vice versa. After all is said and done, therefore, the status quo remains intact in its deep structure. Although modified by lay participation, Catholic ministry will continue to be characterized by sacerdotal sacramentalism. In the Catholic tradition, the priest embodies the fullness of both hierarchic and hierophanic power. Thus, the or-dained priesthood will always be given a higher level of power and authority than the laity. The surface structure of the priesthood, however, will be radically transformed as male celibate monopoly of control collapses. This will happen in two stages. Because male exclusivity has deeper ramifications for patriarchal so-ciety as a whole, celibate exclusivity will be the first to go. But then the married priesthood will provide an opening through which the Church will subsequently drop male exclusivity. How and when will this climactic breakthrough occur?

The Breakthrough Scenario

The Church will open the priesthood to married men in the lifetime of the cur-rent generation. Ostensibly this move will be motivated by pastoral concerns, but official permission will be granted because of economic pressure and polit-ical expediency. Here is the likely scenario.

Within a decade, pressures for a lasting solution to the priest shortage come to a head as the priesthood population continues to dwindle. Progressive coali-tions in certain parts of the Catholic world step up their activity, gaining solidar-ity, visibility, and political expertise. Encouraged by coalitional support, scores of individual bishops and several national bishops conferences contact the next pope soon after his election. They ask permission to ordain qualified married men when celibate priests are not available to provide the Mass and sacraments. They document the emergency situation and explain that they are motivated by pastoral concern for the spiritual needs of their dioceses.

The new pope and his advisers consider the mounting evidence. In their deliberations they give the most weight to economic arguments. The Church needs a competent workforce to provide religious services to almost a billion Roman Catholics. Lay participation notwithstanding, the ordained priesthood remains the technical core of ministry. Besides, in developed countries lay ministers have proven ineffective and unmanageable because of high turnover and related problems. Without a sufficient supply of priests and reliable professional ministers, religious services will have to be drastically cut, not only in quantity and but also in quality. The threat to Catholicism's well-being looms large.

Thus, economic considerations also interact with political factors. The hierarchic sacerdotal priesthood is the Catholic response to the need for centralized control, a fundamental requirement of organized religion; hence ordained priests can be replaced by lay ministers only up to a point. The unrestrained appointment of lay ministers would inevitably result in excessive lay participation in decision-making. The new papal coalition concludes, therefore, that the ordination of married men would, in effect, solve both the economic and political problems. Accordingly, the new pope begins to grant limited permission for bishops to ordain qualified married men when extreme circumstances warrant it. Ideological considerations stemming from traditional Catholic theology are cited to legitimate the change, underplaying the political-economic motives behind the decision.

In reality, the compromise solution is reached as a result of mounting conflict between coalitions of bishops, priests, religious, and laity. Rome is well aware of the tensions and counterpressures. Coalitions that form in countries with longer and unbroken histories of democracy favor the papal compromise: for example, blocs of progressive Catholics in the United States, Canada, France, England, Belgium, and the Netherlands. Progressive coalitions in liberal democratic countries ally themselves with those from countries where the preferential option for the poor has the support of the majority or a significant minority. For example, Catholic coalitions in Latin America and Africa will supply ideological and emotional resources needed for a successful challenge to celibate exclusivity. These will galvanize the pastoral concerns of prophetic coalitions in liberal democratic countries able to supply material and organizational resources.

Progressive coalitions are opposed by those from countries with histories of authoritarianism and challenges to democratic government, either fascist or communist: principally, Germany, Austria, Italy, Spain, and Poland, along with other eastern European countries. The emerging dominance of progressive coalitions, however, is supported by growing worldwide opposition to authoritarian governments in general. The totalitarian regimes of the Soviet Union have broken up, and those of the People's Republic of China and Cuba seem increasingly to teeter on the brink of collapse.

Catholic progressive coalitions receive additional support from the trend toward greater democracy not only in political but other societal institutions as well. Catholicism by definition aspires to be a universal form of religion. It is open to everyone, even infants, who submit to the waters of baptism. Ironically, compulsory celibacy and male dominance have become organizational obstacles to universalism as it is now defined by modern ideology and plausibility struc- tures. In modern democratic countries, ascriptive barriers to high office in most institutions are illegal. The ideology of equality (the foundation stone of demo- cratic citizenship) becomes more widespread through consciousness-raising ef- forts of the feminist movement, the civil rights movement, and liberation theol- ogy. Fewer and fewer mature Catholics will be drawn to the ideology that supports and makes political sense of male celibate exclusivity of the priesthood.

The Roman Catholic Church remains one of the last strongholds of authori- tarian monarchy in the modern world. In fact, the degree to which rigid central- ized control marks its internal workings and spiritual ministry is unprecedented in its long history.[6] Conservative coalitions can no longer sustain it. As the politi- cal-economic pressure of the priest shortage and its consequences escalates, pro- gressive coalitions gain dominance over conservative coalitions supporting the status quo. With dwindling support from fading authoritarianism in its ecological niche and the increasing failure to recruit and retain sufficient leadership re- sources, the Catholic Church decides to reform its technostructure to survive.

Papal permission to ordain married men in extreme circumstances proves to be the camel's nose under the tent. The problem is too widespread to be ad- dressed with scattered improvements. Local churches are not content to suffer from a priest shortage when a solution is there for the asking. As poor recruit- ment and retention of celibate priests continues, the pope is forced to relax the definition of "extreme circumstances." More and more individual dioceses and then entire national bishops conferences seek permission to ordain married men. As ordination rates increase, resignation rates subside, and laypeople be- come comfortable receiving priestly services from married men, the radical breakthrough is gradually routinized. Thus, a steady supply of priestly leader- ship will be available in the future as long as dioceses and religious orders can recruit and retain sufficient married and celibate men for ordination to the priesthood.

Conclusion

I do not want to suggest that this transformation will be painless. The solution to one set of conflicts often sets off another cycle of organizational turmoil. Un- forseen conflicts are likely to emerge. Despite the growing pains, however, most Catholics will have little trouble saying farewell to celibate fathers and welcome to married fathers in the priesthood. The transformed priesthood will restore their right to the Mass and sacraments, once again allowing the People of God to go up to Jerusalem and offer proper, pleasing sacrifice. Then they will begin to wonder about saying goodbye to father-rule and hello to gender equality. The big question—which I address in the concluding chapter—will loom larger than ever: When will the demise of male exclusivity in the Catholic priesthood occur, and what will be its impact on dismantling patriarchy in society?

14

GOODBYE FATHER

You must call no one on earth your father, since you have only one Father,
and he is in heaven.

Mt. 23:9

In the 1944 movie *Going My Way,* Bing Crosby played an astute young priest,
Father O'Malley, and Barry Fitzgerald a seasoned pastor, Father Fitzgibbon.
Both were admired and loved by parishioners and friends and still are by video
viewers two generations later. The film's nostalgic scenes remind us that calling
a priest Father is as Catholic as the rosary and as American as apple pie. Similarly, Catholics and the whole world know Karol Wojtyla as Pope John Paul II, a
title with the same etymology as *father.*[1] In most Romance languages the connotation is even more evident: The word for pope is *papa,* identical to the af-
fectionate term for father. Many address the pope simply as Holy Father. Thus,
whether referring to parish priest or supreme pontiff, the same title signifying
monarchical control, patriarchal respect, reverential fear, and filial affection is
used worldwide and has been for almost two millennia.

This book challenges Catholics and society at large to say goodbye to *Father.*
Not, I insist, goodbye to the sacerdotal sacramentalism of priestly ministry, but
to what the title *Father* has come to symbolize: male celibate exclusivity.

Of the ideal-typical traits characterizing Catholic ministry, two will endure
and two will fall away. Sacerdotal and sacramental dominance will continue, but,
one day soon, celibate and male exclusivity will no longer distinguish the Catholic priesthood. Of the two that will eventually disappear, patriarchal control
attached to male exclusivity is a much more critical problem than the marital-
status inequality attached to celibate exclusivity. I agree with those who find the
ban against ordaining women to be theologically untenable and morally out-
rageous. Moreover, demeaning women by excluding them from positions of full
power makes no political or economic sense in a voluntary organization whose
membership is predominantly female. Overall, male exclusivity in the Catholic
priesthood is more detrimental to authentic religion than celibate exclusivity.
Granted, the enormity of the problem created by male exclusivity demands the
Church's full attention, and the problem of celibate exclusivity pales in comparison. Nevertheless, the forces of history and the dynamics of social change dic-

tate that the Catholic Church will settle the problem of celibate exclusivity first, before it attempts to address male exclusivity. The door of exclusivity is locked with two bars, one on top of the other. Only by lifting the bar of celibate exclusivity will the incongruity of the bar of male exclusivity be exposed.

Speaking personally as a lifelong, faithful, and loyal Roman Catholic, I say: My own theology, sense of justice, and personal spiritual practice convince me that patriarchal dominance is, by far, a greater obstacle to the Christian ideal than mandatory celibacy. Good sociology, however, shows that the Church must and will deal with the issues serially, first permitting the ordination of married men and later the ordination of women. This book argues that a married priesthood is all but a *fait accompli*. A gender-inclusive priesthood, however, faces a long uphill climb. Both are inevitable. One will unfold in a generation, the other in the foreseeable future.

The aim of this final chapter is to address the remaining issues raised by these sociological conclusions and convictions. Because of the nature of these topics, this chapter is more speculative and personal than the others. It begins with the question: Why must the Catholic Church handle the problem of mandatory celibacy before it addresses the ordination of women? I then ask: If the ordination of married men is so imminent, why does the papal coalition oppose it so adamantly?

In answering these questions I explain that priestly celibacy reinforces patriarchal dominance in the Church and society at large. In order, eventually, to say farewell to father-rule, Catholics will first have to say goodbye to celibate fathers. The authoritarian triumphalistic papacy has mounted its last hurrah over both issues. The discussion leads to a final scenario and a résumé of the overall argument. The scenario: The ordination of women to the Catholic priesthood will occur within our grandchildren's lifetime.

Compulsory Celibacy Now, Patriarchy Later

Why will the Catholic Church settle the problem of celibate exclusivity in the ministry before it addresses male exclusivity? Because the institution of compulsory celibacy for priests is more shallowly embedded, more narrowly diffused, more deeply debated, and less widely opposed than the institution of patriarchal ministry. In a word, patriarchal ministry is a much stronger institution than celibate ministry, and deconstructing patriarchy will take significantly more time and effort than dropping celibate exclusivity.

Embeddedness

Consider, first, that the historical embeddedness of patriarchy far exceeds that of compulsory celibacy. Scholars reckon the age of patriarchy by including the two millennia of the common era and the prehistoric period in which it emerged. Thus, they estimate that patriarchy has dominated for at least five millennia and its influence has been strongly felt for an additional five. The transition from hunting and gathering to agriculture-based economies is dated around 8000 to 10000 B.C.E. This axial period witnessed the shift from matrilineal societies, in which divine forces were imaged predominantly with mother goddess symbols, to patriarchal societies, in which the female images began to be replaced with father god symbols. Simultaneously, control of religious ministry gradually passed from females to males.

If the period is restricted to the epoch in which father-rule dominated civilization, then patriarchy has existed for about five millennia. Archaeologists recognize that neolithic groups are predominantly patriarchal societies around the middle of the fourth millennium (3500) B.C.E. Exclusively male ministry becomes dominant in Greek and Hebrew religions and remains so in practically all organized religions until the end of the second millennium of the Christian Era.

In contrast with the five to ten millennia of male dominance in religious ministry, exclusively celibate ministry, as it is known in the Christian West, has existed for only four to eight centuries. (This calculation ignores early Christianity, when priests were married, and the period between the fourth and eleventh centuries, when bishops tried in vain to impose celibacy on secular priests.) Mandatory celibacy for all Latin rite priests became viable during the Gregorian Reform (ca. 1050–1150), although even then with rampant concubinage and countless married priests. Compliance increased notably after the Second Lateran Council in 1139 and the Fourth Lateran Council in 1215. These councils declared clerical marriage null and void. Despite repeated prescriptions from Church councils, however, mandatory celibacy became universal, in the sense of relatively little concubinage and few married priests, only after seminary reforms mandated by the Council of Trent in 1575. Thus, a uniformly celibate priesthood has existed in the Roman Catholic Church for about the last four centuries.

Diffusion

The strength of patriarchal ministry in comparison to celibate ministry can also be gauged by how extensively each is diffused in organized religion. Clearly, patriarchal ministry is overwhelmingly dominant in the vast majority of religions throughout the world. Indeed father-rule persists worldwide in most other social institutions as well. Celibate exclusivity, however, is limited to a minority of religious functionaries. Although much more widespread than compulsory celibacy, father-rule is under heavy criticism. It is receding, even in religious settings. By no means, however, has patriarchy ceded dominance to gender inclusivity.

Male exclusivity is on the wane in Protestant churches, in Zen Buddhism in the United States, and in some new religious movements like Wicca. In a recent study, Mark Chaves shows that half of large Protestant denominations have granted full ministerial rights to women.[2] Similarly, he argues convincingly that the feminist movement and other pressures external to the churches have succeeded in providing women opportunities for religious ministry in practice that far exceed the rights granted by the rules. He cites the growing population of Protestant and Catholic women in seminaries, the large number of ministerial jobs held by both Protestant and Catholic women, and the many church leadership positions filled by women, especially in mission activities.

At the same time, however, male dominance is still strong, even where women have been given full ministerial privileges by denominational rules. Most of the research reports that female ministers are definitely discriminated against—offered lower-level jobs, less pay, less prestige, and so on than their male colleagues.[3] Gender equality in religious ministry is struggling for a place in the sun. But the evidence shows that the sunshine is melting only the tip of an enormous iceberg. Below the surface, patriarchal dominance fills the waters of religious ministry.

In comparison, the exclusively celibate Catholic priesthood is an ice cube in an ocean of marital-status inclusivity. Only Catholicism, of all world and ancestral religions, restricts full ministerial privileges to unmarried men. The Roman Catholic Church confines the entire priesthood, from pope to curate, to those who try to practice lifelong celibacy. The Orthodox churches limit the episcopacy to celibates but allow the lower clergy to marry. In addition, the vow of chastity, which assumes celibacy, is taken in monosexual religious communities of the Eastern and Western Christian churches and those of monastic Buddhism in the Far East.

At the dawn of a new millennium, celibate ministers are a distinct and declining minority. Gender exclusivity, however, is the mirror image of celibate exclusivity. Worldwide, the vast majority of religious functionaries with full ministerial privileges are men, and only a distinct, though growing, minority are women.

Debate

The theological, pastoral, and legal pros and cons of marital-status exclusivity have been debated at much greater length than those of gender exclusivity. Great controversies over the morality of marriage and the value of celibacy were waged between the Apostolic Church and the Gnostic sects.[4] These were continued in Church councils, beginning as early as the Spanish Council of Elvira in 306 and the ecumenical Council of Nicea in 325. Nicea was the first ecumenical council in the Church's history, and the bishops assembled there refused to make the local ruling against married priests promulgated at Elvira a universal requirement.

Obviously, the scriptural and theological issues were quickly settled in favor of marriage, otherwise the new religious movement would have died out.[5] Nor were any theological or biblical grounds found to forbid priests from marrying. During early Christianity, most of the apostles and most priests were married, and clerical marriage and concubinage were tolerated until the end of the Middle Ages.

James Coriden lists a score of councils and major papal decrees between Elvira and Trent that dealt with the troublesome issue of clerical celibacy.[6] Steven Ozment describes the prolific discussion on the topic following Luther's posting of his 95 theses: "The reformers set out to demonstrate not only in theological but in personal and social terms the superiority of a married to a celibate clergy."[7] Note the nuance of the discussions. They hinged on the *pastoral superiority* of marriage over celibacy for priests, not whether theology or Scripture *allowed* priests to marry. That was never an issue in the Roman Catholic or any other Christian church.

John Lynch summarizes the major debates over legal and pastoral issues just prior to the Reformation and Counter-Reformation.[8] He also describes the decrees of the Council of Trent that reasserted universal compulsory celibacy and the unmitigated "frontal attacks" on the discipline that continued from Trent to the Second Vatican Council and beyond. Popes, emperors, kings, and cardinals, along with major and minor theologians and clergy, all had their opinions. The tracts, memoranda, decrees, books, and other publications spelling out the fine points of the debate number in the thousands. It is not an exaggeration to say that the theological, pastoral, and legal refinement of the mandatory celibacy issue began roughly 17 centuries ago and has continued unabated ever since.

In contrast, the debate over patriarchal control in religious ministry was initiated only one and a half centuries ago. With rare exceptions, it never entered anyone's mind to question male dominance in prior ages. Why this long and dark silence? Under patriarchy, men write the history of society. In fact, men control all symbol systems, including religion. Throughout Western civilization, from the beginning of the historical period until almost the twentieth century, women were not allowed either to make history or to know it. In her analysis of the rise of patriarchy, Gerda Lerner shows that "male hegemony over the symbol system took two forms: educational deprivation of women and male monopoly on definition."[9] Women did not know they could aspire to independent positions of power because history contained no examples of women acting autonomously. Men had defined that all positions of dominance were held exclusively by males:

> There had never been any woman or group of women who had lived without out male protection, as far as most women knew. There had never been any group of persons like them who had done anything significant for themselves. Women had no history—so they were told; so they believed. Thus, ultimately, it was men's hegemony over the symbol system which most decisively disadvantaged women.[10]

Thus, ideological support for male exclusivity is rooted in two millennia of taken-for-granted patriarchal hegemony in the Christian churches, plus the several millennia of male dominance that preceded Christianity. This is, indeed, a decisive disadvantage for abolishing male exclusivity in religious ministry.

Women had to find a way to break the silence. The first wave of the feminist movement is traced to a group of Protestant laywomen at a women's rights convention held in Seneca Falls, New York, in 1848. One of the resolutions called for "the overthrow of the monopoly of the pulpit."[11] Catholics entered the fray only about three decades ago. Leonard Swidler credits a Catholic laywoman with bringing the issue of female priests into the public forum.[12] In 1962, Gertrude Heinzelman, a Swiss lawyer, petitioned the Preparatory Commission of the Second Vatican Council to discuss the possibility. By 1970, four scholarly studies of male exclusivity in the Catholic priesthood appeared—all concluding in favor of female priests.[13] Even a report of the Pontifical Biblical Commission, issued in 1976, concluded that the Christian Bible leaves the question open.[14]

Documents from the Second Vatican Council spoke eloquently about gender equality in the Church, theological studies supported the ordination of women, and the pope's own Biblical Commission said the Bible does not oppose female priests. Late in 1976 Rome responded to the growing debate. The Congregation for the Doctrine of the Faith issued *Inter Insigniores,* the "Declaration on the Question of the Admission of Women to the Ministerial Priesthood." It said that the "Church, in fidelity to the example of the Lord, does not consider herself authorized to admit women to priestly ordination."[15]

An unsigned commentary issued with the declaration recounts the events leading up to its publication.[16] The Catholic magisterium's interest was sparked in 1958 when the Swedish Lutheran Church admitted women to the priesthood. Concern mounted when the Episcopalian Church began ordaining women in the early 1970s. The flame was fanned in 1975 when the United Nations sponsored International Women's Year and Catholic nuns, clergy, and laity held a national conference in Detroit entitled "Women in the Future: Priesthood Now, a Call to Action."

Inter Insigniores spawned a rash of reactions contesting the Vatican's narrow opinion and indecisive scholarship. In the process, it became apparent that despite the flurry of reports and publications, from a theologian's viewpoint the issue of female priests remained woefully unexamined. The declaration itself acknowledged that "we are dealing with a debate which classical theology scarcely touched upon" and that the magisterium never had to defend male exclusivity in the priesthood because it was "a principle . . . not attacked . . . a law . . . not challenged."[17] The noted theologian and scripture scholar Carroll Stuhlmueller concludes that "the biblical, patristic, and scholastic basis [for male exclusivity] is not presented as probative . . . the theological debate has only begun."[18]

Most recently, Pope John Paul attempted to quell the debate entirely by pub-

lishing *Ordinatio Sacerdotalis,* "Priestly Ordination Reserved to Men Alone."[19]
But as Yogi Berra would say, the pope's 1994 apostolic letter is déjà vu all over
again. The letter offers nothing new beyond the 1976 Declaration issued by the
Congregation for the Doctrine of the Faith. The only novelty is its strident tone.
In issuing the new document, the pope chooses to ignore the scholarship published in the last three decades, particularly studies called for by the 1976 Declaration, Vatican statements, and bishops concerned about gender equality.[20]

The theological, pastoral, and legal debate in the Catholic Church over female priests is in its infancy. In stark contrast, theological controversy over celibacy was almost nonexistent, because married priests have never been opposed
on scriptural or theological grounds. The real debate has always focused on pastoral, legal, and administrative issues. As such, the debate over compulsory celibacy has been carried on relentlessly since the Council of Elvira.

Opposition

In addition to being more shallowly embedded, more narrowly diffused, and
more deeply debated, compulsory celibacy is more widely opposed than patriarchal ministry. The very term *compulsory* celibacy connotes a history of more
or less flagrant violation and bitter opposition. It supposes that opposition to the
ruling is taken for granted. Recall that compulsory celibacy refers not to the vow
of chastity by monks and members of religious orders but to the universal im-
position of celibacy on all ordained priests of the Roman rite, whether they belong to the diocesan or religious order clergy.

Every poll taken since the Second Vatican Council reports that a majority of
priests and laypeople favors married priests (chapter 2). At the same time, of
course, Rome and the papal coalition oppose any change in the ruling (chapter
11). Although the magisterium offers no scriptural or theological opposition to
married priests, the conservative coalition insists on the ambiguous pastoral and
ascetic *superiority* of celibacy. For example, the short statement on celibacy issued from the Second Vatican Council summarizes the major points currently
stressed by the Catholic magisterium. Coriden lists them as follows: (1) the nature of the priesthood does not demand celibacy; (2) the tradition of married
priests in the Eastern Church should be respected; (3) the source of the obligation is ecclesiastical law, not an "implicit vow"; (4) the motives for celibacy are
not cultic purity or lack of appreciation of marriage and sexuality; and (5) the
positive reasons for celibacy are theological, spiritual, and pastoral—namely, a
sign of the world to come, devotion to Christ, and dedication to apostolic ministry.[21] The first four points all confirm that banning marriage in the priesthood
has no scriptural or dogmatic basis. The fifth point reflects the ambiguity of the
alleged theological, pastoral, and ascetical reasons.

As I have shown in previous chapters (especially 2 and 8), both marriage and celibacy are charismatic signs of the world to come; as such, each is different from but neither is superior to the other. Likewise, the Second Vatican Council clearly says that all Christians, not just priests, are called to full devotion to Christ.[22] That leaves dedication to apostolic ministry as the only unique reason for imposing celibacy on priests. Whether celibate priests are more dedicated to ministry than married ones is a debate settled in favor of marriage by the Protestant churches and celibacy by the Catholic Church.

So who in the Roman Catholic Church is for and who is against mandatory celibacy? The conservative coalition firmly supports mandatory celibacy in pastoral theory and legal practice. In everyday attitude and practice, however, ambiguous or cynical support and widespread opposition still reign supreme. The unbroken tradition of married clergy in the Eastern churches speaks for itself: They firmly oppose compulsory celibacy in theory and in practice. The Reformation sects and denominations emerged vociferously supporting married ministers. Obviously, all Protestant churches are opposed to mandatory celibacy. In their hearts and minds the vast majority of Christians are opposed to compulsory celibacy for priests and ministers.

In comparison, how widespread is opposition to male monopoly of control in religious ministry? The official story is short and simple in the Catholic churches. The Roman Catholic magisterium manifests strong support for male exclusivity. Official statements demonstrate fierce theological opposition to lifting the ban on women priests. The papacy under Paul VI and John Paul II has spoken decisively: The Church must resist any suggestion that male exclusivity is not of divine origin. The Eastern Catholic churches are in firm agreement.

The possibility of women priests would hardly have entered any Catholic's mind before the Second Vatican Council. By 1974, however, a national poll discovered that 29 percent of American Catholics favored women priests. A series of U.S. Gallup polls taken after the 1976 Declaration appeared found steadily increasing proportions of Catholics in favor of women priests over a very short period of time: February 18, 31 percent; March 4, 36 percent; March 18, 41 percent.[23] By the 1990s, national surveys in the United States reported that two-thirds of all adult Catholics and three-fourths of those under 35 favor women's ordination,[24] and German surveys found that support for women priests ranged from 50 to 70 percent in different regions of that country.[25]

As noted earlier, full gender equality is still opposed among large minorities of Protestant Christians. The NORC's 1986 General Social Survey reported that the proportion of U.S. adults who are "against female clergy" ranges from 37 percent in the non-South and nonrural areas to 43 percent in the South and rural areas of the country. Judaism is split on the issue, but the majority of rabbis are male.[26] Islam appears to be intransigent regarding male dominance.[27] A few women have been recognized as Hindu and Buddhist leaders, but support for gender inclusivity comes from voices crying in the wilderness of father-rule.[28]

To recapitulate, despite strong support from Rome, opposition to celibate exclusivity is widespread in the only religious organization where it is required. Moreover, opposition to mandatory celibacy is universal in all other religions. In contrast, opposition to male exclusivity is more ambiguous and considerably less widespread in the Catholic churches, other Christian churches, and other world religions.

Patriarchy: The Real Villain

Celibate exclusivity is on a precarious footing in the Catholic Church. Arguments abound alleging that the ordination of married men is imminent. Given the centuries-long opposition to celibate exclusivity; the negative impact of compulsory celibacy on recruitment and retention in the priesthood during recent decades; the endorsements of the sacramental power of marriage from the personalist movement echoed in the Second Vatican Council; and, above all, the weakening of the eucharistic tradition stemming from the priest shortage, it would seem eminently sensible for the Church to drop the celibacy requirement—the sooner the better. I turn now to the second unanswered question. Why is the papal coalition so adamantly opposed to a married clergy? I believe that the pastoral and ascetic reasons offered are smokescreens hiding the real motive. The most telling and perhaps most unexamined reason is that clerical celibacy provides sacralized support for patriarchy.

The papal coalition is emphatically opposed to tampering with any of the traditional traits of Catholic priesthood, whether sacramental sacerdotalism or male celibate exclusivity. As we have discovered, defending sacerdotal sacramentalism is relatively easy because it is rooted in deep structural elements of authentic religion. Furthermore, almost no one in the Roman Catholic tradition seriously opposes sacerdotal sacramentalism. Celibate exclusivity, however, has been vulnerable since its inception. Today, this vulnerability has increased exponentially because of mandatory celibacy's connection with patriarchy.

Male exclusivity and celibate exclusivity reinforce one another. Letting go of celibate exclusivity would expose male exclusivity in the priesthood for what it is: a historically developed form of gender dominance. If celibate exclusivity is recognized as theologically and pastorally outmoded, then male exclusivity can be subjected to similar criticism, found wanting, and be rejected as well. Celibate exclusivity must be defended at all costs because it provides a sacralized veneer for father-rule. Simply put, father-rule maintains that males rule the family because they rule better than females. Under patriarchy, the superiority of male dominance is extrapolated to all societal institutions. Applied to the Catholic priesthood, only males can be ordained because males rule better than females. By extrapolation, celibate males rule better than married ones because they are free from full relationships with women. Male celibate priests are spiritual fathers, ruling an essentially spiritual community intent not on this world but on the world to come.

According to Hubert and Mauss, all believing communities decide who will embody their sacred symbols by applying the principle of congruity—like attracts like. Ideally, only the finest gifts are offered in ritual sacrifice: first fruits, an unblemished lamb, a *primogenitus* (firstborn), a *unigenitus* (only offspring).[29] Thus, the principle of congruity demands that only those whom the community considers its finest members should be designated to offer the sacrifice. Under the assumptions of strict patriarchy, therefore, only males are allowed to offer sacrifice, for males are superior to females. Hence, as long as patriarchy is taken for granted, male dominance goes unquestioned. Because male dominance is sacralized by its connection with the priesthood, it is even less questionable. The certainty that male dominance is sacred is strengthened further by the institution of compulsory celibacy in the Catholic priesthood.

The sacred symbolic force of celibacy emerges from multiple sources. Because it does not stem from the assumptions of patriarchy, celibacy adds another distinct layer of sacrality to father-rule. Ideally, a commitment to celibacy is grounded in a personal desire for the transcendent emptiness of Infinitely Possible Being (chapter 8). This ideal was institutionalized when Christianity was heavily influenced by principles of other-worldly transcendentalism. The institutionalization resulted in consecrated virginity for women, vowed chastity for monks, and—against great opposition—imposed celibacy for priests.

As I discussed earlier, Christianity ushered in an epoch of other-worldly transcendentalism. In the early Pauline communities, the married person was considered a "half-Christian."[30] The unmarried person was idealized because he or she maintained an undistracted devotion to Christ. Free from this-worldly sexual relations, the unmarried Christian was a sign of the world to come; moreover, the early Christians thought the Second Coming, when Christ would establish this heavenly kingdom, was imminent. Although marriage obviously became the norm, the Christian construction of sexuality overemphasized the transcendent spirit to the neglect of the immanent body, creating a dualistic spiritual superiority.[31] I have labeled the emphasis on spiritual superiority to the neglect of the sacred immanence of the body "other-worldly transcendentalism."

In keeping with the principles of other-worldly transcendentalism, ministers offering the eucharistic sacrifice should remain celibate, for celibates are more devoted to Christ and more clearly signify the world to come than married persons. Following the assumptions of patriarchy, ministers offering the eucharistic sacrifice should be males, for males are superior to women in all leadership positions. And in keeping with the principles of hierarchy and hierophany, ministers offering the eucharistic sacrifice should be ordained priests, for ordination sets a person apart for sacred things.

Thus, male exclusivity, celibate exclusivity, and sacerdotal exclusivity all stem from separate sources of sacrality. Each form of exclusivity reinforces the other because like attracts like. Not only is celibacy further sacralized through its connection with a major sacrament, namely, priesthood, but vice versa, the sacrament of priesthood is further sacralized through its connection with celibacy. Likewise, the sacred character of male exclusivity is reinforced by its link to a celibate priesthood.

Until recently, male exclusivity and celibate exclusivity were perfect together because the patriarchal transcendence of the former reinforced the other-worldly transcendence of the latter. Together they symbolized the sacred taboos inherent in priesthood. Their alliance made perfect sense as long as patriarchy and other-worldly transcendence held sway in the Catholic Church. Both social constructions, however, are now under heavy criticism. I have argued that patriarchy is being gradually replaced by gender equality and interdependence and that other-worldly transcendentalism is receding in the wake of this-worldly personalism. So male and celibate exclusivity are no longer perfect together, because patriarchy and other-worldly transcendentalism no longer form a taken-for-granted holy alliance.

Of the two, ironically, male superiority is the weaker sacred symbol because maleness is an ascriptive attribute. It requires no spiritual asceticism or voluntary choice: a person is born male. Potentially at least, celibate exclusivity has a stronger symbolic force because celibacy can be freely chosen and voluntarily practiced. Removing the symbolic force of celibacy from the priesthood would expose the weaker symbolic force of male superiority, thus endangering the dominance of father-rule. In effect, celibacy provides a sacred shield for patriarchy.

As a social institution, father-rule is a massive structure, solidly based on the millennia-deep, worldwide bedrock of patriarchy. As an authentic religious principle, however, father-rule is a theological house of cards, incapable of withstanding the strong winds of rational criticism. Lerner and others argue convincingly that patriarchy, for all its massiveness, was socially constructed and so is capable of being socially deconstructed.

Farewell to Father-Rule

I have shown that modifying sacerdotal sacramental dominance and eliminating celibate exclusivity will have deep repercussions. Of the four ideal-type traits, male monopoly of control is, by far, the most controversial. Indeed, weakening male exclusivity and eventually eliminating it altogether will have the deepest repercussions of all. The effects of deconstructing patriarchy in the Catholic Church will be felt throughout society. Thus, "dismantling patriarchy" is the ultimate dependent variable in figure 1. All the other segments in the model of social change—the celibacy issue, in particular—bear on this final problem. The celibacy controversy gains urgency because dropping celibate exclusivity is the necessary breach in the patriarchal wall of male dominance. A married priest-hood is the crack that will eventually cause the barrier of gender exclusivity to crumble, first in the Catholic Church and then in other sectors of society.

The main reason why male exclusivity is a long way from the official reform agenda is because the Catholic Church has spent little or no effort developing a theology of gender equality. What passes for Catholic theology of human gen-der and sexuality draws from mostly inaccurate or outdated philosophy, anthro-pology, biology, social science, and history.[32] Moreover, Catholic scholars who suggest new tenets that veer even moderately from Rome's traditional views have been harassed and condemned (chapter 11).[33]

Lerner says it well: It is men's hegemonic control of the symbol system that most decisively disadvantages women. As long as paternalistic celibate men con-trol Catholic theology, gender equality will not get serious attention. As volatile an issue as it is, male exclusivity will be kept off stage as long as celibate exclu-sivity can successfully maintain the status quo in the Catholic priesthood. Celi-bate exclusivity is being used as a foil to avoid confronting the real underlying issue of patriarchal dominance and control.

The connection between institutionalized celibacy and the degradation and domination of women is beginning to receive some scholarly attention. In as-sessing the costs related to compulsory celibacy, Sipe notes:

> In the history of . . . celibacy, we see that the shift sexually was from the essentially horizontal power base of the Gospel . . . to one of male domi-nance over property and women. What Duby describes within the family in 1030 France was paradigmatic of the sexual shift in the whole Church: "What had been an equal association between husband and wife gradually changed into a miniature monarchy in which the man ruled as king."
>
> As celibacy became codified, the power of women and the develop-ment of a Christian theology of sex were sacrificed. In some instances, sexuality and heresy became synonymous, especially in relation to the ho-mosexualities. Women became increasingly associated with sin intrinsi-cally and with witchcraft lustfully. It is hard to overestimate the impor-tance of antifeminism in the formation of the celibate consciousness and priestly development for over two centuries when the discipline of celi-bacy was being solidified (1486 and following).[34]

Uncovering the complex relationships between male monopoly and celibate monopoly in the ministry and the lack of a credible theology of sex remains the work of serious scholarship. A few feminist scholars are providing new impetus and insight in this area.[35]

In the same vein, the auxiliary bishop of Baltimore, Francis Murphy, found much to criticize in the rejected pastoral letter on women in the Catholic Church prepared by U.S. bishops. Murphy argued in favor of rejection mainly because the letter ignored the destructive consequences of patriarchy. He cites the work of feminist scholars in his critique:

> The pastoral is built around the basic assumption, present in our culture as well, "that males should legitimately act as the controlling cultural fathers, while females should appropriately act as dependent minors" (Catherine Spretnak, *States of Grace,* Harper, 1991). . . . Dominance pervades our Church, a dominance that excludes the presence, insights, and experience of women from the "table" where the formulation of the Church's doctrine takes place and the exercise of its power is discerned. It likewise excludes women from presiding at the table where the community is fed. This patriarchy continues to permeate the Church and supports a climate that not only robs women of their full personhood, but also encourages men to be domineering, aggressive, and selfish.[36]

Murphy admits, further, that sexism permeates the Church's history. Augustine's notions about the inferiority of women and the debased nature of sexual intercourse with women as well as the exclusion of women from ordination are "all cut from the same sexist cloth." He believes admission of women to the priesthood is an issue as important as the admission of Gentiles to Christianity. He implies that sexual intercourse with women is not debased and that, perhaps, the exclusion of married men from the priesthood also stems from sexism.

Father-rule deprives women of positions of organizational and spiritual power, thus depriving them of their personhood. Because it helps sacralize father-rule, mandatory celibacy reinforces this deprivation. Patriarchal dominance leads to violence against women: male adults sexually abusing female children, raping adult women, beating wives, and exploiting prostitutes. Because it helps sacralize patriarchal dominance, mandatory celibacy reinforces this violence.

Psychotherapists are also beginning to recognize that mandatory celibacy helps construct the social situation conducive to sexual abuse of women and children. Demetria Martinez writes about the psychic consequences of the disembodied, transcendental view of sexuality:

> For survivors of sexual abuse the body is a distant island that one sailed away from as a child when the trauma of being touched became too much. . . . Holiness is being at home in the body. . . . The preponderance of guilt/sin association with sexuality, a disembodied spirituality symbolized by the male celibate, silence about the pervasiveness of abuse in Catholic families—these factors, despite some heroic efforts at changing the psychic landscape of the Church, militate against recovery.[37]

This is merely an ad hoc list of scholars—Sipe, Duby, Boswell, Murphy, Spretnak, Ruether, Schneiders, Martinez—questioning the relationship between patriarchy and mandatory celibacy. The issue begs for systematic study.

The Last Hurrah

The authoritarian absolutism of the current papacy draws its vehemence from the deep well of patriarchal domination. Seeing Pope John Paul's administration as Catholic triumphalism's last hurrah helps understand the political maneuvers of the papal coalition. In the waning years of John Paul's papacy, Rome has attacked gender equality with awesome fury. Two incidents focused on rejecting inclusive language in English-speaking countries, and a third aimed at rejecting women's ordination forever. This papal administration will have been a grander hurrah and its effects will last longer than most observers imagined. The powerful weight of all those millennia of patriarchal dominance will not be lifted without strenuous exertion.

The apostolic letter "Priestly Ordination Reserved to Men Alone" (*Ordinatio Sacerdotalis*) is a quintessential act of authoritarian father-rule. For example, most of us can recall the power of our father's rule as children. When a little child does not understand the reason for a command and asks her father why, he often replies with "Because I said so." And that ends the discussion. I recognize that I've used the same nonreason with my own children. I'd like to think I did it when the consequences were grave and the reasons too complicated for them to understand. But I can never use that answer with students and colleagues—if I did, I'd be out of a job in short order. Mature adults have a right to know why. This is the basic flaw of the current papal coalition. Mature Catholics, bolstered by decades of personalism and lay involvement, know that any papacy that chooses to follow the strategy of authoritarian patriarchy loses respect. At the same time, many realize that one's father is worthy of love and respect even when his opinions differ or his sources of information are severely limited. After all, the generation gap is nothing new. What is different, however, is the breakneck speed with which knowledge becomes obsolete and whole new areas of unrecognized and therefore unexamined ignorance are uncovered. The tragedy of the modern papacy is that it attempts to teach definitively even in these areas of ignorance.

Apparently, those dominating the Catholic magisterium are unable to recognize the paradigm shift from patriarchal dominance to gender equality occurring in society. Hence, in the view of many who see the emerging evidence, the official teaching body of the Church is acting out of ignorance. For example, early in 1994 Rome finally issued the official English translation of the ("universal") Catechism of the Catholic Church. It had been delayed because the Vatican decided to remove the gender-neutral language that the English-speaking world had submitted for approval. Rome declared that the Church will not allow "humanity" to replace "man" or "mankind" for English-speaking Catholics. Most recently, to the dismay of many Canadian and U. S. bishops, Rome rescinded an earlier approval of the Catholic edition of the New Revised Standard Version of the Bible for the Mass and other official Catholic liturgies. The reason? Because it uses inclusive language like "humanity" instead of patriarchal terms like "mankind."

The meatier pronouncement, sandwiched between these two rejections, was the papal letter declaring that Catholics must forget about women ever being ordained priests. The pope will not permit debate on the subject, admonishing that his views must be "definitively held by all the Church's faithful."[38] In an appendix to the papal letter, he tells the world's Catholic bishops that the teaching excluding women from ordination to the priesthood is "certainly true." The pope adds: "Therefore, since it does not belong to matters freely open to dispute, it always requires the full and unconditional assent of the faithful, and to teach the contrary is equivalent to leading consciences into error."

Whatever their motives or premises, in all three instances the pope and his advisers have exercised pressure politics at its most effective. They have tried to define a burning issue as a nonissue. To evolve at all, a political issue must first be recognized, named, and defined (chapter 13). The pope has declared that the issue of ordaining women will not evolve but die aborning. Furthermore, its grave will be adorned with exclusive patriarchal language.

What is chilling and saddening for many Catholics is the pope's seeming disregard for the well-reasoned and well-documented evidence that calls his views into question.[39] Gerda Lerner and other feminist scholars are uncovering the ignorance of the old patriarchal paradigm, exposing the insidious history and nature of patriarchy, its sedimented massiveness, its horrible destructiveness of women's equality, freedom, and dignity. Instead of seriously considering the opinions of his faithful disciples, his colleagues, his mature adult children, the pope merely replies to those who ask why by saying "Because I said so." And lest they persist, he says: "That's it; no debate." Mature Catholics are either stunned or bemused. He seems to be telling them that good children should be seen but not heard. In effect, the reasons given for the papal view are that it has always been done that way. As proof, John Paul says simply: "The Church has always acknowledged as perennial norm her Lord's way of acting in choosing the 12 men whom he made the foundations of his Church."

This is father-rule at its most powerful. The pope is consciously deciding to treat practicing Catholics as his subjects, expecting blind, unquestioning obedience, as a father treats his immature children. Some of the faithful, he knows, love the Church and her father-ruler so deeply that they can live with such contradictions. No one's father is perfect, so one learns to take the good with the bad. More philosophically, the mature loyalist ponders the mystery of evil, knowing it has no rational solution even in organized religion. Those whose religious vision includes glimpses or sustained awareness of transpersonal consciousness may remember Gamaliel's defense of the Apostles. "Fellow Israelites, be careful what you are about do to these men. . . . For if this endeavor is of human origin, it will destroy itself. But if it comes from God, you will not be able to destroy it; you may even find yourself fighting against God" (Acts 5:35, 38–39). When it comes to banning women from ordination, the pope claims that patriarchal rule "is of God." His letter warns that women must accept the status quo "as the faithful observance of a plan to be ascribed to the wisdom of the Lord of the universe."

Many Catholics, however, are convinced that patriarchal dominance is definitely the plan "of men," and so "it will be overthrown." Some of them will walk away from the Catholic Church, either in shame or disgust. Others will recognize the apostolic letter as patriarchal arrogance and simply ignore it. After all, the pope has no police force other than local bishops and pastors, many of whom will try to soften the blow rather than enforce the letter of the law.[40] Still other Catholics—clergy and laity—will continue the struggle despite the setback, pushing for the new paradigm of full gender equality even in the Catholic priesthood.

The Scenario

Through all the theory, data, distinctions, nuances, and speculations I see the following scenario unfolding. John Paul's letter *Ordinatio Sacerdotalis* sparks further theological debate similar to the discussion following the 1976 declaration *Inter Insigniores*. Efforts of a prophetic coalition spearheaded by groups such as the Women's Ordination Conference, WomanChurch, Call to Action, and other Catholic lay activist groups will continue raise the consciousness of Catholics to be concerned about male exclusivity in the priesthood and keep the issue in the forefront of Church politics.

In the meantime, the priest shortage worsens. Pastorally minded bishops, who are concerned that the faithful are being deprived of the Mass and sacraments, pressure a new pope to allow them to ordain qualified married men. The pope ponders the situation, noting in particular that the dwindling supply of priests severely threatens Catholicism's political and economic well-being. Succumbing overtly to the pastoral pressures, Rome cautiously opens the priesthood to married men but only in well-documented circumstances that warrant the exception. The most compelling reason for ordaining married men, however, is to defuse the antipatriarchy bomb being tossed at the priesthood by the women's ordination movement.

Theological debates will continue to clarify the issue. More and more theologians agree that gender differences have nothing to do with qualifications for the priesthood. Larger majorities of the laity favor women priests. So the pope and his advisers allow the ordination of married men, hoping thereby to preserve sacerdotal sacramentalism and male exclusivity.

A married clergy, however, becomes the camel's nose under the patriarchal tent. Why? Because women and children enter the priest's life space. Abstract philosophical and theological arguments about male superiority are weakened by experiential knowledge of gender equality. Taken-for-granted male privilege recedes when seminaries must accommodate the presence of women as students, girlfriends, and fiancées. Parishes themselves and relationships between bishops and parishes change when both priest and spouse are present. A parish wanting to hire a particular priest may be disappointed to hear the candidate say, "Sorry, I must turn down the offer because my wife and I don't like the schools in your district." A bishop must be more circumspect in making pastoral appointments. Not only educational opportunities but also job possibilities for wives will come into play. When women and children are present, men who are caring and compassionate recognize their equal dignity and want to help satisfy their needs. The myriad forms of accommodating to women and children will themselves weaken patriarchy. Once exclusively male privileges will erode as they are shared with loved ones.

The Catholic Church will ordain married men within our lifetime. This speeds up the acceptance of ordaining women. In interaction with the growing personalist, feminist, and lay movements it takes not three to four centuries to move from ordaining married men to ordaining women, as in the Protestant experience. But it does take three to four generations.

The ordination of married men temporarily dampens the demand for the ordination of women, at least for the hierarchy. For a time, the economic pressure is off because bishops will be able to supply enough priests to meet sacramental demands. Relaxing age-old restrictions, however, can generate a surge of hope and new demands for further change. When the autocratic communist regimes collapsed in the former Soviet Union, for example, people began to chafe at the bit, demanding other long-overdue changes. Hence the coalition supporting women's ordination may redouble its efforts, speeding up the demise of male exclusivity.

In the long run, breaking the status quo of male celibate domination greatly advances the breakthrough to gender inclusivity in the priesthood. An intermediate step is the routinization of the married clergy. The final element of the formal model of social change postulates that the new form of married priesthood becomes prevalent and survives as long as the diocesan niche provides the candidates for ordination and diocesan officials continue to select and retain them. For the radical change in Catholic ministry to persist, it must be legitimated and routinized through bureaucratic or priestly leadership. That is, not only the laity but also diocesan officials and the priests themselves must become comfortable with these new structures. Selecting and retaining those competence elements that continue to reproduce the new form of married priesthood across a few generations of diocesan officials, priests, and laity is a required legitimation and routinization process.

As the married priesthood is routinized, the coalitional forces in favor of gender equality increase their charismatic strength. These forces interact with the experiential knowledge of married priests about female equality. They reach a threshold of strength sufficient to create another breakthrough of radical change in the structural form of Catholic ministry. As a result, the Roman Catholic Church opens the priesthood to women within our grandchildren's lifetime.

Summary and Conclusion

Not surprisingly, the perennial issue of social change is hotly contested as Catholic leaders ponder the status quo defining Catholic ministry. Conflict rages over which aspects of the ideal-type should still be affirmed and which should not. The analysis leads me to side with the conservatives in affirming the necessity of sacerdotal sacramentalism. Both traits are grounded in the principles of hierarchy and hierophany and so pertain to the deep structures of authentic religion; as such, they will continue to be essential elements in Catholic ministry. The same research, however, compels me to side with the progressives in affirming the need to jettison male celibate exclusivity. My analysis concludes that these characteristics are cultural and political accretions. That is, they are dispensable surface structures of ministry.

The logic of my analysis of the situation is represented in figure 1. It begins with the empirical observation, documented extensively in *Full Pews and Empty Altars,* that the Church finds itself unable to reproduce its male celibate priesthood population. When the priest shortage becomes so severe that access to the means of salvation can no longer be satisfactorily provided to Catholics, this old social order defining the Catholic technostructure will disappear. Following the causal chain back one link, we see that mandatory celibacy is a major cause of poor recruitment and retention of priests. Dissatisfaction with celibacy also has antecedent causes. I identified a matrix of social forces that have irreversibly altered the ecological niche of Catholic dioceses rendering compulsory celibacy problematic.

As these transformative forces interact with the priest shortage, a new social order is emerging in the Church. In the language of a Marxist theory of social change, the material conditions of its existence are maturing within the current structure of Catholic ministry. The material forces of production are being altered because (1) the supply of male celibate priests continues to dwindle; (2) the ranks of educated and experienced female career ministers and part-time lay volunteers is constantly growing; and (3) the demand for services from a burgeoning church membership goes unabated.

The Church's inability to recruit enough priests, the basic "material transformation" driving the change, should not be confused with the theological justifications and other cultural and political developments arguing for or against mandatory celibacy and the ordination of women. Just as the priest shortage is caused by antecedent conditions, it is also a prior condition for subsequent effects. The most immediate effect is the formation of Catholic coalitions in which people become conscious of conflict over the priest shortage and fight it out, mainly with ideological weapons.

Coalitions form during periods of change because social transformation no longer occurs behind our backs. Radical change in the Catholic Church must be driven along by the conscious, collective struggle of bishops, priests, religious, and laypersons most affected by the stressful conditions affecting Catholic ministry. Thus, we learned that a conservative Catholic coalition is bent on restoring the priesthood to the status quo ante—hoping to generate high rates of recruitment and retention of male celibates. A progressive coalition assessing the situation thinks a married priesthood is necessary to solve the shortage. Significantly, a key insight has emerged from the ideological struggle between these coalitions: Allowing priests to marry is a more adequate expression of authentic religion in the modern era than demanding that they remain celibate.

The antecedent forces are coming together in a rare balance, providing the driving force for the ordination of married men. By seizing the historical moment, mobilizing its forces, and precipitating change allowing married men to be ordained, the progressive coalition will transform the structure of Catholic ministry.

Allowing women to be ordained, however, is another matter. Celibacy may be easily recognized as a nonessential surface structure, but until recently almost no one has questioned the essential nature of maleness for Catholic priesthood. Most Catholics still give it little thought because, from time immemorial, men have exercised father-rule in religion, economics, politics, and almost all other areas of social privilege. Recently, the pope himself has declared that what has always been the practice must continue forever as an essential mark of the priesthood. Moreover, the Holy Father proclaimed that the official theology of gender inequality in ministry shall remain unexamined and undeveloped. If the papal strategy succeeds, male exclusivity is here to stay—for a long while.

The sociological significance of these events is that the prophets of full gender equality are speaking to deaf hierarchical ears. In my opinion, however, the prophetic vision is correct. Male exclusivity in the priesthood will end some generations hence. Pope John Paul, however, may have increased the number of generations that Roman Catholics will have to wait before women are ordained as priests. In the meantime, he has further isolated Rome from large segments of educated loyal Catholics and weakened their respect for Roman views. At the same time, the supreme pontiff's latest efforts will have consequences that are counterproductive from his point of view. Whereas earlier few Catholics gave male monopoly of control a thought, it has now become a household debate.[41] For many politically astute Catholics, the pope has thrown down the gauntlet and intensified the battle over the status quo. Most probably, the ensuing conflict will result in a more conciliatory strategy between conservatives and progressives during the next papal regime, hastening the ordination of married men.

In comparison to male exclusivity, therefore, letting go of celibate exclusivity appears to be all but a fait accompli. It will certainly not occur during this papacy but probably during the next one. If the charismatic coalition succeeds, married men will be ordained in the lifetime of this generation of Catholic churchgoers. This breakthrough will open the doors to the eventual ordination of women.

For many bewildered Catholics, the Church is running out of time. It needs to adapt its ministerial structures to the modern world. When all is said and done, unless a married priesthood soon breaks the status quo, many sectors of this ancient organization will regress to prerational religion. The demand for blind obedience will replace the demand for the Mass and sacraments. Superstitious magic will displace mystical transcendence. Unbending patriarchy will suffocate the equality and dignity of women. If the Catholic Church cannot say Goodbye Father, many faithful Catholics will have no choice but to say Goodbye Church.

EDITOR'S INTRODUCTION

1. Richard Schoenherr and Lawrence Young, *Full Pews and Empty Altars: Demographics of the Priest Shortage in United States Catholic Dioceses* (Madison: University of Wisconsin Press, 1993).

2. Richard Schoenherr, "Holy Power? Holy Authority? and Holy Celibacy?" in *Celibacy in the Church,* ed. William Bassett and Peter Huizing (New York: Herder and Herder, 1972).

3. From a fragment of the Greek poet Archilochus in Berlin's famous essay "The Hedgehog and the Fox: An Essay on Tolstoy's View of History," in *The Proper Study of Mankind* (New York: Farrar, Straus, and Giroux, 1998), 436.

4. Lawrence Young, "Assessing and Updating the Schoenherr-Young Projections of Clergy Decline in the United States Roman Catholic Church," *Sociology of Religion* 59 (1998):7–23.

5. These and other data on the priesthood are from Bryan Froehle and Mary Gautier, *Catholicism USA: A Portrait of the Catholic Church in the United States* (Maryknoll, N.Y.: Orbis Books, 2000), chapter 6, "Priests."

6. The same is not true of theologate enrollments of religious priesthood candidates, which continue to decline slowly. See Froehle and Gautier, *Catholicism USA,* 117–120, and the *2001 Catholic Ministry Formation Directory* (Washington, D.C.: Center for Applied Research in the Apostolate, 2001).

7. Froehle and Gautier, *Catholicism USA,* 120.

8. Indeed, in addressing the priest shortage themselves, the National Conference of Catholic Bishops took advantage of "the professional skills of the researchers at the Center for Applied Research in the Apostolate," with whose help the bishops were "able to obtain a much more accurate portrait of the fact of fewer priests, and its impact on the pastoral ministry." Bishop Richard C. Hanifen, Introduction to *Study of the Impact of Fewer Priests on the Pastoral Ministry* (Washington, D.C.: National Conference of Catholic Bishops, 2000). In the same paragraph, Bishop Hanifen reiterates his gratitude "to Dr. Bryan Froehle [a sociologist!] and the CARA staff for conducting the three phases of this study."

9. Young, "Assessing and Updating," table 2, 20.

10. Larry Carstens, "The 'Priest Shortage': Natural or Man-(and Woman-) Made?" *New Oxford Review* (June 2000).

11. John F. Quinn, "Priest Shortage Panic," *Crisis* (October 1996), 44. CARA statistics reported in *U.S. Catholic* (January 2002). In a very provocative recent article that I do not have time to fully interrogate here, sociologist Paul Sullins of the Catholic University of America similarly reports a number of statistics that challenge "the supply and demand argument that the Catholic Church is suffering a crisis shortage of priests." For example, there are more priests per parish currently than there were at the turn of the century (figure 6), and the share of churches without a resident priest in the United States consistently declined over the course of the twentieth century, from nearly 40 percent at the beginning of the century to 20 per-

cent by the 1980s (figure 5). Without endorsing all of Sullins's claims, I strongly commend this article to anyone interested in these issues. "Empty Pews and Empty Altars: A Reconsideration of the Catholic Priest Shortage," *Catholic Social Science Review* 6 (October, 2001): 253–270.

12. For an excellent diagnosis of this and related problems, see R. Scott Appleby, "Surviving the Shaking of the Foundations: United States Catholicism in the Twenty-First Century," in *Seminaries, Theologates, and the Future of Church Ministry: An Analysis of Trends and Transitions* by Katarina Schuth (Collegeville, Minn.: Liturgical Press, 1999), 1–23.

13. Andrew Yuengert, "Do Bishops Matter? A Cross-Sectional Study of Ordinations to the U.S. Catholic Diocesan Priesthood," *Review of Religious Research* 42 (March 2001):294–312, quotations from 306.

14. Young, "Assessing and Updating," 18.

15. Quinn, "Priest Shortage Panic," 43–44. These three dioceses were not in the sample drawn by Schoenherr and Young for *Full Pews and Empty Altars*, a scientific sample that replicated the one used for the 1972 National Opinion Research Center survey of diocesan and religious priests. See appendix F of *Full Pews and Empty Altars*, and Andrew Greeley and Richard Schoenherr, *The Catholic Priest in the United States: Sociological Investigations* (Washington, D.C.: United States Catholic Conference, 1972).

16. Albert DiIanni, "A View of Religious Vocations," *America* (28 February 1998):8–12.

17. Michael S. Rose, "Who's Afraid of the 'New Breed' of Priests?" *New Oxford Review* (December 2001):32–34; Dean Hoge, "Get Ready for Post-Boomer Catholics," *America* (21 March 1998), table 4, p. 10; Alessandra Stanley, "U.S. Catholic Seminarians Turning to Orthodoxy," *New York Times* (13 October 1998); Katarina Schuth, *Seminaries, Theologates, and the Future of Church Ministry* (Collegeville, Minn.: Liturgical Press, 1999), 77.

18. Stanley, "U.S. Catholic Seminarians Turning to Orthodoxy"; Jennifer Egan, "The Last Counterculture" (*New York Times Magazine* cover story, 4 April 1999); and Diana Jean Schemo, "Nearing Retirement, Priests of the Sixties Fear Legacy Is Lost," *New York Times* (10 September 2000). See also Laurie Goodstein, "No Longer Eager to Say, 'My Son, the Priest'"; "Religious Careers Lose Luster for Catholic Parents," *New York Times* (19 November 2000).

19. James Davidson, et al., *The Search for Common Ground: What Unites and Divides Catholic Americans* (Huntington, IN: Our Sunday Visitor, 1997), 47.

20. William D'Antonio, James Davidson, Dean Hoge, and Katherine Meyer, *American Catholics: Gender, Generation, and Commitment* (Walnut Creek, Calif.: AltaMira Press, 2001).

21. Jeffrey Hadden, *The Gathering Storm in the Churches: The Widening Gap between Clergy and Laymen* (Garden City, NY: Doubleday, 1969).

22. Compare Wade Clark Roof and William McKinney, *American Mainline Religion: Its Changing Shape and Future* (New Brunswick, N.J.: Rutgers University Press, 1987), and Roger Finke and Rodney Stark, *The Churching of America, 1776–1990: Winners and Losers in Our Religious Economy* (New Brunswick, N.J.: Rutgers University Press, 1992).

23. I cannot help but note that the same relationship exists between faculty (tra-

ditional defenders of "the academic ethic") and students (more progressive) in many colleges and universities. See David Yamane, *Student Movements for Multiculturalism: Challenging the Curricular Color Line in Higher Education* (Baltimore: Johns Hopkins University Press, 2001).

24. Davidson et al., *The Search for Common Ground.*

25. Dean Hoge, William Dinges, Mary Johnson, and Juan Gonzales, Jr., *Young Adult Catholics: Religion in the Culture of Choice* (Notre Dame, Ind.: University of Notre Dame Press, 2001), figure 2.1 and table 3.6. In her study of Catholic identity, Michele Dillon compares data on Dignity (which works for the acceptance of homosexuality within Catholicism), the Women's Ordination Conference, and the abortion rights group Catholics for a Free Choice to data from a survey of members of the Catholic League for Religious and Civil Rights and finds that "although pro-change and conservative Catholics present polarized views on many doctrinal issues, they share a committed attachment to core symbols, meanings, and memories in the Catholic tradition." See *Catholic Identity: Balancing Reason, Faith, and Power* (New York: Cambridge University Press, 1999), 211.

26. Froehle and Gautier, *Catholicism USA.*

27. The 1994 survey is reported in Andrew Greeley, "A Sea of Paradoxes: Two Surveys of Priests," *America* (16 July 1994): 6–7; CARA survey and Hoge results summarized by Roger Schwietz, chairman of the U.S. Bishops" Committee on Vocations, in "Recruiting Vocations," *America* (2–9 July 2001): 8–9.

28. *Study of the Impact of Fewer Priests on the Pastoral Ministry* (Washington, D.C.: National Conference of Catholic Bishops, 2000).

29. "Machine" and "euphemism" are from Chester Gillis, *Roman Catholicism in America* (New York: Columbia University Press, 1999), 246, 255; Msgr. Bergin in Chris Hedges, "Longing for the Past in a Changing Church," *New York Times* (21 February 2001); Francis Dorff, "Are We Killing Our Priests?" *America* (29 April 2000): 7.

30. Eugene Gomulka, "'Home Alone' in the Priesthood," *America* (27 August–3 September 2001): 17.

31. Sullins, "Empty Pews and Empty Altars."

32. Patricia Wittberg, *The Rise and Fall of Catholic Religious Orders: A Social Movement Perspective* (Albany: State University of New York Press, 1994); Froehle and Gautier, *Catholicism USA.*

33. Data summarized in Froehle and Gautier, *Catholicism USA,* table 8.1, p. 142. Reservations reported in Frank DeRego and James Davidson, "Catholic Deacons: A Lesson in Role Conflict and Ambiguity," in *Religion in a Changing World,* ed. Madeline Cousineau (Westport, Conn.: Greenwood Press, 1998), 89–98.

34. *Breaking Faith: The Pope, the People, and the Fate of Catholicism* (New York: Viking Compass, 2001), 24.

35. Philip Lawler, "Murder of the Cathedral," *Catholic World Report* (August/September 2001); Gustav Niebuhr, "Milwaukee Cathedral Plan Draws Ecclesiastical Ire," *New York Times* (14 July 2001).

36. Dillon, *Catholic Identity,* 3–4; Nadya Labi, "Not Doing as the Romans Do," *Time* (30 November 1998); Margot Patterson, "Breakaway Parish Ordains Woman Priest," *National Catholic Reporter* (7 December 2001).

37. See the obituaries I wrote for him with my graduate school colleague Elizabeth Park. David Yamane and Elizabeth Park, "Where Angels Fear to Tread: Rich-

ard Schoenherr (1935–1996)," *American Sociologist* 28 (spring 1997):136–142, and Elizabeth Park and David Yamane, "Life as a Seamless Garment: Richard Schoenherr (1935–1996)," *Sociology of Religion* 57 (fall 1996):319–321.

38. From Tom Baker's presentation on "leadership" at the Commonweal Colloquium on American Catholics in the Public Square, New York, New York, October 27–29, 2000.

ACKNOWLEDGMENTS

1. Richard A. Schoenherr, "Holy Power? Holy Authority? And Holy Celibacy?" in *Celibacy in the Church,* ed. William W. Bassett and Peter Huizing (New York: Herder and Herder, 1972).

2. Peter Blau and Richard Schoenherr, *The Structure of Organizations* (New York: Basic Books, 1971), especially 353–358.

3. For a more detailed, if one-sided and sometimes contradictory account of tensions at NORC during the priest survey, see Andrew M. Greeley, *Confessions of a Parish Priest: An Autobiography* (New York: Simon and Schuster, 1986), ch. 15. For example, he reports that "not a single table" was ready by December 1970. Actually, we had already presented results from scores of tables to a bishops' committee in October. As any researcher knows, no one could create all the tables that appeared in our report in a few weeks' time unless the data had been completely ready for the final runs. Furthermore, the study was much more complicated than the USCC had planned. Although it was my suggestion, everyone had agreed that we must include bishops, major superiors, and resigned priests, none of whom were in the original design. The delays in the final runs of the data, which Greeley angrily complained about, were as much the result of these added complications as they were due to what Greeley characterized as my "slow, cautious, and methodical" work habits.

4. Greeley's biographer, John N. Kotre, reports incorrectly that Greeley was stunned in the autumn of 1970 by my announcement that I was going to get married. See his book *The Best of Times, The Worst of Times: Andrew Greeley and American Catholicism, 1950–1975* (Chicago: Nelson-Hall, 1978). The fact is I had discussed these plans with Greeley six months earlier, at which time I offered to resign as study director if he thought it would jeopardize the credibility of the report. My preference was to continue and to postpone our marriage until after the report was published. Greeley said he wanted me to stay on.

5. See, for example, Robert W. Peterson and Richard A. Schoenherr, "Organizational Status Attainment of Religious Professionals," *Social Forces* 56 (1978):794–822; Robert F. Szafran, Robert W. Peterson, and Richard A. Schoenherr, "Ethnicity and Status Attainment: The Case of the Roman Catholic Clergy," *Sociological Quarterly* 21 (1980):41–51; Richard A. Schoenherr and Eleanor Simpson, *The Political Economy of Diocesan Advisory Councils* (Washington, D.C.: U.S. Catholic Conference Publications, 1978); Richard A. Schoenherr and Annemette Sorensen, "Social Change in Religious Organizations: Consequences of Clergy Decline in the U.S. Catholic Church," *Sociological Analysis* 43 (1982):23–52.

6. Richard A. Schoenherr, "Power and Authority in Organized Religion: Disaggregating the Phenomenological Core," *Sociological Analysis* 47S (1987):52–71.

7. Nathan Keyfitz, "Individual Mobility in a Stationary Population," *Population Studies* 27(1973):335–52.

8. Judah Matras, "Models and Indicators of Organizational Growth, Changes, and Transformations," in *Social Indicator Models,* ed. Kenneth C. Land and Seymour Spilerman (New York: Sage, 1975), 301–318.

9. Gudmun Hernes, "Structural Change in Social Processes," *American Journal of Sociology* 82 (1976):513–547; Howard Aldrich, *Organizations and Environments* (Englewood Cliffs, N.J.: Prentice-Hall, 1979).

10. See Richard A. Schoenherr, Lawrence A. Young, and Jose Pérez Vilariño, "Demographic Transitions in Religious Organizations: A Comparative Study of Priest Decline in Roman Catholic Dioceses," *Journal for the Scientific Study of Religion* 27 (1988):499–523; Richard A. Schoenherr and Lawrence A. Young, "Organizational Demography and Structural Change in the Roman Catholic Church," in *Structures of Power and Constraint,* ed. Craig Calhoun, Marshall Meyer, and Richard Scott (New York: Cambridge University Press, 1990), 235–270, and *Full Pews and Empty Altars: Demographics of the Priest Shortage in U.S. Catholic Dioceses* (Madison: University of Wisconsin Press, 1993), especially ch. 5.

11. Michael T. Hannan and John Freeman, "The Population Ecology of Organizations," *American Journal of Sociology* 82 (1977):929–964, and *Organizational Ecology* (Cambridge, Mass.: Harvard University Press, 1989); John Freeman, Glenn R. Carroll, and Michael T. Hannan, "The Liability of Newness: Age-Dependence in Organizational Death Rates," *American Sociological Review* 48 (1983):692–710; Glenn R. Carroll, "Organizational Ecology," *Annual Review of Sociology* 10 (1984): 71–93, and *Ecological Models of Organizations* (Cambridge, Mass.: Ballinger, 1988).

12. Bill McKelvey and Howard Aldrich, "Populations, Natural Selection, and Applied Organizational Science," *Administrative Science Quarterly* 28 (1983):101–128. It should also be noted that Hannan and Freeman's *Organizational Ecology* brings their model closer to a full sociological theory. Their recent work recognizes technical, legal, political, and other transformative processes along with the natural variation-selection-retention mechanisms of change.

13. Kenneth McNeil, "Understanding Organizational Power: Building on the Weberian Legacy," *Administrative Science Quarterly* 23 (1978):65–90.

14. Paul Goldman and Donald R. Van Houten, "Managerial Strategies and the Worker: A Marxist Analysis of Bureaucracy," *Sociological Quarterly* 18 (1977): 108–125.

15. Charles Perrow, *Complex Organizations: A Critical Essay,* 3rd ed. (New York: Random House, 1986).

16. Gerda Lerner, *The Creation of Patriarchy* (New York: Oxford University Press, 1986).

1. CELIBATE EXCLUSIVITY IS THE ISSUE

1. For an endorsement of the institution of priestly celibacy by a noted sociologist, see Andrew M. Greeley, "In Defense of Celibacy?" *America,* 10 September 1994.

2. Dawn Gibeau, "French Canada: On Road to Church of the Baptized," *National Catholic Reporter,* 5 June 1992, 11.

3. William A. Shannon, "No Circuit-Rider Priests, Please!" *America,* 16 April 1994, 11.

4. Andrew M. Greeley, "Sacraments Keep Catholics High on the Church," *National Catholic Reporter,* 12 April 1991, 12–13. The article reports a survey of 507 Catholics in Chicago and draws from prior studies Greeley analyzed in *The Catho-*

lic Myth (New York: Collier Books, 1990). His main thesis in both publications is that Catholics stay in the Church because they *like* being Catholic, particularly Catholicism's poetic sacramental tradition.

5. Ibid.

6. Mark Granovetter, "Economic Action and Social Structure: The Problem of Embeddedness," *American Journal of Sociology* 91 (1985): 482.

7. See Stephen Bunker and Denis O'Hearn, "Strategies of Economic Ascendants for Access to Raw Materials: A Comparison of the United States and Japan," in *Pacific-Asia and the Future of the World-System,* ed. Ravi Arvin Palat (Westport, Conn.: Greenwood Press, 1993), 83–102.

8. See Richard Fragomeni, "A Vision of the Sacraments: Will the Eucharist Survive?" audiocassette from Future of the American Church Conference (Elkridge, Md.: Chesapeake Audio/Video Communications, 1990).

9. The authorization followed the 1988 promulgation by the Vatican Congregation for Divine Worship of the *Directory for Sunday Celebrations in the Absence of a Priest* (Washington, D.C.: U.S. Catholic Conference, 1988). Later, the U.S. bishops issued their own version of the Vatican's directory: *Gathered in Steadfast Faith: Statement on Sunday Worship in the Absence of a Priest* (Washington, D.C.: United States Catholic Conference, 1991).

10. Jeffrey Pfeffer and Gerald Salancik, *The External Control of Organizations: A Resource Dependence Perspective* (New York: Harper and Row, 1978).

11. Yeheskel Hasenfeld and Richard A. English, eds., *Human Service Organizations* (Ann Arbor: University of Michigan Press, 1974), 1.

12. Max Weber, *Economy and Society,* ed. Guenther Roth and Claus Wittich, 2 vols. (Berkeley: University of California Press, 1978), 400.

13. Talcott Parsons, introduction to Max Weber, *The Sociology of Religion,* trans. Ephraim Fischoff (Boston: Beacon Press, 1963), xix–lxvii, xxviii.

14. For a conceptual model of religious participation based on assumptions of rational economic behavior, see Rodney Stark and William Sims Bainbridge, *A Theory of Religion* (New York: Peter Lang, 1987).

15. Weber, *Economy and Society,* ch. 6.

16. Joachim Wach, *Sociology of Religion* (Chicago: University of Chicago Press, 1944).

17. Weber, *Economy and Society,* ch. 3.

18. John Kenneth Galbraith, *Economics and the Public Purpose* (Boston: Houghton Mifflin, 1973).

2. COMPULSORY CELIBACY AND THE PRIEST SHORTAGE

1. A full analysis of the large data set and details of methods used are in Richard A. Schoenherr and Lawrence A. Young, *Full Pews and Empty Altars: Demographics of the Priest Shortage in United States Catholic Dioceses* (Madison: University of Wisconsin Press, 1993).

2. Net migrations are the surplus of in-migrations over out-migrations resulting from the movement of priests from one diocese to another, between dioceses and religious orders, and between other countries and the United States.

3. See Schoenherr and Young, *Full Pews and Empty Altars,* appendix B, for a description of the adjustments and a fuller discussion of the assumptions used.

4. See ibid., figure 2.2 and table 2.2.

5. For an operational definition of organizational transformation, see Howard E. Aldrich, *Organizations and Environments* (Englewood Cliffs, N.J.: Prentice-Hall, 1979), 203.

6. Roger Finke and Rodney Stark, *The Churching of America, 1776–1990* (New Brunswick, N.J.: Rutgers University Press, 1992).

7. For data up to 1980, see Wade Clark Roof and William McKinney, *American Mainline Religion: Its Changing Shape and Future* (New Brunswick, N.J.: Rutgers University Press, 1987); also see Tom W. Smith, "America's Religious Mosaic," *American Demographics* 6 (1984): 18–23.

8. American Institute of Public Opinion, *Gallup Opinion Index,* no. 259 (Princeton, N.J.: Princeton Religion Research Center, 1987). See the discussion of "Growth in the U.S. Hispanic Population, 1980–2005," in Schoenherr and Young, *Full Pews and Empty Altars,* 299–301.

9. Dean R. Hoge, Joseph J. Shields, and Mary Jeanne Verdieck, "Changing Age Distribution and Theological Attitudes of Catholic Priests, 1970–85," *Sociological Analysis* 49 (1988):264–280.

10. Dean R. Hoge, Jackson W. Carroll, and Francis K. Scheets, *Patterns of Parish Leadership: Cost and Effectiveness in Four Denominations* (Kansas City, Mo.: Sheed and Ward, 1988).

11. Ibid.

12. C. Joseph O'Hara, ed., *CARA Seminary Directory: 1995–96* (Washington, D.C.: Center for Applied Research in the Apostolate, Georgetown University, 1995).

13. For a review of the numerous studies that investigated how to recruit priesthood candidates for best results, see Dean R. Hoge, Raymond H. Potvin, and Kathleen M. Perry, *Research on Men's Vocations to the Priesthood and the Religious Life* (Washington, D.C.: U.S. Catholic Conference, 1984). These authors found that one of the most extensive and frequently cited surveys was Joan L. Fee, Andrew M. Greeley, William C. McCready, and Teresa A. Sullivan, *Young Catholics in the United States and Canada: A Report to the Knights of Columbus* (New York: Sadlier, 1981).

14. Dean R. Hoge, *The Future of Catholic Leadership: Responses to the Priest Shortage* (Kansas City: Sheed and Ward, 1987), 132. The "encouragement factor" is the effect of being encouraged to go to the seminary by a priest, religious sister, or parent.

15. Ibid., 119.

16. Fee et al., *Young Catholics.*

17. Eugene F. Hemrick and Dean R. Hoge, *Seminarians in Theology: A National Profile* (Washington, D.C.: U.S. Catholic Conference, 1986). Also see Hoge, *Future of Catholic Leadership.*

18. Raymond Potvin and Antanas Suziedelis, *Seminarians of the Sixties* (Washington, D.C.: Center for Applied Research in the Apostolate, 1969).

19. Raymond Potvin, *Seminarians of the Eighties* (Washington, D.C.: National Catholic Educational Association, 1985). Raymond Potvin and Felipe Muncada, *Seminary Outcomes: Perseverance and Withdrawal* (Washington, D.C.: Institute of Social and Behavioral Research, Catholic University of America, 1990).

20. See "Desire to Marry Called 'Major Factor' for Ex-Seminarians," *National Catholic Reporter,* 13 April 1990.

21. Joe Feuerherd, "Survey Shows Priesthood Deterrents," *National Catholic Reporter,* 13 April 1990, 13. For the original study, see Fran Gillespie and Eleace King, *Attitudes of Minority Students toward Jesuits, Religious Life, and the Ordained Priesthood* (Washington, D.C.: Center for Applied Research in the Apostolate, 1989).

22. Thomas F. O'Dea, *The Catholic Crisis* (Boston: Beacon Press, 1968); Andrew M. Greeley, William C. McCready, and Kathleen McCourt, *Catholic Schools in a Declining Church* (Kansas City, Mo.: Sheed and Ward, 1976).

23. Andrew Greeley and Richard A. Schoenherr, *The Catholic Priest in the United States: Sociological Investigations* (Washington, D.C.: United States Catholic Conference, 1972). As noted earlier, the study coincided with my final years of graduate school at the University of Chicago.

24. Richard A. Schoenherr and Andrew M. Greeley, "Role Commitment Processes and the American Catholic Priesthood," *American Sociological Review* 39 (1974):407–426.

25. Richard A. Schoenherr and José Pérez Vilariño, "Organizational Role Commitment in the Catholic Church in Spain and the USA," in *Organizations Alike and Unlike: International and Interinstitutional Studies in the Sociology of Organizations,* ed. Cornelis Lammers and David J. Hickson (London: Routledge and Kegan Paul, 1979), 346–372.

26. Mary Jeanne Verdieck, Joseph J. Shields, and Dean R. Hoge, "Role Commitment Processes Revisited: American Catholic Priests 1970 and 1985," *Journal for the Scientific Study of Religion* 27 (1988): 533.

27. Additional data and further arguments supporting the plausibility of moderately high resignations are discussed in Schoenherr and Young, *Full Pews and Empty Altars.* For a similar assessment, see Michael Gaine, "The State of the Priesthood," in *Modern Catholicism: Vatican II and After,* ed. Adrian Hastings (New York: Oxford University Press, 1991), 246–255.

28. Eugene C. Kennedy and Victor J. Heckler, *The Catholic Priest in the United States: Psychological Investigations* (Washington, D.C.: U.S. Catholic Conference, 1972).

29. This and the preceding three quotations: ibid., 128–129.

30. Ibid., 119.

31. For a discussion of the stages of psychosexual development and the crises of identity, intimacy, and mutuality as they apply to men, see Daniel J. Levinson, *The Seasons of a Man's Life* (New York: Ballantine Books, 1978). For an application of this line of theory and research to Christian spirituality, see Evelyn Eaton Whitehead and James D. Whitehead, *Christian Life Patterns* (Garden City, N.Y.: Doubleday, 1979).

32. See Schoenherr and Young, *Full Pews and Empty Altars,* table 9.4 and figure 9.3.

33. Herbert Richardson, "The Symbol of Virginity," in *The Religious Situation 1969,* ed. Donald R. Cutler (Boston: Beacon Press, 1969), 802.

34. For an extended discussion of the sacredness of sexuality, see Andrew M. Greeley, *Unsecular Man: The Persistence of Religion* (New York: Schocken Books,

1972), especially ch. 7, "Religion and Sex"; also see Andrew M. Greeley, *The Catholic Myth* (New York: Collier Books, 1990).

35. Walter M. Abbott, *The Documents of Vatican II* (New York: America Press, 1966), 250–258.

36. For the traditional view see Joseph H. Fichter, *America's Forgotten Priests: What They Are Saying* (New York: Harper and Row, 1968). For a discussion of the mystical potential of celibacy, see Henri J. Nouwen, *Clowning in Rome: Reflections on Solitude, Celibacy, Prayer, and Contemplation* (Garden City, N.Y.: Image Books, 1979). For an analysis of the impact of Council statements about marriage on mandatory celibacy, see John Seidler and Katherine Meyer, *Conflict and Change in the Catholic Church* (New Brunswick, N.J.: Rutgers University Press, 1989).

37. Edward Schillebeeckx, *Ministry* (New York: Crossroad, 1981), 93.

38. Fichter, *America's Forgotten Priests.*

39. Greeley and Schoenherr (NORC), *Catholic Priest.*

40. Potvin, *Seminarians of the Eighties.*

41. Verdieck et al., "Role Commitment Processes Revisited."

42. Dean R. Hoge, Joseph J. Shields, and Douglas L. Griffin, "Changes in Satisfaction and Institutional Attitudes of Catholic Priests, 1970–1993," *Sociology of Religion* 56 (1995):195–213.

43. Kennedy and Heckler, *Catholic Priest,* 13.

44. Richard Sipe, *A Secret World: Sexuality and the Search for Celibacy* (New York: Brunner/Mazed, 1990).

45. See Potvin and Muncada, *Seminary Outcomes.*

46. James G. Wolf, ed., *Gay Priests* (New York: Harper and Row, 1989), 7. For related discussions, see Richard Hasbany, ed., *Homosexuality and Religion* (New York: Harrington Park Press, 1989), especially Robert Nugent and Jeannine Gramick, "Homosexuality: Protestant, Catholic, and Jewish Issues," 7–46. For a valuable overview of the scriptural and theological questions, providing compelling arguments for the acceptance of ethically responsible homosexual relationships, see John McNeill, *The Church and the Homosexual* (Kansas City, Mo.: Sheed Andrews and McMeel, 1976). McNeill, a Jesuit priest for four decades, was forced to leave the order because he publicly dissented from official Catholic teaching on homosexuality.

47. Andrew Greeley, "Bishops Paralyzed over Heavily Gay Priesthood: One Result Is Double Standard on Celibacy," *National Catholic Reporter,* 10 November 1989; Richard P. McBrien, "Homosexuality and the Priesthood," *Commonweal,* 19 June 1987; Tim Unsworth, "In the 1990s, Seminaries Still Struggling to Come to Terms with Sexuality Issues," *National Catholic Reporter,* 13 May 1994; Katie Leishman, "Heterosexuals and AIDS," *Atlantic Monthly* 259, no. 2 (1987). See also "Theologians Call for Older and More Heterosexual Priests," *National Catholic Reporter,* 26 April 1991.

48. For a discussion of this issue, see Wolf, *Gay Priests,* especially 112, 128.

49. John Boswell, *Homosexuality, Religious Life, and the Clergy: An Historical Overview* (Mt. Rainier, Md.: New Ways Ministry, 1985).

50. Jung, quoted in Wolf, *Gay Priests,* 113.

51. R. Edwards, "Invisible Gifts: The Experience of Gay Priests," in Wolf, *Gay Priests,* 112.

52. Ibid., 103.

3. TOWARD A THEORY OF SOCIAL CHANGE IN ORGANIZED RELIGION
    1. [Editor's Note: I have deleted a discussion of Karl Marx's theory of conflict and social change in modern capitalist society that provided some background to Schoenherr's treatment of Weber in this chapter. Those familiar with Marx will recognize the traces of his thought that remain.]
    2. Michael T. Hannan and John Freeman, *Organizational Ecology* (Cambridge, Mass.: Harvard University Press, 1989); Charles Perrow, *Complex Organizations: A Critical Essay,* 3rd ed. (New York: Random House, 1986).
    3. This part of Weber's analysis received little notice among American sociologists until recently. Kenneth McNeil was one of the first organization analysts to call attention to Weber's well-developed theory of organizational power. See his "Understanding Organizational Power: Building on the Weberian Legacy," *Administrative Science Quarterly* 23 (1978):65–90. John Kenneth Galbraith's analysis of monopolistic firms brought Weberian explanations of organizational power to the attention of economists. See his *Economics and the Public Purpose* (Boston: Houghton Mifflin, 1973). Although Weber's organization-level analysis is still most often cited for its treatment of bureaucratic efficiency, nevertheless, its major emphasis is on bureaucratic mechanisms of control.
    4. Weber analyzes authority or legitimate domination as part of his broad theory of organizational control. See his *Economy and Society,* especially ch. 3, "The Types of Legitimate Domination." For an analysis of unobtrusive mechanisms of control that are embedded in organizational structures, see Perrow, *Complex Organizations,* ch. 4.
    5. Peter M. Blau, *Bureaucracy in Modern Society* (New York: Random House, 1956).
    6. Galbraith, *Economics and the Public Purpose.*
    7. Philip Selznick ignored most of the political implications of the distinction. See his *TVA and the Grass Roots* (Berkeley: University of California Press, 1949). Perrow and other theorists have elaborated Selznick's original insight. See Perrow, *Complex Organizations,* ch. 5.
    8. The corporate group or *Verband* is the term Weber gives to organization as a genus, of which his three types of bureaucracies are species. See his *Economy and Society,* chs. 1 and 3.
    9. See Weber's discussion of routinization of charisma in *Economy and Society,* ch. 3.
    10. Karl Marx and Friedrich Engels, *On Religion* (New York: Schocken Books, 1964), 41.
    11. This overriding dilemma facing organized religion was the subject of Troeltsch's study of the evolution of sociological forms of Christianity. See his *Social Teachings.* For a treatment of five dilemmas endemic to modern churchlike forms that advances Troeltsch's analysis, see Thomas O'Dea, *The Sociology of Religion* (Englewood Cliffs, N.J.: Prentice-Hall, 1966).
    12. Perrow, *Complex Organizations.*
    13. I relied heavily on Aldrich's and McKelvey's population perspective for an initial understanding of social change in the Catholic priesthood. See Aldrich, *Organizations and Environments;* Bill McKelvey and Howard Aldrich, "Populations, Natural Selection, and Applied Organizational Science," *Administrative Science Quarterly* 28 (1983):101–128. For a discussion of their contributions to this analy-

sis, see Schoenherr and Young, *Full Pews and Empty Altars.* Michael Hannan and John Freeman, however, have contributed most extensively to the population ecology approach. See their *Organizational Ecology.*

14. Aldrich, *Organizations and Environments,* 28.

15. For a critical review of the research on leadership, see Richard H. Hall, *Organizations: Structure and Process,* 4th ed. (Englewood Cliffs, N.J.: Prentice-Hall, 1987).

16. McKelvey and Aldrich, "Populations," 112.

17. Perrow, *Complex Organizations,* 260–261.

4. THE TRANSPERSONAL PARADIGM

1. For a view of modern society as a network of formally structured organizations, see Charles Perrow, "A Society of Organizations," *Theory and Society* 20 (1991):725–762. For another treatment of the same view and a description of the social revolutions that ushered in the organizational society, see James S. Coleman, "The Rational Reconstruction of Society: 1992 Presidential Address," *American Sociological Review* 58 (1992):1–15.

2. Early applications of the population approach were based on an explicit assumption of prerational behavior, namely, that social change results from random chance and blind forces. See Michael T. Hannan and John Freeman, "The Population Ecology of Organizations," *American Journal of Sociology* 82 (1977):929–964. Later versions incorporate a model of both prerational and rational organizational behavior; see Hannan and Freeman, *Organizational Ecology.*

3. In *Economy and Society,* Weber analyzes the important distinction between substantive rationality (*wertrationalität*) and instrumental rationality (*zweckrationalität*). He introduced the metaphor of the iron cage to describe the ominous results of overemphasizing the latter. See his book *The Protestant Ethic and the Spirit of Capitalism,* trans. Talcott Parsons (New York: Charles Scribner's, 1958).

4. For an elaboration of the consequences of overreliance on instrumental rationality, see Karl Mannheim, *Man and Society in an Age of Reconstruction,* trans. Edward Shils (London: Routledge and Kegan Paul, 1980). According to Mannheim, the two essential traits of instrumental rationality are an agreed-on, prestated goal and a calculus for determining the best or better means for achieving it. See his *Man and Society.* Instrumental rationality, therefore, deals with the question of *how* to reach a goal but not *why* the goal is worth reaching; the latter is an issue stemming from substantive rationality.

5. For a critical review of the institutional school, see Perrow, *Complex Organizations,* 265–72.

6. Practical considerations for not espousing the transrational worldview begin with loss of esteem from social science colleagues, most of whose philosophical assumptions derive from a rational worldview. Other considerations include difficulties in gaining financial support and developing replicable methodologies for one's research.

7. Weber, *Economy and Society,* 1111.

8. Ibid., 1164.

9. Abraham Maslow is the pioneer of transpersonal psychology. For a description of its early beginnings, see his posthumous *The Farther Reaches of Human Na-*

ture (New York: Viking Press, 1971). For a treatment of the various meanings of transpersonal, a history of the development of this new paradigm, and a summary of applications and further potential for empirical research, see Francis E. Vaughan, "The Transpersonal Perspective: A Personal Overview," *Journal of Transpersonal Psychology* 14 (1982):37–45. In a series of seminal publications, Ken Wilber tries to lay out the basic contours of transpersonal sociology, drawing mainly from classic psychological research on developmental structuralism. His is the most successful attempt to introduce serious scholars to the new comprehensive paradigm. See especially his *A Sociable God: Toward a New Understanding of Religion* (Boulder, Colo.: New Science Library, 1983); also see his *Eye to Eye: The Quest for the New Paradigm,* expanded ed. (Boston, Mass.: Shambhala, 1990).

10. Many American scholars were introduced to this topic by Aldous Huxley, *The Perennial Philosophy* (New York: Harper, 1945). Leibniz coined the phrase "perennial philosophy," which Huxley describes as an immemorial and universal metaphysics "first committed to writing more than twenty-five centuries ago" (vii).

11. Arthur Lovejoy, *The Great Chain of Being* (Cambridge, Mass.: Harvard University Press, 1964). Huxley examines the *philosophia perennis* from many angles, citing passages from a wide sample of its written forms drawn mainly from world religions. For recent discussions, see Huston Smith, *Forgotten Truth* (New York: Harper and Row, 1976); also see Fritjof Schuon, *The Transcendent Unity of Religions* (New York: Harper and Row, 1976). The comparative historian of religion Mircea Eliade provides a comprehensive empirical analysis of the deep structure of local ancestral myth systems, which coincides with the basic tenets of the perennial philosophy expounded by world religions. For an introduction to his magisterial works, see *Myths, Rites, Symbols: A Mircea Eliade Reader,* 2 vols., ed. Wendell C. Beane and William G. Doty (New York: Harper, 1975). The mythologist Joseph Campbell further documents the extensive evidence supporting the transcendent worldview prominent in living religious myth systems. See *The Masks of God* (New York: Viking Press, 1968); *The Hero with a Thousand Faces* (Princeton, N.J.: Princeton University Press, 1972); *The Power of Myth* (Garden City, N.Y.: Doubleday, 1988).

12. Wilber, *Eye to Eye,* 216. See his extended discussion and examples of the pre/trans fallacy, 215–260.

13. For a treatment of the Enlightenment's impact on moral philosophy and social science pertinent to this discussion, see Alisdair MacIntyre, *After Virtue* (South Bend, Ind.: University of Notre Dame Press, 1981).

14. The second group includes, for example, Alfred Schutz, "On Multiple Realities," in *Collected Papers,* vol. 1 (The Hague: Nijhoff, 1962), and other phenomenologically oriented and interpretive social scientists.

15. The third group includes previously cited authors such as Maslow, Wilber, Bellah, Anthony and Robbins, Huxley, Turner, Smith, Eliade, and Campbell; classic scholars like Rudolf Otto and Martin Buber; and a growing number of contemporary sociologist who study the experiential dimensions of religiosity, notably Andrew Greeley, James Spickard, and Mary Jo Neitz. For references and a critical review of the most recent empirical research on the experience of ultimate reality, see David Yamane and Megan Polzer, "Ways of Seeing Ecstasy in Modern Society: Experiential-Expressive and Cultural-Linguistic Views," *Sociology of Religion* 55 (1994):1–25.

16. In the widest possible yet valid understanding of science, Wilber proposes

that the scientific enterprise in all its forms has three essential strands: the injunc-
tive, apprehensive, and confirmational. See his *Eye to Eye,* especially ch. 2, "The
Problem of Proof." The first strand is always a methodological injunction: If you
want to know this, do this. The second is grasping the percept, that is, apprehending through direct experience the data needed for knowing. The third is confirmation of the knowledge by sharing the method and apprehension with a qualified
group and thus arriving at a consensus about the truth. If one accepts that a datum
is "any *directly apprehended experience,"* then these three strands of science apply
equally to experiences of sensory, mental, or spiritual percepts (39).

17. Empirical-analytic thinking is the realm of "regular science." It yields explanations that follow the rules of rational linear logic and physical-sensory proof.
Phenomenological-hermeneutic thinking is the realm of empathetic interpretation.
It yields explanations that make rational sense to insiders, that is, to an intersubjec-
tive and interpretive circle familiar with the symbols and other mental data being explained. The "hermeneutic circle" is like the "scientific observer" in that both rely on
rational tools for interpreting directly perceived data. They differ, however, because
empirical-analytic explanations admit only those data verifiable by the senses, while
phenomenological-hermeneutic explanations admit mental data, that is, ideas and
thought processes that can be directly perceived by the mind and not by the senses.

Paradoxical-mandalic thinking is the realm of spiritual knowledge. It yields explanations that make sense to adepts or spiritual virtuosi, that is, those who experience the direct perception of spirit by spirit. It also provides maps for those interested in finding the path to spiritual knowledge. Paradoxical reason understands
reality as the coincidence of opposites: male/female, light/dark, immanence/tran-
scendence, and so on. The phrase *mandalic reason* can be used interchangeably with
paradoxical reason. It derives from *mandala,* "a Hindu or Buddhist graphic symbol
of the universe" (Webster's Tenth New Collegiate Dictionary, s.v. "mandala"). Mandalic thinking is a mapping or cartography of spiritual reality that cannot be expressed in rational conceptual thought. Paradoxical-mandalic thinking, therefore, is
unlike both empirical-analytic and phenomenological-hermeneutic thinking because it admits data that cannot be directly perceived by either the mind or the
senses but only by the human spirit. Hence it is called transrational, translogical,
transpersonal, or transcendent knowledge. For an extended discussion of these notions, see Wilber, *Eye to Eye;* also see Carl Jung, "Concerning Mandala Symbolism,"
in *The Archetypes and the Collective Unconscious* (Princeton, N.J.: Princeton University Press, 1968).

18. For an accessible treatment of Piaget's research, see H. Gruber and J.
Voneche, eds., *The Essential Piaget* (New York: Basic Books, 1977). Note: *Discovery*
is put in quotation marks because centuries earlier these levels of human consciousness were described in Hindu, Buddhist, and other versions of the perennial
philosophy.

5. THE SPECIAL CHARACTER OF ORGANIZED RELIGION

1. See my "Power and Authority in Organized Religion: Disaggregating the Phenomenological Core," *Sociological Analysis* 47 (1987):52–71.

2. The need to externalize interior, unobservable religious experiences is treated
by Rudolf Otto, *The Idea of the Holy* (London: Oxford University Press, 1969); Mar-

tin Buber, *I and Thou* (New York: Scribner, 1970); Mircea Eliade, *The Sacred and the Profane* (New York: Harcourt, Brace, and World, 1961); and Joachim Wach, *Types of Religious Experience: Christian and Non-Christian* (Chicago: University of Chicago Press, 1951). I use the term *unobservable* in its usual connotation, meaning not able to be perceived by the five senses. Following Ken Wilber, I also admit of experiential data that are unobservable by the senses or the mind but are observable by the human spirit, through the eye of contemplation; see his *Eye to Eye*.

3. Eliade, *Sacred and the Profane*. For another analysis of creation myths and those dealing with the order of the cosmos, see Campbell, *Masks of God*. For a popular, illustrated, reliable collection of creation myths, see Virginia Hamilton, *In the Beginning: Creation Stories from Around the World* (San Diego: Harcourt Brace Jovanovich, 1988).

4. For a psychological explanation of different perceptions of time and space, see Maslow, *Toward a Psychology of Being* (Princeton, N.J.: Van Nostrand, 1962). He describes the perception that occurs in moments of peak experience as B-cognition, in which the percept does not occupy the normal time-and-space grid. Similarly, Wach explains that a religious experience, though not verifiable by an observer, tends universally toward expression. Only the external expression is verifiable because it, not the subjective experience itself, occurs in normal time and space. See his *Types of Religious Experience*.

5. For a discussion of the universality of sacrament, see Suzanne Langer, "Life-Symbols: The Roots of Sacrament," in *Theories of Society*, ed. Talcott Parsons, Edward Shils, Kaspar D. Naegele, and Jesse R. Pitts, vol. 2 (Glencoe, Ill.: Free Press, 1961), 1179–1189.

6. For an analysis of the importance of sacrifice, see Robertson Smith, "On Sacrifice," in Parsons et al., *Theories of Society*, 1096–1097. He notes that "in ancient religions all the ordinary functions of worship are summed up in the sacrificial meal . . . the ordinary intercourse between gods and men [sic] has no other form" (1096).

7. Henri Hubert and Marcel Mauss, *Sacrifice: Its Nature and Function*, trans. W. D. Halls (Chicago: University of Chicago Press, [1898] 1964).

8. For a similar argument of the centrality of sacrifice not only in ancient religions but also in contemporary Christianity, see W. H. Frere, *The Principles of Religious Ceremonial* (1928): "The Eucharist was to sum up and supersede all older rites and sacrifices; and it has been from the first the central Christian sacrament, *not significant only, but efficacious*" (quoted in Langer, "Life-Symbols," 1186).

9. Abbott, *Documents of Vatican II*, "Constitution on the Sacred Liturgy," no. 10.

10. Herbert Richardson, "The Symbol of Virginity," in *The Religious Situation 1969*, ed. Donald R. Cutler (Boston: Beacon Press, 1969), 775.

11. Eliade, *Sacred and the Profane*.

12. Wilber, *Eye to Eye*, 171.

13. Ibid., 171–172. The Absolute "is *nirguna*, without attributes, or *sunya*, void of characterization. Since there is no place outside the absolute, there is no place you could take up a stance so as to describe it. If you could get outside it, it would cease to be the absolute" (172).

14. Joan D. Chittister, *The Rule of Benedict: Insight for the Ages* (New York: Crossroad, 1992), 64.

15. Eliade uses the term *symbol* in the sense described by Ernst Cassirer. See

Cassirer, *The Philosophy of Symbolic Forms,* trans. Ralph Mannheim (New Haven: Yale University Press, 1953). Symbol is a unique and irreducible form of human communication distinct from the rational concept. This usage is close to the term *sacrament* as used in my analysis.

16. Eliade, *Sacred and the Profane,* 95.

17. Ibid., 101.

18. For a chilling account of the modern consequences of forgetting the myth, see Václav Havel, "Thriller," in *Living in Truth* (London: Faber and Faber, 1989).

19. Weber, *Economy and Society,* 223.

20. See, for example, the Zen lineage charts in the *Shambhala Dictionary of Buddhism and Zen* (Boston: Shambhala, 1991).

21. For a classic source of such accounts, see William James, *The Varieties of Religious Experience: A Study in Human Nature* (Cambridge, Mass.: Harvard University Press, 1985).

22. Abbott, *Documents of Vatican II,* "Constitution on the Sacred Liturgy," no. 10.

23. Buber, *I and Thou.*

24. Emil L. Fackenheim, "Martin Buber's Concept of Revelation," in *The Philosophy of Martin Buber: The Library of Living Philosophers,* vol. 12, ed. Paul A. Schilpp and Maurice Friedman (LaSalle, Ill.: Open Court, 1967), 279.

25. In their theory of social action, Talcott Parsons and Edward Shils assume that the manner in which actors orient themselves to a situation takes three operative forms, although one usually dominates. See their book *Toward a General Theory of Action* (New York: Harper and Row, 1951). Thus, part of the orientation to any situation is cognitive—the actor understands it rationally; part is cathectic—the actor has positive or negative feelings about it; and part is evaluative—the actor gives it a valence in a hierarchy of values. When a hierophanic event is part of the situation, the orientation takes on a fourth form, which operates along with the cognitive, cathectic, and evaluative orientations, but may very well dominate. For want of a better term, I call this the fideistic orientation to action. See my "Power and Authority in Organized Religion."

26. For a recent critical review of research on dominant coalitions, see W. Richard Scott, *Organizations: Rational, Natural, and Open Systems,* 3rd ed. (Englewood Cliffs, N.J.: Prentice-Hall, 1992), especially ch. 11, "Goals, Power, and Control."

27. See Gene Burns, "The Politics of Ideology: The Papal Struggle with Liberalism," *American Journal of Sociology* 95 (1990):1123–1152.

28. Joseph Frings, quoted in Yves Congar, *Power and Poverty in the Church* (Baltimore: Helicon, 1964), 147–148.

29. See Burns, "Politics of Ideology."

30. The contemporary Roman Curia consists of a vast array of bureaucratic offices:

1. Secretariat of State, which handles the daily business of the Holy See and diplomatic and other relations with civil governments.

2. Nine congregations or governing agencies (named the Congregation for: Doctrine of the Faith; Oriental Churches; Bishops; Divine Worship and Discipline of the Sacraments; Causes of Saints; Clergy; Institutes of Consecrated Life and Societies of Apostolic Life; Seminaries and Catholic Institutes of Study; and Evangelization of Peoples).

3. Five interagency curia commissions for matters involving more than one congregation (named the Interdepartmental Standing Commission for: Appointments to Local Churches; Institutes of Consecrated Life; Candidates for Sacred Orders; Catholic Education; and Church in Eastern Europe).

4. Three tribunals or judicial agencies: Apostolic Penitentiary (for internal matters of conscious and dispensations), Apostolic Signatura (the supreme court of the Church and Vatican City), and Roman Rota (for ordinary legal appeals, especially marriage cases).

5. Eleven councils or promotional agencies (named Pontifical Council for: Laity; Promoting Christian Unity; Family; Justice and Peace; "Cor Unum" [human aid and development]; Pastoral Care of Migrants and Itinerant Peoples; Pastoral Assistance to Health Care Workers; Interpretation of Legislative Texts; Inter-religious Dialogue; Culture; and Social Communications).

6. Seven offices or specialized service agencies (Apostolic Chamber, Prefecture of the Papal Household, Administration of the Patrimony of the Apostolic See, Central Office of Statistics of the Church, Prefecture for the Economic Affairs of the Holy See, Office of the Liturgical Celebrations of the Supreme Pontiff, and Archives of the Second Vatican Council).

31. For an excellent theological and canonical description of both episcopal and papal authority, see Patrick Granfield, *The Limits of the Papacy* (New York: Crossroad, 1987).

32. *1995 Catholic Almanac* and *1994 Official Catholic Directory.*

33. For a description of organizational restructuring that occurred after the Council, see Gertrude Kim, "Roman Catholic Organizations since Vatican II," in *American Denominational Organization: A Sociological View* (Pasadena, Calif.: William Carey Library, 1980), 84–129.

34. Antonio Gramsci, *Selection from the Prison Notebooks,* ed. and trans. Quintin Hoare and G. N. Smith (New York: International, 1971).

35. For sociological analyses of the Roman Catholic parish, see Joseph Fichter, *Southern Parish: Dynamics of a City Church* (Chicago: University of Chicago Press, 1951); David C. Leege and Joseph Gremillion, eds., "Notre Dame Study of Catholic Parish Life: Report Series 1-15" (Notre Dame, Ind.: Institute for Pastoral and Social Ministry, 1984–1989); Melissa L. Ray, "Blest Be the Ties That Bind: Interpretive Appropriation of External Mandates in an Organizational Culture," Ph.D. diss., University of Wisconsin–Madison, 1991.

36. Weber, *Economy and Society,* ch. 6.

6. FORCES FOR CHANGE IN CATHOLIC MINISTRY

1. See Schoenherr and Young, *Full Pews and Empty Altars.*

2. Pluralism is one of the most significant themes treated in the documents issued by the Second Vatican Council. See Adrian Hastings, "The Key Texts," in *Modern Catholicism: Vatican II and After* (New York: Oxford University Press, 1991), 56–67.

3. Bellah, *Beyond Belief: Essays on Religion in a Post-Traditional World* (New York: Harper and Row, 1970).

4. *Webster's Tenth New Collegiate Dictionary,* s.v. "dogma."

5. See Eliade, *Sacred and the Profane.*

6. Bellah, "Religious Evolution," in *Beyond Belief,* 20–50.

7. Monism is the view that the cosmos is a single whole. Dualism is the view that the cosmos is composed of irreducible paired elements: good/evil, heaven/earth, spirit/matter, and so on.

8. Bellah, "Religious Evolution," 42.

9. David Hume argued that reason can go so far but no farther; he did not claim that something "better" than reason could explain all of reality. See his book *The Natural History of Religion,* ed. H. E. Root (Stanford, Calif.: Stanford University Press, 1956).

10. Friedrich Schleiermacher, *On Religion: Speeches to Its Cultured Despisers* (New York: Harper, [1799]1958).

11. Herbert A. Hodges, *The Philosophy of Wilhelm Dilthey* (London: Routledge and Kegan Paul, 1952); Otto, *Idea of the Holy;* Herbert Spiegelberg, *The Phenomenological Movement* (Boston: Martinus Nijhoff, 1982); Joseph M. Kitagawa and Charles H. Long, *Myths and Symbols:Studies in Honor of Mircea Eliade* (Chicago: Chicago University Press, 1969); Wendell C. Beane and William G. Doty, *Myths, Rites, Symbols: A Mircea Eliade Reader,* 2 vols. (New York: Harper Colophon, 1975).

12. Peter Berger, *The Heretical Imperative* (Garden City, N.Y.: Doubleday, 1980).

13. See H. Gruber and J. Voneche, eds., *The Essential Piaget* (New York: Basic Books, 1977). For an excellent summary of Piaget's research, see Roger Brown, *Social Psychology* (New York: Free Press, 1965).

14. Brown, *Social Psychology,* 233.

15. Erik H. Erikson, *The Life Cycle Completed: A Review* (New York: Norton, 1982). For an excellent summary of Erickson's research, see David M. Wulff, *Psychology of Religion* (New York: Wiley, 1991).

16. Lawrence Kohlberg, *The Philosophy of Moral Development: Moral Stages and the Idea of Justice* (San Francisco: Harper and Row, 1981); James W. Fowler, *Stages of Faith: The Psychology of Human Development and the Quest for Meaning* (San Francisco: Harper and Row, 1981).

17. Berger, *Heretical Imperative.*

18. Fowler, *Stages of Faith,* 197.

19. Paul Ricoeur, *Freud and Philosophy: An Essay on Interpretation,* trans. D. Savage (New Haven: Yale University Press, 1965).

20. Ibid., 28. For an accessible treatment of Ricoeur's analysis, see Wulff, *Psychology of Religion.*

21. From a homily delivered by Gary Meyer at St. Benedict Center, Middleton, Wisconsin.

22. Robert Wuthnow, *The Restructuring of American Religion* (Princeton, N.J.: Princeton University Press, 1988).

23. John A. Hannigan, "Social Movement Theory and the Sociology of Religion: Toward a New Synthesis," *Sociological Analysis* (1991):311–331, 325–326.

24. Avery R. Dulles, *Models of the Church: A Critical Assessment of the Church in All Its Aspects* (Garden City, N.Y.: Doubleday, 1974).

25. For a discussion of deep ecumenism, see Matthew Fox, *The Coming of the Cosmic Christ* (San Francisco: Harper and Row, 1988).

26. For an excellent analysis of the Catholic Church's transformation from a Eurocentric religion to a world Church of six continents, see Walbert Bühlmann, *The Church of the Future: A Model for the Year 2001* (Maryknoll, N.Y.: Orbis Books, 1986).

27. Ibid.

28. Ibid.

29. Ibid.

30. Ibid.

31. Ibid., 7.

32. It is important to repeat that, generally, religious order priests do not have a history of hostility toward institutionalized celibacy like that of the secular clergy. Full-fledged members of religious communities take the perpetual vows of poverty, chastity, and obedience as single persons. The vow of chastity implies a lifelong commitment to remain unmarried. In that sense celibacy is institutionalized in religious communities whether the member is ordained or not.

Diocesan priests do not take religious vows. Hence they are called secular clergy (Latin *saecula,* world) because they "live in the world" among the ordinary people. Religious order priests are called regular clergy (Latin *regula,* rule) because they "leave the world" to live in a monastery or other organized fellowship, where they follow the rule imposed by vows of poverty, chastity, and obedience. Mandatory celibacy for all priests, whether secular or regular, is institutionalized by a juridical declaration. Until recently, canon law declared that if any priest attempted marriage the Church not only considered the act sacrilegious but also null and void (no marriage at all) and imposed ipso facto excommunication. For a brief description of the pertinent canons and history of their origins, see Coriden, "Celibacy, Canon Law," in Bassett and Huizing, eds., *Celibacy,* 109–124. The revised Code of Canon Law, promulgated in 1983, is more humane regarding offenses and penalties in general. The law of mandatory celibacy for priests is retained, but if a priest marries he is not ipso facto excommunicated. He is suspended *a divinis* (from sacramental functions) and threatened with further penalties.

33. Sipe, *Secret World,* 283.

34. Ibid., 290.

35. Abbott, *Documents of Vatican II,* 250–258. For an interpretation of the critical consequences of reformulating the goals of marriage, see Theodore Davey, "Marriage and Sexuality," in *Modern Catholicism: Vatican II and After,* ed. Adrian Hastings (London: Oxford University Press, 1991), 267–271.

36. Herbert Richardson, "The Symbol of Virginity," in *The Religious Situation, 1969,* ed. Donald R. Cutler (Boston: Beacon Press, 1969), 775–811.

37. For a brief but reliable analysis of medieval courtly love, see Jamake Highwater, *Myth and Sexuality* (New York: Meridian, 1991).

38. For a discussion of the impact of personalism on the Second Vatican Council, see Edna McDonagh, "The Church in the Modern World (*Gaudium et Spes*)," in Hastings, *Modern Catholicism,* 96–112. McDonagh observes that "The influence of personalism was a dominant and in many ways a welcome influence at the Council" (102). According to council doctrine, companionate marriage, established in a

free and equal loving relationship, is the ideal. A commitment based on personalism becomes the proper context for procreation. For careful documentation of a growing emphasis on companionate marriage from the 1940s to the 1990s, see Gay C. Kitson with William M. Holmes, *Portrait of Divorce: Adjustment to Marital Breakdown* (New York: Guilford Press, 1992).

39. For a far-reaching attempt to reform the theology of sexuality, commissioned by the Catholic Theological Society of America, see Anthony Kosnik, William Carroll, Agnes Cunningham, Ronald Modras, and James Schulte, *Human Sexuality: New Directions in American Catholic Thought* (New York: Paulist Press, 1973).

40. E.g., see Paul Wilkes, "Profiles: Archbishop Weakland," *New Yorker,* 2 parts (15 July 1991, 22 July 1991); "Sex More Controversial Than Drugs at Bishops' Meeting," *National Catholic Reporter,* 23 November 1990; Bishop Frank Murphy, "Let's Start Over," *Commonweal,* 25 September 1992; Robert McClory, "Bishops Buck Criticism, Attend Gay Symposium in Chicago," *National Catholic Reporter,* 10 April 1992; Tom Roberts, "He's Not Disordered, He's My Brother," *National Catholic Reporter,* 4 November 1994.

41. See Philip Rieff, *The Triumph of the Therapeutic: Uses of Faith after Freud* (New York: Harper and Row, 1966); Robert Wuthnow, *The Consciousness Reformation* (Berkeley: University of California Press, 1976); Christopher Lasch, *The Culture of Narcissism* (New York: Warner Books, 1979).

42. Peter Hebblethwaite, "Theologians Offer Menu of Worldviews for a New Europe," *National Catholic Reporter,* 24 April 1992.

43. Mieth, quoted in Hebblethwaite, "Theologians Offer Menu."

44. Erik Olin Wright argues that if gender oppression is defined in terms of different *formal rights* for women and men, then progress in eliminating gender oppression is fairly evident. See his "Explanation and Emancipation in Marxism and Feminism," *Sociological Theory* 11 (1993):39–54. Legally, women have full citizenship and the right to an education, abortion, job, and so on, which they did not have in prior centuries and decades. According to Wright, if one takes the position that the elimination of gender oppression means the equalization of social power and material welfare across genders, then the emancipation of women has a long way to go and, indeed, may seem utopian.

45. Edward C. Lehman, *Gender and Work: The Case of the Clergy* (Albany: State University of New York Press, 1993).

46. For an account of the reform of U.S. religious orders of women, see Helen Rose Ebaugh, *Out of the Cloister* (Austin: University of Texas Press, 1977); also see Marie Augusta Neal, *From Nuns to Sisters: An Expanding Vocation* (Mystic, Conn.: Twenty-Third, 1990).

47. Marie Augusta Neal, *Catholic Sisters in Transition from the 1960s to the 1980s* (Wilmington, Del.: Michael Glazier, 1984), and *Nuns to Sisters.*

48. Helen Rose Ebaugh, *Women in the Vanishing Cloister: Organizational Decline in Catholic Religious Orders in the United States* (New Brunswick, N.J.: Rutgers University Press, 1993); Patricia Wittberg, *The Rise and Fall of Catholic Religious Orders: A Social Movement Perspective* (Albany: State University of New York Press, 1994).

49. Leonard Swidler and Arlene Swidler, eds., *Women Priests: A Catholic Commentary on the Vatican Declaration* (New York: Paulist Press, 1976), 38.

50. Swidler and Swidler, eds., *Women Priests*, contains the full range of reaction; also see Sandra M. Schneiders, *Beyond Patching: Faith and Feminism in the Catholic Church* (New York: Paulist Press, 1991).

51. For a critical analysis of feminism in the Catholic Church, see Schneiders, *Beyond Patching*.

52. The classic theological treatment of the clergy–lay split can be found in Yves Congar, *Lay People in the Church* (London: Geoffrey Chapman, 1965).

53. See "Declaration of Religious Freedom," in Abbott, *Documents of Vatican II;* see also Gene Burns, *The Frontiers of Catholicism: The Politics of Ideology in a Liberal World* (Berkeley: University of California Press, 1992).

54. "Decree on the Apostolate of the Laity," in Abbott, *Documents of Vatican II.*

55. According to Catholic theology, in an emergency anyone with the right intention and using the correct form can baptize, but only an ordained priest can validly celebrate Eucharist and confirmation; preferably a bishop celebrates confirmation.

56. Leege and Gremillion, "Notre Dame Study"; Peter Gilmour, *The Emerging Pastor* (Kansas City, Mo.: Sheed and Ward, 1986); Ruth A. Wallace, *They Call Her Pastor: A New Role for Catholic Women* (Albany: State University of New York Press, 1992).

57. See Zeni Fox, "The Rise of Lay Ministry in the Years Since Vatican II," in *The Church in the Nineties: Its Legacy, Its Future,* ed. Pierre M. Hegy (Collegeville, Minn.: Liturgical Press, 1993).

58. Thomas P. Walters, *National Profile of Professional Religious Education Directors/Coordinators* (Washington, D.C.: National Conference of Diocesan Directors, 1983).

59. Philip Murnion, David DeLambo, Rosemary Dilli, and Harry Fagan, *New Parish Ministers* (New York: National Pastoral Life Center, 1992).

60. Wallace, *They Call Her Pastor,* 141.

61. For an analysis of the importance of this document, see Lester R. Kurtz, *The Politics of Heresy: The Modernist Crisis in Roman Catholicism* (Berkeley: University of California Press, 1986).

62. Greeley and Schoenherr (NORC), *Catholic Priest,* 143.

63. Bühlmann, *Church of the Future.*

64. For a description of ecclesial base communities and references to the literature analyzing their social impact on organized religion in Latin America, see Madeleine Adriance, *Opting for the Poor: Brazilian Catholicism in Transition* (Kansas City, Mo.: Sheed and Ward, 1986), and "The Post–Vatican II Church in Latin America," in *Vatican II and U.S. Catholicism,* ed. Helen Rose Ebaugh (Greenwich, Conn.: JAI Press, 1990), 233–245.

65. Richard Fragomeni, "A Vision of the Sacraments: Will the Eucharist Survive?" audio cassette from Future of the American Church Conference (Elkridge, Md.: Chesapeake Audio/Video Communications, 1990).

66. Ibid.

7. UNITY AND DIVERSITY

1. Contemporary intimations of transcending the dualistic, world-rejecting theology of historic religions can be found in recent developments in creationist theology. For a treatment strongly affirming the goodness of the world as created by God,

see Matthew Fox, *Original Blessing: A Primer in Creation Spirituality* (Santa Fe, N.M.: Bear, 1983). For data showing that Catholics believe the world and its events are something like God and therefore society is sacramental, natural, and good, see Andrew M. Greeley, "Protestant and Catholic: Is the Analogical Imagination Extinct?" *American Sociological Review* (1989):485–502.

2. In the very earliest Christian tradition, Pentecostal proselytizers proclaimed that the Spirit of the Risen Christ is available universally; there are no barriers of race, ethnicity, class, gender, status, age, and so on. See Daphne Hampson's treatment of Galatians 3: 28 in her *Theology and Feminism* (Cambridge, Mass.: Blackwell, 1990).

3. The principal document on religious freedom is titled *Dignitatis Humanae,* but three others—*Unitatis Redintegratio* on ecumenism, *Nostra Aetate* on other (non-Christian) religions, and *Orientalium Ecclesiarum* on the Eastern Catholic Churches—spell out the implications of the doctrine. See Abbott, *Documents of Vatican II.* For analyses of these documents, see chapters 8E-H in Hastings, *Modern Catholicism.*

4. See the discussion of second naivete in chapter 6, particularly the contributions of Paul Ricoeur and James Fowler.

5. Daniel J. Boorstin, *The Discoverers: A History of Man's Search to Know His World and Himself* (New York: Random House, 1983), 47.

6. Lao Tsu, *Tao Te Ching,* trans. Stephen Mitchell (New York: Harper Perennial, 1992), ch. 21. All quotations from the *Tao Te Ching* are from this source. Mitchell's translation contains 81 numbered sections; following him, I refer to them as chapters.

7. Philo, quoted by Mitchell, *Tao Te Ching,* 104.

8. Paul declares, "I live now not with my own life but with the life of Christ who lives in me" (Gal 2:20).

9. See Otto, *Idea of the Holy;* Wilber, *Eye to Eye.*

10. *Tao Te Ching,* ch. 1.

11. The Cartesian revolution established the power of reason, positing an absolute world out there to be known. The question is, How does the knower get in the right relationship to know the external world? The knowing subject relies on human reason to identify and define objects. Cartesian logic demands a subject–object distinction and produces an objective view of reality. The Kantian revolution started from the other side. The questions become: What do we know about the knower? What can the knower gain knowledge of? Thus, objects are defined by what the knower can know. Kantian logic leads to subject–object reciprocity and produces a subjective view of reality.

12. For a discussion of relativism and modern religion, see Peter Berger, *The Heretical Imperative: Contemporary Possibilities of Religious Affirmation* (Garden City, N.Y.: Anchor Books, 1980), and *A Far Glory* (Glencoe, Ill.: Free Press, 1992).

13. On the need for dogma in historical, rational religions, see Alfred North Whitehead, *Religion in the Making* (New York: Macmillan, 1926).

14. Eliade, *Sacred and the Profane.*

15. Otto, *Idea of the Holy;* Wilber, *Eye to Eye.*

16. Wilber, *Eye to Eye.* See also Roberts, *The Experience of No-Self: A Contemplative Journey* (Boston: Shambhala, 1982); *The Path to No-Self: Life at the Center* (Boston: Shambhala, 1985); and *What Is Self?: A Study of the Spiritual Journey in Terms of Consciousness* (Austin, Tex.: Mary Botsford Gains, 1989).

17. Maslow, *Farther Reaches;* Wilber, *Eye to Eye;* Ricoeur, *Freud and Philosophy;* Fowler, *Stages of Faith.*

18. For descriptions of the split between science and religion and accounts of its consequences, see Robert N. Bellah, "Between Religion and Social Science" pp. 237–259 in *Beyond Belief* (New York: Harper and Row, 1970). Abraham Maslow, *Religion, Values, and Peak Experiences* (Columbus: Ohio State University Press, 1964).

19. John Welch, *Spiritual Pilgrims: Carl Jung and Teresa of Avila* (New York: Paulist Press, 1982), 73–74.

20. Ibid., especially 86–87.

21. Abraham Maslow, *Toward a Psychology of Being,* rev. ed. (Princeton, N.J.: Van Nostrand, 1968).

22. In Western mysticism this state of being is referred to as the unitive way or living in the presence of God. In the Eastern tradition it is satori, samadhi, nirvana; see Wilber, *Sociable God.*

23. For such statements by Catholic mystics, see Thomas Merton, *Mystics and Zen Masters* (New York: Dell, 1967); Thomas Keating, *The Heart of the World: An Introduction to Contemplative Christianity* (New York: Crossroad, 1988); David Steindl-Rast, *Gratefulness, the Heart of Prayer: An Approach to Life in Fullness* (New York: Paulist Press, 1984).

24. Michael Hill, *The Religious Order* (London: Heinemann, 1973). Thomas Merton, *The Wisdom of the Desert* (New York: New Directions, 1960).

25. Monasticism flourished in both Eastern and Western churches. For an account of Eastern monasticism, see Timothy Ware, *The Orthodox Church* (New York: Penguin, 1993).

26. For a discussion of how the Catholic tradition uses contemplation, liturgy, and charity to help practitioners negotiate the passage to mature adulthood, see David B. Burrell, "The Church and Individual Life," *Toward Vatican III: The Work That Needs To Be Done,* ed. David Tracy with Hans Küng and Johann B. Metz (New York: Seabury Press, 1978), 124–133.

For the deep roots of the three pillars of Catholic piety, see the ancient variable prayers of the Latin Mass (Collect, Secret, and Postcommunion) developed and recorded from the third to the sixth century C.E. See Joseph A. Jungmann, *The Mass of the Roman Rite: Its Origins and Development,* trans. Francis A. Brunner (New York: Benziger, 1951), especially part 3, ch. 1.

27. Jung and Teresa of Avila, quoted in Welch, *Spiritual Pilgrims,* 81–82. See Teresa of Avila, *The Interior Castle,* trans. Kieran Kavanaugh and Otilio Rodriguez (New York: Paulist Press, 1979).

28. For example, the hegemony of the Dutch, Spanish, British, and United States empires followed one after the other. See Immanuel Wallerstein, *The Second Era of Great Expansion of the Capitalist World-Economy, 1730–1840s* (San Diego: Academic Press, 1989).

29. Bühlmann, *Church of the Future,* 7.

8. IMMANENCE AND TRANSCENDENCE

1. Eliade, *Sacred and Profane;* Campbell, *Masks of God;* Lerner, *Creation of Patriarchy;* Highwater, *Myth and Sexuality.*

2. In the Roman Catholic tradition, the philosophical formulation of personalism

is ascribed to Jacques Maritain and its elaboration to Thomas Merton. See Anne Carr, *A Search for Wisdom and Spirit: Thomas Merton's Theology of the Self* (Notre Dame, Ind.: University of Notre Dame Press, 1988) and Thomas M. King, *Merton: Mystic at the Center of America* (Collegeville, Minn.: Liturgical Press, 1992).

3. Wilber, *Eye to Eye*.

4. Peter Brown, *The Body and Society: Men, Women and Sexual Renunciation in Early Christianity* (New York: Columbia University Press, 1988).

5. In the deutero-Pauline letters to the Ephesians and the Hebrews, the author of the epistle corrects this notion and raises marriage to a Christian ideal. See Brown, *Body and Society*, 57.

6. Brown, *Body and Society*, 49; see ch. 2 in its entirety. See also Henry Charles Lea, *History of Sacerdotal Celibacy in the Christian Church* (New Hyde Park N.Y.: University Books, 1966), for an earlier and decidedly polemical analysis drawing similar conclusions.

7. *Tao Te Ching*, ch. 11.

8. Highwater, *Myth and Sexuality*, 117. Highwater gives a succinct description of the impact of Manichaean doctrine on the Christian (hence Western) conception of sexuality.

9. Elaine Pagels, quoted in Highwater, *Myth and Sexuality*, 122.

10. Lehman, *Gender and Work*; Chaves, *Ordaining Women: Culture and Conflict in Religious Organizations* (Cambridge, Mass.: Harvard University Press, 1997); Paula Nesbitt, *Feminization of the Clergy in America: Occupational and Organizational Perspectives* (New York: Oxford University Press, 1997).

11. Wallace, *They Call Her Pastor*. Also see Jane Redmont, *Generous Lives: American Catholic Women Today* (Liguori, Mo.: Triumph Books, 1993), especially ch. 18, "'You're a *What?*' Catholic Women as Ministers." For an archbishop's strong endorsement of gender inclusivity in top administrative positions of the Catholic Church, see Rembert G. Weakland, "Out of the Kitchen, Into the Vatican," *New York Times*, 6 December 1992.

12. David Gonzalez, "Endorsing Growing Practice, Vatican Approves Altar Girls," *New York Times*, 15 April 1994.

13. Fox, "Rise of Lay Ministry"; Hoge, *The Future of Catholic Leadership;* Murnion et al., *New Parish Ministers.*

14. Weber found that religions of the nonprivileged classes tend to allot equality to women more than religions of the elite classes. See his *Economy and Society*, ch. 6. Nevertheless, men appropriated the positions of power and control even in the religions of the unprivileged.

15. For a treatment of types of transcendence that incorporates the major theories of psychosocial development with recent advances in transpersonal psychology, see Wilber, *Eye to Eye*.

9. HIERARCHY AND HIEROPHANY

1. See Madeleine Adriance, *Opting for the Poor: Brazilian Catholicism in Transition* (Kansas City, Mo.: Sheed and Ward, 1986); W. E. Hewitt, *Base Christian Communities and Social Change in Brazil* (Lincoln: University of Nebraska Press, 1991); Christian Smith, *The Emergence of Liberation Theology: Radical Religion and Social Movement Theory* (Chicago: University of Chicago Press, 1991).

2. See Jay P. Dolan, *The Immigrant Church* (Notre Dame, Ind.: University of Notre Dame Press, 1983), and *The American Catholic Parish: A History from 1850 to the Present*, 2 vols. (New York: Paulist Press, 1987).

3. Andrew Greeley, "The Demography of American Catholics: 1965–1990," in *Vatican II and U.S. Catholicism*, ed. Helen Rose Ebaugh (Greenwich, Conn.: JAI Press, 1991); Walters, *National Profile;* Fox, "Rise of Lay Ministry"; Hoge, *Catholic Leadership;* Wallace, *They Call Her Pastor;* Murnion et al., *New Parish Ministers.*

4. Literally, the phrase is translated "by the work having been performed" and can be taken to mean that the mere accurate performance of a sacramental rite guarantees its desired effect.

5. I studied in a Catholic seminary from 1953 to 1961. In the academic year 1959–60, less than two years before my ordination to priesthood, the entire student body was electrified by a crash course in higher biblical criticism. Our Scripture professor confessed to us that, until recently, he had not been fully aware of developments in the field. To remedy the situation, he invited renowned biblical scholars to give an intensive workshop. We were absolutely flabbergasted to hear Catholic scholars teaching that the world had not been created in six calendar days, that Eve and Adam had not encountered a physical snake and eaten an actual apple, that the story of the Magi was midrash, that the deeper spiritual events recounted in miracle stories were more miraculous and real than the superficial physical events. The impact could hardly have been more earth-shattering. In a few short weeks we had participated in the ending of an era for the Catholic Church and the beginning of a new one.

6. See E. T. Gomulka, "The Priest Shortage: Remaining 'Semper Fi' with Fewer Priests," *America*, 16 April 1994; William H. Shannon, "No Circuit-Rider Priests, Please!" *America*, 16 April 1994.

7. Henri Hubert and Marcel Mauss, *Sacrifice: Its Nature and Function*, translated by W. D. Halls (Chicago: University of Chicago Press, 1964).

8. Other Protestant denominations retained sacerdotal and sacrificial elements of the Eucharist, though they disputed the Catholic formulation of transubstantiation. Lutherans and Episcopalians, for example, emphasize priestly ordination as a requisite for presiding at the Eucharist.

9. Victor Turner, *The Ritual Process: Structure and Anti-structure* (Chicago: Aldine, 1969).

10. See Mathieu Deflem, "Ritual, Anti-Structure, and Religion: A Discussion of Victor Turner's Processional Symbolic Analysis," *Journal for the Scientific Study of Religion* 30 (1991): 1–25.

11. Victor W. Turner, "Social Dramas and Stories About Them," pp. 137–64 in *On Narrative*, edited by W. J. T. Mitchell (Chicago: University of Chicago Press, 1981), quote on 143.

12. Ibid., 144.

13. Gerardus Van der Leeuw, *Religion in Essence and Manifestation* (New York: Macmillan, 1938); Eliade, *Sacred and Profane;* Wilber, *Sociable God.*

14. For example, most of the critical works in liberation theology have been written by priests pursuing pastoral ministries in base communities. See Madeleine Adriance, "Agents of Change: The Roles of Priests, Sisters, and Lay Workers in the Grassroots Catholic Church in Brazil," *Journal for the Scientific Study of Religion* 30 (September 1991):292–305. For a grassroots description of how U.S. parish priests

negotiate between the needs of the faithful and the demands of the diocesan chancery, see Tim Unsworth, "Parish Priests Cope with Mess; Chanceries Tangled up in Rules," *National Catholic Reporter,* 20 May 1994.

15. Some feminist scholars find female images of divinity in Judaeo-Christian scriptures, citing the feminine aspects of Wisdom (Sophia) and the Holy Spirit. See, for example, Rosemary Radford Ruether, *Sexism and God-Talk: Toward a Feminist Theology* (Boston: Beacon Press, 1983). In *Theology and Feminism,* Daphne Hampson takes issue with this view: "That the God of Judaism and of Christianity is in conception profoundly male is clear. It may be more honest to face this for what it is. The various attempts to find female aspects to the tradition can retrieve very little" (96). I agree that the Judaeo-Christian mythic tradition is deeply patriarchal and that male hegemony is ubiquitous in its contemporary social forms. I disagree with Hampson that the Judaeo-Christian tradition must be jettisoned (as if such a choice were sociologically possible). Rather, we should recognize Judaism and Christianity as living myth systems that, along with the rest of society, are increasingly recognizing and celebrating the reality of gender interdependence.

10. Bureaucratic Counterinsurgency in Catholic History

1. Lester Kurtz, *The Politics of Heresy: The Modernist Crisis in Roman Catholicism* (Berkeley: University of California Press, 1986).

2. Studies of coalitional conflict abound in the sociological literature. Several researchers have investigated power struggles in religious settings. For a study of coalition conflict in the Southern Baptist Conference in which the conservatives win, see Nancy Tatom Ammerman, *Baptist Battles: Social Change and Religious Conflict in the Southern Baptist Convention* (New Brunswick, N.J.: Rutgers University Press, 1990). For an analysis of coalition formation reporting that conflict between Protestant liberals and evangelical conservatives has been increasing since World War II, see Robert Wuthnow, *The Struggle for America's Soul: Evangelicals, Liberals, and Secularism* (Grand Rapids, Mich.: Eerdmans, 1989).

3. Gene Burns, "The Politics of Ideology: The Papal Struggle with Liberalism," *American Journal of Sociology* 95 (1990):1123–1152. For a Catholic theologian's carefully nuanced but generally similar view of the expansion of papal control inside the Church during the twentieth century, see Granfield, *Limits of the Papacy.*

4. For a parallel treatment of the same issues, see O'Dea, *Catholic Crisis.*

5. Burns, "Politics of Ideology," 1123.

6. The doctrine of papal infallibility was hotly debated, strongly opposed by a prominent minority of bishops, and confirmed despite a boycott of the final vote by over 10 percent of the bishops attending the First Vatican Council. See Thomas Bokenkotter, *A Concise History of the Catholic Church* (Garden City, N.Y.: Image Books, 1979, especially 332–338). It remains controversial among Catholic theologians to this day; see, for example, Hans Küng, *Infallible?* trans. Edward Quinn (Garden City, N.Y.: Doubleday, 1971).

7. Liberalism in its classic sense "was not, of course, simply one movement, but a number of more or less similar trends, associated with the rise of bourgeois classes and modern states, which affected the Catholic Church throughout Europe. Liberal economics (in the form of capitalism), liberal politics (especially republican forms

separating church and state), and liberal ideology (e.g., freedom of conscience, free-dom of religious practice) all threatened the ancien regime privileges of the Church" (Burns, "Politics of Ideology," 1125).

8. Kurtz, *Politics of Heresy.*

9. Ibid., 7.

10. Ibid., 9.

11. Ibid., 8.

12. John D. Stephens, "Democratic Transition and Breakdown in Western Europe, 1870-1939: A Test of the Moore Thesis," *American Journal of Sociology* 94 (1989):1019-1077.

13. Burns, "Politics of Ideology," 1135-1136.

14. Stephens, "Democratic Transition," 1038.

15. Burns, "Politics of Ideology," 1138.

16. Stephens, "Democratic Transition," does not argue that conservative forces in the Catholic hierarchy were a major element in the breakdown of democracy in Italy. He documents that a coalition among landlords, the state, and the bourgeoisie played the key role; ideological hegemony was less important in the Italian case. In Spain, the Church was allied with the large landowning class and thus remained a crucial element of the conservative bloc supporting the Franco dictatorship. As in Italy, however, "ideological hegemony of the authoritarian (upper-class) forces did not play such a crucial role in the Spanish case" (1063).

17. Bokenkotter, *Concise History.*

18. Burns, "Politics of Ideology," and Granfield, *Limits of the Papacy,* support this interpretation.

19. The cult of the person of the pope has its roots in ultramontanism, which came to a crescendo in the late nineteenth century. "The Ultramontanes were Rome-centered Catholics who in contrast with the Gallicans, their adversaries, saw a strong papacy as the only salvation of the Church in an age of godless, anti-Christian, and anticlerical liberals" (Bokenkotter, *Concise History,* 327). The ultra-montane enthusiasm of Pope Pius IX and his fervent supporters prompted the arch-bishop of Rheims to condemn ultramontanism as "idolatry to the papacy" (331).

20. Roger Haight, "Modernism: Vatican Had to Create It to Condemn It," *National Catholic Reporter,* 27 July 1990.

21. Bernard Cooke, *Ministry to Word and Sacrament: History and Theology* (Philadelphia: Fortress Press, 1976), vii.

11. PRIESTLY COALITION

1. The emergence and contrasting functions of the priestly and prophetic role in organized religion have been analyzed at length by Weber, *Economy and Society,* ch. 6.

2. Abbott, *Documents of Vatican II,* 43.

3. Weber, *Economy and Society,* 986.

4. Ibid., 985-986.

5. For a description of *Opus Dei* and *Comunione e Liberazione,* see Michael J. Walsh, "Aspects of Church Life Since the Council: The Conservative Reaction," in Hastings, *Modern Catholicism,* 283-288. For a radical critique of these conservative Catholic lay groups and the Knights of Malta, see Penny Lernoux, *People of God: The Struggle for World Catholicism* (New York: Penguin Books, 1989). Pope John

Paul II is so enthusiastic in his support of *Opus Dei* that he revised canon law to give the group unprecedented powers. See Knut Walf, "The New Canon Law—The Same Old System: Preconciliar Spirit in Postconciliar Formulation," in *The Church in Anguish: Has the Vatican Betrayed Vatican II?* edited by Hans Küng and Leonard Swidler (San Francisco: Harper and Row, 1987), 91–105.

6. For a generally pessimistic but informative account of attempts to reform the Roman curia, see Peter Hebblethwaite, "The Curia," in Hastings, *Modern Catholicism,* 175–181.

7. Ibid., 177.

8. Hebblethwaite, "The Curia." The general outline of a program to "restore" the Catholic Church was presented earlier by Cardinal Josef Ratzinger, *Report on the Faith,* which was issued in preparation for the 1985 Extraordinary Synod on Vatican II. The synod's agenda was to be an evaluation of the council but instead, according to Hans Küng and many other demoralized liberals in the Church, it became a platform for a peculiar kind of "restoration program." *Pastor Bonus* became a strong plank in the papal platform. See his "Cardinal Ratzinger, Pope Wojtyla, and Fear at the Vatican: An Open Word after a Long Silence," in Küng and Swidler, *Church in Anguish,* 58–74.

9. Josef Ratzinger is described by critics and admirers as a talented and once-liberal theologian who became Pope John Paul's right-hand man. See Peter Hebblethwaite, "John Paul II," in Hastings, *Modern Catholicism,* 447–456. As cardinal prefect of the Sacred Congregation for the Doctrine of the Faith and chairman of the International Theological Commission, he is the most powerful person in the Catholic Church after the pope.

10. Stephens, "Democratic Transition."

11. All but 15 percent of the Synod of Bishops' members are to be elected by episcopal conferences. See Peter Hebblethwaite, "The Synod of Bishops," in Hastings, *Modern Catholicism,* 200–209. The pope calls the synod, sets its agenda, confirms its membership, appoints its president and secretary, determines how its results are to be communicated, and presides over it through a delegate. Nevertheless, since the majority of members are elected and the pope may grant it "deliberative power" if he so chooses, it has potential as a mechanism of collegiality.

12. Ibid.

13. Ibid., 203.

14. Ibid.

15. For the almost unbelievable account of how curialists cunningly influenced the pope to go against the findings of his theological commission and the majority of cardinals and bishops appointed to study the birth control issue, see Philip Kaufman, *Why You Can Disagree and Remain a Faithful Catholic* (Bloomington, Ind.: Meyer Stone Books, 1989); also see Robert McClory, *Turning Point: The Inside Story of the Papal Birth Control Commission* (New York: Crossroad, 1995).

The overwhelming advice given Paul VI was to revise official teaching and remove the prohibition against birth control. To the shock of the Catholic world, *Humanae Vitae* did just the opposite. This was one of the most stunning victories of the conservative coalition since the Second Vatican Council. Given the widespread use of birth control by Catholic couples in recent decades, it is also one of the most lethal blows to papal teaching authority in the history of the Church. For data on the use of contraceptives among Catholics, see William Mosher and Gerry Hendershot, "Religion and Fertility: A Replication," *Demography* (1984):185–191.

16. For the United States, see Greeley and Schoenherr (NORC), *Catholic Priest;* Eugene Kennedy and Victor Heckler, *The Catholic Priest in the United States: Psychological Investigations* (Washington, D.C.: U.S. Catholic Conference, 1972); John Tracy Ellis, *The Catholic Priest in the United States: Historical Investigations* (Collegeville, Minn.: St. John's University Press, 1971). A paperbound edition of the NORC report was available for the American bishops attending the 1971 synod.

17. Edward Schillebeeckx, *The Church with a Human Face: A New and Expanded Theology of Ministry,* trans. John Bowden (New York: Crossroad, 1985).

18. Hebblethwaite, "Synod of Bishops."

19. Paul VI, *Insegnamenti,* vol. 9 (Vatican City: Vatican Polyglot Press, 1971), 873.

20. Hebblethwaite, "Synod of Bishops," 206.

21. Schillebeeckx, *Church with a Human Face,* 221, 231.

22. Ibid., 218.

23. Bühlmann, *Church of the Future,* 6.

24. Hebblethwaite, "Synod of Bishops," 206–207.

25. For critiques of the Extraordinary Synod, see Granfield, *Limits of the Papacy;* Hebblethwaite, "John Paul II."

26. For a critical analysis of the 1994 synod, see Peter Hebblethwaite, "Religious Charisma on Tightrope at Synod," *National Catholic Reporter,* 21 October 1994.

27. Doris Gottemoeller, quoted in "Women Religious Breathe Life into Roman Synod," *Bread Rising: A Report from Terry Dosh* 4 (November–December 1994):3.

28. For an analysis of the theological and ecclesiological problems faced by delegates to the Synod on Africa, emphasizing the thorny issues of inculturation, liberation theology, and black theology, see Peter Hebblethwaite, "Developing a Theology Tied to African Cultures," *National Catholic Reporter,* 22 April 1994.

29. See Alan Cowell, "At Vatican, Talk Is of the Harsh Realities of Africa," *New York Times,* 1 May 1994.

30. Ibid., 6.

31. Hebblethwaite, "Synod of Bishops," 207.

32. Bokenkotter, *Concise History.*

33. Granfield, *Limits of the Papacy,* see especially 75–76.

34. Some U.S. bishops have protested the pope's disdain for the tradition of consulting the local church when appointing new bishops. For example, in a letter to the U.S. pronuncio archbishop Agostino Cacciavillan, Archbishop Rembert Weakland wrote that he and other American bishops felt "that it is totally useless to present names, and find it offensive that one is expected to go through a procedure that is a charade." He complained further that he and his colleagues "had hoped that the appointment of bishops would not continue to be controlled by Cardinal Law, Cardinal O'Connor, and Cardinal Krol"; quoted in Paul Wilkes, "Profiles: Archbishop Weakland," *New Yorker,* part 2, 22 July 1991, 65.

35. See John Thavis, "Orthodoxy First among Episcopal Perquisites," *National Catholic Reporter,* 26 February 1988; also see Hebblethwaite, "'Secret' Criteria Sets Bishops' Appointments," *National Catholic Reporter,* 4 February 1994.

36. Quoted in Granfield, *Limits of the Papacy,* 28. For the full account, see *Origins,* 13, no. 24 (24 November 1983).

37. Granfield, *Limits of the Papacy*. For a full account, see *Origins*, 13, no. 14 (15 September 1983).

38. Walsh, "Conservative Reaction," 287.

39. Tim Frasca, "Secretary Sodano Does It Vatican's Way," *National Catholic Reporter*, 21 December 1990.

40. Robin Taylor, "Most Mexican Bishops Who Champion Poor Do It Secretly," *National Catholic Reporter*, 15 March 1991.

41. Conflict between the conservative Archbishop Cardoso Sobrinho and liberal-minded priests and parishioners resulted in an open clash with police. The popular pastor of Morro da Conceicao parish in Recife was ousted by Archbishop Cardoso. His successor, a conservative priest, was booed at Mass after showing up with eight carloads of priests to take the church building away from the laypeople who were occupying it in protest. See Ken Serbin, "Brazilians Celebrate Mass, Defy Prelate," *National Catholic Reporter*, 16 November 1990.

42. Hebblethwaite, "John Paul II," 455.

43. Gary MacEoin, "Struggle for Latin America's Soul Quickens: How Vatican Applies Bureaucratic Brakes to Lively Local Churches," *National Catholic Reporter*, 22 February 1991, 18.

44. Ibid.

45. For a description of the monarchical rights of bishops, see Granfield, *Limits of the Papacy*, 115.

46. For a full account and documentation of events, see Thomas J. Reese, *Archbishop: Inside the Power Structure of the American Catholic Church*, (San Francisco: Harper and Row, 1988). For a brief parallel account and further documentation, see Gerald P. Fogarty, "The Effect of the Council on World Catholicism: North America," in Hastings, *Modern Catholicism*, 326–333.

47. "French Bishop Is Fired for Challenging Vatican," *New York Times*, 14 January 1995.

48. See Craig R. Whitney, "Thousands in France Protest Dismissal of Leftist Bishop," *New York Times*, 23 January 1995. See also John Skinner, "Protests Follow French Bishop's Removal," *National Catholic Reporter*, 27 January 1995; editorial, "Vatican Loses Credibility When It Abuses Authority," *National Catholic Reporter*, 27 January 1995.

49. For an account of the listening sessions and excerpts from the ensuing pastoral letter, see Mary Gorski, "Weakland Urges Abortion Shifts," and "Abortion Issue Far from Black-and-White," *National Catholic Reporter*, 1 June 1990.

50. Marie Rhode, "Vatican Snub Sends Signal to Weakland," *Milwaukee Journal*, 11 November 1990. Also see Pat Windsor, "Vatican Vetoes Doctorate for Weakland," *National Catholic Reporter*, 16 November 1990. After the snub Weakland was supported by many U.S. bishops. See Pat Windsor, "Vatican's Weakland Veto Hot Topic in Corridors," *National Catholic Reporter*, 23 November 1990.

51. Rhode, "Vatican Snub," A20.

52. Ken Serbin, "Which Gospel for Brazil's Poor? Vatican-ordered Seminary Closings Threaten Schism," *National Catholic Reporter*, 22 September 1989, and "Vatican Stands Firm on Closing Recife Seminaries," *National Catholic Reporter*, 6 October 1989. For a theological analysis of the closings, emphasizing the place of reasoned dissent and dialogue in the history of the Church, see Leonard Swidler,

"Dissent an Honored Part of Church's Vocation," *National Catholic Reporter,* 22 September 1989.

53. For reports on how the papally mandated study was conducted in the United States, see "Background: The Study of U.S. Seminaries" and "Vatican Letter on Study Centers and Houses of Formation," *Origins* 19, no. 45 (April 12, 1990).

54. For an account and documentation of relevant events, see Leonard Swidler, "A Continuous Controversy: Küng in Conflict," in Küng and Swidler, *Church in Anguish,* 193–204.

55. For a transcript of the court decision against Curran, see *Origins* 18, no. 40 (March 16, 1989). For media accounts, see Mary Fay Bourgoin, "Canon Law Keeps Creeping into Curran Case," *National Catholic Reporter,* 30 December 1988, and "Final Hours of Curran Testimony Bring Surprises," *National Catholic Reporter,* 13 January 1989; Robin Taylor, "Curran Loses CUA Lawsuit," *National Catholic Reporter,* 10 March 1989. For a penetrating evaluation of the Curran affair by a prominent moral theologian, see Bernard Häring, "The Curran Case: Conflict Between Rome and the Moral Theologian," pp. 64–66, in *The Church in Anguish,* edited by Küng and Swidler.

56. One source claims the Catholic archdiocese in the area influenced the tenure decision at Auburn University. See Pat Windsor, "Curran Is Denied Tenure at Auburn," *National Catholic Reporter,* 21 September 1990, and "Auburn Faculty May Censure President over Curran," *National Catholic Reporter,* 7 December 1990. For details on the Southern Methodist University appointment, see Pat Windsor, "Curran Finds a Place to Lay His Academic Head," *National Catholic Reporter,* 21 December 1990.

57. Ratzinger has been prefect of the congregation since 1981. Hermann Häring, Ratzinger's former student and now professor of theology at the University of Nijmegen, the Netherlands, claims that Ratzinger's theology rejects the modern age, historical-critical exegesis, the emerging hermeneutical movement, and scholarly dialogue in general. See his "Joseph Ratzinger's 'Nightmare Theology'," in Küng and Swidler, *Church in Anguish,* 75–90.

58. For a short account and documentation of events surrounding Boff's harassment, see Granfield, *Limits of the Papacy,* 13–14. For a personal evaluation, see Leonardo Boff and Clodovis Boff, "Summons to Rome," in Küng and Swidler, *Church in Anguish,* 223–234.

59. For a short account and documentation of events in the Schillebeeckx case, see Granfield, *Limits of the Papacy,* 11–13. For a close-up analysis by a Flemish colleague, see Ad Willems, "The Endless Case of Edward Schillebeeckx," in Küng and Swidler, *Church in Anguish,* 212–22.

60. For accounts of harassment of all these scholars except Fox, see Granfield, *Limits of the Papacy.*

61. Joseph Feuerherd, "Theologians Tossing Vatican's Latest Hot Potato," *National Catholic Reporter,* 13 July 1990; Peter Hebblethwaite, "Alternative of Cowed Silence Strange Way to Defend Faith," *National Catholic Reporter,* 13 July 1990.

62. Certain statutes in the *Code of Canon Law* forbid priests and religious to hold public office that involves use of civil power. Others allow participation in political parties only if competent church authorities deem it necessary for the benefit of the Church or the common good. See canons 285, 287, 672 and 739; the first two of these apply to clerics and the second two to religious. For a discussion of the rel-

evance of these canons and documentation on the four cases, see Granfield, *Limits of the Papacy.*

63. For their personal account of the affair, see Barbara Ferraro and Patricia Hussey with Jane O'Reilly, *No Turning Back* (New York: Poseidon Press, 1990).

64. For a strong criticism of the new *Code,* see Walf, "The New Canon Law."

65. Marie Augusta Neal, *From Nuns to Sisters: An Expanding Vocation* (Mystic, Conn.: Twenty-Third, 1990).

66. Ibid., 94–95.

67. Ibid., 89.

12. PROPHETIC COALITION

1. On abortion, see the section on Archbishop Rembert Weakland hereafter; on gay love, see Tom Roberts, "He's Not Disordered, He's My Brother," *National Catholic Reporter,* 4 November 1994.

2. Weber, *Economy and Society,* 1111.

3. Weber, *Economy and Society,* 1114; Meng-tsu, quoted by Weber, *Economy and Society,* 1115.

4. Paul Wilkes, "Profiles: Archbishop Weakland," *New Yorker,* part 1, 15 July 1991, 39.

5. See John Walcott, "Catholics Stunned by Seattle Archbishop Hunthausen's Decision to Leave His Post," *National Catholic Reporter,* 5 July 1991.

6. Wilkes, "Archbishop Weakland," part 2, 53.

7. Ibid., part 1, 51.

8. Ibid.

9. Ibid.

10. *Origins* 17, no. 16 (1 October 1987).

11. Wilkes, "Archbishop Weakland," part 1.

12. See Pat Windsor, "Weakland Willing to Propose Married Priests," *National Catholic Reporter,* 18 January 1991.

13. For the bishops in Africa, see Adrian Hastings, "Celibacy in Africa," in *Celibacy in the Church,* ed. William Bassett and Peter Huizing (New York: Herder and Herder, 1972), 151–156. In Brazil, see Ken Serbin, "Brazilian Bishops Heed Warnings from Rome," *National Catholic Reporter,* 24 February 1989. In Indonesia, see Karl Beru, "Long Road from Iranian Jaya to Rome Paved with Good Intentions, Snubbed Cultures," *National Catholic Reporter,* 22 March 1991. In Canada, see John Thavis, "Bishops Ask Pope to Allow Married Priest," *National Catholic Reporter,* 1 October 1993; Dawn Gibeau, "Pope Addresses Canada's Bishops," *National Catholic Reporter,* 19 November 1993.

14. Weber, *Economy and Society,* 1112.

15. Wilkes, "Archbishop Weakland," part 1, 58.

16. Ibid., 56.

17. Weber, *Economy and Society,* 1112.

18. Wilkes, "Archbishop Weakland," part 2, 50.

19. Ibid., 64.

20. Ibid.

21. Bruce Murphy, "A Monk for All Seasons," *Milwaukee Magazine,* July 1991, 55.

22. Francis Quinn, quoted by Mary Beth Murphy, "Married Priests Idea Gets Warm Reception," *Milwaukee Sentinel,* 9 January 1991.

23. "Saginaw Priests Encourage Study of Weakland Draft," *National Catholic Reporter,* 19 April 1991.

24. Wilkes, "Archbishop Weakland," part 2, 52.

25. Murphy, "Monk for All Seasons," 55.

26. All quotations of Bishop Lucker are from Wilkes, "Archbishop Weakland," part 2, 52.

27. Ibid., part 1, 56.

28. Ibid., part 1, 57.

29. Ibid., part 2, 65.

30. Ibid., part 2, 65.

31. Ibid., part 1, 58.

32. Ibid., part 2, 53.

33. Ibid., part 1, 56.

34. Ibid., part 2, 53.

35. Václav Havel, "Power of the Powerless," in *Living in Truth,* edited by Jan Vladislav (London: Faber and Faber, 1986), 55.

36. For a biographical sketch of Bishop Untener, see Peter Hebblethwaite, "Saginaw Bishop Folksy, Bright," *National Catholic Reporter,* 23 October 1992. I thank Sister Theresa Byrne, O.P, for sharing her file of media clippings on Bishop Untener.

37. Wilkes, "Archbishop Weakland," part 2, 50.

38. For an account of events leading up to *Humanae Vitae,* see Philip Kaufman, *Why You Can Disagree and Remain a Faithful Catholic* (Bloomington, Ind.: Meyer Stone Books, 1989).

39. Kenneth Untener, "Forum: The Ordination of Women: Can the Horizons Widen?" *Worship* 65 (1991): 50–59.

40. Ibid., 56.

41. See Meyer, "Forum: The Ordination of Women: Responses to Bishop Kenneth Untener," *Worship* 65 (1991):256–62; Sheets, "Forum: The Ordination of Women," *Worship* 65 (1991):451–461; Legrand, *"Traditio Perpetuo Servata?* The Non-Ordination of Women: Tradition or Simply an Historical Fact?" *Worship* 65 (1991):482–508.

42. David Crumm, "Bishop Advocates Women as Priests," *Detroit Free Press,* 12 November 1991. All quotations in the next four paragraphs are from this source.

43. James Ricci, "Jane Eschweiler Is as Worthy of Priesthood as Any Man," *Detroit Free Press,* 17 November 1991.

44. See Robert McClory, "A Silenced Woman," *Chicago Reader,* 3 January 1992.

45. Mary Beth Murphy, "Married Priests Idea"; Pat Windsor, "Weakland Willing"; editorial, "Eucharist, Not Celibacy at Heart of the Church," *National Catholic Reporter,* 18 January 1991.

46. Terence Dosh, "German Bishops Question Church Policies," *Bread Rising,* January–February 1992.

47. Ken Serbin, "Vatican's Man Elbowing over Oaxaca Archbishop," *National Catholic Reporter,* 30 November 1990. A later report claims that "as many as 75 percent of Oaxacan priests violated their celibacy oaths"; Robin Taylor, "Most Mexican Bishops Who Champion Poor Do It Secretly," *National Catholic Reporter,* March 15 1991.

48. Beru, "Long Road from Iranian Jaya."

49. Windsor, "Weakland Willing." Also see "More Openness to Ordaining Women, Married Priests," *Churchwatch,* June–July 1991.

50. Hastings, "Celibacy in Africa."

51. P. Francis Murphy, "Let's Start Over: A Bishop Appraises the Pastoral on Women," *Commonweal,* 25 September 1992.

52. Michael H. Kenny, "Which Way the Pastoral?" *America,* 22 August 1992.

53. Rembert Weakland, "American Culture and History Birthing a New Catholicism," *National Catholic Reporter,* 29 May 1992.

54. *Churchwatch,* "More Openness."

55. Dosh, "German Bishops."

56. Kenny, "Which Way," 77.

57. Alan Riding, "Theologians in Europe Challenge Pope's Conservative Leadership," *New York Times,* 14 July 1989.

58. Pat Windsor, "Theologians' Statement Benign Yet Critical of Vatican," *National Catholic Reporter,* 21 December 1990.

59. Deane Jordan, "NFPC Recommends Ordination of Women, Married Men," *National Catholic Reporter,* 17 May 1991.

60. "Canon Lawyers Launch Study of Married Priesthood," *National Catholic Reporter,* 8 November 1991.

61. Terence Dosh, "Signs of Hope," *Bread Rising* 1, no. 2 (1991).

62. Officially established in 1959 as the Conference of Major Superiors of Women, it took its present name in 1971; it now represents 380 U.S. religious orders of women. See Tim Unsworth, "Women Religious Still Force to Reckon With," *National Catholic Reporter,* 9 September 1994. Much to the chagrin of the LCWR, Rome recently created the Council of Major Superiors of Women Religious (CMSWR) for those congregations who dislike the confrontational activities of the LCWR. Reportedly, the new CMSWR prefers loyal submission to Rome's patriarchal control over its member congregations. The LCWR sees approval of the new group as a strategy of divide and conquer on the part of the Vatican. For documentation on the establishment of the CMSWR, see *Origins* 22, no. 9 (23 July 1992). For an account of tensions created by its establishment, see Dorothy Vidulich, "Sisters Say New Nuns' Group Could Spell Trouble," *National Catholic Reporter,* 3 July 1992.

63. Tom Roberts, "Fusing Vision, Tradition in Call to Action," *National Catholic Reporter,* 18 November 1994; editorial, "Breath of Fresh Air for a Suffocating Church," *National Catholic Reporter,* 18 November 1994.

64. Arthur Jones, "WOC's Prelate, Fitzpatrick, on Steady March to Ordination," *National Catholic Reporter,* 17 June 1994; also see *Call to Action News,* August 1992.

65. See Laura Session Stepps, "Catholics Urge Bishops to Debate Tenets," *Washington Post,* 12 November 1991; Virginia Culver, "Catholic Group Decries Lack of Priests, *Denver Post,* 6 September 1991.

66. Ari L. Goldman, "As Bishops Meet, Catholics Voice Differences with Church's Doctrine: Poll Finds Backing of Female Priests," *New York Times,* 19 June 1992. The Gallup organization polled 802 Catholics on May 5–17, 1992; the margin of sampling error was ± 4 percentage points. See *National Survey of Catholic Opinion* (Princeton, N.J.: Gallup, May 1992).

67. Arthur Jones, "New Germany, New Church: Group Says No to Status Quo," *National Catholic Reporter,* 7 June 1991.

13. THE COLLAPSE OF CELIBATE EXCLUSIVITY

1. For a sharp criticism of attempts to deprive organized religion of its tax-exempt status, see Robert Bellah, *The Broken Covenant: American Civil Religion in the Time of Trial,* 2nd ed. (Chicago: University of Chicago Press, 1992).

2. An article in the Catholic press reports: "Two employees and a trustee of St. George's Church in Guilford, Conn., were required to resign from their positions last month for attending the wedding of the parish's ex-pastor." Archbishop Whealon of Hartford also suspended priests "who attended the wedding of a priest in the diocese." See Steve Burkholder, "Parish Employees Fired for Attending Former Pastor's Wedding," *National Catholic Reporter,* 15 February 1991.

3. See Katie de Koster, ed., *Child Abuse: Opposing Viewpoints* (San Diego: Greenhaven Press, 1994).

4. Rhys Williams and N. Jay Demerath III, "Religion and Political Process in an American City," *American Sociological Review* 56 (1991):417–431.

5. Rhys A. Williams and N. Jay Demerath III, "Cultural Resources in Local Politics: 'Cultural Power' and Prophetic Challenge" (paper presented at the annual meeting of the American Sociological Association, Washington, D.C., August 11–15, 1990).

6. Burns, "Politics of Ideology."

14. GOODBYE FATHER

1. *Webster's Tenth New Collegiate Dictionary,* s.v. "father" [ME *fader,* L *pater,* G *pater*]; s.v. "papa": father.

2. Mark Chaves, *Ordaining Women: Culture and Conflict in Religious Organizations* (Cambridge, Mass.: Harvard University Press, 1997).

3. See Jackson W. Carroll, Barbara Hargrove, and Adair Lummis, *Women of the Cloth: A New Opportunity for the Churches* (San Francisco: Harper and Row, 1983); Sherryl Kleinman, *Equals before God: Seminarians as Humanistic Professionals* (Chicago: University of Chicago Press, 1984); Paula D. Nesbitt, "Dual Ordination Tracks: Differential Benefits and Costs for Men and Women Clergy," *Sociology of Religion* 54 (1993):13–30; Edward C. Lehman Jr., "Pattern of Lay Resistance to Women in Ministry," *Sociological Analysis* 41 (1980):318–338, "Organizational Resistance to Women in Ministry," *Sociological Analysis* 42 (1981):101–118, and *Gender and Work: The Case of the Clergy* (Albany: State University of New York Press, 1993); Nancy Nason-Clark, "Ordaining Women as Priests: Religious versus Sexist Explanations for Clerical Attitudes," *Sociological Analysis* 48 (1987):259–273; Marjorie H. Royle, "Using Bifocals to Overcome Blindspots: The Impact of Women on the Military and the Ministry," *Review of Religious Research* 28 (1987):341–350. Mark Chaves reviews this and other relevant literature in *Ordaining Women.*

4. Demetrios Constantelos, "Marriage and Celibacy of the Clergy in the Orthodox Church," in Bassett and Huizing, *Celibacy in the Church,* 30–38. See also Brown, *Body and Society;* John Boswell, *Christianity, Social Tolerance, and Homosexuality: Gay People in Western Europe from the Beginning of the Christian Era to the Fourteenth Century* (Chicago: University of Chicago Press, 1980).

5. See Rodney Stark, *The Rise of Christianity* (Princeton: Princeton University Press, 1997).

6. James A. Coriden, "Celibacy, Canon Law, and Synod 1971," in Bassett and Huizing, *Celibacy,* 109–124.

7. Steven Ozment, "Marriage and Ministry in the Protestant Churches," in Bassett and Huizing, *Celibacy,* 39–56, 39.

8. John Lynch, "Critique of the Law of Celibacy in the Catholic Church from the Period of the Reform Councils," in Bassett and Huizing, *Celibacy,* 57–75.

9. Lerner, *Creation of Patriarchy,* 219.

10. Ibid.

11. Cited by Chaves, *Ordaining Women,* 15.

12. Leonard Swidler, "Introduction: *Roma Locuta, Causa Finita?*" pp. 3–18, in *Women Priests: A Catholic Commentary on the Vatican Declaration,* edited by Leonard Swidler and Arlene Swidler (New York: Paulist Press, 1977).

13. For references, see Swidler, Introduction: *"Roma Locuta."* He also cites a dozen articles and an annotated bibliography with over one hundred entries on the topic of women priests in the Catholic Church. See also Anne E. Patrick, "Studies on Women Priests," in Swidler and Swidler, *Women Priests,* 70–74.

14. "Biblical Commission Report. Can Women Be Priests?" *Origins* 6, no. 6 (1 July 1976):92–96. For a brief, cogent analysis of the report, see John R. Donahue, "A Tale of Two Documents," in Swidler and Swidler, *Women Priests,* 25–34. Donahue summarizes the results of the commission's voting on three different formulations of the issue: "(1) a unanimous (17–0) vote that the New Testament does not settle in a clear way and once and for all whether women can be ordained priests, (2) a 12–5 vote in favor of the view that scriptural grounds alone are not enough to exclude the possibility of ordaining women, and (3) a 12–5 vote that Christ's plan would not be transgressed by permitting the ordination of women" (Donahue, "Tale," 25).

15. Paragraph 5 of the Declaration, reprinted in Swidler and Swidler, *Women Priests,* 37–49.

16. "Commentary on the Declaration of the Sacred Congregation for the Doctrine of the Faith on the Question of Admission of Women to the Ministerial Priesthood," in Swidler and Swidler, *Women Priests,* 319–337.

17. *Inter Insigniores,* no. 4, no 8.

18. Carroll Stuhlmueller, "Internal Indecisiveness," in Swidler and Swidler, *Women Priests,* 23–24.

19. For the full text, see *Origins* 24, no. 4 (9 June 1994).

20. For example, one of the major documents issued by the Second Vatican Council says: "Every type of discrimination . . . based on sex . . . is to be overcome and eradicated as contrary to God's intent" (*Gaudium et Spes,* no. 29). Similarly, in his 1988 "Meditation on the Dignity of Women" Pope John Paul II presents an exegesis of Genesis 3:16, explaining that rule of man over woman is sinful patriarchy, not normative but disruptive. For a bishop's earnest plea for an international commission to study the women's ordination issue, see P. Francis Murphy, "Let's Start Over: A Bishop Appraises the Pastoral on Women," *Commonweal,* 25 September 1992.

21. Coriden, "Celibacy," 110. He notes that these points are elaborated in Pope Paul VI's 1967 letter *Sacerdotalis Caelibatus.* For an excellent, short theological discussion of celibacy, arguing that the alleged reasons for its superiority are Manichaean, Platonizing, and dualistic, see F. J. Laishley, "Unfinished Business: Celibacy," in Hastings, *Modern Catholicism,* 235–239.

22. One of the most important documents of the Second Vatican Council, *Lumen Gentium,* declares that the whole Church is called to holiness, not just the ordained and religiously professed. See Richard P. McBrien, "The Church (*Lumen Gentium*)," in Hastings, *Modern Catholicism,* 84–95.

23. The 1974 poll is cited by Swidler, "Introduction: *Roma Locuta,*" 3, and also by Richard N. Ostling, "The Second Reformation," *Time* (22 June 1992), 57. Gallup Poll data reported in *Origins* 8, no. 47 (12 May 1977), 742.

24. Two 1992 surveys were widely reported in the media. One, a national poll sponsored by Catholics Speak Out, was executed by Gallup and released at a press conference during the U.S. bishops' 1992 spring meeting. Of the 802 respondents, 67 percent supported the ordination of women; the margin of error was ±4 percent. See Goldman, "As Bishops Meet." The other was a telephone poll of 145 U.S. Catholic women undertaken for *Time/CNN* on June 3–4, 1992, by Yankelovich Clancy Shulman with a sampling error of ±8 percent. These data showed that 59 percent believe "women should be allowed to be priests." See Richard N. Ostling, "Cut from the Wrong Cloth," *Time,* 22 June 1992. The data from the two surveys are fairly consistent, given their margins of error. A 1993 survey reports that 64 percent of U.S. adult Catholics favor women's ordination. See William V. D'Antonio, James Davidson, Dean R. Hoge, and Ruth A. Wallace, *Laity, American and Catholic: Transforming the Church* (Knoxville, Tenn.: John Knox Press, 1996).

25. See "Papstin mit Recht auf Heirat," *Der Spiegel,* 21 December 1992.

26. The first woman was admitted to the rabbinate in 1972. See Chaves, *Ordaining Women.*

27. For a theoretically informed and empirically rooted analysis of Islam, stressing the pervasiveness of patriarchal dominance, see Martin Riesebrodt, *Pious Passion: The Emergence of Modern Fundamentalism in the United States and Iran,* trans. Don Renau (Berkeley: University of California Press, 1993).

28. For experiences and opinions of over 85 female Buddhist practitioners regarding male hegemony, see Sandy Boucher, *Turning the Wheel: American Women Creating the New Buddhism* (San Francisco: Harper and Row, 1988). The women admit that the prevailing structure is patriarchal, but they claim they are striving to transform American Buddhism to include full gender equality.

29. Hubert and Mauss, *Sacrifice.*

30. In the deutero-Pauline letters to the Ephesians and the Hebrews, the author of the epistle corrects this notion and raises marriage to a Christian ideal. See Brown, *Body and Society,* 57.

31. Ibid., 49; see ch. 2 in its entirety. For an earlier and decidedly polemical analysis but yielding the same conclusion, see Lea, *History of Sacerdotal Celibacy.*

32. For recent attempts in the social sciences to reexamine the social construction of gender, particularly the normative acceptance of heterogender, see Chrys Ingraham, "The Heterosexual Imaginary: Feminist Sociology and Theories of Gender," *Sociological Theory* 12 (July 1994):203–219. Michel Foucault, pioneer in poststructural critique of orthodox theories of sexuality, exposes each and every "sexual regime as a political and social event." See Steven Seidman, "Queer Theory/Sociology: A Dialogue," *Sociological Theory* 12 (July 1994):171.

33. For a serious attempt to update the Catholic Church's theology of sexuality, see Kosnik et al., *Human Sexuality.* For a brief account of the repudiation of this re-

port by the Vatican Congregation for the Doctrine of the Faith and the U.S. National Conference of Catholic Bishops, see Granfield, *Limits of the Papacy*. Most recently, the Salvatorian priest Robert Nugent and the School Sister of Notre Dame Jeannine Grammick have been investigated by Rome for their work promoting moral acceptance of gay people's sexual activity. See Robin T. Edwards, "Ministry to Gays Investigated," *National Catholic Reporter,* 27 May 1994.

34. Sipe, *Secret World,* 50.

35. For an analysis of Christianity's negative attitude about marriage and, indeed, all sexual activity, in contrast to its positive attitude about celibacy, see Rosemary R. Ruether, "Homophobia, Heterosexism, and Pastoral Practice," in *Homosexuality in the Priesthood and the Religious Life,* ed. Jeannine Grammick (New York: Crossroad, 1989). Also see Schneiders, *Beyond Patching.*

36. Murphy, "Let's Start Over," 13.

37. Demetria Martinez, "Eroticism: Reconnecting Faith and Flesh for God's Sake and Ours Also," *National Catholic Reporter,* 22 March 1991.

38. Alan Cowell, "Pope Rules Out Debate on Women as Priests," *New York Times,* 31 May 1994. All citations of the apostolic letter are from this source.

39. Studying the Scriptures and testimony of early Christians, these scholars find evidence that Jesus himself preferred gender equality, gave apostolic authority to the woman at the well, and inspired Paul to declare that in Christ there is neither Jew nor Greek, slave nor free, male nor female. These arguments and other relevant evidence against the ban on women priests are presented in Swidler and Swidler, *Women Priests.*

40. For example, Archbishop Rembert Weakland pledged obedience to the pope's decision but with grave concerns. His reaction reflected more empathy with the people in the pews, most of whom are women, than enthusiasm for the papal pronouncement. The archbishop's written statement puts his reaction in the form of questions: "How, as a bishop, am I to deal with the anger and disillusionment which will inevitably result? What can I do to instill hope in so many women who are now living on the margins of the church?" quoted by Peter Steinfels, "Future of Faith Worries Catholic Leaders," *New York Times,* 1 June 1994. For similar examples of "creative obedience," in this instance by parish priests dealing with rigid bureaucratic decisions of their bishops, see Tim Unsworth, "Parish Priests Cope with Mess," *National Catholic Reporter,* 20 May 1994.

41. The issue dominated radio talk shows for several days after the letter "On Reserving Priestly Ordination to Men Alone" was released.

International Federation of Married
   Catholic Priests, 179
intimacy, priests' sexuality and, 22–23,
   224n.31
involution, in spiritual priority, 108–109
Islam, male exclusivity in, 204, 252n.27
I-You, 59–60, 108, 127

Jansenism, 78
John Paul II
   on bishop appointment/promotion,
      151–153, 244n.34
   on celibate exclusivity, xxiii–xxiv,
      149–151
   curia reform and, 145, 243n.9
   on gender equality, 202–204,
      210–211, 215, 251n.20
   Synod of Bishops under, 149–151
John XXIII, curia reform and, 145–146
Judaism, male exclusivity in, 252n.26,
   204, 253n.39

Kant, Immanuel
   on religion, 70, 97–98, 237n.11
knowing
   human development of, 47–48, 101
   spiritual realm of, 47, 229n.17-n.18

labor. See division of labor
laity. See lay ministry movement
language, gender-neutral, 210–211
Latin America, bishop appointments in,
   17, 152–153, 245n.41
law, in social change theory, 32
lay ministry movement
   attitude gap of, xviii–xix, 219n.23,
      219n.25
   breakthrough scenario, 193–195
   in Catholic Tragedy, 127–128, 191
   clericalism vs., 117–119; balancing
      tensions, 121–123; narrowing gap
      with, 83–85
   doctrinal statement on, 83–84
   John Paul II impact on, 149
   as priest shortage answer, 3–4, 87
   as prophetic coalitions, 161,
      178–180, 212

rise of, xii, xvi, xxi, xxviii, 9, 192
   as women's issue, 83–85
lay-sacrificer, 54
Leadership Conference of Women
   Religious (LCWR), 179, 249n.62
legitimization
   of charismatic leaders, 162
   of organizational authority, 39–40,
      119
   as religion's role, 48–49, 213
   in social change theory, 32–33,
      226n.4
liberalism
   papal battle against, 135–138,
      241n.6-n.7
   rise of, xviii–xix, 135, 152
liberation movement, 74, 81, 195
life cycle development, sexuality and,
   22–23
literalism, 74
liturgical movement
   as Catholic change force, 85–89;
      balancing sacrament and word,
      88–89; demographic boost,
      87–88; historical developments,
      86–87, 103, 238n.26; opposition
      in, 117–118; worship services,
      85–86, 192
   Eucharist survival with, 10–11,
      222n.9
   rise of, xii, xvi, xxi, xxviii, 9
Liturgy of the Word, 85–87, 120–123
localism
   balance of, 13, 87, 104–105
   as change force, 94, 103–104
logical positivism, in social evolution, 47
loneliness, detrimental effect of, xx-xxi,
   21
loose organization, of charismatic
   leadership, 163, 170–171
love
   Christian, 103, 190
   developmental psychology of, 22–23,
      101
   integration with sexual intercourse,
      80
   marriage as symbol of, 78–79

DATE DUE ON LINE 2/03

MAR 0 4 2003	
JUN 2 8 2003	
JUL 1 4 2003	
OCT 1 4 2003	

GAYLORD   PRINTED IN U.S.A.